D1593121

Philosemitism in History

Too often philosemitism – the idealization of Jews and Judaism – has been simplistically misunderstood as merely antisemitism "in sheep's clothing." This book takes a different approach, surveying the phenomenon from antiquity to the present and highlighting its rich complexity and broad impact on Western culture. *Philosemitism in History* includes fourteen essays by specialist historians, anthropologists, literary scholars, and scholars of religion, ranging from medieval philosemitism to such modern and contemporary topics as African American depictions of Jews as ethnic role models, the Zionism of Christian evangelicals, pro-Jewish educational television in West Germany, and the current fashion for Jewish "kitsch" memorabilia in contemporary east central Europe. An extensive introductory chapter offers a thorough and original overview of the topic. The book underscores both the endurance and the malleability of philosemitism, drawing attention to this important but widely neglected facet of Jewish–non-Jewish relations.

Jonathan Karp is Associate Professor in the History and Judaic Studies Departments at Binghamton University, SUNY, and Director of the American Jewish Historical Society. He is the author of *The Politics of Jewish Commerce: Economic Thought and Emancipation, 1638–1848* (Cambridge University Press, 2008), and coeditor, with Barbara Kirshenblatt-Gimblett, of *The Art of Being Jewish in Modern Times* (2007).

Adam Sutcliffe is Senior Lecturer in European History, Department of History, King's College London. He is the author of *Judaism and Enlightenment* (Cambridge University Press, 2003) and coeditor, with Ross Brann, of *Renewing the Past, Reconfiguring Jewish Culture: From Al-Andalus to the Haskalah* (2004).

Philosemitism in History

Edited by

JONATHAN KARP

Binghamton University, State University of New York

ADAM SUTCLIFFE

King's College London

CAMBRIDGE UNIVERSITY PRESS
Cambridge, New York, Melbourne, Madrid, Cape Town,
Singapore, São Paulo, Delhi, Tokyo, Mexico City

Cambridge University Press
32 Avenue of the Americas, New York, NY 10013-2473, USA

www.cambridge.org
Information on this title: www.cambridge.org/9780521695473

© Cambridge University Press 2011

First published 2011

Printed in the United States of America

A catalog record for this publication is available from the British Library.

Library of Congress Cataloging in Publication data
Philosemitism in history / edited by Jonathan Karp, Adam Sutcliffe.
p. cm.
Includes bibliographical references and index.
ISBN 978-0-521-87377-2 (hardback) – ISBN 978-0-521-69547-3 (pbk.)
1. Philosemitism – History. I. Karp, Jonathan, 1960– II. Sutcliffe, Adam.
DS148.5.P55 2010
305.8924–dc22   2010030602

ISBN 978-0-521-87377-2 Hardback
ISBN 978-0-521-69547-3 Paperback

Contents

Notes on Contributors

Yaakov Ariel is Professor of Religious Studies at the University of North Carolina at Chapel Hill. He has published extensively on contemporary Judaism as well as on Christian-Jewish relations. His book *Evangelizing the Chosen People* (2000) won a prize from the American Society of Church History.

Robert Chazan is the Scheuer Professor of Jewish History at New York University. He has written extensively on the Jews of medieval Christian Europe and is the author of *The Jews of Medieval Western Christendom* (2006) and *Reassessing Jewish Life in Medieval Europe* (2010).

Lars Fischer is Academic Director of the Centre for the Study of Jewish-Christian Relations in Cambridge. His publications mainly focus on Jewish–non-Jewish relations in nineteenth- and twentieth-century Europe and include *The Socialist Response to Antisemitism in Imperial Germany* (2007).

Ruth Ellen Gruber is an American journalist and author based in Europe, who has published widely on contemporary Jewish issues. Her books include *Virtually Jewish: Reinventing Jewish Culture in Europe* (2002).

Wulf Kansteiner is Associate Professor of European History at Binghamton University, SUNY. He has published widely in the fields of media history, memory studies, and historical theory. His books include *In Pursuit of German Memory: History, Television, and Politics after Auschwitz* (2006).

Jonathan Karp is Associate Professor in the History and Judaic Studies Departments at Binghamton University, SUNY, and Director of the American Jewish Historical Society. He is the author of *The Politics of Jewish Commerce: Economic Thought and Emancipation in Europe, 1638–1848* (2008), and numerous articles on Jewish cultural, intellectual, and economic history.

Alan T. Levenson is Schusterman Professor of Jewish Religious and Intellectual History at the University of Oklahoma. His books include *Between Philosemitism and Antisemitism: Defenses of Jews and Judaism in Germany, 1871–1932* (2004).

Julian Levinson is the Samuel Shetzer Professor of American Jewish Studies and Associate Professor of English at the University of Michigan. His book *Exiles on Main Street: Jewish American Writers and American Literary Culture* (2008) won the National Jewish Book Award for American Jewish Studies.

Howard Lupovitch is the Waks Family Chair in Jewish History at the University of Western Ontario. He has published numerous articles on the Jews of Hungary and the Habsburg monarchy and is the author of *Jews at the Crossroads: Tradition and Accommodation during the Golden Age of the Hungarian Nobility* (2007) and *Jews and Judaism in World History* (2009).

Abraham Melamed is Professor of Jewish Philosophy at the University of Haifa, where he holds the Wolfson Chair for the Study of the Jewish Cultural Heritage. He has published widely on medieval and Renaissance Jewish intellectual history and political philosophy. His books include *The Philosopher-King in Medieval and Renaissance Jewish Political Thought* (2003) and *The Black in Jewish Culture: A History of the Other* (2003).

Alyssa Goldstein Sepinwall is Associate Professor of History at California State University, San Marcos. She is the author of *The Abbé Grégoire and the French Revolution: The Making of Modern Universalism* (2005).

Adam Shear is Associate Professor of Religious Studies at the University of Pittsburgh. His research focuses on early modern Jewish intellectual and cultural history, and he is the author of *The Kuzari and the Shaping of Jewish Identity, 1167–1900* (2008).

Adam Sutcliffe is Senior Lecturer in European History at King's College London. He has published widely on western European Jewish history and intellectual history in the seventeenth and eighteenth centuries and is the author of *Judaism and Enlightenment* (2003).

Nadia Valman is Senior Lecturer in English at Queen Mary, University of London. She has published many essays and edited volumes on discourses and debates concerning Jews in nineteenth-century Britain. She is the author of *The Jewess in Nineteenth-Century British Literary Culture* (2007).

Introduction

A Brief History of Philosemitism

Adam Sutcliffe and Jonathan Karp

Q: Which is preferable – the antisemite or the philosemite?
A: The antisemite. At least he isn't lying.

Is there such a thing as philosemitism? The concept is often met with skepticism, as this characteristically terse Jewish joke exemplifies. The term is certainly an awkward one, and it has an awkward history. Coined in Germany in 1880 as the antonym to another neologism – antisemitism – the word "philosemitism" was invented by avowed antisemites as a sneering term of denunciation for their opponents. Almost all late nineteenth-century opponents of antisemitism strenuously sought to defend themselves from the charge of philosemitism, insisting instead that they regarded the Jews neutrally and were untainted by prejudice either for or against them.[1] This normalization of attitudes toward Jews has remained the aim of almost all liberal engagements in the field of Jewish–non-Jewish relations, both by Jews and by non-Jews, and from this dominant perspective philosemitism is almost always regarded as deeply suspicious, sharing with antisemitism a trafficking in distorted, exaggerated, and exceptionalist views of Jews and Judaism. Taking these distortions as the essential hallmark of antisemitism, it has seemed reasonable to many to regard philosemitism as a counterfeit benevolence, and philosemites, as Daniel Goldhagen has described them, as "antisemites in sheep's clothing."[2]

---

[1] Wolfram Kinzig, "Philosemitismus Teil I: Zur Geschichte des Begriffs," *Zeitschrift für Kirchengeschichte* 105 (1994): 208–28, esp. 210–17; Lars Fischer, *The Socialist Response to Antisemitism in Imperial Germany* (Cambridge: Cambridge University Press, 2007), 21–36, and his essay in this volume. On the extensive discussion of philosemitism by Wilhelm Marr, the key figure in the popularization of the term "antisemitism," see Moshe Zimmermann, *Wilhelm Marr: The Patriarch of Anti-Semitism* (New York: Oxford University Press, 1987), 118–32.

[2] Daniel Goldhagen, *Hitler's Willing Executioners: Ordinary Germans and the Holocaust* (New York: Vintage, 1997), 58.

Yet this negative assessment of philosemitism is itself one-sided and prejudicial. Since the period of antiquity favorable characterizations of the Jewish people have recurrently formed a quiet counterpoint to the more familiar hostile stereotypes. Jews have been idealized not only, in the Christian tradition, as "God's chosen people," but also for such imputed virtues as their superior intelligence, economic acumen, ethnic loyalty, cultural cohesion, or familial commitment. These idealizations have at times had a significant impact on historical events, often directly affecting Jews' status and standing, and for this reason have in some contexts been directly encouraged or even induced by Jews themselves. The vast human cost of antisemitism, and of the Nazi genocide in particular, does not warrant the simple conflation of these idealizations into their negative shadow. Historians must seek to explain not only the expulsions and forced conversions of Jews, but also the numerous times when Jewish settlement has been welcomed and even solicited. Similarly, non-Jewish support for the Zionist idea and for the state of Israel demands explanation and analysis not simply as theological fantasy or political expediency, but as in some cases reflecting genuine sympathy for Jews' historical victimization and admiration of their presumed collective qualities, such as moral refinement, advanced civilization, and will to survive. The normalization of the status of Jews and Judaism in the world, meanwhile, remains an elusive and perhaps unattainable aspiration, and "normality" therefore an unhelpfully simple and ahistorical yardstick for the evaluation of non-Jewish attitudes toward Jews. If we are to understand the meanings and associations with which Jews have long been freighted in Western culture, we must recognize their complexity and approach them from all angles, without a predetermined assessment of their underlying essence as monolithically negative.

The word "philosemitism" remains inevitably tainted by etymological association with its antonym. Why should we continue to echo late nineteenth-century prejudices in associating "Semitism," however it may be prefixed, specifically with Jews? Both "isms" also problematically suggest an underlying fixity in attitudes to Jews. However, although these issues have been widely highlighted and debated by scholars, as has the wider question of the relationship of antisemitism to the broader category of racism, the term "antisemitism" remains firmly entrenched as a category of analysis for ancient and medieval as well as modern history.[3] Language is

---

[3] See, e.g., Richard Levy and Albert Lindemann, *Antisemitism – a History* (New York: Oxford University Press, 2010); Gavin Langmuir, *Toward a Definition of Antisemitism* (Berkeley and Los Angeles: University of California Press, 1990), esp. 311–52; Peter Schäfer, *Judeophobia: Attitudes toward the Jews in the Ancient World* (Cambridge, MA: Harvard University Press, 1997), 197–211. For a recent reflection on the relationship of antisemitism to color-coded forms of racism, see George M. Fredrickson, *Racism: A Short History* (Princeton, NJ: Princeton University Press, 2002), 40–7, 156–68.

a messy, hand-me-down artifact: in the main we necessarily use the words already in common circulation. Whatever misgivings we may have about the origins or the imprecision of the word "antisemitism," this concept remains overwhelmingly dominant in transhistorical thinking on relations between Jews and non-Jews, and attempts to broaden approaches to this subject must start from an engagement with this reality. "Philosemitism" is as problematic a term as "antisemitism." However, given that antisemitism is a firm fixture in our lexicon and in our thinking, if we are to stretch the subtlety of this inescapable terminology we must think more carefully about the meaning and nature of philosemitism also. This word is uniquely serviceable as a discursive balancer, drawing attention to those facets of attitudes to Jews that are most egregiously misinterpreted or overlooked within a paradigm that recognizes antisemitism alone.

To speak of philosemitism, then, certainly does not imply an unreserved endorsement of the word. Nor does it entail the claim that philosemitism can be or should be neatly separated from antisemitism. Indeed, an intricate ambivalence, combining elements of admiration and disdain, has arguably been by far the most common feature of non-Jewish constructs of Jews and Judaism, while the philosemitism of many Christians has been motivated by a conversionist desire ultimately to erase Jewish distinctiveness altogether. The use of this term as a transhistorical category also should not suggest a belief that it possesses some unchangingly eternal essence. Analogously, the bracketing together as antisemitic of, say, medieval blood libel accusations, Voltaire's antibiblical tirades, and the Soviet treatment of Jewish refuseniks does not imply the existence of some quasi-genetic connection of these phenomena, though it may open up the possibility of identifying certain echoes or common traits. In similar fashion, it is our hope that this volume will bring to attention various lines of continuity and influence, recurrent patterns, and other disparate echoes that link different instances of the positive valorization of Jews or Judaism. By joining these episodes under the analytically imperfect but functionally illuminating rubric of philosemitism, we are better able to explore the nature and scope of these transhistorical resonances and assess the endurance, development, and historical impact of this significant but understudied phenomenon.

A small scholarly literature on philosemitism does now exist, made up of a handful of synoptic surveys as well as some more detailed case studies.[4] The impact of this work has, however, been almost entirely

---

[4] For existing overviews of the history of philosemitism, see Salomon Rappaport, *Jew and Gentile: The Philosemitic Aspect* (New York: Philosophical Library, 1980); Alan Edelstein, *An Unacknowledged Harmony: Philo-Semitism and the Survival of European Jewry* (Westport, CT: Greenwood, 1982); William D. Rubinstein and Hilary Rubinstein, *Philosemitism: Admiration and Support for Jews in the English-Speaking World, 1840–1939* (Basingstoke, UK: Palgrave Macmillan, 1999). The most notable general articles are Wolfram Kinzig, "Philosemitismus Teil I" and "Philosemitismus Teil II: Zur

drowned out by the vastly greater focus on antisemitism as a keynote in relations between Jews and non-Jews. This fixation was long ago critiqued by Salo W. Baron in his argument against the "lachrymose conception" of Jewish history.[5] In the charged contemporary environment, passionate debates over the existence or otherwise of a "new antisemitism" in Europe intersect with even more passionate controversies over the identification as antisemitic of some strands of anti-Zionist or anti-Israeli politics.[6] Against this backdrop it seems particularly important to highlight the significance of more positive attitudes to Judaism, which have been occluded or distorted when viewed through the dominant historiographical lens of antisemitism.

Much of the existing work on philosemitism is marred by an analytical reductiveness, commonly assuming one of two diametrically opposed alternatives: either that philosemitism is the exact opposite of antisemitism, or that it is itself a form of antisemitism. The first limits the term to rare cases of disinterested, pure, and sincere admiration for Jews, forgetting that all thought is shaped by interests of one kind or another, and that perfect objectivism in the perception of other ethnic groups is, at the very least, extremely unusual. Scholarship in this vein tends to be commemorative in character, celebrating the achievements of philosemites and sometimes admonishing Jews for their failure to appreciate and remember them.[7] The second approach, however, in viewing philosemitism as merely the reverse side of the antisemitic coin, almost inevitably goes too far in the opposite direction, routinely discounting any possible element of sincerity or authenticity in philosemitic utterances. Frank Stern's study of philosemitism in the very particular environment of postwar West Germany thoughtfully examines the ways in which philosemitic speech was shaped by an unspoken but ubiquitous consciousness of antisemitism – but this does not warrant his interpretation of all instances of apparent philosemitism in this context as

historiographischen Verwendung des Begriffs," *Zeitschrift für Kirchengeschichte* 105 (1994): 360–83; David S. Katz, "The Phenomenon of Philo-Semitism," in *Christianity and Judaism: Papers Read at the 1991 Summer Meeting and the 1992 Winter Meeting of the Ecclesiastical History Society* (Oxford: Blackwell, 1992), 327–61; Jacques Berlinerblau, *On Philo-Semitism* (2007), posted at http://pjc.georgetown.edu/docs/philo-semitic.pdf. Most recently, and appearing too late to be fully considered in this volume, see Irene A. Diekmann and Elke-Vera Kotowski, eds., *Geliebter Feind, gehasster Freund: Antisemitismus und Philosemitismus in Geschichte und Gegenwart* (Berlin: VBB, 2009).

[5] Salo W. Baron, *A Social and Religious History of the Jews* (Philadelphia: Jewish Publication Society of America, 1937), 2:32; "Newer Emphases in Jewish History," in his *History and Jewish Historians: Essays and Addresses* (Philadelphia: Jewish Publication Society of America, 1964), 90–108.

[6] Among many recent publications see Matti Bunzl, *Anti-Semitism and Islamophobia: Hatreds Old and New in Europe* (Chicago: Prickly Paradigm, 2007); Jeffrey Herf, ed., *Anti-Semitism and Anti-Zionism in Historical Perspective* (London: Routledge, 2007).

[7] See, e.g., Rappaport, *Jew and Gentile*, 134; Rubinstein and Rubinstein, *Philosemitism*, 203.

simply masking an underlying antisemitism.[8] It is also surely unreasonably suspicious and sweeping to follow Phyllis Lassner and Lara Trubowitz, who, echoing the Jewish joke with which we started, characterize philosemitism as a more insidiously dangerous threat than "transparent antisemitism," which at least can be easily recognized.[9] The varying motives and mentalities of apparent philosemites require careful exploration, even when they conceptualize Jewishness in clearly exaggerated, idealized, or reified ways. Our aim should not be to expose "false" or self-interested philosemites, or to identify "true" ones, but rather to comprehend the significance and function of positive perceptions of Jews and Judaism within their broader intellectual frameworks.

The assumption underlying all entrenched attitudes toward Jews, whether admiring or hostile, is that Jews are in some profound sense different from others. The sociologist Zygmunt Bauman has very usefully advanced the evaluatively neutral word "allosemitism" – derived from *allos*, the Greek word for "other" – as an apt term for this belief.[10] In both the premodern and modern worlds, Bauman has argued, Jews have characteristically occupied intermediary, analytically incongruous roles, standing out as anomalous in the social order, and, in the eyes of modernity's discontents in particular, the representatives par excellence of the invisible "sliminess" of the forces of change. Allosemitism itself, Bauman recognizes, is attitudinally ambivalent. Jewish difference is not necessarily a negative observation, and nor, indeed, is it necessarily untrue – though the negative casting of the Jews as "ambivalence incarnate" and as a perpetual source of disruption and disorder is, he shows, central to the history and underlying dynamics of antisemitism.[11] Bryan Cheyette's exploration of the "semitic discourse" that pervaded representations of Jews in late nineteenth- and early twentieth-century English literature is another notable example of the use of analytically neutral critical terminology to draw attention to the ways in which Jewishness can inspire contradictory associations within a given cultural context.[12] But neither the resort to "ambivalence" nor the subsuming of positive prejudices toward Jews in negative ones can account adequately for

---

[8] Frank Stern, *The Whitewashing of the Yellow Badge: Antisemitism and Philosemitism in Postwar Germany* (London: Heinemann, 1991).

[9] Phyllis Lassner and Lara Trubowitz, eds., *Antisemitism and Philosemitism in the Twentieth and Twenty-First Centuries* (Newark: University of Delaware Press, 2008), 7–8.

[10] Zygmunt Bauman, "Allosemitism: Premodern, Modern, Postmodern," in Bryan Cheyette and Laura Marcus, eds., *Modernity, Culture and "the Jew"* (Cambridge: Polity Press, 1998), 143–56.

[11] Ibid., 151–4; *Modernity and the Holocaust* (Cambridge: Polity, 1989), 37–60; *Modernity and Ambivalence* (Cambridge: Polity Press, 1991), esp. 18–52.

[12] Bryan Cheyette, *Constructions of "the Jew" in English Literature and Society: Racial Representations 1875–1945* (Cambridge: Cambridge University Press, 1993), 8–12, 268–75.

the singularity and richness of philosemitic themes in Western discourse on Jews. And even in those cases where such approaches are justified, the philosemitic strand, so often neglected or dismissed, requires clear articulation. We can only reach an understanding of ambivalence toward Jews if we patiently pick apart its contrasting and sometimes contradictory component threads.

A key aim of *Philosemitism in History*, then, is to explore the complex interplay of positive and negative attitudes toward Jews, highlighting the often highly problematic character of many currents of idealization of Jews and Judaism while taking seriously the significance of non-Jewish impulses to befriend, defend, support, or learn from Jews. The essays in this volume represent a wide range of views of and approaches to this topic. Rather than striving for unanimity, we have invited our contributors to engage critically with this central concept, with no predetermined consensus or constraint. Drawing on a range of disciplinary traditions as well as of regional and chronological specializations, these essays enter into dialogue with each other and together, we hope, offer a salutary and stimulating range of approaches to the topic. Cumulatively, while certainly not definitively pinning down the nature and scope of philosemitism, they do, we believe, convincingly show that the subject they address is broad, complex, and worthy of attention.

Are there any useful generalities to be observed about philosemitism? Despite its many different guises and metamorphoses over space and time, there are nonetheless a number of recurrent motifs and themes that suggest a strong degree of transhistorical integration. It would clearly be reductive to seek to identify a single underlying cause or theory of philosemitism, but it is surely worthwhile to try to make some analytical sense of its internal continuities and connections. Several scholars have already presented their own rough typologies of philosemitism, in which a similar cluster of classifications generally recur: economic, utilitarian, millenarian, humanistic, romantic, intellectual, liberal, Christian, and Zionist.[13] These categories, which overlap with each other and can be grouped together in a number of meaningful ways, provide a heuristically useful listing of the main currents into which philosemitism in the *longue durée* can be divided.

Typologies, however, are limited by their descriptive character. While it is helpful to break down the complexity of philosemitism into more focused components, this does not in itself advance an understanding of the relationships and reactions between these various elements. As a more promising alternative we will in the following pages organize our introductory exploration of the broad transhistorical contours of philosemitism

---

[13] Hans Joachim Schoeps, *Philosemitismus im Barock* (Tübingen: Mohr, 1952); Rappaport, *Jew and Gentile*, 2–4; Rubinstein and Rubinstein, *Philosemitism*, 111–85; Kinzig, "Philosemitismus Teil I," 227–8.

under three analytical headings: its underlying roots, intellectual content, and historical impact. Each of these, at least for the purposes of this brief survey, can be divided into two loosely countervailing elements, which we will try in the following paragraphs briefly to characterize and exemplify (with an emphasis on instances not covered in the chapters to follow).

The sine qua non of philosemitism is the notion of the Jews as a resolutely distinct people, with distinctively admirable characteristics. Several ancient Greek and Roman writers subscribed to this belief, and the existence of philosemitism in antiquity demonstrates the independence of the phenomenon from Christianity, but the deep roots of philosemitism must equally be situated in the supercessionist but also dependent structural relationship of Christianity with Judaism. The substantive arguments marshaled by philosemites can be roughly split into "pure" and "applied" approaches. There is a long philosophical tradition, most interestingly exemplified by Friedrich Nietzsche, of admiring Jews as themselves particularly intellectually impressive, while economists and policymakers have in many different contexts attempted to harness the wealth-generating commercial utility of Jews. This flows naturally into our third heading: the uses and impact of philosemitism through history. The central theme here is the invocation of Judaic models of political governance or national identity, particularly but not only in the British imperial world. Collective identification with Jews has been a significant element in the self-understanding of many different nations. A special case, demanding independent scrutiny, is the political role of philosemitism in support of Zionism, through which it has been a significant force in shaping modern Jewish history as well.

The close relationship of Christianity to philosemitism raises the question of what role philosemitism may have played in Muslim and Arab cultures. Nineteenth-century Jewish historians, underscoring the history of Christian intolerance by juxtaposing it with the relatively favorable treatment of Jews under Islam, coined the term "the Golden Age of Spain" to highlight the capacity of Jews to thrive in the atmosphere of religious tolerance and cultural integration that had prevailed, they argued, in medieval al-Andalus. There are indeed numerous examples of Muslim rulers welcoming Jews to their lands for the skills and services they could provide. For example, the Ottoman Sultan Bayezid II (1491–1512), to whose lands many Sephardim fled after 1492, reportedly ridiculed the Spanish king Ferdinand for expelling such a valuable population. "Can you call such a king wise and intelligent?" remarked Bayezid. "He is impoverishing his country and enriching my kingdom."[14] That this quotation derives from a contemporary Jewish chronicle and not an Islamic source, however, suggests an important point. While prominent Muslim authorities

---

[14] Quoted in Esther Benbassa and Aron Rodrigue, *Sephardi Jewry: A History of the Judeo-Spanish Community, 14th–20th Centuries* (Berkeley: University of California Press, 2000), 7.

sometimes advocated philosemitic policies, they did not necessarily articulate philosemitic viewpoints. This seems to stem from the lesser distinctiveness of Jewish populations living under Muslim as opposed to Christian
rule. Jews in Christendom bore a unique theological and sociological
status, whereas the Jews of Islam were never the focus of a comparable
singularity, being invariably only one among several similarly designated
religious minorities (categorized as tolerated *dhimmi*), usually less prominent or problematic than Christians in Spain or Turkey or Zoroastrians
in Persia. As Marc Cohen points out, "Islamic law lacked a specific focus
on Jews."[15] Nevertheless, a definitive evaluation of Islamic philosemitism
requires more thorough investigation, unfortunately not possible here.

Prior to the emergence of Christianity and Islam, the earliest manifestations of philosemitism are to be found in the period of Greco-Roman
antiquity, when Judaism became an object of admiration, and even partial allegiance, among a handful of Greek authors and a larger number
of pagan "God Fearers." As part of Hellenism's fascination with the East,
authors such as Hecataeus of Abdera (fourth century B.C.E.) and Marcus
Varro (first century B.C.E.) depicted Jews as particularly philosophically
sophisticated, and Judaism as a venerable cult imbued with exemplary customs and a refined monotheism. According to Louis Feldman, Jews were
in the third century B.C.E. widely seen as a "philosophical people," admir-
ingly described by Aristotle's successor Theophrastus as "philosophers by
birth."[16] Judaism was notably successful in the Hellenistic and Roman periods in winning not only converts but also "sympathizers" – non-Jews who,
without converting, adopted certain Jewish practices and whom we might
consider as an early type of philosemite. Feldman suggests three reasons
for this admiration. The antiquity of the Jews was widely acknowledged,
and this was considered an important source of cultural authority in the
ancient world. The Jews were also associated, by several writers, with the
cardinal virtues of courage, temperance, justice, piety, and (above all) wisdom. Finally, there was a strong ancient tradition of admiration for Moses,
who was frequently esteemed, alongside Minos and Lycurgus of Sparta, as
one of the greatest leaders and lawgivers.[17]

Praise for the excellence of the Mosaic polity, by authors such as Strabo
in his *Geography* (first century C.E.), was widely picked up the early modern era, when this current of political commentary became complicatedly
entangled with another idea derived from ancient sources: the ascription

[15] Marc Cohen, *Under Crescent and Cross: The Jews in the Middle Ages* (Princeton, NJ: Princeton
University Press, 1995), 54.
[16] Louis H. Feldman, *Jew and Gentile in the Ancient World* (Princeton, NJ: Princeton University
Press, 1993), 201–3.
[17] Feldman, *Jew and Gentile*, 177–287, 429–35. See also his "Philo-Semitism among Ancient
Intellectuals," *Tradition* 1 (1958–9), 27–38; John Gager, *The Origins of Anti-Semitism: Attitudes
toward Judaism in Pagan and Christian Antiquity* (Oxford: Oxford University Press, 1983), 73.

of Egyptian origins to the Jews. Strabo and Diodorus Siculus (first century B.C.E.) both put forward this notion, claiming that Moses had been initiated into the Egyptian priesthood.[18] For early modern scholars such as John Spencer and John Toland – to say nothing of Sigmund Freud's adoption of this idea in his *Moses and Monotheism* (1939) – the Egyptianization of Moses took on a complicated and ambivalent significance, serving in part to critique the inaccuracy and hubris of the Jews' own account of their origins.[19] There certainly circulated in the ancient world implicitly or explicitly hostile counternarratives to the Jewish Bible, locating the Jews' origins in places such as Crete or Ethiopia and explaining their migration as due to their unpopularity or disease. The most famous summary of these views, in the fifth book of Tacitus's *Histories* (c. 110 C.E.), has almost exclusively been interpreted by scholars as an antisemitic source text and has often been used as such, though strains of philosemitism have also been identified in it.[20] In ascribing Egyptian roots to the Jews and their religious practices, however, authors such as Strabo and Diodorus did not intend to denigrate them. From their pagan perspective, unconcerned (unlike Christians) with the validity of the biblical narrative, this lineage rather reaffirmed the prestige of the Jews, associating them, and Moses in particular, with a familiar and venerable tradition of Egyptian priestly magic.

Prevailing attitudes toward Jews in the Hellenistic and Roman worlds were complex and variegated, and certainly not unremittingly hostile. Judaism, as John Gager has argued, "provoked among Christians and pagans alike profound internal divisions."[21] The cultural influence of the Jews was also significant: according to Arnaldo Momigliano, it was the Jews, rather than the Greeks, who provided the key model for late antique historians' attempts to write "national" histories.[22] Indeed, the anti-Judaic sentiment that did pervade much Roman literature from the first century C.E. can be interpreted as a conservative reaction to the considerable success of Judaism in attracting admirers and sympathizers, even in the highest echelons of the Roman aristocracy. Jews in the ancient world were structurally distinctive in ways that differ significantly but not unrecognizably from the most characteristic features of their distinctiveness in modern history: they were a relatively tightly defined subgroup, with a particularly textual and aniconic religious life and a detailed and deep sense of

[18] See Gager, *Origins of Anti-Semitism*, 67–73.
[19] On this intellectual tradition see Jan Assmann, *Moses the Egyptian: The Memory of Egypt in Western Monotheism* (Cambridge, MA: Harvard University Press, 1997).
[20] Louis H. Feldman, "Pro-Jewish Intimations in Tacitus' Account of Jewish Origins," *Studies in Hellenistic Judaism* (Leiden: E. J. Brill, 1996), 377–407.
[21] Gager, *Origins of Anti-Semitism*, 269.
[22] Arnaldo Momigliano, *The Classical Foundations of Modern Historiography* (Berkeley and Los Angeles: University of California Press, 1990), 85.

their cultural origins. It is not, then, surprising that in both eras the Jews inspired both admiration and resentment, and that this dual response was embedded within a wider cultural uncertainty over how to accommodate and value difference within an ostensibly unified and universalist political and social system.

The issue of difference also lies at the heart of the knotty relationship between Christianity and Judaism, formed in the historical separation process of these two religions in the first few centuries of the Christian era. The central concern of Paul, as many scholars have argued, was to reformulate Judaism as a universalistic message, open to all. In interpreting the Jewish law as an allegorical prefiguring of the coming of Christ, which he regarded as having annulled its validity, Paul's underlying concern was with the overcoming of all particularities, of which Jewish particularity stood as emblematic. Paul thus crucially opposed Jewish difference against Christian universalism. In doing so, he was not the originator of antisemitism (as some would have it), but he did reformulate the older Greek antipathy to Jewish distinctiveness, placing the Jews' assimilation within a bold new eschatological schema. Paul indeed retained an intense concern for his Jewish kin and continued to accord the Jews a uniquely meaningful place in history, writing in his Epistle to the Romans that "to them belong the adoption, the glory, the covenants, the giving of the law, the worship, and the promises" (Romans 9:4). His emphasis on the still-favored status of a Jewish "remnant," and on the ultimate restoration of Israel to its former glory (Romans 11:26–32), initiated a current of philosemitic theology that has endured within Christianity ever since.[23]

Medieval Christian attitudes toward Jews and Judaism, most succinctly and influentially captured in the "witness people" doctrine elaborated by Augustine, were shot through with ambivalence and paradox. While interpreting the Jews' dispersal and suffering as God's just punishment for their rejection and crucifixion of Jesus, Augustine regarded Jewish survival as imbued with unique meaning and purpose: the Jews' preservation of their own religious texts and practices provided peripatetic proof of the biblical prophecies that pointed the way to Christianity.[24] This was of course in no sense a philosemitic doctrine, and it coexisted with a sharply anti-Judaic *Adversus Iudaeos* tradition, stridently exemplified by Augustine's fourth-century contemporary John Chrysostom, that demonized medieval Jews as insults to Christianity and emphasized the disjunction between them

---

[23] For a less universalist interpretation of Paul's relation to Jews and Judaism, see Alan F. Segal, *Paul the Convert: The Apostolate and Apostasy of Saul the Pharisee* (New Haven, CT: Yale University Press, 1990), and especially Daniel Boyarin, *A Radical Jew: Paul and the Politics of Identity* (Berkeley: University of California Press, 1994).

[24] For a succinct and authoritative summary of this doctrine and its influence, see Jeremy Cohen, *Living Letters of the Law: Ideas of the Jew in Medieval Christianity* (Berkeley and Los Angeles: University of California Press, 1999), esp. 23–65.

and their scriptural texts.[25] However, the theology of Jewish witness both denigrated and elevated Jews and in particular ways laid the foundations of some of the key strains of Western philosemitism. Most basically, the commitment to Jewish survival – based on the biblical prooftext "Slay them not" (Psalms 59:11), which was taken as an injunction not simply against the killing of Jews, but also against preventing their observance of Judaism – underwrote the continuance of a Jewish presence in medieval Christendom and indirectly made possible their availability to rulers as vulnerable, and therefore all the more valuable, niche economic operators.

More abstractly, the casting of Jews as, in Jeremy Cohen's phrase, "living letters of the law" – the blindly literalist custodians of textual truths, the figurative significance of which they could not see – placed them at the heart of profound hermeneutical controversies that intensified in the late medieval and particularly in the early modern period.[26] The humanist and Renaissance recovery of classical learning sometimes entailed an idealization of nonbiblical but putatively Jewish sources as pristine fonts of wisdom and truth. Christian Hebraists in the sixteenth and seventeenth centuries were generally temperamentally ambivalent, in varying hues, toward their subject matter. More mystically inclined ecumenicists, however, such as northern European followers of Jacob Boehme, or Christian Knorr von Rosenroth and Francis Mercury van Helmont, the compilers of the *Kabbalah Demudata* (1677), which presented the Jewish mystical tradition as the key to uncontaminated and universal philosophical truth, were avowedly philosemitic in their idealization of certain strands of Judaism. The logical conclusion of this strain of Christian philosemitism was actual conversion to Judaism, of which there are a number of documented cases in early modern Europe, isolated but nonetheless revealing, particularly in the long Enlightenment period.[27]

Philosemitism has figured particularly in Christian eschatological thought, in which the conversion of the Jews constitutes a key element in the unfolding of prophecies concerning the end of time. Whereas the teachings of both Paul and Augustine did not encourage missionizing among Jews, whose conversion they believed would occur only at the appropriate

---

[25] Ora Limor and Guy Stroumsa, eds., *Contra Iudaeos: Ancient and Medieval Polemics between Christians and Jews* (Tübingen: Mohr, 1996).

[26] Cohen, *Living Letters*, esp. 391–400.

[27] Schoeps, *Philosemitismus im Barock*; Allison P. Coudert and Jeffrey Shoulson, eds., *Hebraica Veritas? Christian Hebraists and the Study of Judaism in Early Modern Europe* (Philadelphia: University of Pennsylvania Press, 2004); Allison P. Coudert, *The Impact of the Kabbalah in the Seventeenth Century: The Life and Thought of Francis Mercury von Helmont* (Leiden: E. J. Brill, 1999); Adam Sutcliffe, *Judaism and Enlightenment* (Cambridge: Cambridge University Press, 2003), 23–41, 148–64; Martin Muslow and Richard H. Popkin, *Secret Conversions to Judaism in Early Modern Europe* (Leiden: E. J. Brill, 2004).

time,[28] serious conversionist efforts began in the thirteenth century and have persisted ever since. While the desire to convert Jews is in itself clearly far from philosemitic, Christian conversionism should nonetheless not be hastily conflated with antisemitism, particularly as many chiliastic movements have emphasized beneficence toward Jews as a prerequisite for their successful conversion, and thus for the Second Coming. An ultimate missionary intent, no matter how much it suggests "ulterior motives," should not in itself preclude applying the philosemitic label. Radical Christian millenarians also not infrequently envisaged a religious transformation that would Judaize Christianity at least as much as it would Christianize Jews. In the mid-seventeenth century, in particular, millenarian sentiment among both Jews and Christians led to a heightened expectancy among religious radicals that a reconciliation of Judaism and Christianity was imminent – a belief that played a significant role in the readmission of Jews to England in 1665–6.[29]

Christian philosemitism was also a notable presence in late eighteenth-century political radicalism. The extension of political rights to Jews in the midst of the French Revolution was a decision heavily charged with both secular and religious symbolism: the "regeneration" of Jews envisaged by the revolutionaries transposed into a new idiom the millenarian resonance of Jewish conversion.[30] In Britain the anti-Catholic radical agitator Lord George Gordon actually converted to Judaism in 1787, while in the following decade the prophets Richard Brothers and Joanna Southcott both attracted support for their rival claims to be the imminent leader of the Jews back to their Promised Land.[31] These individuals have often been dismissed as marginal eccentrics, but their distinct brands of popular millenarian radicalism were significant movements feeding into the rise of British socialist movements in the early nineteenth century. Certainly these

---

[28] Cohen, *Living Letters*, 37; Christopher M. Clark, "The Limits of the Confessional State: Conversions to Judaism 1814–1843," *Past and Present* 147 (1995): 159–79.

[29] Ernestine G. E. van der Wall, "A Philo-Semitic Millenarian on the Reconciliation of Jews and Christians: Henry Jessey and His 'The Glory and Salvation of Jehuda and Israel' (1650)," in *Sceptics, Millenarians and Jews* (Leiden: E. J. Brill, 1990), 161–84; Gordon M. Weiner and Richard H. Popkin, eds., *Jewish Christians and Christian Jews: From the Renaissance to the Enlightenment* (Dordrecht: Kluwer, 1994); David S. Katz, *Philo-Semitism and the Readmission of the Jews to England, 1603–1655* (Oxford: Oxford University Press, 1982).

[30] See Ronald Schechter, *Obstinate Hebrews: Representations of Jews in France, 1715–1815* (Berkeley and Los Angeles: University of California Press, 2003), 150–93, esp. 164–5.

[31] Marsha Keith Schuchard, "Lord George Gordon and Cabalistic Freemasonry: Beating Jacobite Swords into Jacobin Plowshares," in Muslow and Popkin, *Secret Conversions*, 183–232; Eitan Bar-Yosef, *The Holy Land in English Culture 1799–1917* (Oxford: Oxford University Press, 2005), 46–60; Ian McCalman, "New Jerusalems: Prophecy, Dissent and Radical Culture in England, 1786–1830," in Knud Haakonssen, ed., *Enlightenment and Religion: Rational Dissent in Eighteenth-Century Britain* (Cambridge: Cambridge University Press, 1996), 312–35.

radicals' associations with Jews and Judaism were often fanciful, but their engagements were serious and sustained. They drew in Jewish associates and contributed to the development of a wider early nineteenth-century cultural environment in which a variety of Christian millenarian preoccupations, utopian projections, and conversionist endeavors often cross-fertilized with more politically mainstream campaigns for Jewish material uplift and political emancipation, even if they did not straightforwardly align with them.[32]

Admiration for and fascination with Judaism, then, are present in Greco-Roman intellectual culture and have deep roots within Christianity. Both traditions associated Jews with great antiquity, bookishness, and – most importantly – a determination to preserve a particular identity and set of cultural practices. While the Christian tradition, and especially its ambiguous Pauline heritage, is most often advanced in academic discussions of philosemitism, it is actually the Greek and Hellenistic legacies to which the most vital and variegated expressions of modern philosemitism owe their allegiance. To the extent that Hellenistic philosophy concerned itself with Judaism, it sought to address the relationship between universality and particularism. Philosophers in the modern Western tradition have retained this preoccupation, with Jewishness not infrequently continuing to present itself as a key test case. The late seventeenth-century Huguenot encyclopedist Pierre Bayle, for example, engaged so deeply with Judaism that his twentieth-century editor, Richard Popkin, speculated that he may even have been a "secret Jew," though his fascination was fundamentally philosophical in nature: he regarded Jews, because they were the unique recipients of God's directly revealed commandments, as alone standing outside the otherwise insoluble tension between the incommensurable demands of Christian faith and universal reason.[33] Gotthold Ephraim Lessing's famously philosemitic plays *The Jews* (1754) and above all *Nathan the Wise* (1779) self-consciously invert negative Jewish stereotypes, associating their Jewish heroes with Lessing's own Enlightenment values of universalist virtue, humanity, and wisdom.[34] Contrastingly, in some recent postmodern thought Judaism has represented an alluringly communitarian and poetic escape from the cold rationalism of Western philosophy.[35]

[32] Mel Scult, *Millennial Expectations and Jewish Liberties* (Leiden: E. J. Brill, 1978), 90–142.

[33] Richard H. Popkin, introduction to *Pierre Bayle – Historical and Critical Dictionary: Selections* (Indianapolis: Hackett, 1991), xxvi; Adam Sutcliffe, "Bayle and Judaism," in Wiep van Bunge, ed., *Pierre Bayle (1647–1706), Le Philosophe de Rotterdam: Philosophy, Religion and Reception* (Leiden: E. J. Brill, 2008), 121–34.

[34] Ritchie Robertson, "'Dies hohe Lied der Duldung'? The Ambiguities of Toleration in Lessing's *Die Juden* and *Nathan der Weise*," *Modern Language Review* 93 (1998): 105–20; Willi Goetschel, *Spinoza's Modernity: Mendelssohn, Lessing and Heine* (Madison: University of Wisconsin Press, 2004), 230–50.

[35] See Gillian Rose, *Judaism and Modernity* (Oxford: Blackwell, 1993).

Philosophical philosemitism can be most fruitfully explored, however, through the writings of Friedrich Nietzsche, whose legacy with regard to Judaism continues to generate much controversy and confusion and, for this reason, merits particularly close attention.[36] The young Nietzsche certainly casually imbibed and expressed antisemitism. However, the anti-antisemitism of his mature work was a key feature of his philosophical opposition to the politics of the herd. The vengeful and bitter popular sentiment of *ressentiment* was, he repeatedly noted, most frequently and crudely directed against Jews, both in the foundational era of early Christianity and in the nationalist demagoguery of his own era.[37] Jews were, however, in Nietzsche's eyes centrally responsible for the introduction of *ressentiment* into Western culture, as a consequence of the "slave rebellion in morals" that they initiated with their prophets' valorization of meekness and poverty over nobility and strength.[38] Nietzsche expressed admiration both for preprophetic Judaism, with its ennobling emphasis on the divine strength of Yahweh, and for modern Judaism. His critiques focused on the prophets and their priestly successors, whom he viewed as paving the way for Christianity, which he reviled. He nonetheless regarded the life-denying *ressentiment* morality as in essence profoundly un-Judaic, explaining in his late work that in the era of Isaiah the Jews turned to this negation of their natural values as a final, tough-minded act of "self-preservation" in the face of impossible circumstances.[39] There is thus a backbone of intense, awed admiration of the vital spirit of the Jewish people even – indeed particularly – in Nietzsche's ascription to them of this most profoundly negative development in the history of civilization.

Nietzsche's attitudes to Judaism and Jews are elusive and complicated, and – in keeping with his general intellectual style – expressed in mobile and at times inconsistent fashion. However, the characterization of his stance as fundamentally ambivalent is misleading.[40] Nietzsche regarded

[36] See Steven E. Aschheim, "Thinking the Nietzsche Legacy Today," in his *In Times of Crisis: Essays on European Culture, Germans, and Jews* (Madison: University of Wisconsin Press, 2001), 13–23; *The Nietzsche Legacy in Germany, 1890–1990* (Berkeley and Los Angeles: University of California Press, 1992).

[37] Friedrich Nietzsche, *The Anti-Christ* (1888), trans. R. J. Hollingdale, §40; *On the Genealogy of Morals* (1887), trans. Walter Kaufmann, §2:11, 3:14.

[38] Friedrich Nietzsche, *Beyond Good and Evil* (1886), trans. Walter Kaufmann, §195; *Genealogy of Morals*, §1:7.

[39] Nietzsche, *Anti-Christ*, §24. For a helpful analysis see Michael F. Duffy and Willard Mittelman, "Nietzsche's Attitudes toward the Jews," *Journal of the History of Ideas* 49 (1988): 301–17; Weaver Santaniello, *Nietzsche, God, and the Jews* (Albany: State University of New York Press, 1994); "A Post-Holocaust Re-Examination of Nietzsche and the Jews," in Jacob Golumb, ed., *Nietzsche and Jewish Culture* (London: Routledge, 1997), 21–54.

[40] For this characterization see Yirmiyahu Yovel, *Dark Riddle: Hegel, Nietzsche, and the Jews* (Cambridge: Polity Press, 1998), esp. 177–9; "Nietzsche and the Jews: The Structure of an Ambivalence," in Golumb, ed, *Nietzsche and Jewish Culture*, 117–34.

the Jews in superlative terms, as a uniquely resilient, intellectually energetic, and historically significant people, closely aligned with his positive moral values, whereas his German contemporaries in the main stood against them. Antisemitism appalled him, but it would be wrong to regard him simply as an anti-antisemite, neglecting his pointedly affirmative evaluations of Jews. His admiration for the Jews was most fundamentally intellectual, based on a characterization of their core values as strong and life affirming. He also admired the Jews as a sociopolitical collectivity of supreme cohesion and fortitude, celebrating their particularity (in anticipation of later postmodern responses). There was in addition a concretely political aspect to his admiration: although he was not at all interested in the Jews as an economic asset, he cast them, in quasi-millenarian fashion, as potentially the crucial agents of a future revivification of Europe.[41]

Philosemitism has had a significant historical impact in the realm of politics as well as philosophy. Christian Hebraist scholarship in early modern Europe exerted a considerable influence on the legal and constitutional thought of the period, with Moses commanding widespread admiration as a supreme lawgiver. The importance of "political Hebraism," however, which can be discerned in almost all major early modern political thinkers, has only recently begun to receive close scholarly attention.[42] The deployment of Hebraic themes has also often served to advance political arguments. John Milton, for example, strongly identified the prophetic tradition in Judaism, which he used in support of his antiepiscopalian politics, and juxtaposed against the Jewish priesthood, which he associated with his Laudian opponents. Milton's split view of Judaism, widely shared in the mid-seventeenth century, is thus clearly ambivalent – but this does not diminish the strikingly Hebraic idiom of his positive political thought.[43] Milton's contemporary, the scholar and parliamentary leader John Selden, viewed the Mishnaic tradition (which postdated Christ) as a model of religious toleration within an enlightened polity.[44]

---

[41] Nietzsche, *Beyond Good and Evil*, §251; *Human, All Too Human* (1878), trans. R. Hollingdale, §1I:475.

[42] See Lea Campos Boralevi, "Classical Foundation Myths of European Republicanism: The Jewish Commonwealth," in Martin van Gelderen and Quentin Skinner, eds., *Republicanism: A Shared European Heritage*, vol. 1, *Republicanism and Constitutionalism in Early Modern Europe* (Cambridge: Cambridge University Press, 2002), 247–62; also the new journal *Hebraic Political Studies*, published in Jerusalem since 2006.

[43] See Douglas A. Brooks, ed., *Milton and the Jews* (Cambridge: Cambridge University Press, 2008), esp. the essays by Nicholas von Maltzahn, "Making Use of the Jews: Milton and Philo-Semitism," 57–82, and Achsah Guibbory, "England, Israel and the Jews in Milton's Prose, 1649–1660," 13–34; Jeffrey S. Shoulson, *Milton and the Rabbis: Hebraism, Hellenism and Christianity* (New York: Columbia University Press, 2001).

[44] See Jason Rosenblatt, *Renaissance England's Chief Rabbi: John Selden* (Oxford: Oxford University Press, 2006), 141–65.

Politics more broadly construed encompasses a view of Jews as testing the limits of eligibility for citizenship, both in themselves and by providing a model for the further extension of the franchise to other, even more marginal groups. One thinks, for instance, of the mutual impact of efforts to grant Jews and Catholics citizenship in nineteenth-century Britain, or the troubled relationship of a legally privileged Jewish population to French colonial Algeria under the 1870 Crémieux Decree, or the political incorporation of Hungarian Jews to provide the ruling Magyars with electoral majorities in the face of peasant Romanian and Slavic opposition. In a different vein, one might also cite the curious case of Leopold von Sacher-Masoch, whose accounts of central European Jewish ghetto life provide a particularly striking example of the potential political resonance of a gendered philosemitism. Sacher-Masoch, an acute observer of the Hasidic world to which he was exposed during his youth in mid nineteenth-century Galicia, was fascinated by Jewish women, whom he portrayed as alluring, strong, and sensuous. His interest in the humanization and emancipation of Jews, and above all Jewesses, was both fetishistically eroticized and connected to his broader support for the emancipation of women, and of the erotic imagination in general.[45]

The malleability of Jewishness in the Western political imagination is such that the Jews have served to exemplify both the primacy of the nation as well as its cosmopolitan transcendence. Perceptions of Jews as particularly culturally cohesive or loyal have offered grist not only for attacks on their particularist exclusivity but also for admiring ruminations on their powerful sense of collective identity and belonging. In the early modern Protestant polities of northwest Europe, where both economic prosperity and political Hebraism were most heavily concentrated, emergent ideals of nationhood were closely modeled on the Hebraic biblical exemplar. Theorists of modern nationalism have emphasized the importance of the "biblical prototype" in the development of a covenantal, sacral notion of nationhood, first articulated in post-Reformation England, and not long afterward in Dutch and German Pietist ideals of national or linguistic community.[46] In the nineteenth and twentieth centuries this idiom of collective political imagination was exported around the world. Afrikaner nationalists, for example, strongly identified with the Jews, whom they imagined as a similarly small, isolated, and pious nation, while in the mid-Victorian period many Maori converts to Christianity enthusiastically adopted the

[45] David Biale, "Masochism and Philosemitism: The Strange Case of Leopold von Sader-Masoch," *Journal of Contemporary History* 17 (1982): 305–23; Irving Massey, *Philo-Semitism in Nineteenth-Century German Literature* (Tübingen: Niemeyer, 2000), 17–60, 165–9.

[46] Anthony D. Smith, *Chosen Peoples* (Oxford: Oxford University Press, 2003), esp. 44–65; Adrian Hastings, *The Construction of Nationhood: Ethnicity, Religion and Nationalism* (Cambridge: Cambridge University Press, 1997), 35–65; Colin Kidd, *British Identities before Nationalism* (Cambridge: Cambridge University Press, 1999), 9–33.

theory – first suggested by British missionaries and linguists – that they were of Jewish descent.[47]

Hebraic identification also influenced the perspective from the British imperial metropole. The British Israelite movement, which claimed that the British were the descendants of the ten lost tribes of Israel, reached its peak of influence during Britain's late Victorian imperial zenith. Loosely derived from Richard Brothers's prophetic claims in the 1790s, the British Israelites not only asserted Hebraic authenticity for their own Saxon lineage but denied the legitimacy of contemporary Jews, whom they derided as mongrel impostors. Although they attracted significant support, the British Israelites were always a marginal group, widely ridiculed by mainstream Anglicans and others, and their theology was a particularly confused mix of self-declared philosemitism and racialized antisemitism. Nonetheless, their claims fitted well with the expansionist agenda of British imperialism. The British Israelites agitated vocally for British colonial involvement in Palestine, and, as Eitan Bar-Yosef has argued, their Hebraic identitarianism was eccentric only as a literalist expression of the widespread Victorian conviction that the British had in some sense inherited from the Jews the mantle of providential election.[48]

In the twentieth and early twenty-first centuries, while predominantly American "Christian Identity" movements have fashioned British Israelite theology into a virulently racist and antisemitic fringe credo, the rhetoric of national chosenness in mainstream political discourse in the United States has, as in nineteenth-century Britain, often intertwined with an identification with Israel, since 1948 concretized as the state of Israel.[49] Other currents of philosemitism in twentieth-century Europe arose, developed, and endure in relation to particular local political polarities. Liberalism in Spain from its nineteenth-century inception tended to espouse an element of philosemitism as a marker of contrast to the dominance of Catholic conservatism, and in the early twentieth century a small but not insignficant

[47] Smith, *Chosen Peoples*, 77–85; Rappaport, *Jew and Gentile*, 135–41; Tony Ballantyne, *Orientalism and Race: Aryanism in the British Empire* (Basingstoke, UK: Palgrave Macmillan, 2002), 58–62, 164–7.

[48] Bar-Yosef, *Holy Land*, 199–202; "Christian Zionism and Victorian Culture," *Israel Studies* 8 (2003): 18–44; Colin Kidd, *The Forging of Races: Race and Scripture in the Protestant Atlantic World, 1600–2000* (Cambridge: Cambridge University Press, 2006), 203–14; Tudor Parfitt, *The Lost Tribes of Israel: The History of a Myth* (London: Weidenfeld & Nicholson, 2002), 52–65; David S. Katz and Richard H. Popkin, *Messianic Revolution: Radical Religious Politics to the End of the Second Millennium* (London: Penguin, 1999), 170–89.

[49] Kidd, *Forging of Races*, 218–26; Katz and Popkin, *Messianic Revolution*, 189–204. On the highly ambivalent representation of Jews in the avowedly Zionist and philosemitic Left Behind Christian novel series by Timothy LaHaye and Jerry Jenkins, leading best sellers in the United States since 1995, see Jonathan Freedman, "Antisemitism without Jews: *Left Behind* in the American Heartland," in Lassner and Trubowitz, eds., *Antisemitism and Philosemitism*, 154–74.

filosefardismo movement emerged, arguing that the Spanish race and economy would be regenerated by the return of Sephardim to the country. In 1931 the progressive government of the new Second Republic swiftly moved to promote this return, in response to which, in part, the preoccupation of the Spanish Right with Judeo-Masonic-Bolshevik conspiracy was consolidated.[50]

While some anti-Jewish nationalists insisted that the Jews' tribal cohesiveness corroded that of non-Jewish peoples, cosmopolitan liberals and socialists also occasionally praised Jews (or specific currents within Jewish life) for defying all forms of national chauvinism. Well before Isaac Deutscher – scion of Polish rabbis – had coined the term "the non-Jewish Jew," V. I. Lenin and Maxim Gorky celebrated the "great, universally progressive traits in Jewish culture."[51] The overrepresentation of Jews in various liberal and socialist causes was to be explained, Lenin insisted, by the "internationalism" of Jewish culture and "its responsiveness to the advanced movements of the age."[52] Gorky went further, locating the sources of Jewish universalism not in a nebulous "Jewish culture," but in a transposed idealism rooted in the biblical prophets. The Jews, Gorky asserted, "disturb the peace of the satiated and self-satisfied and shed a ray of light on the dark sides of life. With their energy and enthusiasm, they have given people the gift of fire and the tireless pursuit of truth. They have been rousing nations, not letting them rest, and finally – and this is the main thing! – this idealism has given birth to the scourge of the powerful; the religion of the masses, socialism."[53]

The Jews' contribution to commerce and capitalism, rather than to socialism, has also possessed its philosemitic dimension. While medieval antisemitism owed much to the growing identification of Jews and usury, the Jews' very presence in northern Europe was significantly premised on their assumed (and often indeed proven) economic utility. The idea that Jews were reputed to generate economic benefits does not sit well with the standard notion that during the Middle Ages they were deliberately forced into commercial and moneylending occupations as a way of excluding them from the landholding elite or from membership in urban guilds.

---

[50] Michael Alpert, "Dr Angel Pulido and Philo-Sephardism in Spain," *Jewish Historical Studies* 40 (2005): 105–21; Isabelle Rohr, *The Spanish Right and the Jews, 1898–1945* (Brighton: Sussex Academic Press, 2007), 14–49. For an analysis of much earlier Spanish philosemitism in terms of a broadly similar political antagonism see David L. Graizbord, "Philosemitism in Late Sixteenth- and Seventeenth-Century Iberia: Refracted Judaeophobia?" *Sixteenth-Century Journal* 38 (2007): 657–82.

[51] Isaac Deutscher, *The Non-Jewish Jew and Other Essays* (Oxford: Oxford University Press, 1968).

[52] Hyman Lumer, ed., *Lenin on the Jewish Question* (New York: International Press, 1974), 107.

[53] See Yuri Slezkine, *The Jewish Century* (Princeton, NJ: Princeton University Press, 2004), 163–4.

While some Jews did own land well into the medieval period, most were invited to settle precisely because they were understood to be commercial or financial specialists. The very shift from commerce to finance and moneylending, occurring in western Europe between the eleventh and late twelfth centuries, was not necessarily the result of the Jews' exclusion from more mainstream occupations, but rather of the fact that the medieval commercial revolution made financial occupations especially attractive to those with the capital and skills to undertake them: that is, among others, to Jews.[54] Few of the numerous medieval privileges granted to Jews overtly sing their praises (the famous one issued by Bishop Rudiger of Speyer in 1084 is exceptional in this regard), but the favorable terms often specified in these documents suggest a very high valuation of Jewish presence indeed.[55]

In early modern Europe this favorable regard for Jewish commercial utility sometimes found expression in the emerging literature of political economy, a phenomenon that some historians have labeled "mercantilist philosemitism." The application of mercantilist principles to Jewish settlement was often inspired by arguments found in contemporary Jewish apologetic works, such as those of Simone Luzzatto and Menasseh ben Israel, which offer a clear indication that Jews themselves often sought to induce philosemitic beliefs as a matter of self-interested pragmatic policy. Such notable figures as Josiah Child, John Toland, Joseph Addison, and Josiah Tucker in Britain, and Jean-Baptiste Colbert, Montesquieu, Ange Goudar, and Jean-Baptiste Say in France enumerated the benefits of Jewish commerce. Naturally, in doing so they were concerned to combat the more prevalent attitude of hostility toward Jewish "usury" and "middleman activity"; nevertheless, their voices were often influential, creating an enduring if tense symbiosis between economic liberalism and Jewish emancipation.[56]

The most contentious but arguably the most materially significant realm in which philosemitism has played a prominent role is the history of modern Zionism. From the 1830s onward, evangelical Christians in England, especially those associated with the Clapham sect and the followers of the leading evangelical social reformer Lord Shaftesbury, sustained a strong interest in the "restoration" of the Jews to the Holy Land.[57] In the late 1870s, immediately after the publication of George Eliot's explicitly

[54] Michael Toch, "Economic Activities of the Jews in the Middle Ages," in Michael Toch and Elizabeth Müller-Luckner, eds., *Wirtschaftsgeschichte der mittelalterlichen Juden: Fragen und Einschätzungen* (Munich: Oldenberg Verlag, 2009), 187–8.

[55] For a sampling, see Robert Chazan, ed., *Church, State, and Jew in the Middle Ages* (New York: Behrman House, 1980), 57–94.

[56] See Jonathan Karp, *The Politics of Jewish Commerce: Economic Thought and Emancipation in Europe 1638–1848* (Cambridge: Cambridge University Press, 2008), esp. 91–3.

[57] Donald M. Lewis, *The Origins of Christian Zionism: Lord Shaftesbury and Evangelical Support for a Jewish Homeland* (Cambridge: Cambridge University Press, 2010).

Zionist novel *Daniel Deronda* (1876), millenarian Victorians saw the crisis in the Turkish Empire known as the "Eastern Question" as an opportunity to promote British intervention in Palestine. This restorationist agenda, however, intersected with attacks on Prime Minister Disraeli's insufficient response to massacres of Bulgarian Christians by Turkish militia, spearheaded by Disraeli's adversary, Gladstone, and tinged with antisemitism. At this stage Jews in Britain and beyond were focused on the civil rights and safety of their brethren in southeast Europe, and not on Palestine, and thus stood politically at odds with Christian Zionists.[58] With the emergence of the Jewish Zionist movement, however, this began to change.

The Balfour Declaration of November 1917, affirming British support for a Jewish homeland in Palestine, has largely been interpreted under the sign of antisemitism, focusing on the British elite's stereotypical fantasies of the extreme power of Jews, both as American bankers and as Russian socialists, who they hoped might swing the support of their respective countries behind the Entente side in World War I.[59] These stereotypes, however, were ambivalent, encompassing notes of admiration at least as much as hostility. While primarily shaped by strategic realpolitik, the Balfour Declaration was imaginable in no small measure due to the British tradition of Bible-based identification with the Jews. As David Lloyd George himself stated, explaining the roots of the declaration in an address to the Jewish Historical Society of England in 1925: "It was undoubtedly inspired by natural sympathy, admiration, and also by the fact that, as you must remember, we had been trained even more in Hebrew history than in the history of our own country."[60] British policy toward Zionism in the early twentieth century should certainly be seen in the context of the ethnically oriented thinking that dominated among diplomatic elites in this period, which culminated in the redrawing of the map of Europe in 1918.[61] The Jews, however, were not simply one small nation among many others: their unique cultural and political significance in the eyes of the British enabled the Zionist leadership to command an unrivaled degree of high-level attention. The Balfour Declaration was not, as some would have it, an instance of "pure" philosemitism, shaped by an altruistic concern for the welfare of Jews.[62] The predominant mind-set of its framers

---

[58] David Feldman, *Englishmen and Jews: Social Relations and Political Culture, 1840–1914* (New Haven, CT: Yale University Press, 1994), 94–105; Bar-Yosef, *Holy Land*, 202–25.

[59] David Vital, *A People Apart: A Political History of the Jews in Europe, 1789–1939* (Oxford: Oxford University Press, 1999), 687–702, esp. 698–9; Mark Levene, "The Balfour Declaration: A Case of Mistaken Identity," *English Historical Review* 107 (1992): 54–77; James Renton, "The Historiography of the Balfour Declaration: Toward a Multi-Causal Framework," *Journal of Israeli History* 19 (1998): 109–28.

[60] Cited in Bar-Yosef, *Holy Land*, 182.

[61] James Renton, *The Zionist Masquerade: The Birth of the Anglo-Zionist Alliance, 1914–1918* (Basingstoke, UK: Palgrave Macmillan, 2007), 11–42.

[62] Rubinstein and Rubinstein, *Philosemitism*, 149–70.

and their cultural world was nonetheless in the final analysis largely positive toward Jews, and it was by recognizing and appealing to this that Chaim Weizmann and the Zionist leadership were able to secure what they wanted.

Philosemitism thus played an important role in this key diplomatic event in modern Jewish history, and it continues to be a factor in the global politics of the Middle East conflict, though precisely how and to what extent remains a hotly contested issue. How has the broader history of Zionism and Israel related to the philosemitic dynamic? The intertwinement of the political, cultural, and religious strands of philosemitism discussed here, and their penetration into Jewish life, are perhaps most powerfully highlighted by the absorption into Jewish Zionism, as Gabriel Piterberg has recently argued, of the theologically charged colonialist arguments of Protestant restorationist philosemitism. An apt emblem of this is the encounter in November 1895 between Theodor Herzl and Colonel Albert Goldsmid, an Anglo-Jew who had been raised as a Christian by his baptized parents but had returned to Judaism in early adulthood, which Herzl records in his diary as having been deeply moving for both men. Goldsmit, Herzl notes, enthusiastically embraced his Zionist vision as "the idea of my life," proudly declaring to him, "I am Daniel Deronda."[63]

This brief overview of trends and themes in the history of philosemitism complements and foreshadows the essays presented in this volume, which proceed in broad chronological order. The first three chapters offer synoptic overviews of philosemitism in the medieval and early modern periods. Robert Chazan's opening essay shows how the New Testament and the patristic legacy outlined a protected space for Jews within a Christian order, which remained doctrinally operative through much of the Middle Ages, despite intensifying persecution and expulsions. Chazan demonstrates that medieval Christendom provided the basic framework of papal protections, intellectual engagement, and economic utilization, which, however "episodic and specific," would grow into a more variegated and full-fledged philosemitism in postmedieval Europe. Abraham Melamed describes how Renaissance humanism restored the West's connection to the Greek and Hellenistic strain of ancient philosemitism, focusing specifically on the notion, prevalent in the sixteenth century, that ancient Judaism was the original font of all worldly and spiritual wisdom. Melamed is careful to insist that such attributions of Jewish priority were often deployed for distinctly non-philosemitic ends (supercessionist, missionary, polemical, etc.), yet he conjectures that the long-term effect of the Renaissance preoccupation with Jewish sources fed the impulse toward political accommodation

---

[63] Gabriel Piterberg, *The Returns of Zionism: Myths, Politics and Scholarship in Israel* (London: Verso, 2008), 244–57; John M. Picker, "George Eliot and the Sequel Question," *New Literary History* 37 (2006): 361–88, esp. 382.

with Jews. In similar fashion, Adam Sutcliffe questions the extent to which even at its mid-seventeenth-century peak early modern philosemitism had much to do with positive attitudes toward contemporary Jews. Focusing on Holland and England, Sutcliffe emphasizes the importance of the philosemitic phenomenon for the articulation of philosophical and especially political doctrines connected with republican theory and contemporary nationalism and patriotism.

Following these introductory overviews a trio of portrait essays focuses on the philosemitism of several individual thinkers: William Whiston in England (1667–1752), the abbé Grégoire in France (1750–1831), and Mór Jókai in Hungary (1825–1904). Adam Shear describes Whiston, a Newtonian theologian and the English translator of Josephus, as a "Judeocentric" Christian who affirmed the legitimacy of Jewish law to primitive Christianity and viewed the restoration of Jews to Palestine, the reconstruction of the Temple in Jerusalem, and the full practice of Mosaic law as essential features of the millennium. Grégoire, in Alyssa Goldstein Sepinwall's account, is an especially ambiguous case of philosemitism. A leading champion of Jewish emancipation during the French Revolution, he jealously guarded his reputation as a friend of the Jews and indeed was lionized by the Franco-Jewish community itself. However, despite praising certain Jewish mores (such as marital fidelity, parental devotion, and charity), Grégoire disparaged the Jewish religion and represented Jews as a degenerate population in need of moral and physical regeneration. No such debunking exercise is involved in Howard Lupovitch's exposition of the philosemitism of the Magyar novelist Jókai. As Lupovitch sees it, Jókai's attitude to Jews was unusual in two respects. It was the product of a conversion, so to speak – a painful and self-conscious effort to expunge the anti-Jewish attitudes he had absorbed in his youth – and it was characterized by a resistance to viewing Jews as positive symbols and a commitment instead to depicting them as flesh and blood human beings, albeit almost always virtuous ones.

The next three essays take a more broadly analytical approach to nineteenth- and early twentieth-century European philosemitism. Nadia Valman explores the rise to prominence in Victorian England of the figure of the beautiful, virtuous, and self-sacrificing Jewess. Through a close and striking reading of two key novels of the 1870s – Anthony Trollope's *The Way We Live Now* and George Eliot's *Daniel Deronda* – Valman shows how representations of Jewish women in both narratives are indebted to a long-standing Christian evangelical fascination with the Jewess as a figure of exceptional spirituality and significance. The essays by Lars Fischer and Alan T. Levenson engage in an at times contentious conversation with each other on philosemitism in late imperial Germany. Arguing against treatments that accept the philosemitism of German Social Democrats at face value, Fischer makes the point that since in contemporary political parlance "antisemitism" was a far-ranging rightist program, socialist opposition to it should not necessarily be confused with a defense of Jews. On the contrary, according to Fischer, both antisemites and their opponents concurred on the point that the label "philosemite" was a taint. Levenson, in contrast, rejects this characterization as too extreme (after all, there was even a journal named *Der Philosemit*). While acknowledging philosemitism's many weaknesses (its admixtures of prejudice and overemphasis on assimilation), he regards it as a genuine tendency often reflecting sincerely held beliefs, the existence of which ought to warn us against assuming pervasive anti-Jewish attitudes in imperial German culture.

Although the next trio of chapters shift the locale from Europe to North America, they maintain a significant thematic continuity with the previous essays. Jonathan Karp's contribution focuses on the philosemitism of three major figures in early and mid-twentieth century African American life: the educator Booker T. Washington, who depicted Jews as a model of economic self-help that blacks should emulate; the writer Zora Neale Hurston, who was steeped in the tradition of political Hebraism exemplified by Machiavelli, Toland, and others; and the singer and activist Paul Robeson, whose identification of Jews as a source of both Negro folk music and black spirituality recalls the Renaissance doctrine on the Jewish origins of worldly and sacred knowledge. The transfiguration of these older motifs to suit African American ideologies underscores both the extreme malleability and the enduring continuity of many philosemitic themes. Yet while much philosemitism seems impervious to the actual doings of contemporary Jews, this was certainly not the case in the post–World War II America examined by Julian Levinson. Here the rise of Jewish American writers such as Saul Bellow, Delmore Schwartz, and Alfred Kazin (to name but a few) was greeted by some non-Jewish artists as a source of fresh vitality within American culture, marking a new sensibility that exalted marginality, nonconformity, and victimhood in combination with intellectual intensity and depth. Levinson traces these themes in the writings of non-Jews like the poets Robert Lowell, Sylvia Plath, and John Berryman, all of whom in one form or another epitomized the artist as symbolically or archetypically a Jew. Philosemitic continuity is still more apparent in Yaakov Ariel's study of the relationship between late twentieth-century Christian millenarianism and the state of Israel. Although Ariel traces the long historical trajectory of evangelical pro-Zionist views, his study focuses mainly on developments among American millenarians from William Blackstone in the late nineteenth century to the present. American evangelical activism for Israel since the 1967 Six Day War, although contradictory and problematic, has produced a degree of religious-based support for Jews that Ariel sees as unprecedented in the history of Jewish-Christian relations.

The final two essays examine the nature of philosemitic popular and mass culture in post–World War II European consciousness. Wulf Kansteiner treats the delicate topic of self-consciously philosemitic television programming in West Germany from the 1960s to the 1980s. While noting the extreme awkwardness of many of the televisual efforts to present Jews in an exclusively positive light, Kansteiner argues that it was the media's growing awareness of these "faux pas" that ironically helped nudge German public consciousness toward a more normalized view of Jews. Ruth Ellen Gruber adopts a similar approach in surveying the flourishing industry of Jewish kitsch souvenirs and tourist sites in Eastern Europe. These objects include wooden figurines of Hasidic Jews with stereotypical Jewish features and even images baked of marzipan. Gruber argues that despite their grotesque aspect, these statues possess a talismanic aura for many of their purchasers, whose outlook on Jews she judges to be a peculiar combination of sentimentality, fashionableness, bemusement, and devotion. The "Jewish" tourism industry in places like Kazimierz, Poland, has grown enormously in recent years, even where Jews themselves compose only a small percentage of those in attendance. Yet here too Gruber shows that the temptation to ridicule should be resisted: not only are Jews themselves prominent among the promoters and entrepreneurs driving this market, but their material success has often led to a revival of Jewish settlement in locales from which they had been eradicated during the Holocaust. Jews' simultaneous discomfort with and interest in promoting philosemitism thus remain as potent as ever.

The essays in this volume together offer, we hope, a broad and varied range of philosemitic case studies, illuminating both continuities and contrasts in the ways in which this phenomenon has manifested itself in different times and places. They certainly do not constitute a comprehensive overview. The positive attitudes toward Judaism of several prominent thinkers touched upon in this introduction, such as Gottfried Lessing, George Eliot, or Friedrich Nietzsche, might each have been the subject of a chapter of their own.[64] Much more might have been said about the eighteenth- and nineteenth-century roots of the particularly intense American tradition of philosemitism, in relation to both religion and politics.[65] We have also not found room to discuss instances of literary philosemitism in Russia, for example in the work of Maxim Gorky, briefly discussed earlier, or Vladimir Nabokov.[66] Finally, with the important exception of Ruth Ellen Gruber's essay on Jewish "kitsch" philosemitism in contemporary

[64] Most recently on Eliot see Alan T. Levenson, "Writing the Philosemitic Novel: *Daniel Deronda* Revisited," *Prooftexts* 28 (2008): 129–56.

[65] See Eran Shalev, "'A Perfect Republic': The Mosaic Constitution in Revolutionary New England, 1775–1788," *New England Quarterly* 82 (2009): 235–63; Robert K. Whalen, "'Christians Love the Jews!': The Development of Christian Philosemitism, 1790–1860," *Religion and American Culture* 6 (1996): 225–59.

[66] Shalom Goldman, "'Nabokov's Minyan': A Study in Philo-Semitism," *Modern Judaism* 25 (2005): 1–22.

Europe, this volume does not address the philosemitic phenomenon within Western popular culture, from radio and television shows like *The Goldbergs* to the "Jewish" identification of such soccer clubs as England's Tottenham Hotspur and Holland's Ajax.[67] Indeed, a truly exhaustive study of philosemitism in history would necessarily be voluminous, underscoring – if further evidence were needed – that the topic is neither a minor nor a marginal one. This volume's aspiration, though, is to be stimulating and suggestive rather than encyclopedic. If nothing else, we hope that we have assembled a convincing case that philosemitism, far from being a mythical or empty category, does indeed have a deep, complex, and significant history, and one that is worthy of serious scholarly attention.

In the contemporary world the significance of philosemitism shows no sign of abating. Admiring popular histories, such as Thomas Cahill's bestselling *The Gifts of the Jews* (1998) or Steven L. Pease's *The Golden Age of Jewish Achievement* (2009), reach a wide readership.[68] From within academic Jewish history, meanwhile, some recent prominent studies have put forward controversially bold claims for the centrality of Jews in the emergence and development of modernity. Yuri Slezkine, in his analysis of twentieth-century history focused on the experience of Russian Jewry, has declared that, as Jews have been the key entrepreneurial, mobile, and urban minority in European history, "modernization ... is about everybody becoming Jewish"; for Yirmiyahu Yovel, meanwhile, the roots of modern subjectivity are to be found in the split identity of the Iberian Marranos.[69] While these rhetorically dispassionate scholarly studies should not be considered in themselves straightforwardly philosemitic, they share with philosemitism a strong emphasis on the positive historical importance of Jews and reflect the recent development of the "Jewish contribution to civilization" tradition of Jewish scholarship from assimilatory apologetics to intellectually ambitious assertiveness.[70] In a very different context, there has in the past decade been a notable rise of philosemitic rhetoric on the European Far Right. From Norway to Romania and from the United Kingdom to Latvia Far Right political parties have been distancing themselves from

---

[67] See Franklin Foer, *How Soccer Explains the World: An Unlikely Theory of Globalization* (New York: Harper, 2010), 77–88.

[68] Thomas Cahill, *The Gifts of the Jews: How a Tribe of Desert Nomads Changed the Way Everyone Thinks and Feels* (New York: Random House, 1998); Steven L. Pease, *The Golden Age of Jewish Achievement: The Compendium of a Culture, a People and Their Stunning Performance* (Sonoma, CA: Deucalion, 2009). In this genre see also Ernest Van den Haag, *The Jewish Mystique* (New York: Stein and Day, 1969); Paul Johnson, *The History of the Jews*, 2nd ed. (London: Weidenfeld & Nicholson, 2001).

[69] Slezkine, *Jewish Century*, 1; Yirmiyahu Yovel, *The Other Within: The Marranos: Split Identity and Emerging Modernity* (Princeton, NJ: Princeton University Press, 2009).

[70] On this tradition, see Jeremy Cohen and Richard I. Cohen, eds., *The Jewish Contribution to Civilization: Reassessing an Idea* (London: Littman, 2008).

their antisemitic pasts and adopting assertively pro-Israeli policies, often also placing Jewish members in positions of prominence and positioning themselves as the strongest advocates for the security of Jews in the face of perceived threats from both Middle Eastern and European Muslims.[71] This development is a striking reminder of the precariousness and the malleability of the relationship between philosemitism and antisemitism, and of the intensely political context in which these terms find their meaning.

The geopolitical sensitivity of the unresolved conflict in the Middle East ensures that the history of relations between Jews and non-Jews will remain for the foreseeable future a charged and controversial subject, inescapably colored by differing perceptions of the interrelationships between such distinct but overlapping categories as Jews, Judaism, Zionism, and Israel. Consequently, this volume, written in a spirit of dispassionate scholarly rigor by leading period specialists, must necessarily engage not only with historical but also with contemporary debates. The fourteen essays that follow offer a diverse and in places conflicting range of perspectives on the phenomenon of philosemitism. Collectively, however, they clearly underscore the inadequacy of interpreting Jewish–non-Jewish relations only through the prism of an all-pervasive antisemitism. The multifaceted and intricate history of laudatory responses to Jews and Judaism is indubitably a real and significant subject. Without a clear-sighted analysis of this philosemitic tradition we are liable to fall into a distorted understanding not only of the past but also of the present.

[71] See Yves Patrick Pallade, "Proisraelismus und Philosemitismus in rechtspopulistischen und rechtsextremen europäischen Parteien der Gegenwart," in Diekmann and Kotowski, eds., *Geliebter Feind*, 409–36.

PART I

MEDIEVAL AND EARLY MODERN FRAMEWORKS

1

Philosemitic Tendencies in Medieval Western Christendom

Robert Chazan

Medieval Christendom would seem an unlikely venue for philosemitic tendencies. It has regularly been portrayed as the most negative of environments for Jewish life – a setting of unremitting hostility and violence toward Judaism and Jews, indeed the context in which the major motifs of modern antisemitism were adumbrated. Medieval Christians, modern Christians, medieval Jews, and modern Jews have all agreed, for differing reasons, on this assessment of the relationship between medieval western Christendom and its Jews.

Medieval Christians were heirs to a theology that posited Jewish suffering as divine punishment for Jewish sins; hence Jewish travails were regularly highlighted and emphasized. Some modern Christians have maintained allegiance to this theology; other modern Christians, seeking the roots of modern antisemitism in their own tradition, have focused with deep regret on medieval western Christendom as the setting for church teachings that contributed to the Holocaust. Medieval Jewish observers were moved in part by the normal human predilection to report the violent and the negative and by the sense that an accumulation of suffering would eventually end with messianic redemption. Modern Jewish observers have been deeply influenced by their medieval predecessors and by the inclination to contrast the liabilities of societies dominated by religious institutions and attitudes with the blessings of modern secular societies. For diverse reasons then, a consensus as to Jewish suffering in medieval western Christendom and to the baneful stance of the medieval Christian majority toward the Jewish minority in its midst has long held sway.

In 1928, as a young historian, Salo Baron challenged the regnant view of a sharp contrast between the totally negative features of Jewish life in premodern western Christendom and the thoroughly positive features of Jewish life in the wake of emancipation. Baron challenged both elements in the contrast, arguing (well before the Holocaust) that emancipation

had not been an unmixed blessing and – our focus – that Jewish circumstances in medieval western Christendom were hardly as dire as the popular view projected.[1] Baron continued to make both cases – especially the
latter – throughout his subsequent magisterial works, and this perspective has been developed and expanded by his students and successors.

The most significant datum advanced on behalf of the Baron view
is the widely acknowledged fact that, during the period when western Christendom was allegedly so inhospitable to Jews, world Jewish
population was slowly but steadily shifting from its prior center in the
Islamic Near and Middle East to Christian Europe. An environment
unceasingly hostile and harmful should hardly have been growing in
the number of Jews and the percentage of world Jewish population it
housed.[2]

Medieval western Christendom produced nothing like a cohesive ideology of philosemitism, along the lines of modern antisemitism. Rather, a
number of discrete factors on the medieval scene moved members of the
Christian majority to see Judaism and Jews in a positive light. The central factors that gave rise to philosemitic tendencies in medieval western
Christendom included New Testament imagery of Judaism and the Jews
and the formal church doctrines that flowed out of that imagery; well-
established ecclesiastical policies relative to Judaism and the Jews; lacunae
in the European economy, which Jews were perceived as capable of filling;
needs of the governing authorities, which Jews were again viewed as useful in meeting; and – finally and occasionally – respect for Jewish thinking and warm feelings toward specific Jews. The last of these factors will
be the most difficult to analyze but will be projected as notable realities
nonetheless.

All the factors that fostered philosemitic tendencies regularly went
hand-in-hand with traditional anti-Jewish perspectives and often engendered anti-Jewish images and actions. Again, the positive factors by no
means coalesced into an ideology of philosemitism. The philosemitic
tendencies operating in medieval western Christendom were specific
and sporadic. It is, however, important to acknowledge their presence
and influence, if the objective is fuller comprehension of the Jewish
experience in medieval western Christendom, better understanding of
the growth and evolving centrality of this set of Jewish communities on
the world Jewish scene, and a more nuanced grasp of the complex history of Christian-Jewish relations.

---

[1] Salo Baron, "Ghetto and Emancipation: Shall We Revise the Traditional View?" *Menorah
Journal* 14 (1928): 515–26.

[2] For a broad overview of Jewish circumstances in medieval western Christendom, see Robert
Chazan, *The Jews of Medieval Western Christendom* (Cambridge: Cambridge University Press,
2006).

NEW TESTAMENT IMAGERY AND FORMAL
CHURCH DOCTRINE

Christianity from its earliest stages was deeply engaged with the problem of distinguishing itself from the Jewish matrix out of which it evolved. The New Testament, Christianity's authoritative sacred source, advances a rich set of images relative to Judaism and Jews. Complicated needs eventuated in complex imagery, including both negative and positive elements. Formal church doctrine was intimately linked to the New Testament, evolving out of the web of images bequeathed in the Gospels and the Pauline corpus. Subsequently, the church's formal doctrine spawned in turn further imagery. Formal ecclesiastical doctrine was especially influential with the leadership of the Roman Catholic Church; the imageries had enormous impact on the Christian masses; the combination shaped in significant ways Jewish fate in medieval western Christendom.

Christian imagery and doctrine concerning Judaism and the Jews were, from the outset, highly charged and deeply ambivalent. While it is easy to highlight the negative in this imagery and doctrine, in fact ambivalence was omnipresent and influential. This is true, for example, for the first great Christian thinker whose writings have reached us. Paul left a legacy that is baffling and has given rise to sharp division among recent commentators. For some, Paul was the progenitor of the supersessionist view of Judaism that has had harmful impact on Jews over the ages; for others, Paul remained positive throughout his career to the people from which he originated.[3] Jeremy Cohen, in his comprehensive analysis of Christian views of Judaism and the Jews from late antiquity through the Middle Ages, suggests convincingly that the data that have given rise to such polarized views are in fact suffused with ambivalence, with destructive negativism on the one hand and with positive elements on the other. According to Cohen, this early ambivalence is reprised in the thinking of major figures across late antiquity and the medieval centuries. Alongside images and doctrines that emphasized the sinfulness of the Jews and their rejection by God, there existed positive images and doctrinal views that were in constant tension with the negative.[4]

The positive views and images tended to be removed from the contemporary scene and to cluster around the future and the past. Paul himself set the tone for the subsequent Christian focus on the future, specifically an eventual reconciliation between God and the Jews, rooted in the special relationship between God and the Jewish people that was a feature of the distant past. In his Epistle to the Romans, Paul alerts his gentile audience

---

[3] For the diverse views on Paul, see John Gager, *Reinventing Paul* (New York: Oxford University Press, 2000).

[4] Jeremy Cohen, *Living Letters of the Law: Ideas of the Jew in Medieval Christianity* (Berkeley: University of California Press, 1999).

to the unbroken relationship between God and the Jewish people. "I ask, then: Has God rejected his people? Of course not! I am an Israelite myself, of the stock of Abraham, of the tribe of Benjamin. God has not rejected the people he acknowledged of old as his own."[5] This is followed by complex discussion of sin and punishment, of a new dispensation and punishment for God's first people. The conclusion of these convoluted ruminations is the inevitability of God's eventual salvation of the Jews. "Judged by their response to the gospel, they are God's enemies for your sake; but judged by his choice, they are dear to him for the sake of the patriarchs; for the gracious gifts of God and his calling are irrevocable."[6] For subsequent church policy, eventual salvation of the Jews became a cornerstone for insistence on their preservation. God's planned redemption of the Jews necessitates their ongoing existence, and Christian rulers and societies were obligated to assure that ongoing existence.[7] For later Christian imagery, the implications of the Pauline view were equally profound. As sinful as the Jews might have been or might currently be, they remained an object of love to God, must hence have had much that was good and virtuous in their past, and will enjoy a renewed relationship with the divine in the future.

In the late eleventh century, Christian warriors began the long and arduous process of reconquering the Iberian Peninsula from the Muslims, in a campaign that in many ways presaged the development of the crusading ideal and movement at the close of the same century. A letter written by Pope Alexander II to the bishops of Spain indicates that the campaign against the Muslims evoked anti-Jewish sentiment and some measure of anti-Jewish violence. The pontiff expresses pleasure at the reports he has heard concerning the bishops, that they had protected endangered Jews. They were correct in so doing because of God's eventual plan of redeeming the Jews. Pope Alexander II describes the erring Christian warriors in the following terms: "These warriors, moved surely by foolish ignorance and strongly by blind cupidity, wished to bring about the slaughter of those whom divine charity has predestined for salvation."[8] The papal condemnation of anti-Jewish violence rests in the first instance on the future salvation intended by God for the Jews.

As noted, positive sentiments about the Jews and their future were specific and episodic during the Middle Ages and could be expressed hand-in-hand with harshly negative views. Thus, Pope Alexander II, after insisting that Jews must be preserved because of divine commitment to them and their future, reinforces his argument for Jewish safety with imagery

---

[5] Romans 11:1–2.
[6] Romans 11:28–29.
[7] See the discussion of ecclesiastical policy in the following section.
[8] Robert Chazan, *Church, State, and Jew in the Middle Ages* (West Orange, NJ: Behrman House, 1980), 100.

that is harshly negative. "In the same manner, Saint Gregory also admonished those agitating for annihilating them, indicating that it is impious to wish to annihilate those who are protected by the mercy of God, so that, with homeland and liberty lost, in everlasting penitence, damned by the guilt of their ancestors for spilling the blood of the Savior, they live dispersed throughout the various areas of the world."[9] To juxtapose the positive and the negative in this manner is characteristic of medieval thinking concerning Judaism and the Jews, since again there was nothing like a cohesive ideology of philosemitism.

The early-eleventh-century attacks against the Jews of Spain stimulated by the protocrusading campaign of reconquest serve as a revealing harbinger of the more serious violence that erupted in the wake of the papal call to the First Crusade in 1095. The bishops of the Rhineland areas affected by the violence of 1096 emulated their Spanish predecessors in attempting to shield Jews from the animus unleashed by popular interpretations of the crusading mission; they seem to have been less effective than their Spanish predecessors, sometimes succeeding and sometimes failing. Unfortunately, we are not privy to the thinking that animated these bishops or to the arguments they marshaled against those determined to spill Jewish blood. We have reports, Jewish and Christian, on the actions of the Rhineland bishops, but we lack the reflective statements that would clarify their thinking.[10]

As the Second Crusade was organized, all observers – those in the Christian majority and those in the Jewish minority – were fully aware that crusading bore the potential for evoking powerful anti-Jewish thinking and action. Early during the period of recruitment to the crusade, this potential began to manifest itself. The spiritual leader of the enterprise, Bernard of Clairvaux, who had begun to address to all corners of western Christendom messages intended to present the case for joining the crusade, quickly became aware of the incipient anti-Jewish violence. He thus began to append an addendum to his crusading missives, highlighting the danger of anti-Jewish thinking and violence and mounting a multifaceted case against such thinking and behavior. Like Pope Alexander II, Bernard of Clairvaux advanced simultaneously arguments that demeaned the Jews and arguments that dignified them. The place of the philosemitic tendencies incorporated in his letters warrants analysis.

On the one hand, Bernard begins his case on a demeaning note, citing the line of thinking advanced earlier by Pope Alexander III. He opens with a powerful argument from scripture, citing the vivid imagery of Psalm 59. "Do not kill them, lest my people be unmindful. With your power, make wanderers of them." Bernard explicates this verse in the following

---

[9] Ibid.
[10] For more on the 1096 violence, see the discussion in the following section.

fashion: "The Jews are for us the living words of Scripture, for they remind us always of what our Lord suffered. They are dispersed all over the world, so that by expiating their crime they may be everywhere the living witnesses of our redemption."[11] All this hardly constitutes positive imagery of the Jews. Yet, interestingly, Bernard shifts gears right in the midst of this demeaning reading of Psalm 59. While the psalm itself seems to proceed to increasingly harsh condemnation of the enemy figures depicted by the psalmist, Bernard takes the Latin "convertantur ad vesperam" and decontextualizes it, moving it in a diametrically opposed positive direction. "Under Christian princes they endure a hard captivity, but they only wait for the time of their deliverance."[12] Thus, negative and positive readings of the same biblical passage are advanced simultaneously.

Bernard moves from this bold and to an extent internally inconsistent reading of the passage from Psalm 59 to the Pauline admonition grounded in God's enduring love for his wayward people. "We are told by the Apostle that, when the time is ripe, all Israel shall be saved. ... If the Jews are utterly wiped out, what will become of our hope for their promised salvation, their eventual conversion."[13] Again, then, Paul is invoked for his imagery of the Jews as retaining grace in God's eyes and of the divine intention to eventually reclaim his people as his own, all of which bespeaks a decidedly positive view of the Jews.[14]

Such ambivalent views of the Jews, expressed with respect to their future, abound in medieval popular culture as well. Visions of the projected future redemption were widespread throughout medieval popular culture, and Jews often appeared in them. For example, popular theater regularly portrayed the dynamics of future redemption. On the one hand, the place of the Jews in these depictions is often negative, involving their destruction and disappearance. On the other hand, Jewish recognition of Christian truth and massive acceptance of Christianity by Jews often serve in these plays as harbingers of redemption. While this role may have done little to enhance the image of medieval Jews, it did create a popular sense of Jewish potential, of what Jews might become, and it did reinforce some popular and positive sense of what Jews had once been.

It is the distant past that – for Paul, Bernard of Clairvaux, and many other Christian thinkers – won the Jews a relationship with God that is ultimately unwavering. Paul led the way and set the tone. We recall his indication that the Jews "are dear to him [God] for the sake of the patriarchs." Slightly earlier in his Epistle to the Romans, Paul had depicted in fuller detail the glorious past that served as warrant for God's enduring love.

[11] Chazan, *Church, State, and Jew*, 103.
[12] Ibid.
[13] Ibid.
[14] For further themes in this important missive, see the discussion in the following section.

"They are descendants of Israel, chosen to be God's sons; theirs is the glory of the divine presence, theirs the covenants, the law, the temple worship, and the promises. The patriarchs are theirs, and from them by natural descent came the Messiah."[15] This is a striking litany of positives. The Jews, so often vilified by Paul and subsequently by the Gospel authors, are portrayed here in glowing terms, involving both abstractions, such as the covenants, the law, and the promises. In more immediate and perhaps moving terms, they are portrayed in terms of beloved figures, commencing with the patriarchs and culminating with the person of Jesus himself.

Returning to the letters of Bernard of Clairvaux calling Christian warriors to the Second Crusade and warning them against anti-Jewish agitation and violence, we note readily the direct impact of the Pauline view of the meritorious Jewish past. After making his dual case for preservation of the Jews from Psalms 59, Bernard proceeds to argue on empirical and reasonable grounds for preservation of the Jews. He concludes this new argument with an a fortiori claim. It would in all instances be "an act of Christian piety to vanquish the proud and also to spare the subjected." This is far more obviously the case for the Jews, "from whom we have a law and a promise, and whose flesh was shared by Christ, whose name be forever blessed."[16] The roots of this final element of Bernard's case in the Epistle to the Romans are patent. It is further striking that this is the note on which Bernard chose to conclude his carefully argued brief for Jewish safety. Those poised to attack the Jews grounded their violence in the widely shared sense of the Jews as historic enemies of Christianity and Christendom; against this perception Bernard advances a different perception of the Jewish past, a past of Jewish acceptance of God and acceptance of the Jews by God, a past that included spawning the figure accepted and adored by Christians as their Redeemer.

Positive imagery of the Jews, grounded in the past and the future, was bequeathed to medieval western Christendom by the New Testament. This positive imagery formed one side of a complex equation. It served to counterbalance the decidedly negative imagery that was likewise the legacy received by medieval western Christendom from its sacred sources. The positive imagery, whatever its relationship to the negative, served as anchor for a fully articulated doctrine that posited a place – to an extent a dignified place, to an extent merely a useful place – for Judaism and the Jews within Christian society. The imagery worked in considerable measure on the minds of all medieval Christians, members of the upper strata of Christian society and the lower strata as well. The doctrine was more abstract – effective with the learned leadership group that dominated the Roman Catholic Church, somewhat less effective with the lay leadership of

[15] Romans 9:4–5
[16] Chazan, *Church, State, and Jew*, 104.

medieval Europe, and little understood by the masses. Ecclesiastical policy, firmly grounded in both imagery and formal doctrine, became a major safeguard for the Jews of medieval western Christendom; the executors of ecclesiastical policy became important guardians of Jewish well-being.

ECCLESIASTICAL POLICY

The imageries and doctrines identified thus far laid the foundation for a clearly articulated policy that demanded recognition of the legitimacy of Judaism and a protected place for Jews within Christian societies. Once such a policy emerged, it necessitated compliance by the leadership and populace of western Christendom. The Roman Catholic Church was deeply committed to a carefully defined set of regulations for the governance of corporate and individual life; it insisted upon adherence to this structure of laws; and that meant inter alia insistence on safety for the Jews as well. While the underpinnings of the policy – which we have seen to be rooted in imagery of the Jewish past and the Jewish future – were important, adherence to the law became an ideal and an objective in its own right.

Fundamental ecclesiastical policy was regularly spelled out by the popes of the Middle Ages in a document known as the *Constitutio pro Judeis*, the basic provision for the Jews in medieval Christian society.[17] The *Constitutio*, which can be traced back into the twelfth century and perhaps has roots even earlier, decrees "that no Christian shall use violence to force them to be baptized, so long as they are unwilling and refuse." Provision for willingness on the part of Jews for conversion is then spelled out. From the spiritual plane, the papal document proceeds to protections of Jewish physical well-being. "Without the judgment of the authorities of the land, no Christian shall presume to wound their persons or to kill them or to rob them of their money or to change the good customs which they have thus far enjoyed in the places where they live." Jewish festivals and sacred spaces are similarly protected. The sum of these protections is impressive. Ecclesiastical policies, grounded in authoritative imagery and doctrine, are intended to assure the Jews safety in medieval western Christendom. Of course, the critical question is whether adherence to this policy was in fact demanded or whether it remained simply a set of lofty statements. In fact, the former is very much the case.

The negative imagery of Judaism and the Jews, some of which we have already noted, evoked anti-Jewish passions that could often lead to violence. The church policy that posited the fundamental right of Jews to live safely within Christian society necessitated ongoing opposition to popular

[17] Solomon Grayzel, ed. and trans., *The Church and the Jews in the XIIIth Century*, 2 vols. (Philadelphia and New York: Dropsie College and Jewish Theological Seminary, 1933–89), 1:93–5.

anti-Jewish sentiment. It was in consonance with this explicit policy that Pope Alexander II commended the bishops of Spain for the protection offered in the face of anti-Jewish agitation and Bernard of Clairvaux insisted on safety for the Jews during the Second Crusade. During the elaborate preparations for the Third Crusade, Emperor Frederick I convened a major gathering of warriors and churchmen in the town of Mainz for acceptance of the crusading cross. Leading Jews endangered themselves by remaining in town to plead their case before this impressive assemblage of lay and ecclesiastical leadership. The Jewish efforts were successful, as both the emperor and the assembled bishops took a resolute stand against anti-Jewish crusading violence.[18]

In many instances, ecclesiastical insistence on adherence to the policy that guaranteed Jewish safety could be highly unpopular and could expose churchmen themselves to popular violence. Thus, for example, a Jewish source reports that, during the tumultuous months of spring 1096, crusaders and townsmen in Trier agitated for vengeance against the Jews of the town. The bishop, a relative newcomer, took an adamant stance against such violence, a stance so unpopular that he himself was forced to flee the wrath of the townspeople of Trier.[19] Standing up to popular passions in the name of ecclesiastical policy was no simple matter.

Crusading anti-Jewish violence was set in motion largely by imagery of the Jews as historic enemies of Christianity and Christians. During the middle decades of the twelfth century, popular imagery of Jewish animosity evolved from the past into the present. Jews were increasingly portrayed as contemporary enemies as well, ever poised to bring harm upon the Christian society that hosted them. The most threatening element in this imagery involved projection of Jews as murderers, with subsequent accusations of ritual murder and use of Christian blood emanating from the core notion of Jewish murderousness. These canards created a new set of dangers to Jewish safety and thus activated once again traditional ecclesiastical insistence on safety for the Jews. When the notion of Jewish ritual use of Christian blood surfaced in the 1230s, for example, Pope Innocent IV responded with condemnation of the allegation on grounds of its lack of reasonability and concluded with renewed insistence on safety for the Jews.[20]

We shall shortly engage Jewish fulfillment of economic and political needs as further sources of philosemitic tendencies in medieval western Christendom. Positive tendencies could be intimately linked to negative

[18] See Robert Chazan, "Emperor Frederick I, the Third Crusade, and the Jews," *Viator* 8 (1977): 83–3.
[19] Robert Chazan, *European Jewry and the First Crusade* (Berkeley: University of California Press, 1987), 289.
[20] Grayzel, *Church and the Jews*, 1:269–71.

developments as well. A combination of economic and political needs turned many of the rulers of medieval western Christendom into strong supporters of Jewish moneylending activities, as we shall shortly see. However, ecclesiastical concerns, popular hatred of the Jewish moneylender, and sheer cupidity on the part of many rulers by the early thirteenth century transformed erstwhile supporters of Jewish banking into opponents of the practice and despoilers of the practitioners. In the face of cruel treatment they were suffering, Jews appealed to Pope Gregory IX for assistance, and the assistance was quickly forthcoming, in the form of a compassionate letter to the archbishops and bishops of France, where the new governmental policies and cruelty were most in evidence.[21]

Pope Gregory IX begins his missive by establishing precisely the grounding for humane treatment of the Jews we have already identified. "They [the Jews] are not to be destroyed, God forbid, by his own creatures, especially by believers in Christ. For no matter how perverse their midway position may be, their forefathers were made friends of God, and their remnant shall be saved." Considerations of past and future serve to balance out what are perceived to be present Jewish shortcomings and to buttress Jewish rights. These preliminary considerations are followed by an extensive depiction of Jewish suffering, a depiction steeped in anger over Christian cruelty and sympathy for the plight of the Jews. The papal stance is unequivocal. Pope Gregory IX urges the bishops to "make every effort, in our name, to warn all faithful Christians in your dioceses and to induce them not to harm the Jews in their persons, nor to dare rob them of their property, nor for the sake of plunder to drive them from their lands."

Thus, the papacy and the rest of the leadership of the medieval Roman Catholic Church recurrently insisted on scrupulous execution of ecclesiastical policy with respect to Judaism and the Jews. In fact, on occasion popes could even intervene to protect Jews against initiatives of the church itself. A striking example is provided by the innovative ecclesiastical program with respect to the Talmud. Up until the mid-thirteenth century, the church knew little about the Talmud and its contents. In the 1230s a convert from Judaism to Christianity was received in the papal court, contending that the Talmud was replete with blasphemies against Christianity and antisocial teaching with respect to Christians. The same Pope Gregory IX sent this informer, Nicholas Donin by name, to the court of King Louis IX of France, where he launched a full-scale investigation of the Talmud that eventuated in trial, condemnation, and burning.

This effort was applauded by Gregory IX's successor, Innocent IV, with admonition to the pious king of France that he continue his support for this important new initiative. Subsequently, however, Jewish leaders appeared before Pope Innocent IV and argued that the Talmud was essential to

---

[21] Ibid., 201–3.

Jewish religious life. Thus, prohibition of the Talmud was tantamount to outlawing Judaism itself. To be sure, anti-Christian materials could not be condoned. Thus, Pope Innocent IV attempted to accept the Jewish argumentation, at the same time protecting Christianity and Christian society from blasphemy. The compromise involved returning to the Jews those parts of the Talmud that were free of anti-Christian materials and removing those other parts of the Talmud that were deemed blasphemous.[22] Censorship of Jewish writings thus became a staple of subsequent ecclesiastical policy. The mitigation of the attack on the Talmud once again indicates church commitment to the preservation – within limits – of Judaism.

PERCEIVED LACUNAE IN THE EUROPEAN ECONOMY

The ecclesiastical authorities of western Christendom struggled to balance a received tradition of imagery, doctrine, and policy vis-à-vis Judaism and the Jews with the needs of medieval life; the lay authorities of medieval western Christendom enjoyed far greater latitude in the policies they might adopt with respect to the Jews. This is not to say that the lay authorities were completely free to innovate with regard to Jewish circumstances. On the one hand, they were deeply affected by ecclesiastical tradition and by the demands of church leadership; at the same time, they had to be cognizant of the pressures of a variety of societal forces – their external rivals; their internal competitors, including the lesser barons and the urban elites; and the populace at large. When compared, however, to the leaders of the Roman Catholic Church, the lay authorities of medieval western Christendom encountered far fewer constraints as they sought to lead the societies they ruled to a higher level of material achievement and power.

Medieval western Christendom was engaged, from the eleventh century on, in a furious effort first to equal and then to surpass the rival power blocs of eastern Christendom and Islam. Ultimately, the key to success in this effort lay in the realm of the economy, in the capacity to build a more powerful society grounded in successful exploitation of the resources of the rich European continent. To be sure, circumstances differed markedly between southern Europe, heir to traditions bequeathed from the halcyon days of Roman rule, and northern Europe, seeking to initiate a more sophisticated economy and culture.

In the areas of the south, the drive toward advancement involved, first of all, military aggression intended to drive Muslims out of Europe and to eliminate Muslim enclaves on the continent. These efforts were concentrated on the Italian and Iberian Peninsulas. In Italy, the Muslim presence was more limited, and its elimination took place quite quickly; in Spain, Muslim rule was more firmly entrenched and the process of reconquest

[22] Ibid., 275–7.

stretched out over a lengthy period, completed only at the end of the fifteenth century. In these areas of southern Europe, large Jewish populations had developed over the centuries of Muslim rule. For the Christian conquerors, eager to maintain the economy and civilization of the areas acquired through military achievement, the Jews were perceived as potential allies of great value. They were thoroughly integrated into the societal structures newly conquered and knew them well. At the same time, they had not been displaced from power and authority and harbored no aspirations for resuming the status quo ante; they could thus be trusted.

From the Iberian Peninsula, numerous charters extended by the conquering Christian kings indicate a strong desire to convince Jewish residents of the conquered territories to remain in place and to contribute to the preservation and enhancement of the economies of the newly Christianized areas.[23] Enticements offered by these conquering rulers included grants of land and homes, tax relief, special economic privileges, legal safeguards, and protection against onerous ecclesiastical limitations. The sum of all these stipulations was a set of favorable circumstances that would encourage prior Jewish residents to stay and Jews living elsewhere to immigrate. Underlying these stipulations was the conviction that Jews could contribute notably to economic stabilization and growth. By and large, the efforts of the conquering Christian kings toward winning Jewish assistance were successful, and the Jewish population of the Iberian Peninsula, which had prospered under Muslim rule, made a smooth transition to the new Christian hegemony.[24]

In northern Europe, the situation was quite different. Northern Europe had, prior to the onset of vitalization in the late tenth and eleventh centuries, harbored no significant Jewish population. Its backwardness had created no incentives for Jews to venture forth into new areas of settlement. As northern Europe began its remarkable surge forward, its most progressive rulers saw in the Jews and in Jewish immigration a valuable source of economic stimulation. It was anticipated that Jews familiar with the more advanced economies of the Byzantine and Muslim worlds could bring their expertise with them into the areas struggling to develop as rapidly as possible.

A number of sources – sketchy but useful – indicate the commitment of some northern European authorities to attracting Jews. The count of Flanders is portrayed in a Hebrew source as inviting a Jewish leader and his associates to his realm; Duke William of Normandy, who became King William the Conqueror of England, is reported in a Latin chronicle to

---

[23] Chazan, *Church, State, and Jew*, 69–75.

[24] For a sense of the successes of Jewish communities transplanted from Muslim to Christian rule, see Yom Tov Assis, *The Golden Age of Aragonese Jewry: Community and Society in the Crown of Aragon, 1213–1327* (London: Littman Library of Jewish Civilization, 1997).

have invited Jews from his continental domain to his island kingdom in the wake of the conquest; and the bishop of Speyer invited Jews to settle in his town in 1084. The latter case is the best attested, since we have both a Hebrew report of the invitation and the Latin charter of invitation itself.[25]

The latter source is highly illuminating. At the outset, Bishop Rudiger indicates the basis for his initiative: "When I wished to make a town out of the village of Speyer, I Rudiger, surnamed Huozmann, bishop of Speyer, thought that the glory of our town would be augmented a thousandfold if I were to bring Jews." While Bishop Rudiger does not elaborate on what he means precisely by augmenting the glory of Speyer, he surely was focused on the economic contribution that Jews might make in this rapidly evolving area of the Rhineland. At the end of his charter, Bishop Rudiger spells out his technique for attracting Jews: "In short, in order to achieve the height of kindness, I have granted them a legal status more generous than any that the Jewish people have in any city of the German kingdom." Competition moved the bishop of Speyer to outdo his peers in the benefits extended to potential Jewish settlers. These benefits included a grant of land for residence and additional land for burial of the dead, enclosure of the Jewish settlement area with a protective wall, trade rights, legal protections, and a number of safeguards against ecclesiastical restrictions. The sum of these benefits is impressive, and an enduring Jewish community was in fact created in the developing town of Speyer.

In southern Europe, Jewish economic activity under Muslim rule was highly diversified, and thus the Jewish contribution anticipated by the new Christian authorities was seen in diversified terms as well. In northern Europe, the Jews attracted were heavily concentrated in commerce and trade, reflected in the business privileges accorded them. As western Christendom matured economically during the twelfth century, a new Jewish specialization emerged, involving lending money at interest. The way for this Jewish specialization was paved by two critical factors: The rapidly evolving economy of Christian Europe required the movement of capital, while the Roman Catholic Church was deeply committed to a campaign against what it perceived as the sin of Christian usury, that is, Christians' taking interest of any kind from fellow Christians. In the face of the conflicting pressures of economic need for movement of capital and ecclesiastical opposition to Christian exaction of interest, the way was opened for Jews – unfettered by the strictures of canon law against the giving to or taking from Christians of usury – to fill the economic void, and once again far-sighted rulers supported this useful Jewish contribution to economic development in their realms.[26]

[25] Chazan, *Church, State, and Jew*, 57–9.
[26] For full discussion of Jewish moneylending, see Joseph Shatzmiller, *Shylock Reconsidered: Jews, Moneylending, and Medieval Society* (Berkeley: University of California Press, 1990).

To be sure, this positive development from the perspectives of the European economy, of many of the rulers of Christian Europe, and of the Jews themselves was at the same time bound up with significant negatives as well. The church quickly became cognizant of and concerned with the new Jewish economic specialty that it had played a major role in creating, while the populace at large developed the normal feelings in all societies and ages toward moneylending and moneylenders – appreciation at the time of extension of the loan and animosity when the time comes for repayment of the obligation. From a purely economic perspective, this new Jewish contribution to the economic maturation of western Christendom was significant, and the authorities that supported Jewish moneylending in fact performed a useful service for the societies over which they ruled.

There was yet one more twist to the medieval European philosemitic tendencies grounded in perceived Jewish economic usefulness. While the previously backward areas of northwestern and north-central Europe began their rapid maturation rather quickly, the areas of northeastern Europe lagged noticeably in this process. By the thirteenth century, these areas – particularly the kingdoms of Hungary and Poland – began to embark on a delayed, somewhat slower, but nonetheless perceptible process of economic development. Once again, the Jews were perceived as useful agents of positive economic change. In this case, the reservoir of Jewish population to be tapped was no longer the more advanced Byzantine and Islamic worlds, but rather the Jewish settlements that had developed in the Germanic lands. The economic needs of the emerging eastern European kingdoms coincided with deteriorating circumstances for the Jews farther westward. Thus, as the eastern European authorities contemplated following the precedent of Bishop Rudiger of Speyer, there was in fact within western Christendom a Jewish population prepared to migrate in search of better life circumstances. Once again, the immigrant Jews made a significant contribution to economic maturation; once again, their contribution was by no means universally appreciated.

NEEDS OF THE GOVERNING AUTHORITIES

In the successful effort to move medieval western Christendom forward, economic development was one key – perhaps the most important key. At the same time, political maturation was critical as well. More cohesive and effective political units constituted a crucial dimension of progress in medieval western Christendom, and once again great success was achieved. Indeed, economic development and political maturation were intimately bound one to the other; economic development fostered the emergence of more effective polities, and more effective polities reinforced and encouraged economic development.

Here too the Jews were perceived as useful allies in the effort to foster more effective political units in Christian Europe. One of the major obstacles encountered by the political authorities in medieval western Christendom involved the need for enhanced financial resources and the lack of flexible taxation mechanisms that might provide such resources. The projects undertaken by the European authorities were increasingly ambitious and expensive, while the taxation system at their disposal remained highly traditional and inflexible. Traditional taxation systems rested on custom and changed little; what was required by the rapid maturation of medieval western Christendom was taxation innovation, which would produce an expanding stream of revenue to meet new and more expansive needs and projects.

The Jews were viewed by many of the most far-sighted rulers of medieval Europe as a societal element that might assist considerably in production of the much-needed revenues. Two factors conspired to project the Jews as politically useful producers of innovative and expansive revenue. The first was the newness of the Jews in many areas, especially in the northern sectors of Europe. Where Jews were new, there could be no real insistence on the limitations of traditional taxation, and rulers could innovate freely with respect to the Jewish contributions to their treasuries.

More important was Jewish dependence on the authorities. For a number of reasons, significant popular hostility to the Jews developed quickly and lastingly. The reasons included newness of the Jews in some sectors of Europe, the accumulated legacy of potent Christian anti-Jewish imagery, and the innovativeness of the Jewish economic activities, prized by some but deeply resented and feared by others. In the face of popular hostility, the Jews regularly had recourse – as we have seen – to the ecclesiastical leadership; on an everyday basis, the lay leadership of medieval western Christendom was even more vital to Jewish well-being. The depth of their needs put the Jews in a difficult negotiating position with respect to the fiscal demands imposed by the authorities. In effect, governmental demands could rarely be resisted.

This flexibility in taxation of the Jews was problematic for the Jewish partners to the alliance; it was quite positive from the perspective of the rulers of medieval Europe, offering them precisely the kind of flexible and expanding income they required. The Jews of medieval western Christendom in effect served as a conduit for the secular authorities, offering them access to valuable fiscal resources. To be sure, these fiscal resources lay ultimately in the Christian majority. The Jews, through their business activities and the tax burden they bore, enabled their ruler-protectors to access funds that would otherwise have been closed to them. In terms of the consolidation of effective European polities and thus the further maturation of European civilization, the Jewish role was highly useful, but once again its utility was by no means realized or appreciated by many in society. To the contrary, like the Jewish economic contribution, this political impact also was deeply resented in many quarters. A vicious cycle ensued – Jewish insecurity fostered deep dependency on the political authorities, which created a powerful and a useful alliance, which in turn intensified the original insecurity.

We have seen repeatedly that positive elements in the Christian majority–Jewish minority relationship could often go hand-in-hand with negative factors; we have also noted that positive elements could often spawn negative by-products as well. The utility of the Jews to the ruling class and thus to the consolidation of political power in medieval western Christendom offers yet another instance of a positive factor that gave rise to negative offshoots. As the rulers of medieval Christian Europe focused increasingly on the revenues their Jews might produce, they almost inevitably became concerned with maintaining control over these valuable resources. Insistence on stabilization of Jewish population movement emerged, with a variety of techniques essayed to ensure that revenue-producing Jews not slip away into neighboring realms. This eventuated in imagery of "Jewish serfdom." While Jews were in fact quite different in their status from serfs, what was common to both groups was the desire and intention of those in power to maintain control through limitation on movement.

The important Jewish contribution to the coffers of the ruling class could eventually lead in disastrous directions. Since the rulers of medieval Europe were regularly under heavy financial pressure, the temptation to exploit Jewish resources was almost irresistible in many instances. To be sure, rulers understood that excessive exploitation of the Jews would ultimately exhaust their funds and hence their usefulness. Nonetheless, the combination of fiscal pressures and the availability of Jewish resources often led to exploitation that did in fact exhaust Jewish capacities. Robert Stacey, for example, has documented the taxation policies of the English monarchy in the 1240s and has argued that at that point excessive royal exactions in fact destroyed the economic foundations of the Jewish community.[27] Once again, positive perceptions and inclinations could lead ultimately to negative results.

RESPECT FOR JEWISH THINKING AND SENTIMENTS OF FRIENDSHIP

The philosemitic tendencies noted thus far in medieval western Christendom have all been related either to ecclesiastical imagery, doctrine, and policy or to Jewish economic and political utility. These philosemitic tendencies clashed with powerful anti-Jewish sentiments that developed

---

[27] Robert Stacey C., *Politics, Policy, and Finance under Henry III: 1216–1245* (Oxford: Oxford University Press, 1987), 143–59.

out of preexistent negative imageries and problematic medieval realities. The problematic medieval realities included the newness of the Jews in many areas of Europe, the innovativeness of Jewish economic activity (as noted, positive and useful but at the same time regularly resented), and the complications of Jewish political circumstances (again positive and useful but resented in many circles). It was the preexistent Christian legacy that was decisively negative and harmful. The New Testament, especially the Gospels, bequeathed to medieval western Christendom imageries of Jewish opposition and malevolence that deeply colored medieval (and modern) Christian perceptions of Judaism and Jews. During the Middle Ages, the negativity of the legacy was much intensified, as motifs of Jewish disbelief, irrationality, murderousness, ritual murder, blood libel, host desecration, and well poisoning reflected a deepening sense of the Jews as error-prone and evil. Nonetheless, medieval western Christendom was far from homogeneous in its perceptions of Jews. While many – perhaps most – medieval European Christians probably did see their Jewish contemporaries as irrational and malevolent, a minority saw Jews as thoughtful and creative; on occasion genuinely warm relations developed between Christians and Jews, with Christians viewing Jewish neighbors as friends. These perceptions of Jewish thoughtfulness and creativity and these warm human feelings toward Jews are somewhat difficult to reconstruct, since no everyday literature of letters and memoirs has survived. Here and there, however, evidence remains of Christians' viewing Jews positively, not for their distant past and their distant future and not for their contemporary fiscal or political value, but for their wisdom and goodness. We shall examine a number of examples of this respect for Jewish wisdom and goodness.

As medieval western Christendom matured and its horizons expanded, interest developed in the traditions of others, especially Muslims and Jews. The predominant stance toward the religious literature of other faiths was denigration; new knowledge was exploited to show the superiority of Christianity to its rivals. As Jewish postbiblical literature became known, it was also sometimes used for missionizing purposes, with Christian preachers arguing that the rabbis of old – when read carefully – evidenced recognition of key Christian truths. At the same time, there was a lesser, but by no means insignificant inclination to value postbiblical Jewish knowledge and writings for their own sake.

Especially as a new tendency surfaced during the twelfth century toward reading biblical texts in their original languages and seeking the straightforward historical truth of these texts, some medieval Christians committed to this new trend turned to Jewish experts for fuller knowledge of Hebrew. References to consultation with Jews or rabbis expert in Hebrew begin to emerge. Beyond the linguistic, some Christian exegetes began to seek illumination from the Jewish exegesis and Jewish exegetes as to the meaning of important biblical passages. During the second half of the twelfth century, in particular, disinterested valorization of Jewish biblical exegesis was expressed by a number of major Christian exegetes and thinkers. This valorization of Jewish biblical exegesis for its own sake, as a repository of religious insight and truth, suggests an alternative stance to the majority sense of Jewish error and irrationality.[28]

Equally significant is the limited evidence of the realities of Christian-Jewish amity, of Christians and Jews simply living in proximity to one another and treating each other respectfully and even warmly. Again, evidence for such contacts is limited, but it does exist. Paradoxically, some of this evidence derives from narratives that depict anti-Jewish violence and are suffused with deep anti-Christian sentiments on the part of the Jewish authors.

The anti-Jewish violence that spun out of the call to the First Crusade stimulated intense Jewish responses, new forms of Jewish martyrdom, and innovative Jewish historical narration.[29] The earliest of the Hebrew First Crusade narratives reconstructs carefully the onset of the crusade, the passage of French crusaders into the Rhineland and their exploitation of Jewish fears, the development of sporadic and unorganized anti-Jewish violence, and then the organized assault that resulted in the destruction of the venerated Jewish community of Mainz. The very first of the 1096 attacks – directed against the Jews of Speyer (settled by Jews, as we have seen, a scant twelve years earlier) – involved an ad hoc coalition of random crusaders and Speyer townsmen. It was put down effectively by Bishop Rudiger's successor. As word of the Speyer attack spread, Jews along the Rhine began to fear for their safety.

In nearby Worms, the Jewish community – not yet fully cognizant of how profound the danger was – divided into two segments, one turning to the bishop for security and the other seeking the assistance of Christian neighbors. The narrator, knowing of the eventual destruction of both Jewish groups, castigates the burghers of Worms. "The burghers promised them vainly and cunningly; they are splintered reeds, for evil and not for good, for their hand was with the crusaders in order to destroy our name and

[28] Important work on this tendency has been done by Beryl Smalley; see her *The Study of the Bible in the Middle Ages*, 3rd ed. (Notre Dame, IN: University of Notre Dame Press, 1978). For a detailed and valuable study of one of the major Christian exegetes who valued Jewish thinking, see Deborah L. Goodwin, *"Take Hold of the Robe of a Jew": Herbert of Bosham's Christian Hebraism* (Leiden: E. J. Brill, 2006).

[29] For the violence and the Jewish responses, see Chazan, *European Jewry and the First Crusade*; for Jewish martyrdom, see Shmuel Shepkaru, *Jewry Martyrs in the Pagan and Christian Worlds* (Cambridge: Cambridge Univerity Press, 2006); for the new Jewish history writing, see Robert Chazan, *God, Humanity, and History: The Hebrew First Crusade Narratives* (Berkeley: University of California Press, 2000) and Jeremy Cohen, *Sanctifying the Name of God: Jewish Martyrs and Jewish Memories of the First Crusade* (Philadelphia: University of Pennsylvania Press, 2004).

remnant."[30] The modern reader has to wonder whether the Jews of Worms were fools, taken in by promises that the burghers had no intention of fulfilling or alternatively whether in fact the Jews of Worms had deep confidence in their neighbors, a confidence that proved illusory in the face of dangers that neither the Jews nor their burgher friends were in a position to assess properly.

A curious story in the later *Solomon bar Simson Narrative* reinforces the latter possibility. After presenting an embellished version of the *Mainz Anonymous* account of the destruction of the Jewish community of Mainz, the narrator portrays the special travails of the head of that ill-fated Jewish community. Kalonymous, the *parnas* of Mainz Jewry, led a group of armed Jewish men to safety in the basement of the archbishop's palace during the slaughter that took place there. When the archbishop – who had found safety on the other side of the Rhine River – heard of the survival of Kalonymous and his band, he sent an armed contingent to extricate these Jews, an interesting reflection of concern that seems to go beyond ecclesiastical policy. When the Jews and their armed protectors reached the other side of the river, the later Jewish narrator tells us that "the archbishop was exceedingly happy over R. Kalonymous, that he was alive, and intended to save him and the men who were with him."[31] This later narrator knew of course that the effort failed and that this group of Jews eventually perished, yet the story of the archbishop's genuine human concern for Kalonymous seems to have been sufficiently well known to allow – or perhaps to force – the later narrator to acknowledge the prelate's positive feelings for the Jewish leader Kalonymous.

In this connection, the Jewish sources recurrently mention pleas on the part of friendly Christians to Jews, urging the latter to convert in order to save themselves. These pleas do not seem to have been inspired by genuine missionizing ardor. Rather, they seem to reflect the simple desire of Christians to save Jewish neighbors at all costs. The story of the Jews of Regensburg is told elliptically in the *Solomon bar Simson Narrative*: The burghers of Regensburg "pressed them [the Jews of the town] against their will and brought them into a certain river. They made the evil sign in the water – the cross – and baptized them all simultaneously in that river."[32] The fact that the Jews of Regensburg are reported to have returned almost immediately to Judaism reinforces the sense of an act performed by well-intentioned burghers in order to save endangered Jewish neighbors.

Curious and intriguing evidence of warm Christian-Jewish relations is available from more peaceful circumstances as well. Joseph Shatzmiller has studied in depth an unusual court record from fourteenth-century

---

[30] Chazan, *European Jewry and the First Crusade*, 228.
[31] Ibid., 269.
[32] Ibid., 293.

Marseilles.[33] There, a Jewish moneylender named Bondavid was accused of attempting to collect a debt twice and chose to defend his reputation in court. During the protracted deliberations, Bondavid brought on his behalf a set of Christian witnesses, who testified to his exceptional character and generosity. Human relations are always reciprocal. The testimony offered by the Christian witnesses attests to Bondavid's warmth and generosity toward Christians in need. In return, the Christian witnesses to his largesse took the trouble to make court appearances and to praise Bondavid's character lavishly.

Bondavid was regularly portrayed by his Christian defenders as the very best of the Jews of his community, a fact that is allegedly acknowledged far and wide. Beyond that, one witness, Petrus Columbi, testified that Bondavid was scrupulously ethical and would never alter his behavior, no matter what the sums to be gained or lost might be. Another, Arnauld de Baux, asserted that he would trust Bondavid as he would his own brother. The most extreme of the praise lavished on Bondavid came from a member of the clergy, Guillelmus Gasqueti, who said the following: "And actually [Bondavid is] more righteous than anybody he ever met in his life. He does not believe that there is [one] more righteous than he in the whole world. For, if one may say so, he never met or saw a Christian more righteous than he."[34] Clearly, Bondavid was unusual and elicited unusual reactions among his Jewish and Christian associates – unusual but surely not unique.

Medieval western Christendom was a difficult setting for medieval Jewish life, with obstacles abounding. Nonetheless, the vitality of the area persuaded those Jews absorbed into it by conquest to stay and convinced other Jews to immigrate. All these Jews encountered serious difficulties – popular hostility, recurrent violence, and eventual expulsion from the more westerly and advanced sectors of Europe. These difficulties were real and painful; they should not, however, obscure countervailing tendencies that favored Jews and Jewish life. The brute reality is that, despite the serious obstacles, the Jews became a European people during the Middle Ages, a tribute to the dynamism of medieval western Christendom and to the existence of significant and influential philosemitic tendencies.

---

[33] Shatzmiller, *Shylock Reconsidered.*
[34] Ibid., 118.

2

The Revival of Christian Hebraism in Early Modern Europe

Abraham Melamed

Nihil quod nostrum esse in philosophia quod non ante Iudaeorum fuerit.

Reuchlin, *De arte cabalistica*, 130

Renaissance and early modern philosemitism, inasmuch as it existed, resulted directly from the renewed interest of Renaissance humanists in the ancient past, and particularly from the emergence of Christian Hebraism.[1] Early modern Christian Hebraism and the myth of the Jewish or Hebrew origins of human knowledge were a direct outcome of Renaissance humanism. The scholars who created this field of study, mostly participants in the northern Renaissance beyond the Alps, widened the original humanistic definition of classical learning beyond the Greek and Roman sources beloved by Italian Renaissance humanists, to ancient Hebrew, among other eastern sources. This Hebraic tendency joined the general antiquarian movement of that period that enthusiastically, even

[1] See in the old discussions of G. H. Box, "Hebrew Studies in the Reformation Period and After: Their Place and Influence," in E. R. Bevan and C. Singer, eds., *The Legacy of Israel* (Oxford, 1948), 315–75; F. Rosenthal, "The Rise of Christian Hebraism in the 16th Century," *Historia Judaica* 7 (1945): 167–91; L. Roth, "Hebraists and Non-Hebraists in the 17th Century," *Journal of Semitic Studies* 6 (1961): 193–219; S. Ettinger, "The Beginnings of the Change in the Attitude of European Society towards the Jews," *Scripta Hierosolymitana* 7 (1961): 193–219. And see more recently S. G. Burnett, *From Christian Hebraism to Jewish Studies* (Leiden, 1996); A. L. Katchen, *Christian Hebraists and Dutch Rabbis* (Cambridge, MA, and London, 1984); J. Friedman, *The Most Ancient Testimony* (Athens, OH, 1983); G. L. Jones, *The Discovery of Hebrew in Tudor England* (Manchester, 1983); F. E. Manuel, *The Broken Staff: Judaism through Christian Eyes* (Cambridge, MA, and London, 1992), chaps. 1–4; A. Sutcliffe, *Judaism and Enlightenment* (Cambridge, 2003); A. P. Coudert and J. S. Shoulson, eds., *Hebraica Veritas? Christian Hebraism and the Study of Judaism in Early Modern Europe* (Philadelphia, 2004); H. A. Oberman, "Three Sixteenth Century Attitudes to Judaism: Reuchlin, Erasmus and Luther," in B. D. Cooperman, ed., *Jewish Thought in the Sixteenth Century* (Cambridge, MA, 1983), 326–64; P. T. Van Rooden, *Theology, Biblical Scholarship and Rabbinical Studies in the Seventeenth Century* (Leiden, 1989), chap. 4.

obsessively, collected, cataloged, and compared knowledge on cultures and societies. These they considered exotic, whether they were forgotten esoteric ancient cultures or those recently unearthed in the great voyages of exploration.[2]

The English seventeenth-century scholar Ben Jonson chose to put the following words, so descriptive of this widespread phenomenon, into the mouth of a madwoman:

> For except
> We call the rabbins, and the heathen Greeks
> To come from Salem, and from Athens,
> And to teach the people of Great Britain
> To speak the tongue of Eber and Javan,
> We shall know nothing ...
> And so we may arrive by Talmud skill,
> And profane Greek, to raise the building up
> Of Helen's house against the Ismaelite,
> King of Thogarma, and his habergions
> Brimstony, blue and fiery; and the force
> Of king Abaddon, and the beast of Cittim;
> Which rabbi David Kimchi, Onkelos,
> And Aben Ezra do interpret Rome.[3]

The scholars who participated in this movement borrowed ideas and literary forms from postbiblical Hebrew literature and adapted them to their cultural and religious needs as Christians. They developed tools for the study of the Hebrew language, translated many Hebrew literary sources, and made them available to a wider reading audience. They renewed the old myth of the Jewish origins of philosophy and science[4] and endeavored to appropriate the treasures of the Jewish culture. They thus created a new academic field, Hebraic studies. Its influence upon the development of early modern European culture was enormous, far beyond the limited number of scholars who participated in this movement. What started as an esoteric interest of a small group in the late fifteenth century became within a hundred years a defined and respected academic discipline. At an early stage in its development, we already find evidence of the great impression it made upon contemporary Jewish scholars. Abraham ben Eliezer Halevi, a Spanish refugee who settled in Jerusalem, wrote in a letter dated 1525:

---

[2] A. Momigliano, "Ancient History and the Antiquarian," in his *Contributo alla storia degli studi classici* (Roma, 1954), 67–102; M. T. Hodgen, *Early Anthropology in the Sixteenth and Seventeenth Centuries* (Philadelphia, 1971), chap. 4.

[3] Quoted in Roth, "Hebraists and Non-Hebraists," 205.

[4] See Abraham Melamed, *A History of the Myth of the Jewish Origins of Human Knowledge* [in Hebrew] (Jerusalem, 2010); see esp. chap. 12, dealing with Christian Hebraism.

And who knows the Divine intentions which influenced the heart of many people in the lands of the gentiles to study the holy language and the books of Israel, and they turn and turn them as much as they can.[5]

As far as he was concerned, this was indisputable evidence of the imminent coming of the Messiah. As Zephaniah prophesied (3:9): "For then will I turn to the peoples a pure language, to serve Him with one consent." As far as Halevi was concerned, "a pure language," *safah berurah* (שפה ברורה), must have meant the Hebrew language and its culture.

During the seventeenth century Christian scholars investigated the rabbinic literature perhaps more than in any other period. This culminated with Johannes Buxdorf's (1564–1629) magnum opus, the *Bibliotheca Rabbinica*, which was so well received that some Jewish scholars contemplated translating it into Hebrew, assuming that even the Jewish scholar could benefit from it.[6] His son and scholarly heir, Johannes Buxdorf Jr. (1599–1664), translated two of the most important Jewish medieval texts into Latin: Maimonides' *Moreh Nevukin* (*Doctor Perplexum*, 1629), and Judah Halevi's *Kuzari* (*Liber Cursi*, 1660).[7] Two additional major bibliographies published in this period following Buxdorf Sr. were the four-volume *Bibliographia Magna Rabbinica* (*Kiriat Sefer* is the Hebrew title) by the Italian Hebraist Jiulio Bartolocci (1613–87) and the *Bibliotheca Hebraea* by the German Hebraist Johann Christoph Wolf (1683–1739) (three volumes, Hamburg, 1715–33). These two bibliographies became indispensable tools for every aspiring Hebraist in this period.[8]

The Christian scholar who virtually created this new academic field was Johann Reuchlin (1455–1522), who transmitted the embryonic Renaissance interest in Hebrew sources, as it developed since Manetti and Pico della Mirandola,[9] to the northern Renaissance. Reuchlin met Pico during his visit to Italy in 1490 and took over from him the mission of developing the study of the Hebrew language and culture. He studied with Jewish teachers, among them Ovadiah Sforno, and consequently added the knowledge of Hebrew to his mastery of Greek and Latin. Thus he achieved full command of the three classical languages, the sources of Christianity. For his

---

[5] I. Robinson, "Two Letters of Abraham ben Eliezer Halevi," in I. Twersky, ed., *Studies in Jewish History and Literature* (Cambridge, MA, 1984), 2:403–22.

[6] See n. 1.

[7] Burnett, *From Christian Hebraism*, 22, 148, 160; Manuel, *Broken Staff*, 88–90.

[8] See Sutcliffe, *Judaism and Enlightenment*, 16, 37–9; Melamed, *History of the Myth*.

[9] See J. L. Blau, *The Christian Interpretation of the Cabala in the Renai*ssance (New York, 1944); D. P. Walker, *The Ancient Theology* (Surrey, UK: 1972); M. Idel, "Hermeticism and Judaism," in I. Merkel and A. G. Debus, eds., *Hermeticism in the Renaissance* (Washington, DC, London, and Toronto, 1988), 59–76; Idel, "Prisca Theologia in Marsilio Ficino and in Some Jewish Treatments," in M. J. B. Allen and V. Rees, eds., *Marsilio Ficino: His Theology, His Philosophy, His Legacy* (Leiden, 2002), 137–78. And see the detailed discussion in Melamed, *History of the Myth*, chap. 8.

admirers he became the *miraculum trilingue* (the miracle of the three languages). Reuchlin had a great interest in Hebrew philology and composed textbooks of the Hebrew language. Following Pico, his main interest was the Kabbalah, which he understood in its wider sense, namely, as part of the chain of tradition. He identified a chain of transmission of esoteric knowledge beginning with Adam, who supposedly received it from an angel following the exile from Eden. Here too he followed Pico and transmitted the so-called "Christian Kabbalah," the Christian interpretation of the Jewish Kabbalistic traditions, from the Italian to the northern Renaissance. Reuchlin's two main Kabbalistic works are *De verbo mirifico* [On the word making wonders, 1494] and *De arte cabalistica* [The art of Kabbalah, 1517]. In the former, Hebrew is presented as the first written language, created by Moses and antedating the Egyptian script.[10] *The Art of Kabbalah* provides an important instance of transmitting the myth of the Jewish origins of human knowledge to contemporary Christian culture. A central purpose of this treatise was to prove the basic affinity of Pythagorean philosophy with Kabbalah. Pico had already advanced this idea and Reuchlin developed it further.[11] From this premise he went on simply to conclude that Pythagoras received his esoteric knowledge from ancient Hebrew scholars. Reuchlin cites the old Hellenistic tradition linking Pythagoras and Plato, who studied with ancient eastern thinkers, one that completely identifies Jewish Kabbalah with Greek philosophy, further arguing that "philosophy" is the Greek term Pythagoras gave to the esoteric knowledge he received from those eastern scholars, and especially from the Jews.[12] Reuchlin presented the myth of the Jewish origins of knowledge in its most radical terms: "There is nothing in our philosophy that was not developed by the Jews first."[13] He describes the scholars who took from the Jews as *plagiatores*, who purposely concealed the Jewish origins of their knowledge.

Another important scholar connected to the tradition of Christian Kabbalah was Guillaume Postel (1510–81). Like Ficino, Pico, and Reuchlin, he too assumed that the Pythagorean and Platonic ideas complemented Kabbalistic traditions. This necessarily also assumed the ancient Hebrew sources of all wisdom. Unlike other humanist scholars, Postel was ambivalent concerning Greek culture. On one hand, he argued, following Plato

---

[10] See Blau, *Christian Interpretation of the Cabala*, 43–4; Y. Dan, "Reuchlin's Theory of Kabbalah and Its Historical Meaning," in A. Ravitzky, ed., *From Rome to Jerusalem: Festschrift in Memory of J. B. Sermoneta* [in Hebrew] (Jerusalem, 1998), 455–85.

[11] G. Lloyd Jones, introduction to Johannes Reuchlin, *On the Art of the Kabbalah, De Arte Cabalistica*, trans. M. Goodman and S. Goodman (New York, 1983); Blau, *Christian Interpretation of the Cabala*, chap. 4; Friedman, *Most Ancient Testimony*, esp. 24–8, 56–7, 71–98; Manuel, *Broken Staff*, 19–20, 44–6; Oberman, "Three Sixteenth Century Attitudes"; Dan, "Reuchlin's Theory."

[12] Reuchlin, *On the Art of the Kabbalah*, 127–31; also 185–7, 249, 255.

[13] Ibid., 130.

(*Epinomis*, 987), that "whatever Greeks acquired from foreigners is finally turned by them into something nobler," and he ascribed to them an important role in transmitting knowledge from east to west. On the other hand, in later writings his enthusiasm for Greek philosophy waned, and he accused it of corrupting and debasing the original Kabbalistic knowledge from ancient times in the transmission process. Postel identified the beginning of knowledge in the age of Noah, not Adam, who was personally tainted with original sin. It was Noah who first established the centers of learning in the east and later in Italy. Postel took these stories from Josephus's Latin translation of *Contra Apionem* and Ibn Yahia's *Chain of Tradition* (*Shalshelet ha-Kabbalah*, 1587), among other sources. Typical of Renaissance syncretism, he tried to gather Jewish and pagan traditions into one system. Noah established a system of law that was the basis for the Mosaic laws that were later transmitted, albeit in corrupted form, to the great pagan lawmakers. Noah transmitted his knowledge to Japhet, who carried it with him to France and Spain. The language in which Noah thought was of course Hebrew, and Postel assumed that the various European languages, especially the French, developed from this progenitor of all human language. The main Noachitic achievement was the wisdom called Kabbalah, the Jewish origin of all ancient religious sensitivities. In his *De Originibus* (1553) Postel reemphasized the old myth of the ancient eastern, mainly Hebrew, source of human knowledge. He related every idea in Greek culture to eastern, usually Jewish sources. Plato received his knowledge from the Chasdeans and the Hebrews, and the core Platonic term "idea" came to him from the Hebrew. He found the fullest expression of the Platonic theory of the ideas in the classic Kabbalistic text, the *Zohar*, and in his view this book represented a tradition far older then Plato's. Thus even Plato's wisdom was second-hand, and the philosophical originality of the Hebrews was established.[14]

Christian Hebraism of the fifteenth and sixteenth centuries rejected the oral Torah but was fascinated by the Kabbalah. The scholars within this school of thought saw Kabbalah as a hidden esoteric tradition originating with Adam, who deciphered the secrets of creation and the divinity, wherein hints at the basic tenets of Christianity could be identified. In the seventeenth century, however, the Kabbalistic enthusiasm that Pico, Reuchlin, and Postel nurtured waned.[15] The focus of the study of Judaism moved from Kabbalah to Halakhah, to Jewish history and to philosophy.[16] The interest in the Halakah, including the regime of the ancient Jewish

---

[14] See W. J. Bouwsma, *Concordia Mundi: The Career and Thought of Guillaume Postel* (Cambridge, MA, 1957), 48–52, 252–61.

[15] But see A. P. Coudert, *The Impact of the Kabbalah in the Seventeenth Century: The Life and Thought of Francis Mercury van Helmont (1614–1698)* (Leiden, 1999).

[16] Manuel, *Broken Staff*, 38–9, 146.

state, was typical of the antiquarian tendencies of this period and served the needs of early modern political philosophy, from Machiavelli to Rousseau. Many of these scholars were intensively, even obsessively occupied in investigating ancient chronology and tried in various ways to resolve the obvious discrepancies between biblical and the other eastern chronologies such as the Egyptian, Babylonian, Persian, and Indian. Most preferred the biblical chronology, which assumes the primacy of the people of Israel. Acceptance of biblical chronology was of course a basic assumption within the myth of the Jewish origins of all wisdom. Later, with the advent of deism and the culture of the Enlightenment, the biblical chronology would be undermined, a development that would contribute to the final collapse of the myth of the Jewish origins of human knowledge.

Jean Bodin's (1529/30–96), *Colloquium of the Seven about the Sublime* (*Colloquium heptaplomeres de rerum sublimum arcanis abditis*, 1588) is a kind of intermediate stage between the Kabbalistic interests of the previous generations and the later quest for the deist common denominator among the monotheistic religions. This treatise was not published until the nineteenth century but was widely circulated during the author's lifetime, and its scandalous radical tendencies created an uproar. The book is a dialogue among seven sages of various religious and philosophic tendencies. Not by coincidence is the oldest participant the Jew Solomon. His age represents the antiquity of his culture and religion, while his name hints his proverbial supreme wisdom. Thus even stating his name and age expresses belief in the antiquity and originality of Judaism among the monotheistic cultures. Indeed this Solomon is represented as the most learned of all the participants; he is respected by all and is the central figure in the dialogue. He argues that the Mosaic laws, the most ancient of all, are still the most perfect: he does not even hesitate to reject Christological interpretations of the Torah and the Prophets forcefully. Quite apart from the disputed question as to which participant represents Bodin's own views, the vast knowledge of Jewish sources that the Jew Solomon displays proves just how great Bodin's interest in Hebraic studies was, and how much knowledge he acquired from them.[17] Against this background, he put into the mouth of one participant a paraphrase of Horatius's famous saying that ultimately conquered Greece culturally overpowered triumphant Rome ("Graecia capta ferum victorem cepit," *Epist.* II, i.156). He argues that the proof of Judaism's antiquity, and the fact that all monotheistic religions originated

[17] M. Leathers Daniels Kuntz, introduction to Jean Bodin, *Colloquium of the Seven about the Sublime*, trans. and with an introduction by M. Leathers Daniels Kuntz (Princeton, NJ, and London, 1957); J. Guttman, "Uber Jean Bodin in seinen Beziehungen zum Judentums," *MGWJ* 49 (1905): 315–48, 459–89; Ettinger, "The Beginning," 197–8; Manuel, *Broken Staff*, 54–6; M. Yardeni, "The Attitude towards the Jews in the Literary Controversy in the Age of the French Religious Wars" [in Hebrew], *Ziyyon* 28 (1963): 83–4.

from it, similarly proves that "Conquered Judah finally conquered its vicious conqueror" [Judea capta ferum victorem cepit].[18]

Bodin's other works (likewise very influential even in his own time) express basic ideas of the myth of Jewish origins of human knowledge, this time in the sphere of political thought. In his *Method of the Easy Comprehension of History* (*Methodus ad facilem historiarum cognitionem*, 1566) and especially *Six Books on the Republic* (*Six livres de la République*, 1576), Bodin often refers to the Mosaic law and the ancient Hebrew regime. He repeatedly insists on the antiquity of the people of Israel, its religious and cultural superiority, and the unique image of Moses, the first legislator, who, unlike the legislators of other peoples, thought all humans were brothers since they all originated from the same father.[19]

Blaise Pascal (1623–62) was not a typical scholar of Christian Hebraism, but a mathematician and a skeptic. His religious inclinations, though, led him to relate to Christianity's parent, and consequently he made impressive use of the myth of the Jewish sources of human knowledge. His famous *Pensées*, a collection of references prepared for a work he planned to write in defense of the Christian faith, was published by his friends after his death. Here Pascal relates to Judaism from a traditional Christian point of view typical of the Church Fathers, as expressed in the Middle Ages. The Jews sinned in refusing to accept the Messiah, in executing the Son of God, and thus were eternally punished, but they are still identified as the first ancestors of Christianity. Thus, Pascal uses the proof of Israel's priority to any other people and its religious and cultural superiority to defend the church itself, precisely as Eusebius, Clement of Alexandria, and Augustine had done.[20]

Pascal relates to all the basic tenets of the myth of the Jewish origins of wisdom: Jewish priority in time to the Greeks (more than a thousand years!), Judaism's religious and political superiority, having a direct divine origin, and the fact that the greatest nations on earth, among them Greece and Rome, copied directly from the Jews. Pascal's criticism of Islam and the Chinese religion, the Romans and the Egyptians, seems to be a reaction against the countermyth, which reappeared in this period.

---

[18] *Colloquium*, 236, introduction, xlv, and n. 84. Also A. Hertzberg, *The French Enlightenment and the Jews* (New York, 1969), chap. 3.

[19] Jean Bodin, *Method of the Easy Comprehension of History*, trans. B. Reynolds (New York, 1969), introduction, xxiii–xxiv, and esp. 81, 107, 279–82, 340. Also his *The Six Books of a Commonweal*, facsimile reprint of the English translation of 1606, ed. and with an introduction by K. D. McRea (Cambridge, MA, 1962), esp. 116, 211, 293, 303, 319, 325. Hodgen, *Early Anthropology*, 318–19; J. W. Allen, *A History of Political Thought in the Sixteenth Century* (London and New York, 1960), pt. 3, chap. 8.

[20] Blaise Pascal, *Pensées*, trans. and with an introduction by H. F. Stewart (London, 1950), par. 619. Hertzberg, *French Enlightenment and the Jews*, chap. 3; Sutcliffe, *Judaism and Enlightenment*, 189–90.

The countermyth, which will be influential in the deistic thought of the early Enlightenment, argued that the Egyptians, Romans, or Chinese predated the Hebrews.[21] Pascal, then, tried to undermine the credibility of the historical annals of the Greeks, Egyptians, and Chinese, arguing that they were composed hundreds of years after the events they relate took place and so were unreliable. Homer's great works were initially composed as legends and should be treated as such. Books attributed to ancient mystical philosophers, such as the Sibyls and Hermes Trismegistus, to which Renaissance humanists related with the utmost reverence, were nothing but forgeries in his view. The validity of the holy books of the Jews, on the other hand, could not be denied, since they were composed when the events they describe took place, and they originated directly from the people itself.[22] Pascal based himself here on the two Jewish-Hellenistic sources at the basis of the myth, Josephus and Philo, whose words he accepted without doubt, and the Church Fathers, Eusebius and Tertullian. The anti-Jewish references in the *Pensées* are based on Raymondus Martini's *Pugio fidei*.[23] The final proof of Israel's ancient origins and its superiority to all ancient religions serves here to reinforce the legitimacy of its lawful successor, the Christian Church. By inheritance Christianity thus acquires priority and superiority over all other religions. Pascal's defense of Judaism, then, does not stem from any philosemitic tendencies beyond those of traditional Christian motivations.

Among English scholars, Isaac Newton (1642–1727) is definitely the most prominent and interesting Hebraist. Alongside his scientific activities, he was busy throughout his life with ancient history, chronology, astrology, alchemy, and other esoteric matters. As Pascal's theological speculations bewildered French deists, who expected a more philosophic-rational, "scientific" approach from him, so Newton's esoteric theological speculations embarrassed English scholars, who could not fathom the interest of the founder of modern natural science in such weird matters. Newtonian scholars still struggle with this issue.[24] Newton fully accepted the myth of the Jewish sources of human knowledge. Especially in his *The Chronology of Ancient Kingdoms Amended* (1728), published posthumously, he discussed ancient chronology at length. The main aim of these investigations, based on Puritan theological assumptions, was to prove the supremacy

[21] On the popularity of the myth of Egypt in this period see E. Iverson, *The Myth of Egypt and the Hieroglyphs in European Tradition* (Princeton, NJ, 1993). On China see B. Guy, *The French Image of China before and after Voltaire* (Geneva, 1997).
[22] *Pensées*, par. 628.
[23] Ibid., par. 635.
[24] See F. E. Manuel, *Isaac Newton, Historian* (Cambridge, MA, 1963), 4; K. J. Knoespel, "Newton in the School of Time: *The Chronology of Ancient Kingdoms Amended*, and the Crisis of Seventeenth Century Historiography," *Eighteenth Century, Theory and Interpretation* 30 (1989): 19.

and originality of the Hebrew culture above all other ancient cultures. As Frank Manuel summarized at the end of his book on Newton's activity as a historian:

Newton's fierce Judaic monotheism was a secret faith. To show that the Israelites rather than the heathen were the first founders of the humanity of the ancient world was the one historical end to which the long astronomical calculations and the reams of literary analysis were ultimately subservient.[25]

This position, which praises the cultural achievements of the distant past, stood in stark contradiction to the theory of scientific progress of which Newton was a prime advocate. However, Newton's position on the question of scientific progress was ambivalent to say the least. In various places in his writings he presents himself as a scientific innovator who discovered the principles of the physical world and forcefully struggles against whoever he thought attempted to deprive him of his scientific birthright. Elsewhere, by contrast, he admits that ancient scientists, not only Moses, but also Greek mathematicians like Apollonius and Pythagoras, discovered some physical principles, albeit in a different manner. Modern scientists, himself included, thus did not discover the principles of nature ex nihilo; they rediscovered what was already known to ancient scholars, but was forgotten and distorted in the vicissitudes of time. This moderate theory of progress is aptly expressed in Newton's familiar use of the old parable of dwarfs standing on the shoulders of giants. The parable traditionally paralleled the moderns to dwarfs who stand on the shoulders of ancient giants and thus are able to see further. In Newton's version, the advantage of the moderns over the ancients is due to their ability to build on the knowledge acquired from the ancients. This moderate interpretation of the theory of scientific progress enabled Newton to use the myth of ancient knowledge, particularly that of the Hebrews, yet still support the principles of scientific progress and consider himself to be one of its main protagonists.[26]

As indicated, most of the Christian savants of the sixteenth and seventeenth centuries based their world chronologies upon biblical history. The biblical genealogy was the only one that gave a full and continuous description of the order of historical events, to a degree exceptional in ancient historical documentation. Scholars built quite fantastic arguments and counterarguments concerning its smallest details; delved into Egyptian, Greek, Chaldean, and Chinese chronologies; and exerted themselves in mighty efforts to synchronize these with biblical chronology. None of them, however, ever questioned the superiority of the latter or sought to replace it

---

[25] Manuel, *Newton*, 193, and see the discussion, esp. chaps. 3, 6. Also M. Goldish, *Judaism in the Theology of Sir Isaac Newton* (Dordrecht, 1998).

[26] Manuel, *Newton*, 18. See on the whole issue, A. Melamed, *On the Shoulders of Giants* [in Hebrew] (Ramat Gan, 2003), chap. 6.

with any of the others. To question this principle would have meant breaking with the tradition of the Church Fathers. The possibility that any of these cultures antedated Israel, or, alternatively, developed simultaneously with it, was unacceptable and inherently heretical. The Christian point of view had to assume the existence of one and only one ancient people, the people of Israel, the primogenitor of Christianity. Arguments that the world had existed longer than five or six thousand years, or that it had existed forever, and that the Greeks predated the Hebrews in the development of human society, were tantamount to undermining the very basis of the Christian faith. The biblical chronology was to be discredited only in the next generation, with the advent of deism, which had a completely different agenda.

Newton too accepted the priority of biblical chronology and did not even imagine the possibility of undermining it. In this respect he was a traditionalist. All the complicated chronological and astronomical calculations and his ongoing disputes with his contemporaries on these issues were intended to verify biblical chronology once and for all. He made considerable use of his astronomical knowledge to clarify and establish it and was not the first to enlist knowledge of astronomy for this purpose (e.g., Joseph Scaliger and others predated him).[27] Through such astronomical calculations Newton endeavored to undermine all pagan chronologies including the competing Greek records. Synchronizing the biblical and other chronologies, now including the Chinese, was even more complicated once the Jesuits opened China up to Europe. It was even more complicated because, unlike clear and continuous biblical chronology, many of these others were obscure, with many long periods remaining hidden in the historical mist and based on lists of generations or dynasties, quite unlike the continuous lists of the Hebrews. Newton sharply criticized the other ancient chronologies, arguing that the oldest testimonies were lost and the later ones were full of mistakes, if not completely invented. He did not base the priority of the biblical chronology on the argument of Divine Providence, but upon historical credibility. He accused Egyptian, Babylonian, Greek, and other chroniclers of attempts to fabricate historical lists to prove their antiquity, since according to their cultural mentality – which he himself still shared – the older a tradition, the more authentic it is considered to be.

In the fragment *The Original of Monarchies* Newton deals with the problems of the antiquity of the kingdoms of Assyria and Egypt in comparison with the people of Israel. The problem here was especially tough, since some contemporary scholars assumed that the Assyrians and Egyptians predated the Hebrews, and the biblical text itself, which Newton accepted as historical truth, describes Egypt's greatness in Moses' time all too

---

[27] A. T. Grafton, "Joseph Scaliger and Historical Chronology: The Rise and Fall of a Discipline," *History and Theory* 14 (1975): 156–85.

clearly, when the Hebrews were merely slaves. Newton made ingenious use of every possible hint from the prophetic literature to decrease the importance of Assyria and prove that Israel and Judea did not receive the arts and sciences from the pagans. Rather the opposite was true: their own wisdom spread among the nations. The Egyptian case was the most problematic, especially since the interest in Egyptian antiquities was very strong in contemporary intellectual circles.[28] Newton himself was ambivalent on this point, and he performed ingenious textual, chronological, and etymological acrobatics in order to prove that the Hebrews antedated and were superior to the Egyptians. Although Newton tended to distinguish sharply between pagan and Hebrew beliefs, he often argued that those of the pagans were nothing but a distortion of an originally Jewish monotheism. Thus, in the *Chronology* he argued, on the basis of an old etymological exercise, that the Zoroastrian religion was merely a pagan distortion of the Abrahamic tradition transmitted through "Brachmans," that is, Brahmins, whose name was derived from the descendents of Abraham. This tradition, which etymologically, and hence historically, connected the Jews (*Iudaeos*) and the Indians (*Indoi*), and the Abrahamites with the Brahmins, has a long history, from Hellenistic times,[29] and Newton obviously derived his argument from it. He also tended to look for the origins of Greek and eastern stories and mythological personalities in biblical literature. In his *Theologiae gentile origins philosopicae*, he tried to show the possibility of identifying all the pagan divinities with Noah and his descendants. Noah is identified with Saturn, and his three sons with the three sons of Saturn.[30]

It is important to understand that with Newton too the whole discussion of the Jewish antiquities was directly connected to his Christian Weltanschauung and was deliberately used in the Christian religious battles of this period. It came not from any love of Israel or from pure scientific motivation. It represented a clearly Puritan tendency, steeped in the New Testament. The Puritan believer felt a deep connection to ancient Israel. He identified ancient Christianity, before it was tainted by the papacy, as the direct legitimate heir of biblical Israel, which Puritan Christianity was rehabilitating and reviving. The papacy was viewed as the heir to Egyptian blasphemies and Greek distortions. The true object of Newton's severe critique of the Egyptians and the Greeks was Catholic Rome.

---

[28] See n. 20.

[29] See Manuel, *Newton*, 111. On these traditions, with additional bibliography, see A. Melamed, "The Image of India in Medieval Jewish Culture: Between Adoration and Rejection," *Jewish History* 20 (2006): 299–314.

[30] See examples in Manuel, *Newton*, 116–18; R. S. Westfall, "Isaac Newton's *Theologiae Gentile Origines Philosophicae*," in W. W. Wagner, ed., *The Secular Mind: Essays Presented to F. L. Baumer* (New York, 1982), 15–34; J. E. Force, "Biblical Interpretation, Newton and English Deism," in R. H. Popkin and A. Vanderjagt, eds., *Scepticism and Irreligion in the Seventeenth and Eighteenth Centuries* (Leiden, New York, and Köln, 1993), 282–305.

Such arguments and traditions appeared in the writings of many scholars connected with Christian Hebraism, who had antiquarian tendencies and were concerned with ancient chronologies. Among them are the French scholar Jacques Gaffarel (1601–81),[31] and the Englishmen Henry More (1614–87),[32] Theophilius Gale,[33] Thomas Hyde,[34] Humphery Prideaux,[35] William Warbutron,[36] and John Toland.[37]

The most outstanding in this loose group of scholars was Giambattista Vico (1670–1744), a native of Naples, whose heavy tome, *La scienza nuova* (*The New Science*), became a cornerstone of modern history of philosophy, and whose influence was widespread. Like Newton, Vico too mixed novel ideas with the etymological and chronological gymnastics so beloved of his contemporaries. Sometimes they were fascinating but more often peculiar, occasionally obscuring his many original insights. Most important among these was the endeavor to uncover the fundamental structures of human culture. In the history of philology he identified a symbolic expression of human consciousness in its historical development. The mythological tales of ancient peoples were a symbolic expression of their original consciousness. In his opinion such mythological philology had a central role in the religious battles of his time. As a devout Catholic he enthusiastically joined the debates on ancient chronologies, intending to prove the originality and veracity of the Hebrew in comparison with others, especially the Egyptian, which still fascinated some contemporary scholars, as indicated previously. He strongly objected to the current theories on the antiquity of the Chinese, another people that aroused contemporary scholastic interest, and ridiculed the traditions of peoples he considered primitive, like the Scandinavians or the Flemish, who argued for their own historical antiquity. Moreover, for Vico proof of the antiquity and divine selection of the Hebrews was a necessary precondition for proving the veracity

---

[31] See H. Wirszubski, *Pico della Mirandola's Encounter with Jewish Mysticism* (Cambridge, MA, 1989), 11, 15, 16; H. Y. Yerushalmi, *From Spanish Court to Italian Ghetto* (New York and London, 1971).

[32] J. van del Berg, "Menasseh ben Israel, Henry More and Johannes Hoornebeek on the Pre-Existence of the Soul," in Y. Kaplan et al., eds., *Menasseh ben Israel and His World* (Leiden, 1989), 106.

[33] Manuel, *Newton*, 95–6; D. B. Sailor, "Moses and Atomism," *Journal of the History of Ideas* 25 (1964): 9; S. Ettinger, "Jews and Judaism in the Eyes of English Deists of the Eighteenth Century" [in Hebrew], *Ziyyon* 29 (1964): 185n10.

[34] Ettinger, "Jews and Judaism."

[35] Ibid., 186n12, 192–3n43.

[36] Iverson, *Myth of Egypt*, 103; J. Assman, *Moses the Egyptian* (Cambridge, MA, 1997), 91–6.

[37] I. Barzilay, "The Jews in the Literature of the Enlightenment," *Jewish Social Studies* 18 (1965): 243–61; Barzilay, "John Toland Borrowing from Simone Luzzatto," *Jewish Social Studies* 31 (1969): 75–81. Sutcliffe, *Judaism and Enlightenment*, 197–205. Toland, however, as a deist, was already ambivalent concerning the myth of the Jewish origins of human knowledge.

of the Christian faith. Unlike his attitude to the mythical history of all other ancient peoples, he saw biblical stories as true history. The entire *New Science* was directed at modern scholars who denied the veracity of the Bible stories of Creation and argued that other peoples had much older traditions. In this respect he followed the old Catholic distinction between the sacred history of the Hebrews and the profane history of the gentiles but invested it with a new meaning. In one place he went as far as identifying Adam as the forefather of the Hebrews, although the biblical evidence shows Abraham as the genetic father of Israel and Moses as its political founding father. He retraced history to its biblical beginnings to prove the ultimate antiquity of Israel once and for all. He turned the Jews back into Hebrews (as they are called in Italian), to strengthen the argument about the antiquity of the Jews, especially vis-à-vis those who insisted upon the priority of the Egyptians or the Chinese.

However, Vico did not accept the tradition of the Jewish sources of human knowledge literally. Precisely because he insisted upon the inherent difference between the Hebrews and all other ancient peoples, he denied that the sages of the nations studied with the wise men of Israel. He argued that it would be inconceivable to assume that the Jewish sages would have shared their esoteric knowledge with gentiles when their Torah strictly forbids it. In his opinion, while the Jews received their knowledge directly from divine Providence, gentile scholars such as Plato and Aristotle approached divine knowledge through rational investigation. As far as he was concerned, the Jews were the ancient source of Christianity, not of pagan philosophy; they were outstanding in their relationship to divine Providence, not in philosophical knowledge, which was the Greek domain. In this respect he was quite exceptional among his scholarly contemporaries, who concluded from their belief in the antiquity and divinely chosen status of Israel that all human knowledge originated there.[38]

Some scholars not only argued that ancient Greek sages studied with Jewish ones, but even identified the forefathers of the Hebrews with the gods of Greek and Rome. Like Vico, they argued that the ancient gods were originally great rulers and sages who benefited human society and thus were honored by deification after their death. The name of the god Janus, identified as the discoverer of wine, was associated with the Hebrew word *Ya'in* (wine), this being a proof that the Hebrews were the first to produce it. The biblical story of Noah and his son Ham was associated with the Greek god Jove; the biblical hero Nimrod was identified with Saturn; others identified the first Adam too with Saturn, while Cain was associated with Jupiter; Yuval, Tuval, and Tuval Cain were identified with Mercury,

[38] P. Rossi, *The Dark Abyss of Time: The History of the Earth and the History of Nations from Hooker to Vico*, trans. from the Italian by L. G. Cochrane (Chicago and London, 1984), 168–78; F. R. Marcus, "Vico and the Hebrews," *New Vico Studies* 13 (1995): 14–32.

Vulcan, and Apollo, to cite a few examples. Many of these scholars found parallels between the biblical stories of Creation and Greek mythology and concluded that the Greeks borrowed from the Hebrews.[39]

Not only the sources of religious beliefs, philosophic and scientific knowledge, and even the Greek gods were identified in the ancient Hebrew culture, but also the source of human languages. Most contemporary scholars assumed that Hebrew was the language of the first generations of men, and all other languages evolved from it. The development of different languages from the Hebrew, and other languages that evolved from them, was explained either as a result of the accumulated philological distortions of children and simple folk, or as a natural consequence of migration, wars, and the mingling of populations. In any case, many considered Hebrew to be the perfect primordial original language, the one that had expressed the original divine revelation. By contrast, the development of all other languages was seen as a consequence of distortion of and deterioration from the perfect original.[40]

An area in which the myth of the Jewish origins of human culture was most apparent was political philosophy. The arguments that Moses was the first legislator who gave the Hebrews a divine law and established a perfect constitution, which became a model for any future human constitution, and that Solomon (sometimes Abraham and David too) was the perfect archetype of the Platonic philosopher-king, had been basic ideas in Jewish political philosophy since Philo. Jewish scholars always identified in the esoteric layers of the Torah the ancient source of the most up-to-date philosophic ideas and scientific theories. They also found there the origins of the regimes and political theories current in various periods. The very same texts were interpreted as expressing a monarchist or the contrary republican Weltanschauung, depending on time, place, and historical circumstances. In all cases, the ideal constitution, legislator, regime, and rulers of the ancient Hebrew state were considered the perfect archetypes appropriate for any cultured people. Such positions were essentially normative in medieval Muslim and especially Christian political thought as well. With the renewed interest in classical culture in the Renaissance, the classical Hebrew sources also, especially the biblical ones, were identified as major political sources, alongside Plato and Aristotle. Moreover, ancient Hebrew history was considered a significant, relevant source of political lessons, no less then the histories of Greek and Rome. In *Il principe* (*The Prince*) and his *Discorsi* (*Discourses*), Machiavelli made extensive use of biblical sources together with those of Greece and Rome. Moses consistently appears in his political writings as the greatest ancient legislator, who possessed the

---

[39] Hodgen, *Early Anthropology*, 323–5, with additional bibliography.
[40] Ibid., 265; and the collection of papers, A. P. Coudert, ed., *The Language of Adam* (Wiesbaden, 1999).

optimal political *virtú* long before the greatest legislators of Greece and Rome, Solon, Lycurgus, and Romulus. In the last chapter of *The Prince* he describes the plight of the Israelites in Egypt before Moses appeared, as a prototype to be adopted by the oppressed Italian people:

> And if, as I said, the Israelites had to be enslaved in Egypt for Moses to emerge as their leader; ... then, at the present time, in order to discover the worth of an Italian spirit, Italy had to be brought to her present extremity. She had to be more enslaved than the Hebrews, ... leaderless, lawless, crushed, despoiled, torn, overrun.[41]

Machiavelli learned from the biblical stories of David and Solomon how Italian leaders should gain dominion in their city-states and how to keep and establish it. Political thinkers of early modern times, like Bodin, Hobbes, Locke, Filmer, Sydney, Selden, Harrington, Milton, Grotius, and many more, were deeply influenced by Christian Hebraism and the information it provided and adapted it in their political philosophy. They were "political Hebraists," who saw the regime of the Torah as an archetypical model and learned actual political lessons from its stories. Some found in it a monarchical direction; others, the sources of republicanism. The written and oral Torah were both enlisted now in the ideological battles of this period. Core terms of early modern political theory, such as natural law, the state of nature, the idea of sovereignty, the rule of law, and republican values, were originally identified in the Torah and the Talmud.[42] Harrington, for example, argued in the introduction to his *Oceana* (1651) that "ancient prudence was first discovered unto mankind by God himself in the fabric of the commonwealth of Israel,"[43] and the structure of his utopian state has clear Hebraic characteristics. Contemporary utopian political literature, such as More's *Utopia*, Campanella's *Città del sole* [City

---

[41] Machiavelli, *The Prince*, trans. and with an introduction by G. Bull (Baltimore, 1961), chap. 25, 134. See on the whole issue, A. Melamed, *The Philosopher-King in Medieval and Renaissance Jewish Political Thought* (Albany, NY, 2003), chap. 8.

[42] See, for example, in Allen, *Political Thought*, and elsewhere; Ettinger, "The Beginnings"; Melamed, *Philosopher-King*, chaps. 8–9; Sutcliffe, *Judaism and Enlightenment*, chaps. 2, 10; A. Berkowitz, "John Selden and the Biblical Origins of the Modern International Political System," *Jewish Political Studies Review* 6 (1994): 196–203; on Selden's Hebraism, see also recently J. P. Rosenblatt, *Renaissance England's Chief Rabbi: John Selden* (Oxford, 2006); K. Neuman, "Political Hebraism and the Early Modern 'Respublica Hebraeorum': On Defining the Field," *Hebraic Political Studies* 1 (2005): 57–70, and see additional papers in this and subsequent issues. Also on this subject: L. C. Boralevi and D. Quaglioni, eds., *Politeia Biblica* (Firenze, 2002).

[43] *The Political Works of James Harrington*, ed. and with an introduction by J. G. A. Pocock (Cambridge, 1977), 161. See on the whole issue A. Melamed, "English Travellers and Venetian Jewish Scholars: The Case of Simone Luzzatto and James Harrington," in G. Cozzi, ed., *Gli Ebrei e Venezia* (Milano, 1987), 401–13; M. Goldie, "The Civil Religion of James Harrington," in A. Pagden, ed., *The Language of Political Theory in Early-Modern Europe* (Cambridge, 1987), esp. 209.

of the Sun], Harrington's own *Oceana*, and Francis Bacon's *New Atlantis*, are full of Hebraic innuendoes. The capital of Bacon's island-state is called Bensalem; its first legislator is called Salomone and the residence of government is called the House of Salomone, where some of King Solomon's lost scientific writings are apparently stored.[44] J. G. A. Pocock once remarked that Hebrew was one of the main languages in early modern European political discourse, alongside Greek, Latin, and the vernacular.[45] The influence of political Hebraism will be found later in the writings of scholars of the French Enlightenment, such as Montesquieu and Rousseau.[46] With the advent of deism and the Enlightenment, however, the intellectual atmosphere will change, and early modern Christian Hebraism will go out of fashion.

The big question here is whether the emergence and influence of Christian Hebraism in early modern Europe necessarily led to a more tolerant attitude toward the Jews, and additionally to any kind of philosemitism. This is not necessarily the case. The oversimplified and naïve romantic myth that Christian Hebraism created some kind of philosemitic atmosphere cannot be defended. As usual, the picture is ambiguous, and often the renewed interest in Jewish culture intensified antisemitic tendencies, especially in the Germanic environment. As we have observed a few times in the course of this essay, we must bear in mind that the impetus of Christian Hebraism was not any love of Israel and things Jewish, but a combination of the Renaissance urge to uncover the ancient wisdom and the traditional Christian interest in proving itself the legitimate heir of Israel. Christian Hebraists – Catholic and Protestant alike – were by and large ambivalent about the Jews and created conflicting images of the Jew and Judaism. The growing appreciation of the treasures of Jewish literature often strengthened the missionary tendencies of prominent Christian Hebraists and resulted in the rejection of whoever refused to be saved. Christian Hebraists strongly rejected any attempt to baptize forcibly, but many among them saw the dialogue with the Jews as a useful means to persuade their Jewish counterparts to be saved. Their failure led some Christian Hebraists back to the old conclusion that Jews are not just blind but also stubborn, refusing to see the light. In some cases the better knowledge of Jewish sources, especially Talmudic sources, provided more ammunition and made it possible to intensify anti-Jewish propaganda. Reuchlin was a great Hebraist and did indeed plead the case of civil rights, but he never doubted the collective guilt of the Jews or the utility of mass expulsion. Erasmus promoted the cause of tolerance among educated Christians

[44] See H. Morley, ed., *Ideal Commonwealths* (New York, 1901).
[45] J. G. A. Pocock, "The Concept of Language," in A. Pagden, ed., *The Language of Political Theory in Early Modern Europe* (Cambridge, 1987), 20.
[46] Hertzberg, *French Enlightenment and the Jews*, chap. 9; Manuel, *Broken Staff*, 213–15.

and the freedom of research and teaching but at the same time rejoiced that France was free of heretics and Jews. As Heiko Oberman concluded, "the Jews were good for grammar but not for grace – they remained what they were, a miserable scrap of humanity."[47]

The difference between high and mass culture should not be overlooked here. We should always bear in mind that even if Christian Hebraism did create a more favorable attitude toward the Jews, it was limited to a relatively small number of scholars and intellectuals and barely filtered down to mass culture, if it did so at all. It did not touch the vast majority of Christians. Second, even among Christian Hebraists, the favorable interest was limited to high Jewish culture identified with Mosaic and Solomonic knowledge and Kabbalistic mysteries, seen as the primordial source of all human knowledge. Their attitude toward mass Jewish culture remained negative; it was deemed primitive and superstitious.

However, one can still take issue with Oberman's blunt conclusion that "the campaign for the *Veritas Hebraica* was, both philologically and ideologically, not merely a setback but a failure."[48] It is not at all clear what is meant here concerning the setback. A setback compared to what? Was the attitude toward the Jews significantly better at any given earlier period? Regarding failure, as always the picture is ambiguous, and we should avoid unrealistic expectations. But Christian Hebraism did, undeniably, create a meaningful and favorable interest in things Jewish, and a framework for cultural dialogue between Jewish and Christian scholars possibly unprecedented in extent and intensity, and many Christian Hebraists did protect the rights of Jewish colleagues. It can be argued that the very definition of Hebraic studies and its great popularity in early modern culture, together with other factors, helped create a growing – albeit very slow, ambivalent, and conflicting – legitimization and rehabilitation of Jews and Judaism. Or at least it helped create the basis for a future gradual process of more tolerant attitudes during the Enlightenment and the period of Jewish Emancipation. It did have some strong antisemitic ramifications, especially in the Germanic lands, as Oberman correctly cautions, but in other places,

---

[47] H. A. Oberman, *The Roots of Anti-Semitism in the Age of the Renaissance and Reformation*, trans. J. I. Porter (Philadelphia, 1984), esp. epilogue, 138–43; Jones, "Discovery of Hebrew and Discrimination against the Jews: The *Veritas Hebraica* as Double-Edged Sword in Renaissance and Reformation," in A. C. Fix and S. C. Karant-Nunn, eds., *Germania Illustrata: Essays on Early Modern Germany Presented to G. Strauss* (Ann Arbor, 1992), 19–34; the quotation is from 33–4; A. P. Coudert, "Seventeenth Century Christian Hebraists: Philosemites or Antisemites?" in A. P. Coudert et al., eds., *Judeo-Christian Intellectual Culture in the Seventeenth Century* (Dordrecht, 1999), 43–69.

[48] Oberman, "Discovery of Hebrew," 43. Note also that Oberman mainly discusses the Germanic cultural environment. In this respect, the book title is rather misleading. It does not deal with the roots of antisemitism in the Renaissance and Reformation as a whole, but only in the Germanic context, which does not necessarily apply to other western European countries such as England and the Netherlands.

such as England and the Netherlands, it tended toward the other direction. In this respect, Peter Gay's assessment, with which Oberman takes issue, still seems to the point:

The humanists have prepared the way for that solution; their realism made possible a secular view of political power and a secular, or at least no longer specifically Christian, justification for political obligation; their critical philology, combined with their admiration for antiquity, prepared educated men to read Christian documents with skeptical detachment, and pagan philosophies with sympathy; their appeal to nature laid the foundations for ... a style of thought that ordered the world by natural law, natural morality, and natural theology.[49]

Notwithstanding Oberman's justified caution, and his correct insistence on the great ambivalence of the sources, by and large Gay's assessment seems correct still. The admiration for antiquity, with emphasis on Jewish antiquities, combined with increasing secular tendencies, did create the basis for a more tolerant attitude toward the Jews. The process was slow and ambiguous, but it was nonetheless a hesitant step in the right direction.

---

[49] P. Gay, *The Enlightenment: An Interpretation* (New York, 1977), 297. See Oberman's criticism of this view, *Roots of Anti-Semitism*, 138–9.

3

The Philosemitic Moment?

Judaism and Republicanism in Seventeenth-Century European Thought

Adam Sutcliffe

The early seventeenth century witnessed the simultaneous rise of the economic fortunes of European Jewry and of Christian scholarly interest in Jewish texts. Increasingly valued as facilitators of international trade by states and rulers guided by mercantilist economics and *raison d'Etat* pragmatism, Jews extended their geographical presence and deepened their commercial importance, particularly during the turmoil of the Thirty Years' War.[1] Christian Hebraism, meanwhile, having emerged as a facet of Renaissance humanism, and invigorated by the theological rivalries of the post-Reformation era, reached its intellectual high-water mark in the second quarter of the seventeenth century.[2] In Jonathan Israel's words, "philosemitic scholarship was ... born at the same moment, and in the same context, as philosemitic mercantilism."[3]

What, though, was the relationship between these two phenomena? Or, to pose this question slightly differently, what were the politics of seventeenth-century Christian intellectual engagement with Jews and their texts, and in what sense, and to what extent, is it appropriate to consider this endeavor "philosemitic"? The expansion of Jewish settlement from the mid-sixteenth to the mid-seventeenth century – around the North Sea, in Italy and central Europe, and, slightly later, in colonial settlements around the Caribbean – was overwhelmingly driven by commercial

---

[1] See Jonathan Israel, *European Jewry in the Age of Mercantilism 1550–1750*, 3rd ed. (London: Littman, 1998), 44–57, 72–100.

[2] See Adam Sutcliffe, *Judaism and Enlightenment* (Cambridge: Cambridge University Press, 2003), 23–30; Stephen G. Burnett, *From Christian Hebraism to Jewish Studies: Johannes Buxtorf (1564–1629) and Hebrew Learning in the Seventeenth Century* (Leiden: E. J. Brill, 1996); Peter van Rooden, *Theology, Biblical Scholarship and Rabbinical Studies in the Seventeenth Century: Constantijn L'Empereur, Professor of Hebrew and Theology at Leiden* (Leiden: E. J. Brill, 1989).

[3] Israel, *European Jewry*, 46.

motives.[4] However, this expansion placed practical issues related to Jewish settlement on the intellectual agenda, and in these debates economics, politics, and theology inescapably intertwined. The appreciation that a Jewish presence was commercially beneficial to the states that welcomed them itself of course constituted a positive valuation of Jews, and it was an argument vigorously promoted by several Jewish leaders: the first to do so in detail was the Venetian rabbi Simone Luzzatto in 1638.[5] Acceptance of Jews for economic *ragione di stato* fed into a broader discussion concerning the civic utility and loyalty of Jews, and the appropriate terms on which they should be tolerated.[6]

Scholarly discourse on Jewish themes often had little to do with actual Jews, past or present. In early seventeenth-century England in particular, as Eliane Glaser has recently emphasized, Judaism often functioned as a highly versatile polemical resource, widely but inconsistently invoked to score points in theological and factional disputes between Christians.[7] However, since the early Renaissance much Christian Hebraist scholarship had been deeply embedded within the humanist moral and political concerns of liberty and virtue. Biblical figures were read by both Christian and Jewish Italian humanists as exemplary and usable political models, associated not only with wisdom but also with these civic values.[8] The preservation of *libertà* and *virtù* was central to Renaissance republican thought – an intellectual current that emerged in close proximity to Hebraist scholarship.

The Hebrew Bible offers several political models, and in the Jewish interpretive tradition monarchy is usually taken to be the governmental norm.[9] However, over the course of the early modern period Hebraism became increasingly closely associated with republican juristic and political thought. This reached its peak in the seventeenth century, when, in both England and the Dutch Republic, Hebraic texts and Judaic models

---

[4] See Paolo Bernardini and Norman Fiering, eds., *The Jews and the Expansion of Europe to the West, 1450–1800* (New York: Berghahn, 2001); Jonathan Israel, *Diasporas within a Diaspora: Jews, Crypto-Jews and the World Maritime Empires (1540–1740)* (Leiden: E. J. Brill, 2002).

[5] Simone Luzzatto, *Discorso circa il stato de gl'Hebrei e in particolar dimoranti nell'inclita Città de Venetia* (Venice, 1638).

[6] See Benjamin Ravid, *Economics and Toleration in Seventeenth-Century Venice: The Background and Context of the "Discorso" of Simone Luzzatto* (Jerusalem: American Academy for Jewish Research, 1978); Jonathan Karp, *The Politics of Jewish Commerce* (Cambridge: Cambridge University Press, 2008), 12–42.

[7] Eliane Glaser, *Judaism without Jews: Philosemitism and Christian Polemic in Early Modern England* (Basingstoke, UK: Palgrave Macmillan, 2007).

[8] Fabrizio Lelli, "Jews, Humanists and the Reappraisal of Pagan Wisdom Associated with the Ideal of the *Dignitas Hominis*," in Allison P. Coudert and Jeffrey S. Shoulson, eds., *Hebraica Veritas? Christian Hebraists and the Study of Judaism in Early Modern Europe* (Philadelphia: University of Pennsylvania Press, 2004), 49–70.

[9] Abraham Melamed, *The Philosopher-King in Medieval and Jewish Political Thought* (Albany: State University of New York Press, 2003), 7.

were widely used to defend and advance republican and quasi-republican arguments. It is in this republican tradition, I would suggest, that the political core of early modern valorization of Judaism is to be found. This was indubitably a philosemitic tradition, in which we find an intricate but unmistakable relationship between political biblicism and attitudes toward contemporary Jews. Moreover, the tensions internal to early modern republican thought, in particular in relation to land, agriculture, and commerce, were cast into particularly stark relief by the Jewish case.

A key focus of scholarly interest was the ancient Mosaic commonwealth, which served as a major political examplar, uniquely offering a sacred model of republican government.[10] The study of the "Republic of the Hebrews" was a pan-European project in the early modern era, engaging Catholics as well as Protestants: Carlo Sigonio's *Respublica Hebraeorum*, published in Bologna in 1582, was one of the most important early examples of the genre. However, identification with the ancient Hebrews, and fascination with the divinely ordained governmental arrangements of the *respublica Hebraeorum*, appealed most potently to reformed Protestants, themselves engaged in forging new – and, it was hoped, more godly – structures of social and political organization.[11] In the Dutch Republic, where national analogies with the ancient Israelites were most vivid, the most powerful and popular celebration of Mosaic republicanism was the *De republica Hebraeorum* of Petrus Cunaeus, professor of law at the University of Leiden (1617).

In England also collective identification as a "second Israel" – in some sense an elect nation – had particular resonance. The political significance of this identification was, however, rendered more complicated by the fact that, although civic values associated with republicanism were powerfully established in Elizabethan and early Stuart England, the English polity, unlike the Dutch, was not constituted as a republic during this period.[12] Early English

---

[10] For an overview, see Lea Campos Boralevi, "Per una storia della *Respublica Hebraeorum* come modello politico," in V. I. Comparato and E. Pii, eds., *Dalle "Repubbliche" elzeviriane alle ideologie del' 900* (Florence: Olschki, 1997), 17–33; Boralevi, "Classical Foundational Myths of European Republicanism: The Jewish Commonwealth," in Martin van Gelderen and Quentin Skinner, eds., *Republicanism: A Shared European Heritage* (Cambridge: Cambridge University Press, 2002), 1:247–61.

[11] The most important early Calvinist writings on the Mosaic republic were Bonaventure Bertram, *De politia Judaica* (Geneva, 1574), and various writings by Moyse Amyraut (1596–1664), who taught at the Huguenot academy of Saumur. See François Laplanche, *L'Ecriture, le sacré et l'histoire: Érudits et politiques protestants devant la Bible en France au XVII siècle* (Amsterdam: APA Holland University Press, 1986), 496–516.

[12] On the relationship between republican values and monarchy in England see Patrick Collinson, "The Monarchical Republic of Queen Elizabeth I," *Bulletin of the John Rylands Library* 69 (1987): 394–424; John F. McDiarmid, ed., *The Monarchical Republic of Early Modern England* (Aldershot, UK: Ashgate, 2007); Markku Peltonen, *Classical Humanism and Republicanism in English Political Thought 1570–1640* (Cambridge: Cambridge University Press, 1995).

Hebraism was, indeed, sponsored by the royal court, and its most significant outcome was the publication of the King James Bible (1611).[13] The Old
Testament, as scholars such as Christopher Hill and William Lamont have
shown, was an intensely political and contested text in early seventeenth-
century England, and Puritans and Anglicans identified with its Jewish protagonists in markedly different ways.[14] Whereas high church traditionalists
invoked Jewish precedents in support of their own position on theological
and ceremonial issues, their opponents used Jewish examples in a more
explicitly political fashion. For critics of divine right theory and of high
church ceremonialism, the divinely ordained Mosaic republic, enshrined in
Jewish law and explicated and evolved in rabbinic literature, provided the
most powerful basis for their claim that all government should be derived
not from naked authority but from collective consent to a just system of law,
responsive and adaptive to changing needs and conditions.[15]

　　According to the influential though controversial thesis of J. G. A. Pocock's
"Machiavellian moment," the central intellectual thread of European
republican thought in the early modern era runs from Machiavelli and
his contemporaries in Renaissance Florence, via James Harrington and
others in mid-seventeenth-century England, through to the Jeffersonian
republicanism of the early United States. This tradition, which emphasized
citizen involvement in public affairs as the key guarantor of the fundamental but eternally precarious political good of individual and collective
liberty, according to Pocock enshrined humanist notions of civic virtue
at the core of European republican values.[16] A loosely parallel lineage of
Hebraic scholarship and identification is readily apparent, from the roots
of this scholarly endeavor in Renaissance Italy, via the politicized biblicism
of seventeenth-century England, through to the covenantal language of
early America. Hebraism also, as we have already noted, permeated seventeenth-century Dutch political culture – a key chapter in the history of
republicanism, but nonetheless absent from Pocock's intellectual genealogy, as several of his critics have pointed out.[17] At the center of early modern

[13] See Gareth Lloyd Jones, *The Discovery of Hebrew in Tudor England* (Manchester: Manchester
University Press, 1983).
[14] Christopher Hill, *The English Bible and the Seventeenth-Century Revolution* (London: Allen
Lane, 1993); William Lamont, *Godly Rule: Politics and Religion, 1603–60* (London: Macmillan,
1969).
[15] For an excellent analysis of these contrasting uses see Glaser, *Judaism without Jews*, 30–91.
[16] J. G. A. Pocock, *The Machiavellian Moment: Florentine Political Thought and the Atlantic
Republican Tradition* (Princeton, NJ: Princeton University Press, 1975), esp. 49–80, 462–
505. For a useful summary of this text and the debate it provoked, see J. G. A. Pocock, "*The
Machiavellian Moment* Revisited: A Study in History and Ideology," *Journal of Modern History*
53 (1981): 49–72.
[17] Campos Boralevi, "Classical Foundation Myths," 247–8; Jonathan Scott, "Classical
Republicanism in Seventeenth-Century England and the Netherlands," in Van Gelderen
and Skinner, eds., *Republicanism*, 1:61–81.

Hebraist scholarship was a theological aspiration to fortify Christian faith and quell religious conflict by establishing accuracy and certainty in the interpretation of the Bible.[18] However, it was also a political project, and one closely intertwined with the history of republicanism.

It makes sense, indeed, to posit the existence of a "philosemitic moment" in Western republican thought, connecting a sequence of early modern thinkers for whom, in distinct but related ways, republican ideals were articulated in Hebraic terms, through identification with the ancient Jews and admiration for the Mosaic commonwealth. This philosemitic republican tradition – like Pocock's Machiavellian one – was inherently precarious, beset with a sense of vulnerability to the corrupting forces of authoritarianism, faction, and commerce. It is in the unfolding of this republican anxiety that the parallelism between the philosemitic and the Machiavellian "moments" is most illuminating. In the late seventeenth and eighteenth centuries, Pocock has emphasized, Anglo-American republicanism was strongly aligned with agrarian, "country" values, in opposition to the threats believed to emanate from parliamentary centralization and, above all, from commerce.[19] Writers on the Mosaic commonwealth strongly associated this polity, as we shall see later, with agrarian virtue. However, no ethnic group of the seventeenth and eighteenth centuries was more closely associated with commerce than the Jews. Ancient myths and contemporary realities pulled in diametrically opposed directions. In the attempts of various thinkers to harmonize these contrary perspectives on Jews, we witness the complex strains internal both to early modern European republican thought and to the politics of philosemitism.

PETRUS CUNAEUS AND THE REPUBLIC OF THE HEBREWS

The detailed study of the Old Testament as a source of explicitly political inspiration and example emerged in the later sixteenth century as a new genre in humanist scholarship. Machiavelli himself, in his political writings, paid close and admiring attention to Moses, identifying him as the most venerable and one of the most outstanding lawgivers and possessors of *virtù*.[20] Later writings were clearly indebted to Machiavelli, but the explication of the laws and institutions of what became known as "The Republic of the Hebrews" – or, in England, the Mosaic or Jewish

---

[18] See Peter N. Miller, "The 'Antiquarianization' of Biblical Scholarship and the London Polyglot Bible (1653–57)," *Journal of the History of Ideas* 62 (2001): 463–82.

[19] Pocock, *Machiavellian Moment*, 401–552; J. G. A. Pocock, *Virtue, Commerce, and History* (Cambridge: Cambridge University Press, 1985), 51–72, 103–24.

[20] Melamed, *Philosopher-King*, 149–66; John H. Geerken, "Machiavelli's Moses and Renaissance Politics," *Journal of the History of Ideas* 60 (1999): 579–95. See also Gisela Bock, Quentin Skinner, and Maurizio Viroli, eds., *Machiavelli and Republicanism* (Cambridge: Cambridge University Press, 1990).

"Commonwealth" – emerged only in the theologically competitive environment of the post-Reformation era. At least twelve major texts were published in this genre between 1546 and 1710.[21]

It was in the early Dutch Republic that Hebraic politics most firmly took grip. Analogies between the Dutch Revolt and the liberation of the Jews from their enslavement in Egypt appear ubiquitously in the visual and literary culture of the Dutch Golden Age, as Simon Shama has vividly shown.[22] Deeply immersed in Protestant biblicism, and politically formed in struggle with the much mightier Catholic Spain, the Dutch readily identified their young nation as a "New Israel," blessed with divine protection and a special historical destiny. This theological rhetoric was embraced across the political spectrum, but its significance was pointedly contested, particularly during the bitter conflicts in the second decade of the seventeenth century between the Remonstrants and their more strictly Calvinist Counter-Remonstrant adversaries.[23] The Counter-Remonstrants (like the English Puritans) restricted their understanding of collective divine election to the community of true believers in the national Dutch Reformed Church. For the Remonstrants, however (who were also echoed by their fellow Arminians in similar debates across the North Sea), the Dutch "New Israel" was primarily a political notion, identified with the entire nation.[24] The divinely inspired political model of the Hebrew republic took on a particular appeal for the Remonstrants in the context of this intense conflict over the theologicopolitical identity of the new Dutch state.

Hugo Grotius, the intellectual leader of the Remonstrant party, attempted to apply the ancient Hebrew example to contemporary Dutch politics in his earliest piece of extended political writing, *De republica emendanda* [On the emendation of the republic] (in manuscript in 1601, but unpublished during his lifetime).[25] However, he left the more

[21] François Laplanche, "L'Erudition chrétienne aux XVIe et XVIIe siècles et l'état des hébreux," in *L'Ecriture sainte au temps de Spinoza et dans le système Spinoziste* (Paris: Presses de l'Université de Paris Sorbonne, 1992), 133–47.

[22] Simon Shama, *The Embarrassment of Riches: An Interpretation of Dutch Culture in the Golden Age* (New York: Alfred A. Knopf, 1987), 93–125; Campos Boralevi, "Classical Foundation Myths," 248–51.

[23] On this dispute see Jonathan Israel, *The Dutch Republic: Its Rise, Greatness and Fall, 1477–1806* (Oxford: Oxford University Press, 1995), 433–49.

[24] Miriam Bodian, "The Biblical 'Jewish Republic' and the Dutch 'New Israel' in Seventeenth-Century Dutch Thought," *Hebraic Political Studies* 1 (2006): 186–201, esp. 190–6; Sutcliffe, *Judaism and Enlightenment*, 44–6.

[25] Hugo Grotius, "*De republica emendanda*: A Juvenile Tract by Hugo Grotius on the Emendation of the Dutch Republic," in Arthur Eyffinger, ed., *Grotiana* n.s. 5 (1984): 66–121; Arthur Eyffinger, introduction to Petrus Cunaeus, *The Hebrew Republic*, trans. Peter Wyetzner (Jerusalem: Shalem Press, 2006), ix–lxx, esp. xxvii–xxx; Arthur Eyffinger, "'How Wondrously Moses Goes Along with the House of Orange!' Hugo Grotius' 'De Republica

detailed explication of this theme to Petrus Cunaeus, his close friend and Remonstrant ally, whose *De republica Hebraeorum* has been described by Richard Tuck as "the most powerful statement of republican theory in the early years of the Dutch Republic."[26] Published in 1617 at the height of the power struggle between the Arminian and Counter-Remonstrant camps, Cunaeus's text was intended to be read first and foremost as a demonstration of how to preserve civil unity and avoid the perils of factionalism (a danger widely regarded as inherent in the theological exclusivism of the Counter-Remonstrants). His readers did not miss this pointed contemporary argument: in 1619–20, in the aftermath of the Counter-Remonstrant victory at the Synod of Dordrecht, Cunaeus was required to "clarify" certain of his arguments and defend his theological orthodoxy.[27]

The contemporary relevance of Cunaeus's tract is clearly stated in his preface, patriotically dedicated to "the illustrious and mighty States of Holland and Western Frisia":

For your inspection, most illustrious Members of States, I offer a republic – the holiest ever to have existed in the world, and the richest in examples for us to emulate. It is entirely in your interest to study closely this republic's origins and growth, because its creator and founder was not some man sprung from mortal matter, but immortal God Himself.... You will see what it was, in the end, that preserved the Hebrew citizens for so long in an almost innocent way of life, stirring up their courage, nurturing their harmonious coexistence, and reining in their selfish desires.[28]

The downfall of the Hebrew republic, he emphasized, was caused by factionalism, formented by Jeroboam after the death of Solomon, and resulting in the disastrous division of the polity into two.[29] The need to learn from the Hebraic example was urgent, because the Dutch Republic faced a very similar and pressing danger: "Many of your citizens have already split off into factions of one sort or another, and they have been fighting over these differences of opinion ever since they entered into a pointless conflict over obscure issues of religious doctrine which most of them do not even understand."[30]

Emendanda' in the Context of the Dutch Revolt," *Hebraic Political Studies* 1 (2005): 71–109; Guido Bartolucci, "The Influence of Carlo Sigonio's 'De Republica Hebraeorum' on Hugo Grotius' 'De Republica Emendanda,'" *Hebraic Political Studies* 2 (2007): 193–210.

[26] Richard Tuck, *Philosophy and Government 1572–1651* (Cambridge: Cambridge University Press, 1993), 169.

[27] Eyffinger, introduction to Cunaeus, *Hebrew Republic*, xxii–iv.

[28] Cunaeus, *Hebrew Republic*, 3. See also Cunaeus, *De republica Hebraeorum – the Commonwealth of the Hebrews*, ed. Lea Campos Boralevi (Florence: Centro Editoriale Toscano, 1996), which presents face to face the original Latin text and its 1653 English translation.

[29] Ibid., 4, 61–4.

[30] Ibid., 6.

Cunaeus did not regard himself as aligning the Hebraic polity with his own faction against another, but rather as turning to this divinely inspired model as an example of how to transcend faction altogether, by grounding politics in a world of timeless concord. In contrast with the disputatiousness and flux of his own era, Cunaeus situated the ancient Hebrews virtually outside history, living in unchanging simplicity. This, he believed, marked them apart from all their neighbors. While increasing trade intensified the contacts among the various nations around the Mediterranean and eroded the differences between them, only the Jews were immune to this trend: "only the Jews, living in their own land, and content with the wealth that nature produced there, led a life free of commerce. They did not cross the sea, nor did they visit foreigners or receive them."[31] Their economy was exclusively agrarian. There was no such thing as a Jewish craftsmen, which should be regarded as "a great compliment, not a criticism; for how can it be a noble act to invent things that are of no use to respectable citizens?"[32]

The uncompromising agrarianism of Cunaeus's republican vision is striking, and it contrasts with the opinion of Grotius, who regarded commerce and republicanism as mutually supportive.[33] To some extent this extreme position is generated by the nature of Cunaeus's material: the Hebrew republic, utterly unique because underwritten by God, appeared necessarily exceptional in every respect and thus invited exemption from the usual norms of commercial exchange. However, we also see here an early expression of the association of republicanism with agrarianism and stability, in opposition to commerce and innovation. This position was not yet present in Machiavelli (who admired Moses and other political leaders precisely as innovators), but it became a key hallmark of "Machiavellian moment" republican thought from the mid-seventeenth century onward.[34] The idealization of agrarian simplicity and its association with the preservation of a just and virtuous *respublica* had been a prevalent theme in sixteenth-century humanist political thought, exemplified most notably by Thomas More's *Utopia* (1516).[35] Agrarian republicanism was spurred on by the invocation of the ancient Hebraic political example, presented as a biblical idyll juxtaposed against the disputatiousness and instability of contemporary politics. Cunaeus ascribed the instability of his own era not only to theological intolerance and factionalism but also, implicitly, to the disruptive impact of commerce.

[31] Ibid., 20–1.
[32] Ibid., 22.
[33] Tuck, *Philosophy and Government*, 167.
[34] Pocock, *Machiavellian Moment*, 169–72, 183–211.
[35] See Brendan Bradshaw, "Transalpine Humanism," in J. H. Burns, ed., *The Cambridge History of Political Thought 1450–1700* (Cambridge: Cambridge University Press, 1991), 95–131, esp. 116–25.

Cunaeus's preferred brand of republicanism, like that of Grotius, was firmly oligarchic.[36] In the Hebraic republic he discovered a form of government that conformed to this preference. Almost all decisions, he claimed, were taken by a wise elite of judges or elders, who transmitted their authority through the laying of hands ("cherothesia") on new appointees. On rare occasions they called together assemblies to consult "the people," but this occurred only for major decisions such as selecting kings (whose political role is quietly elided by Cunaeus) or deciding whether to wage war.[37]

Authority resided not only with the elders, however, but also, crucially, in law. Although he did not engage in detailed legal exegesis, Cunaeus paid careful attention to the key structures and principles of Jewish law, using, like other Dutch Hebraists in this period, Maimonides' *Mishneh Torah* as his principal guide.[38] He particularly admired the laws that regulated the land redistribution practices of the jubilee, which he regarded as crucial in preventing concentration of landownership and sustaining the social harmony of the Hebrews' agrarian polity.[39] Cunaeus was also the first to introduce into Western European legal thought the key concept, drawn from Maimonides' *Mishneh Torah*, of the seven fundamental and universal Noachide laws, the observance of which was required of all peoples with whom the Jews were to sustain peaceful relations.[40] This notion was further developed in the jurisprudence of Grotius and John Selden, for whom it assumed fundamental importance in marking the distinction between "universal" laws, binding on all nations, and "particular" local laws and regulations, analogous to the "voluntary" divine law that extended beyond the seven Noachide precepts and that was revealed only to the Jews and binding only on them.[41]

Despite his deep respect for the ancient Hebrew polity, Cunaeus showed no particular admiration for the Jews as a people. The ancient Jews, he noted, had been excellent soldiers.[42] However, despite the excellence of their laws and judicial procedures, they had often preferred to believe in superstitions: he reports the usage of a mystical drink to try women accused of adultery, which was believed to cause those guilty "to burst on

---

[36] See Tuck, *Philosophy and Government*, 154–69; Tuck, "Grotius and Selden," in Burns, ed., *Cambridge History of Political Thought*, 499–529, esp. 503–9.

[37] Cunaeus, *Hebrew Republic*, 48.

[38] See Campos Boralevi, "Per una storia," 30–2; Aaron Katchen, *Christian Hebraists and Dutch Rabbis: Seventeenth Century Apologetics and the Study of Maimonides' "Mishneh Torah"* (Cambridge, MA: Harvard University Press, 1984).

[39] Cunaeus, *Hebrew Republic*, 14–16; Jonathan R. Ziskind, "Petrus Cunaeus on Theocracy, Jubilee and the Latifundia," *Jewish Quarterly Review* 68 (1978): 235–54, esp. 243–53.

[40] Cunaeus, *Hebrew Republic*, 128. See also Lea Campos Boralevi, introduction to Cunaeus, *Republica Hebraeorum*, xlvii–xlviii.

[41] Hugo Grotius, *De jure belli ac pacis* (1625); Tuck, *Philosophy and Government*, 190–201; Tuck, "Grotius and Selden," 516–17.

[42] Cunaeus, *Hebrew Republic*, 125–6.

the spot."[43] Some contemporary Jews, he commented, still believed in this "asinine Jewish stupidity."[44] He was particularly scornful of the Jews of his own day. Although in time they would be returned to the "right path," he commented that "all of today's Jews have a slavish and illiberal character," a misery he in part ascribed to their persecution, but also seemed to regard as deeply imbued in their collective character.[45] The political model Cunaeus admired resided in the laws and political structures of the ancient Hebrews, and not in the people themselves.

This distinction could not be so neatly sustained, however. The very practice of Hebraist scholarship was extremely difficult without contact with living Jews, who were by far the most competent teachers of the language: this was one of the reasons advanced by Grotius in support of Jewish settlement in Holland, despite his strong desire to restrict informal contact between Jews and Christians.[46] The political appeal of Cunaeus's turn to the Hebraic republic also lay in the fact that it offered a political model that was not only divinely underwritten but also in some sense visibly alive, because inescapably associated with the Jews of his own era. By 1617 Sephardic Jews were already conspicuously established in Amsterdam, and the simultaneously ancient and contemporary lens through which they were viewed is vividly apparent in the touches of biblicist exoticism that characterize several depictions of them by Rembrandt.[47] Cunaeus's Hebraic politics thus hovered over a confused relationship between imaginary and real Jews, and those of the distant past and of the local present. Moreover, the seventeenth-century Dutch Sephardim could not have been more different from those of the Mosaic republic. Utterly nonagrarian, they were commercial intermediaries par excellence, and it was this, rather than their linguistic skills, that most crucially persuaded the Dutch authorities to look favorably on their settlement. The widespread Dutch unease regarding the cultural and moral impact of their nation's rising commercial prowess was nowhere more potently distilled, in the realm of political theory, than in the diametric contrast between the Jews of utopian fantasy and those of contemporary reality.

JOHN SELDEN AND THE POLITICS OF JEWISH LAW

The most intellectually significant edifice constructed, in part, on Cunaeus's politically engaged approach to Jewish law was Hugo Grotius's *De jure belli ac pacis* [On the law of war and peace] (1625). This text was

[43] Ibid., 51.

[44] Ibid.

[45] Ibid., 71–3.

[46] Hugo Grotius, *Remonstrantie … op de Juden* (1614), ed. Jap Meijer (Amsterdam: N.p., 1949), 111–16; Israel, *European Jewry*, 52–3.

[47] See Michael Zell, *Reframing Rembrandt: Jews and the Christian Image in Seventeenth-Century Amsterdam* (Berkeley: University of California Press, 2002).

of fundamental importance in establishing the key principles of international law on the basis of the distinction between universal principles (for which the Noachite laws served as a blueprint) and local or national laws.[48] However, Grotius did not thrust Hebraic themes to the fore of his writing. His central concern was to present his arguments as logically and rationally as possible: Richard Tuck has aptly described *De jure* as "a manifesto for a new science of morality," emphasizing the very minimal and straightforward nature of morally and theologically necessary beliefs.[49] Jewish law provided Grotius with a key avenue of approach into the jurisprudential distinctions necessary for his argument, but his usage of Jewish legal arguments in *De jure* was somewhat haphazard.[50] Whereas the Noachite laws foreshadowed the universal principles that were fundamental to his "science of morality," the bulk of Jewish law was concomitantly of diminished significance, being relevant only to the Jews themselves – and in any case, as Grotius conventionally emphasized in his *De veritate religionis Christianae* (1627), superseded by the advent of Christianity.

The work of the English legal scholar John Selden, in contrast, was overwhelmingly Hebraic in focus. Almost exact contemporaries, he and Grotius shared a very similar intellectual agenda, as the work of Richard Tuck has emphasized.[51] Like Grotius, Selden was a politically engaged scholar with strong anticlerical instincts. A vigorous parliamentarian and a trenchant critic of Charles I's royal authoritarianism, he was, above all, a historically minded Erastian, committed to the supreme authority of the state, and particularly of its legal institutions and traditions, which, he stressed, must be understood as continually evolving within human history. The ancient Jewish case represented, for Selden, a uniquely authoritative and detailed example of the supremacy and the sophistication of law. Selden's politics were moderate and pragmatic: in his earlier work, written prior to the outbreak of the English Civil War, it was clear he regarded England's immemorial "ancient constitution" as "mixed," based on shared sovereignty of monarch, aristocracy, clergy, and representatives of the people. However, even before his entry into Parliament in 1623 his sympathies were firmly

---

[48] Grotius, *De jure*; Jonathan R. Ziskind, "International Law and Ancient Sources: Grotius and Selden," *Review of Politics* 35 (1973): 537–59; Richard Tuck, *The Rights of War and Peace: Political Thought and the International Order from Grotius to Kant* (Oxford: Oxford University Press, 1999), 78–108.

[49] Tuck, "Grotius and Selden," 520.

[50] Phyllis S. Lachs, "Hugo Grotius' Use of Jewish Sources in *On the Law of War and Peace*," *Renaissance Quarterly* 30 (1977): 181–200, esp. 198–9.

[51] Richard Tuck, *Natural Rights Theories* (Cambridge: Cambridge University Press, 1979), 58–100; *Philosophy and Government*, 205–21; "Grotius and Selden," 522–9. For biographical information on Selden see Paul Christianson, "Selden, John (1584–1654)," *Oxford Dictionary of National Biography* (Oxford: Oxford University Press, 2004).

parliamentarian, and his Hebraic scholarship served as the fundamental intellectual underpinning of his active political engagement.[52]

Selden's central intellectual project was to contribute to the theory of natural law: the exposition of a secure, universal grounding of legal principles, free from clerical meddling and impregnable to arbitrary authority. The key bedrock of his legal theory was provided by the seven Noachite precepts. This concept, ultimately derived from the Talmud (Sanhedrin 56a), was, as we have noted, aired by Cunaeus and significant also for Grotius, but Selden engaged with it much more centrally than either Dutch thinker. In his key work *De jure naturali et gentium juxta disciplinam Ebraeorum* [On the law of nature and of nations according to the doctrines of the Hebrews] (1640), he built his legal arguments firmly on the basis of these principles, universal in their reach, although their divine enunciation was precisely located within Jewish history. The relationship between the universal applicability and the historical specificity of these moral tenets was a slippery issue for Selden and has been the subject of some recent historiographical controversy. Selden did not believe (unlike Grotius) that natural morality was accessible directly by human reason. Morality was, for Selden, part of God's revelation to mankind, and this revelation had concretely occurred as an event in the history of the Jewish people. He was not, however, willing to countenance that prior to the deluge humans had lived without any morals. The Noachite precepts (except for the seventh one, which forbade the eating of live animals) were, he asserted, enjoined upon Adam, and thus upon all mankind.[53]

The Hebraic biblical narrative, hovering ambiguously both within and outside history, thus enabled Selden to situate the roots of legal morality in a similarly ambiguous position. This ambiguity was vital for his broader theory of jurisprudence. For natural law to have any purchase, it needed to be universal in the extent of its authority. However, Selden regarded these basic principles as standing at the outset of a process of legal evolution, the historicity of which was key to his understanding of the essence and strength of the English common law tradition. Selden's interest in the minute detail of Jewish civil law stemmed from his desire to elucidate, by analogy, this relationship between revealed principles and historical adaptation in societies properly regulated by law. Beyond the Noachite precepts,

---

[52] Paul Christianson, *Discourse on History, Law and Governance in the Public Career of John Selden (1610–1635)* (Toronto: University of Toronto Press, 1996), 11–85; see also J. G. A. Pocock, *The Ancient Constitution and the Feudal Law*, rev. ed. (Cambridge: Cambridge University Press, 1987).

[53] J. P. Sommerville, "John Selden, the Law of Nature, and the Origins of Government," *Historical Journal* 27 (1984): 437–47, 439–40, citing John Selden, *De jure naturali* (1640), 109. For Richard Tuck's earlier statement of a different position, and his later response to Sommerville, see Tuck, *Natural Rights Theories*, 96–7; Tuck, *Philosophy and Government*, 215–16.

Jewish civil law, and its rabbinic elucidation and development, in Selden's eyes represented the model for the relationship of all particular, specific, or local legislation to its fundamental principles. This is how he succinctly encapsulated this perspective in his posthumously compiled *Table-Talk*:

God at first gave laws to all mankind, but afterwards he gave peculiar laws to the Jews which only they were to observe. Just as we have the common law for all England, and yet you have some corporations that besides that have peculiar laws and privileges for themselves.[54]

Selden did not directly idealize the agrarianism of the ancient Hebrew polity. However, his earliest and most controversial use of ancient Jewish sources to advance a contemporary political argument was on a fundamental agrarian theme. Selden presented his *History of Tithes* (1618) as a straightforward, objective account of the history of tithing practices. However, the polemical thrust of his scholarship was unmistakable: Selden sought to challenge claims that tithing was guaranteed by divine right, by showing their basis in law, and the historical variation in their practice. His starting point, in pursuing this argument, was the tithe payments of the ancient Jews, which, he showed, altered over time, reflecting changing conditions and according to the consensus of reasoned legal opinion.[55] Selden's deployment of Jewish law ranged over many topics: his extensive and admiring study of Jewish marriage law implicitly contrasted the legal sophistication and purity of this tradition with the more arbitrary accretions of canon law on marriage and divorce, while his final work portrayed ancient Jewish government as a positive model of the Erastian subsuming of religious governance into the broader affairs of state.[56] It is noteworthy, however, that his first engagement addressed the economic and political importance of land tenure.

Jason Rosenblatt, in his recent monograph on Selden, has emphasized the generosity of this highly erudite scholar's approach to Judaism, describing his *De jure* as "surely one of the most genuinely philosemitic works produced by a Christian Hebraist in early modern Europe."[57] Rosenblatt's important study enters deeply into the scholarly texture of Selden's engagement with Jewish sources, stressing his "love of *halacha*" and taking seriously the appropriateness of his status, as described in quasi-jest by a fellow

---

54 John Selden, *Table-Talk*, 3rd ed. (London, 1716), 47.
55 John Selden, *History of Tithes* (1618), in his *Opera Omnia* (London, 1726), 3:1075–88; see also Glaser, *Judaism without Jews*, 49–54.
56 John Selden, *Uxor Ebraica* (1646), ed. and trans. Jonathan Ziskind (Leiden: E. J. Brill, 1991); Selden, *De synedriis & praefecturis juridicis veterum Ebraeorum* (1650–53), in *Opera Omnia* 1:785 9ff.; on the influence of *Uxor Ebraica* on John Milton see also Jason P. Rosenblatt, *Torah and Law in Paradise Lost* (Princeton, NJ: Princeton University Press, 1994), 87–9.
57 Jason P. Rosenblatt, *Renaissance England's Chief Rabbi: John Selden* (Oxford: Oxford University Press, 2006), 161.

Hebraist in correspondence, as England's "chief rabbi."[58] It is certainly reasonable to describe Selden as a philosemite: not only was his approach to Jewish law unfailingly respectful, but it signified for him a blueprint for all legal thinking and governance.

However, it is somewhat misleading to read Selden, as Rosenblatt does, as an apostle for religious toleration who sought to combat prejudice by emphasizing "the humaneness of rabbinical exegesis."[59] Selden's reading of rabbinic literature was certainly animated by a broader political purpose, but this had very little to do with relations between Christians and Jews in his own era. His passion for Hebraic texts was deep and admiring, and his scholarly engagement with them was careful and in large measure open-minded. However, his interest in Hebraica was not purely one of reverential erudition. Selden's scholarship was also shaped by his juridicopolitical commitment to using the resources of the past to advance, in the present, the sophistication and supremacy of the law as a check to the authority of over-mighty monarchs. The foundational status of Jewish law, and the rich-ness of rabbinic interpretations of this legal tradition, made Jewish sources immensely valuable for Selden in advancing these arguments. There was no necessary connection, though – and also very little actual connection in Selden's mind – between this formal use of Hebraic legal exegesis and any particular interest in or concern with attitudes toward the Jews of his own day.

Unlike the leading continental Hebraists, such as the Buxtorfs of Basel, Selden worked without contact with living Jews, toward whom his attitudes were certainly not unambiguously positive. In a brief note on the medie-val history of Anglo-Jewry he endorsed the blood libel, stating that it was "usual amongst them, every year towards Easter" to steal, circumcise, and crucify a young Christian boy, "out of their own devilish malice to Christ and Christians."[60] His brief comment under the heading "Jews" in his *Table-Talk* is not hostile, but not particularly warm either, emphasizing not their religion but their commercial acumen and collective cohesion:

Talk what you will of the Jews, … they thrive where e'er they come, they are able to oblige the Prince of their country, by lending him Money; none of them beg, they keep together, and for their being hated, my life for yours, Christians hate each other as much.[61]

Selden's philosemitism certainly did not entail that he held Jews or Judaism in global positive regard. His Hebraist interests were focused in the dis-embodied realm of Jewish law and legal exegesis. However, although

---

[58] Ibid., 3–5, 276; see also Rosenblatt, *Torah and Law*, 82–96.
[59] Rosenblatt, *England's Chief Rabbi*, 181.
[60] John Selden, *On the Jews Sometimes Living in England*, n.d., in *Opera Omnia* 3:1461.
[61] John Selden, *Table-Talk*, 3rd ed. (London, 1716), 47.

his systematic interest in Jewish law was classically antiquarian, he only partially conformed to Arnaldo Momigliano's pithy definition of this type of scholar as someone "interested in historical facts without being interested in history."[62] The historicity of law, and its mutability within history, was fundamental to Selden's understanding of what Pocock has described as the English "common law mind."[63] His scholarship was also, notwithstanding his occasional strategic protestations to the contrary, unabashedly political, pursued in support of a particular vision of quasi-republican jurisprudential government. Selden's engagement with Jewish law was, thus, not purely systematic, but also historical. However, there were limits to this historical interest, and the Jews of his modern era fell outside them. He evinced little interest in considering contemporary Jews alongside those of the era of his scholarship. The modern theological and commercial realities of Jewish-Christian relations found no resonance in his intellectual world, but generated only an untidy and awkward dissonance.

JAMES HARRINGTON, HEBRAIC REPUBLICANISM, AND THE READMISSION OF JEWS TO ENGLAND

If an incipient republicanism can be discerned in Selden's legal critique of arbitrary rule, the republican vision is explicit in the writings of James Harrington, a mid-seventeenth-century political theorist strongly influenced by Selden and a key figure in the lineage of Pocock's *Machiavellian Moment*.[64] In his *Oceana* (1656) Harrington echoed Selden's Hebraic Erastianism, arguing that in the divinely ordained Mosaic commonwealth there had been no distinction between civil and religious authority. This claim pointedly undermined traditional Christian arguments for the autonomy of the church, which were based on its status as the successor institution to the ancient and divinely instituted Jewish priesthood. Unlike Selden, but similarly to Cunaeus, Harrington explicitly stressed the republican nature of the Mosaic polity and offered it, alongside but above the other venerable constitutions of Athens, Sparta, and republican Rome and the modern exemplar of the Republic of Venice, as the most perfect model for an English republican regime.

The Jews occupied an oddly bifurcated status in Harrington's *Oceana* – as they did for Selden, and in general for seventeenth-century republican thought. On the one hand, Harrington treated the ancient Jews as one political example among many in history, and analyzed them comparatively alongside Sparta, Rome, and Venice. However, as a divinely underwritten

[62] Arnaldo Momigliano, *The Classical Foundations of Modern Historiography* (Berkeley: University of California Press, 1990), 54.

[63] Pocock, *Ancient Constitution*, 30–69.

[64] Pocock, *Machiavellian Moment*, 383–400.

polity, founded on "laws given by God such as were not fit to be altered by men," the "commonwealth of Israel" stood in a category of its own.[65] Both within history and outside it, the Jews blur the boundary between pragmatism and utopianism in Harrington's *Oceana* – a text published amid great political flux and visionary hope in England, and at a time when the nexus between utopianism and pragmatism was particularly brought into focus by the issue of the readmission of Jews to England.

An intricate intertwinement of idealism (whether inspired by political republicanism or religious millenarianism) and economic and strategic pragmatism suffused English thinking about Jews in the era of the readmission. The Jews figure prominently, indeed, in Harrington's own attempt to bridge the gap between vision and reality. He opens his text with a mellifluous hymn to the island of Oceana, which, it is clear, should be understood as England in the immediate post–Civil War future. Harrington then addresses attention to the problems of the fertile but degenerate "neighbour island" of "Panopea" – "the soft mother of a slothful and pusillanimous people": this is clearly Ireland. Panopea, Harrington suggests, should be settled with Jews, who, he confidently proclaims, would flock there in large numbers if allowed to observe "their own rites and laws." In Panopea the Jews would retain their mercantile skills and also rediscover their ancient talent for agriculture, presenting the possibility of a uniquely profitable arrangement both for the tenant Jews and for the landlord Commonwealth of Oceana.[66]

This suggestion is clearly a response to contemporary events both in England – where the issue of Jewish readmission had recently moved center stage – and in Ireland, where Cromwell was attempting to implement a brutal policy of colonial land confiscation and native transplantation. Harrington's position here is implicitly critical both of Cromwell's strategy in Ireland and of the de facto acceptance of Jewish settlement in England, which had effectively been established only a few months prior to the publication of *Oceana* in the autumn of 1656.[67] In contrast to the newly acknowledged Jewish colony living and working in the heart of London, Harrington's proposed plantation of Ireland with Jews was designed to quarantine them from others:

To receive the Jews after any other manner into a commonwealth were to maim it; for they of all nations never incorporate but, taking up the room of a limb, are of no use or office unto the body, while they suck the nourishment which would sustain a natural and useful member.[68]

[65] James Harrington, *The Commonwealth of Oceana* (1656), in J. G. A. Pocock, ed., *The Political Works of James Harrington* (Cambridge: Cambridge University Press, 1977), 174–87, esp. 176.
[66] Ibid., 159.
[67] See David S. Katz, *Philo-Semitism and the Readmission of the Jews to England* (Oxford: Oxford University Press, 1982), 232–8; S. B. Liljegren, "Harrington and the Jews," *Humanistiska Vetenskapssamfundets* (1932): 65–78.
[68] Harrington, *Oceana*, 159.

Harrington was hostile to the settlement of Jews in Oceana proper because he believed that they would introduce with them an economic culture of vigorous financial speculation. This commercial energy was, in his opinion, inimical to the form of virtuous republic he envisaged, in which political power and participation were based on the ownership of landed property, broadly dispersed among the nobility and gentry.[69] Harrington's view of the Jews thus mixed admiration with disdain, and reverence with fear. He idealized the latent agrarian skills of the Jews, which he regarded as part of their timeless collective talents as God's chosen people. He was much less comfortable, however, with the economic specialism manifested by the actual Jews of his own time. Once again, the mythic agrarian Jews of the past clashed uncomfortably with the real, commercial Jews of the present. Whereas Selden for the most part silently evaded this tension, Harrington attempted to reconcile it. In so doing, he drew attention to the contradictory duality of the Jews' association both with the agrarian simplicity that carried such positive connotations in the republican tradition and with the commercial and speculative skills that he and others regarded as deeply corrosive of this political cause.

Here we see very clearly the ambivalence of the "philosemitic moment." From Harrington onward, Pocock has stressed, Anglo-American republican thought was highly suspicious both of parliamentary power and of commercial society and tended to align with "country" propertied interests and agrarian values, against these urban foci of power, which they perceived as a threat to republican virtue. Republicanism, however, was unimaginable without parliamentary authority, and, at least in the context of the seventeenth and eighteenth centuries, unimaginable also without the rise of commerce, which provided the incomes of almost all potential or actual beneficiaries and participants in republican government. Republican thought in the Enlightenment era was, as Pocock has shown, thus caught in a quandary, and beset with anxieties of its own decay and corruption.[70] This tension – between the moral and collectivist ideals of republicanism and the commercial energies it unleashed – was brought into uniquely dense focus by the case of the Jews. While in abstract terms Judaism was very strongly associated with the values and practices of agrarian republicanism, theorists such as Selden and Harrington also accepted the dominant seventeenth-century linkage of Jews with commerce, and with its very different, and in some eyes even diametrically opposed, system of values. Confusion over commerce thus manifested itself in confusion over Jews – with significant consequences for the lives of Jews themselves, who, in the mid-1650s in particular, did their best to navigate this confusion to their advantage.

[69] Ibid., 166–7. See also Pocock, *Machiavellian Moment*, esp. 391; Blair Worden, "English Republicanism," in Burns, ed., *Cambridge History of Political Thought*, 443–75, esp. 450–5.
[70] Pocock, *Machiavellian Moment*, 401–552.

Economics and political theology similarly swirled awkwardly around each other in the debates surrounding the readmission of the Jews to England in 1655/6, as several historians have noted.[71] Established merchants feared Jewish competition and generally argued that their readmission would "enrich Foreigners, and impoverish English merchants," to which advocates responded that Jewish competition would lower prices, and thus benefit most people.[72] The millenarian Baptist preacher Thomas Collier put this argument very forcefully:

> If it should be some loss to some rich Merchants, yet it would be advantage to the people in general. The more is brought in the plentier and cheaper it would be; what a few rich men might lose, a great many poor men might gain, and that would be indeed and in truth no loss at all.[73]

Collier's interest in Jews was not economic but theologicopolitical. Many of the God-fearing English were, he insisted, eagerly "waiting for the redemption of Israel."[74] By treating the Jews with kindness, and welcoming them with open arms, they would show both their true piety and their republican spirit, in sharp contrast to the ungodliness of papism, of the Turks, and of authoritarian royal government.[75] The biblical ideal of the Mosaic republic was far more engaging for Collier than were the commercial activities of contemporary Jews. In order to further his millenarian vision, it made sense to align the cause of Jewish readmission with populism and free trade, against national vested interests and protectionism. This alignment was not, however, stable. While willing to make alliances of convenience against those London merchants opposed to readmission, religiously inspired proponents of Jewish settlement generally shared Harrington's agrarian traditionalism and his suspicion of the untrammeled impact of commerce.

Supporters of Jewish readmission thus variously negotiated the dissonance between the Jews of their biblically based imaginary and those of seventeenth-century reality. However, although the committed agrarians of the Mosaic republic could scarcely be more different from the vigorous intercontinental traders of the Sephardic Diaspora, both images of Jews shared a common assumption that this small minority would make an immense impact wherever they were present. With respect to commerce this assumption was not altogether unwarranted: Sephardic merchants were indeed among the most significant international merchants of the period, their success underpinned by uniquely far-flung networks of cooperation

---

[71] See Katz, *Philo-Semitism*; Glaser, *Judaism without Jews*, 113–29.

[72] [Henry Jessey], *A Narrative of the late Proceeds at White-Hall, Concerning the Jews* (London, 1656), 8–9.

[73] Thomas Collier, *A Brief Answer to Some of the Objections and Demurs Made against the Coming-in and Inhabiting of the Jews in this Common-wealth* (London, 1656), 13.

[74] Ibid., 9.

[75] Ibid., 8.

and trust sealed by tight bonds of kinship and identity.[76] Belief in Jewish power, though, also took other guises and was shared by some of the most ardent critics of readmission. William Prynne, one of the Puritan leaders of this camp, argued in his *Short Demurrer to the Jews* (1656) that "this giddy Apostatizing age" was particularly ill suited for the admission of Jews to England, lest "their company and society should easily seduce the unstable people to their Judaism and Infidelity."[77] Despite his own unremittingly negative view of the influence of Jews, Prynne's ascription of such immense rhetorical and seductive power to them constitutes a certain form of awed idealization, and one that drew on the same pool of assumptions as did his pro-readmission adversaries.

The impact of philosemitism in this debate was multifaceted and double-edged, and can neither be equated with wholly positive views of Jews nor straightforwardly annexed only to one position on the readmission issue. Both supporters and opponents of this campaign – as well as the many people, such as Oliver Cromwell, whose position seems indeterminate – shared a common belief in the political, economic, and theological exceptionalism of the Jews.[78] This gave rise to responses both of admiring enthusiasm and of anxious hostility. Although these countervailing temperaments were closely intertwined and cannot be sharply dissected from each other, it is nonetheless the case that the events of 1655 and 1656 would not have unfolded as they did had it not been for the ultimate dominance of positive attitudes toward Jews among the republican and Puritan leadership in England at this time – attitudes that in both intent and impact can only be classed as philosemitic. Anglo-Jewish historians have since the nineteenth century cast the readmission as characteristic of deep-seated English decency and toleration, in contrast to the antisemitic prejudices rife in continental Europe.[79] It makes more sense, however, to understand the readmission in the context of a particular tradition of biblically inspired republicanism, which was briefly triumphant in England in this unique and tempestuous decade.

EXCAVATING THE PHILOSEMITIC MOMENT

Republican philosemitism remained a vital current of British political thought in the early eighteenth century, most significantly carried

[76] See Israel, *Diasporas within a Diaspora*, esp. 1–41.

[77] William Prynne, *A Short Demurrer to the Jews* (London, 1656), 73.

[78] On Cromwell and readmission see Edgar Samuel, "Oliver Cromwell and the Readmission of the Jews to England in 1656," in *At the End of the Earth: Essays on the History of the Jews in England and Portugal* (London: Jewish Historical Society of England, 2004), 179–89; Glaser, *Judaism without Jews*, 20–7.

[79] See Glaser, *Judaism without Jews*, 7–29; Eliane Glaser and Stephen Massil, "1656 and All That," *Jewish Quarterly* 202 (2006), posted at www.jewishquarterly.org.

forward by John Toland, who was a fascinated admirer of the Mosaic republic, on which he commented in several brief pieces and projected but did not complete a major study.[80] Toland was also strongly influenced by Harrington, whose *Oceana* and other key works he edited and republished in 1700.[81] Toland's 1714 essay arguing for the naturalization of Jews in Britain and Ireland was, as Jonathan Karp has shown, heavily imbued with a Harringtonian republican framework, although Toland proposed a much fuller incorporation of Jews into the national polity, most crucially extending to them the right to own land throughout the realm.[82] Drawing directly from a Jewish source – Simone Luzzatto's Venetian apologetic of 1638 – Toland reiterated the distinction drawn by Cunaeus and Selden between the universal, "natural" core of Judaism and its particularist ceremonial embellishment. While praising the mercantile usefulness of Jews, his emphasis was on their political loyalty and, latent since ancient times, their martial skill.[83] His proposal for Jewish naturalization most centrally aimed, as Jonathan Karp has very aptly put it, to "resurrect their republican capacities" and to harness these primordial Jewish talents in politics, agriculture, and warfare to the contemporary fortunes of republicanism in Britain.[84]

In the increasingly commercial eighteenth century the association between landed agrarian and republican ideals came under considerable strain, and in England (though not in Scotland) concern with the values of civic virtue receded as industrialism advanced. In America, however, as Pocock has compellingly argued, pessimistic anxieties regarding the corrupting force of commerce retained their potency, and the self-sufficient landowning yeoman remained the ideal model of the virtuous citizen.[85] The privileging of agrarian republicanism and the biblical roots of this political ideal are particularly evident in the writings of Thomas Jefferson,

---

[80] See Justin Champion, *John Toland and the Crisis of Christian Culture, 1696–1722* (Manchester: Manchester University Press, 2003), esp. 49–52; Robert Rees Evans, *Pantheisticon: The Career of John Toland* (New York: Peter Lang, 1991), 187ff.; Sutcliffe, *Judaism and Enlightenment*, 197–205, 225–8.

[81] *The Oceana of James Harrington, and His Other Works ... collected, Methodiz'd and Review'd, with an Exact Account of His Life Prefix'd, by John Toland* (London, 1700). See also J. G. A. Pocock, "Historical Introduction" to *Political Works of James Harrington*, 141–7.

[82] John Toland, *Reasons for Naturalizing the Jews in Great Britain and Ireland* (London, 1714); Jonathan Karp, "The Mosaic Republic in Augustan Politics: John Toland's 'Reasons for Naturalizing the Jews,'" *Hebraic Political Studies* 1 (2006): 462–92, esp. 474–85.

[83] Toland, *Reasons*, 11, 16, 50–1.

[84] Karp, "Mosaic Republic," 474; see also Justin Champion, "Toleration and Citizenship in Enlightenment England: John Toland and the Naturalization of the Jews, 1714–1753," in Ole Peter Grell and Roy Porter, eds., *Toleration in Enlightenment Europe* (Cambridge: Cambridge University Press, 2000), 133–56.

[85] Pocock, *Machiavellian Moment*, 506–52.

who in his *Notes on the State of Virginia* (1781) explicitly assumed the mantle of divine election for the nascent American republic:

Those who labour in the earth are the chosen people of God, if ever he had a chosen people, whose breasts he has made his peculiar deposit for substantial and genuine virtue. ... It is the manners and spirit of a people which preserve a republic in vigour. A degeneracy in these is a canker which soon eats to the heart of its laws and constitution.[86]

Considerable scholarly controversy has raged over the question of Jefferson's European intellectual influences, but Pocock's collocation of him as a culminating thinker of the "Machiavellian Moment," although certainly not his only lineage, nonetheless remains persuasive.[87] Although Jefferson does not directly mention Jews here, it is clearly the Judaic position of divine chosenness that he is invoking, in the long-standing tradition of Protestant Hebraist republicanism. His implicit juxtaposition of agrarian virtue against the corrupting forces of urban commerce is, again, not explicitly posed in relation to Jews. However, this political language, which, enshrined in the reverence sustained toward the American "founding fathers," has remained resonant in the United States, carrying forward into the modern era the idealization of notionally Judaic Old Testament agrarian traditionalism, and also the tension between this idealization and the dynamic energy of metropolitan commerce, in which actual Jews have remained significantly concentrated.

The relationship between philosemitic Hebraism and actual living Jews is, then, extremely complicated. Judaism was certainly widely used in the seventeenth century as a form of conceptual token, deployed for its particular rhetorical authority in debates between the adversarial political and theological wings of Dutch and English Protestantism. However, in both countries policies toward Jews were undoubtedly to some degree shaped by these debates: positive associations with ancient Judaism indirectly but indubitably fed into greater openness toward actual Jews. More intangibly, the sustained undercurrent of Hebraic idealization that we see in this period should be recognized as a significant current in shaping underlying cultural attitudes toward Jews and Judaism. John Toland's declaration of proto-Zionism, originally advanced as a suggestion to his patron Prince Eugene of Savoy, was not an utterly anomalous opinion, and nor was the circulation of such ideas in this period utterly unconnected to their overdetermined realization more than two centuries later:

[86] Thomas Jefferson, *Notes on the State of Virginia* (1781), ed. William Peden (Chapel Hill: University of North Carolina Press, 1955), query 19, 164–5; see also Gary Wills, *Inventing America: Jefferson's Declaration of Independence* (New York: Doubleday, 1978); Ronald Hamowy, "Jefferson and the Scottish Enlightenment: A Critique of Gary Wills' *Inventing America*," *William and Mary Quarterly* 36 (1979): 503–23.

[87] Pocock, *Machiavellian Moment*, 532–43.

[If the Jews] ever happen to be resettl'd in Palestine upon their original foundation, which is not at all impossible, they will then, by reason of their excellent
constitution, be more populous, rich and powerful than any other nation now in
the world. I would have you consider, whether it be not both in the interest and
duty of Christians to assist them in regaining their country. But more of this when
we meet.[88]

It is no less misleading to exaggerate than to diminish the association
between real, living Judaism and the rhetorical use made of Jewish texts
by Christians. Fania Oz-Salzberger has recently emphasized the indebtedness of early modern political thinkers to their Jewish sources, claiming
that key concepts, such as federalism, settled boundaries, and a socially
responsible moral economy, were essentially derived from Judaism and
incorporated into modern liberalism, while Eric Nelson has argued that
the uncompromising republicanism introduced into English thought in
the mid-seventeenth century was prompted by Hebraists' encounters with
particular Talmudic commentaries.[89] However, it is inaccurate to claim
primary Jewish ownership of these ideas and oversimplified to interpret
Christian reading of Jewish sources straightforwardly as a process of Jewish
"influence." In parallel with Christian scholars, and similarly influenced by
current political debates in Amsterdam and London, some seventeenth-
century Sephardic writers, such as Miguel Levi de Barrios, also emphasized the republican nature of Jewish political structures, with their roots
in Mosaic law.[90] The exegesis of this tradition was, though, a Christian as
much as a Jewish project. Moreover, scholars such as Cunaeus and Selden
who made extensive use of Jewish interpreters approached their Jewish
sources – usually Maimonides – knowing what they were looking for. Their
commitments to federalism, republicanism, and the authority of law were
derived from their preexisting political perspectives and commitments and
certainly were not "discovered" by them in the Bible or the Talmud.

It is ultimately not illuminating to try to gauge the authenticity of
philosemitic attitudes in early modern Europe, or to associate or disas-
sociate them with Judaism as understood and experienced by Jews. The
deployment of Jewish themes in the thought of this period was extremely
intricate and complicated and stemmed ultimately from the structurally
foundational relationship between Christianity and Judaism. Nonetheless,

---

[88] John Toland, *Two Problems Concerning the Jewish Nation and Religion* (1709), in Justin
   Champion, ed., *Nazarenus* (Oxford: Voltaire Foundation, 1999), 240.
[89] Fania Oz-Salzberger, "The Jewish Roots of Western Freedom," *Azure* 13 (2002): 88–132;
   Eric Nelson, "'Talmudical Commonwealthsmen' and the Rise of Republican Exclusivism,"
   Historical Journal 50 (2007): 809–35; Eric Nelson, *The Hebrew Republic: Jewish Sources and
   the Transformation of European Political Thought* (Cambridge, MA: Harvard University Press,
   2010), 23–56.
[90] Miriam Bodian, "Biblical Hebrews and the Rhetoric of Republicanism: Seventeenth-
   Century Portuguese Jews on the Jewish Community," *AJS Review* 22 (1997): 199–221.

in early modern political thought we discover an engagement with Judaism that, although certainly ambivalent, is in its dominant tenor highly positive. Attention to this tradition serves as an important corrective to dominant assumptions about the nature of Jewish-Christian relations. The charged significance of Judaism in this current of republican thought presents us with a notable ethnoreligious twist to the core tensions that beset this "Machiavellian" lineage. The strain between self-sufficient agrarian stability and commercial growth was nowhere more sharply crystallized than in the dissonance between the Jews of the Mosaic imaginary and those actually encountered by the political admirers of Moses.

PART II

THREE EUROPEAN PHILOSEMITES

4

William Whiston's Judeo-Christianity

*Millenarianism and Christian Zionism in Early
Enlightenment England*

Adam Shear

Jews and Judaism played a crucial role in the thinking of William Whiston
(1667–1752), disciple and popularizer of Isaac Newton, millenarian pam-
phleteer, Josephus translator, coffeehouse lecturer, and antitrinitarian
heretic. Although hardly known today except to specialists in the religious politics and the scientific achievements of early eighteenth-century
England, Whiston was a well-known figure to the eighteenth-century reading public. During his long life, Whiston published more than seventy
books and pamphlets on topics including early Christian theology, ecclesiastical history, navigation, astronomy, geology, and mathematics. Whiston
carried on vigorous polemics in print with contemporaries on many topics,
mainly religious, and revisited his long career in a two-volume autobiography published three years before his death. Whiston, one of Newton's
prominent students at Cambridge in the 1690s, succeeded his teacher as
Lucasian Professor in 1702. During this same period, Whiston's emerging interest in primitive Christianity led him to adopt an antitrinitarian
view of Christianity. His understanding of Jesus as a nondivine teacher and
Messiah was reminiscent of theological views common in the early church
that had been declared heretical by the Council of Nicea in 325 C.E. and
was anathema to the established Church of England. When Whiston publicly preached (and then published) his "Arian" view, he was put on trial
for heresy and was exiled from Cambridge in 1710. After his expulsion, he
moved to London and remained a well-known lecturer and author until
his death.

In the last few decades, as Newton's religious views have been the subject
of a good deal of discussion, his student Whiston has also been the theme
of considerable scholarly interest. Most attention has focused on his relationship to Isaac Newton as a student of Newton's scientific and religious

I am grateful to David Ruderman, Matt Goldish, and Richard Cogley for helpful comments
on earlier versions of this essay.

beliefs, to his trial for heresy in 1710, and to his career as a lecturer after his expulsion from Cambridge.[1] However, very little scholarly attention has been paid to another important interest of Whiston's. Although Whiston was not a Christian Hebraist nor someone who had particularly close relations with Jews, his lifelong project of promoting a restoration of "primitive Christianity" led him toward a profound interest in Judaism as a means of recapturing the Jewishness of early Christianity. The restoration of the Jews to the land of Israel and the reestablishment of a Jewish state, Jewish law, and the Jewish Temple were important elements in his millenarian thinking. Although Whiston's views about the restoration of the Jews and his role as translator of Josephus have been noted, the central role that Judaism plays in his thinking has not been fully explored.[2]

It is apparent that Whiston's discussions with Isaac Newton involved much more than what we would today call "science."[3] It is very likely that Whiston learned his Arianism from Newton; at the least, we can say that Whiston and Newton shared an antitrinitarian view of Christianity along with other prominent Newtonians such as Samuel Clarke.[4] Whiston, however, went public with his Arianism in a way that Newton or Clarke never did, and his trials and expulsion from Cambridge were

---

[1] The major studies of Whiston are Maureen Farrell, *William Whiston* (New York: Arno Press, 1981); James Force, *William Whiston: Honest Newtonian* (Cambridge: Cambridge University Press, 1985); Steven Snobelen, "William Whiston: Natural Philosopher, Prophet, Primitive Christian" (PhD diss., University of Cambridge, 2000). On specific incidents in Whiston's career, see also Eamon Duffy, "'Whiston's Affair': The Trials of a Primitive Christian, 1709–1714," *Journal of Ecclesiastical History* 27 (1976): 129–50; G. S. Rousseau, "'Wicked Whiston' and the Scriblerians: Another Ancients-Modern Controversy," *Studies in Eighteenth Century Culture* 17 (1987): 17–44; Steven Snobelen, "The Argument over Prophecy: An Eighteenth-Century Debate between William Whiston and Anthony Collins," *Lumen* 15 (1996): 195–213. This controversy between Whiston and Collins is also treated in a recent monograph by David Ruderman on Moses Marcus and the role of Judaism in the construction of Christian theology in eighteenth-century England, *Connecting the Covenants: Judaism and the Search for Christian Identity in Eighteenth-Century England* (Princeton, NJ: Princeton University Press, 2007).

[2] Force cites Whiston's views on the restoration of the Jews in a number of places (see *William Whiston: Honest Newtonian*, index, s.v. "Jews") but does not discuss these views in great detail.

[3] On Newton and Whiston, in addition to the works of Force and Snobelen cited previously, see Steven Snobelen, "Caution, Conscience, and the Newtonian Reformation: The Public and Private Heresies of Newton, Clarke, and Whiston," *Enlightenment and Dissent* 16 (1997): 151–84; and Scott Mandelbrote, "Newton and Eighteenth-Century Christianity," in I. Bernard Cohen, ed., *The Cambridge Companion to Newton* (Cambridge: Cambridge University Press, 2002), 409–30. On Newton's views of Judaism, see Matt Goldish, *Judaism in the Theology of Sir Isaac Newton* (Dordrecht: Kluwer, 1998).

[4] In addition to the works cited previously, see Richard Westfall, *Never at Rest: A Biography of Isaac Newton* (Cambridge: Cambridge University Press, 1980), 650. Mandelbrote notes considerable contemporary discussion about whether Newton shared the views of Whiston and Clarke.

well known to his contemporaries.[5] During the last decade of the seventeenth century, there had been sharp debates in England over the nature of the Trinity.[6] Perhaps for this reason, Whiston's contemporaries were particularly on guard against his view that the Son was not divine in the same way as the Father, as expressed in his 1709 collection of *Sermons and Essays upon Several Subjects.* This idea was immediately seen as a revival of the Arian position, and in 1710 Whiston was stripped of his professorship for violating the injunction against teaching unorthodox doctrine.

Whiston's defense did not deny or recant his antitrinitarian position but rather focused on the fact that his sermons in question were not preached at the university and that views expressed in private conversation with colleagues should not count as "teaching."[7] Whiston also argued that his motives stemmed simply from his "Zeal for the pure, original, uncorrupt Doctrines and Duties of Christianity."[8] Like his mentor Newton, Whiston did not divide religion and science into separate spheres; nor did he see his investigation into true religion as fundamentally different from his scientific research. The new empirical methods of science applied just as well to religion. Just as scientific knowledge should be derived from observational and experimental practice and not from "uncertain Systems of Philosophy," so too knowledge of religion should be derived from the study of "original Languages of the Bible, and most ancient Authors" rather than from "Scholastick Disputations about modern Controversies in Divinity."[9] True, knowledge of God was not comparable to science (it had to be derived from historical study rather than experiment). Nevertheless, for Whiston, the knowledge that "Primitive Christianity" is the true religion seemed as obvious as the fact that Newton's discoveries in mathematics offered a true picture of the workings of the physical universe.

After leaving Cambridge, Whiston made his way to London, where he soon found himself on trial before the Convocation of the Church of

---

[5] The best account of Whiston's expulsion from Cambridge remains Duffy, "'Whiston's Affair,'" cited previously. The question of why Whiston was more open about his heretical beliefs is beyond the scope of the essay; on this, see Force, *William Whiston*; Snobelen, "Caution, Conscience, and the Newtonian Reformation"; and Mandelbrote, "Newton and Eighteenth-Century Christianity."

[6] For this background, see Duffy, "'Whiston's Affair,'" 133.

[7] See his own account in *An Historical Preface to Primitive Christianity Revived with an Appendix Containing an Account of the Author's Prosecution at, and Banishment from the University of Cambridge* (1711), 18–19. Unless otherwise noted, the place of publication for all of Whiston's works is London.

[8] Ibid., 12.

[9] "Emendada in Academia," a series of proposals for academic reform, drafted while Whiston was in Cambridge, published in *Memoirs*, 48.

England and excluded by the Tory pastor from his parish church.[10] In the end, however, nothing much came of Whiston's trial, and he was soon able to establish himself in London as a popular, although still somewhat infamous, lecturer on Newtonian physics and religion.[11] He was one of the first to offer public demonstrations of Newtonian physics in his lecture courses, usually presented in coffeehouses. Whiston was able to live off a small income from writing and lecturing, a small estate, and gifts from friends, and he remained a well-known London figure. He became a favorite target for a group of Tory wits known as the Scriblerians for his continual predictions of comets and his millenarianism.[12] His millenarian expectations and espousal of primitive Christianity were so well known that one student of Whiston's impact on culture has suggested that the term "Whistonism" was in common use in London during his lifetime.[13]

What then of Whiston's attitude toward Jews? Whiston's lifetime almost exactly coincides with the first period of Jewish settlement in England in modern times. He was born a decade after the Whitehall Conference of 1656 and died one year before the 1753 debate on Jewish naturalization. During this period, interest in Judaism and the Jews reached new heights among English intellectuals.[14] Although much of this interest was fed by the same sources as that of European-wide Christian Hebraism, in English thought millenarianism, and particularly the belief in the future restoration of the Jews to Palestine, played an outsized role.[15]

[10] See Duffy, "'Whiston's Affair,'" 137, and Whiston's *Account of the Convocation's Proceedings with Relation to Mr. Whiston ...* (1711). For Whiston's account of his removal from his parish church, see *Account of Dr. Sacheverell's Proceedings ...* (1719).

[11] Whiston's career as a lecturer is studied carefully by Snobelen in his PhD thesis. The broader context of coffeehouse lectures and scientific popularization is treated by Steven Snobelen in an earlier work as well, "Selling Experiment: Public Experimental Lecturing in London, 1705–1728" (MA thesis, University of Victoria, 1995).

[12] See G. S. Rousseau, "'Wicked Whiston.'"

[13] Ibid., 33. On the influence of Whiston, see also G. S. Rousseau, "Mysticism and Millenarianism: 'Immortal Dr. Cheyne,'" in Richard Popkin, ed., *Millenarianism and Messianism in English Literature and Thought, 1650–1800* (Leiden: E. J. Brill, 1988), 81–126.

[14] The key works on Christian attitudes to Judaism and Jewish-Christian relations in seventeenth- and eighteenth-century England are Todd Endelman, *The Jews of Georgian England, 1714–1830: Tradition and Change in a Liberal Society* (Philadelphia: Jewish Publication Society, 1979); David Katz, *Philosemitism and the Readmission of the Jews to England, 1603–1655* (Oxford: Clarendon Press, 1982); David Katz, *The Jews in the History of England, 1485–1850* (Oxford: Oxford University Press, 1994); David Ruderman, *Jewish Enlightenment in an English Key* (Princeton, NJ: Princeton University Press, 2000).

[15] On millenarianism and the restoration of the Jews in English thought, see Richard Cogley, "The Fall of the Ottoman Empire and the Restoration of Israel in the Judeo-centric Strand of Puritan Millenarianism," *Church History* 72 (2003): 304–32; Nabil Matar, "The Controversy over the Restoration of the Jews in English Protestant Thought (1701–1753)," *Durham University Journal* 80 (1988): 241–56; Nabil Matar, "The Idea of the Restoration of the Jews in English Protestant Thought between the Reformation and 1660," *Durham University Journal* 78 (1985): 23–35; Nabil Matar, "The Idea of the Restoration of the Jews

Whiston's beliefs about the restoration of the Jews differed in some important ways from those of most of his contemporaries, however, and it is these differences that demonstrate his transformation of some long-standing themes in Christian perceptions of Judaism. For Whiston, an understanding of the "Jewish revelation," as he called it, was important in order to comprehend the true nature of Christianity. Christian Hebraists sought to reclaim Jewish sources for the benefit of Christian self-understanding long before Whiston, of course, and the notion that Christianity was built on some Jewish foundations was as old as Paul. Such attempts did not necessarily correlate with positive feelings toward Jews: on the contrary, Christian efforts to appropriate Jewish sources very often had a polemical edge.[16] Whiston's Christianity, however, was built so firmly on "Jewish" foundations (as he conceived them) that it is no exaggeration to call it "Judeo-Christianity."[17] For Whiston, an understanding of Jewish practice in the time of Jesus is crucial for the reconstruction of "primitive Christianity." Likewise, since for Whiston the millennium consists of the revival of this early form of Christianity, the restoration of the Jews to Palestine takes a form that is, for him, crucial to that revival. Whether this constitutes a form of "philosemitism" is a question to which I shall return explicitly at the end of this essay.

WHISTON'S PRIMITIVE CHRISTIANITY

Whiston centrally advocated a return to "primitive Christianity" – Christianity as practiced at the time of Jesus and shortly afterward. The most important Jewish source for Whiston in arguing for such a Christianity was the first-century Pharisee, general, and historian, Josephus. Although he had been promoting "primitive Christianity" and citing Josephus for decades, it was only in 1737 that Whiston published his translation of

in English Protestant Thought, 1661–1701," *Harvard Theological Review* 78 (1985): 115–48; Peter Toon, ed., *Puritans, the Millennium and the Future of Israel: Puritan Eschatology, 1600–1800* (Cambridge: Cambridge University Press, 1970); and James Force and Richard Popkin, eds., *Millenarianism and Messianism in Early Modern European Culture*, vol. 3, *The Millenarian Turn: Millenarian Contexts of Science, Politics, and Everyday Anglo-American Life in the Seventeenth and Eighteenth Centuries* (Dordrecht: Kluwer, 2001).

[16] For a brief survey, see Jeremy Cohen, "Scholarship and Intolerance in the Medieval Academy: The Study and Evaluation of Judaism in European Christendom," *American Historical Review* 91 (1986): 592–613.

[17] Historians of Judaism, of Christianity, and of Jewish-Christian relations before the twentieth century ought to be suspicious of the formulation "Judeo-Christian" (for perceptive discussion of this term, see Arthur Cohen, *The Myth of the Judeo-Christian Tradition* [New York: Schocken Books, 1970] and Frank Manuel, *The Broken Staff: Judaism through Christian Eyes* [Cambridge, MA: Harvard University Press, 1992], 1). Here, however, I believe it to be an appropriate term to describe the importance of Judaism to Whiston's formulation of Christianity.

Josephus, which remains the most widely circulated version in the English-speaking world. One of Whiston's strongest reasons for seeing Josephus as reliable was his belief that Josephus was a convert to Christianity who became bishop of Jerusalem—a belief shared by few of Whiston's contemporaries.[18] As a convert to Christianity who still observed Jewish ceremonial law, Josephus was, for Whiston, representative of the large group of Jews who accepted Jesus as their Messiah on the basis of Jewish sources[19] and who formed the nucleus of early, or "primitive," Christianity. Whiston also believed that Josephus had used the most reliable copy of the Old Testament possible.[20] In other words, Josephus – properly reconstructed – represented a way back to the original Jewish (i.e., Christian) scripture, uncorrupted by rabbis or by Rome.[21]

Whiston's references to Talmudic and later rabbinic literature are few, and in many places he criticizes the reliability of the rabbis in comparison to that of Josephus. His severe criticism of the accepted (rabbinic) Hebrew text of the Old Testament had sparked a major controversy in the 1720s, reviving not only seventeenth-century debates over the reliability and originality of the Masoretic text but also medieval Christian charges that the rabbis had corrupted the biblical text.[22] Whiston's rejection of the Hebrew Old Testament as a rabbinic corruption represented a departure from his earlier views. In 1702, Whiston had defended the use of the original Hebrew, echoing traditional humanist rhetoric.[23] And in an essay published in 1709 (although most likely written earlier) Whiston advised "students of divinity" to include the 1657 *Biblia Polyglotta* and the Hebrew concordance of the Buxtorfs (strong defenders of the Masoretic text's originality) in even a "small theological library."[24] But already in his Boyle Lectures of

---

[18] Ibid., xxxvii.

[19] Ibid.

[20] See "Dissertation II proving that the Copy of the Books of the Old Testament laid up in Herod's temple, and thence used by Josephus, the Jewish Historian, in his Antiquities, was no other than that most ancient Collection or Library made by Nehemiah, in the days of Artaxerxes, the son of Xerxes; and was free from the several additions and alteration made afterwards in the other copies, which are now extant," in *The Genuine Works of Flavius Josephus, the Jewish Historian, in English*, 1:lv; I consulted the second edition (Dublin, 1751).

[21] According to Whiston, Josephus is only unreliable whenever he has adopted the legal or exegetical interpretations of the Pharisees; see *Genuine Works of Flavius Josephus*, 295, 391. And sometimes Josephus even gave way to Trinitarian Christian views; according to Whiston, Josephus's likening of Jesus to God was merely "a sort of compliance with the Romans and the catholick Christians": ibid., "The Testimonies of Josephus Vindicated," dissertation 1, xlii.

[22] On this controversy, see Ruderman, *Connecting the Covenants*, esp. chap. 4.

[23] See *A Short View of the Chronology of the Old Testament and of the Harmony of the Four Evangelicals* (1702), 2–3.

[24] "Advice for the Study of Divinity with Directions for the choice of a Small Theological Library," in *Sermons and Essays upon Several Subjects* (1709), 320ff.

1707 Whiston maintained that the Samaritan Pentateuch represented the most authentic text of the first five books of the Old Testament.[25] Over the course of the next four decades, Whiston would consistently disdain the Masoretic text as the least reliable in comparison to the Samaritan Pentateuch, the Septuagint, or Josephus. By the 1730s, Whiston was publicly criticizing his mentor Newton for reliance on the Masoretic text.[26] Newton also came under criticism for his use of the Talmud and rabbinic sources and for ignoring Josephus:

> Sir Isaac Newton seldom makes use of the great authority of Josephus, the most learned Jew of the first Century; while he frequently allows the weak Authority, and ill-grounded traditions of the Talmud in the fourth or fifth centuries; and of even the still weaker Authority and more ill-grounded Traditions of the Rabbins afterwards.[27]

Whiston also criticized rabbinic descriptions of the Temple in his own descriptions and models that he discussed in a series of lecture tours and also published.[28]

However, Whiston did not hesitate to cite the Talmud when it supported one of his own interpretations.[29] In addition, certain of the later "Rabbins" met with his approval, particularly Manasseh ben Israel and "the great Maimonides."[30] This apparently hypocritical stance can be related to a specific methodology. Whiston's general approach is to place Jewish sources in a hierarchy of authority based on their chronological proximity to the first Christian century. Thus, Josephus is more reliable than the Talmud. Indeed, Whiston was fairly consistent in applying this approach regardless of the religious identity of the sources. Thus he also places Christian sources in a hierarchy from most authoritative to least based on their chronology: the earliest Christian sources, the New Testament and the earliest

---

[25] *The Accomplishment of Scripture Prophecies* [The Boyle Lectures] (1707), 70.

[26] "A Short View of Sir Isaac Newton's Observations upon the Prophecies of Daniel, and the Apocalypse of Saint John," in *Six Dissertations* (1734), 270.

[27] Ibid., 273.

[28] *Mr. Whiston's Descriptions of the Models of the Tabernacles of Moses; and of Solomon's, Herod's, and Ezekiel's Temples at Jerusalem. Wherein Many Errors of the Talmudists, and Later Rabbins; with Those of the Christians That Follow Them … Are Corrected* (1733); also published in his *The Genuine Works of Flavius Josephus* (1737; 2nd ed., Dublin, 1751). For discussion of his Temple lectures and his polemics with other Temple "reconstructors," see Snobelen, "William Whiston," 204–16. As Goldish shows, Newton also places "scripture," Josephus, and archaeology over the Talmud as sources for the reconstruction of the Temple; see Goldish, *Judaism in the Theology*, chap. 5, "The Temple of Jerusalem in Newton's Thought," esp. 103.

[29] See *The Literal Accomplishment of Scripture Prophecies* (1724), 71–2. This work should not be confused with Whiston's Boyle Lectures, published as *The Accomplishment of Scripture Prophecies* in 1707.

[30] *Accomplishment of Scripture Prophecies* [Boyle Lectures], 85.

Church Fathers (as well as the *Apostolical Constitutions*),[31] are more authoritative than later writings. He states his opposition to the "vain hypotheses, or unnatural Interpretations [of] the Moderns, against the Constant Sense of the Jews and Christians of the first and second centuries."[32] Sometimes, however, later sources faithfully preserve earlier traditions and thus may be used with caution.

Whiston's analogous treatment of Jewish and Christian sources derives from his insistence on the use of "original records."[33] Here, Whiston echoes a vein of Christian argumentation that dates to the humanism of Erasmus and the view of the early reformers. But the result is to place the categories of "Jewish" and "Christian" on provisionally equal footing. From quite early in his career, Whiston made his judgments about the evidentiary value of primary sources in relation to (his perception of) their dating. Primitive or true Christianity is certainly to be preferred to rabbinic Judaism, but rabbinic Judaism is no worse than Roman Christianity.[34] First-century Judaism, as described by Josephus, is as good as the New Testament as a source for primitive Christianity.

Indeed, Whiston recognizes no real distinction between "Judaism" and "Christianity." In his defense of revealed religion against the deist challenge, there are many places in which Judaism and Christianity are defended as one and even referred to in the singular as "Jewish and Christian religion."[35] What is crucial for Whiston is that the earliest Christians were Jews:

For the apostles themselves being Jews, as is well known, together with their Christianity observed the ceremonial laws of Moses: especially when they were in Judea: and permitted their Jewish converts to do the same: provided that there were no necessity laid on them for such its observation; that justification and salvation were not expected by that law, but by the Christian dispensation; and that the Gentile Christians were allowed to be intirely [*sic*] free from that bondage.[36]

Whiston echoes Paul here but then goes one step further. Although gentile Christians did not observe the "ceremonial laws of Moses," Whiston

---

[31] Whiston believed that the *Apostolical Constitutions* were first-century statements of Jesus himself and thus as authoritative as (or more than) the canonical New Testament. He devoted much of his *Primitive Christianity Reviv'd* (1711–12) to arguing for their authenticity and also published *St. Clement's and St. Irenaeus's Vindication of the Apostolical Constitutions* (1715).

[32] *Literal Accomplishment of Scripture Prophecies*, 20.

[33] "Advice for the Study of Divinity," 245.

[34] On this, cf. Newton's negative view of Catholicism as described by Goldish, *Judaism in the Theology of Sir Isaac Newton*, chap. 6.

[35] *Scripture Politicks, or an Impartial Account of the Origin and Measure of Government, Ecclesiastical and Civil ...* (1717), 9. Whiston's arguments against deism are fully described in Force and Snobelen's monographs and in Snobelen, "Argument over Prophecy," cited previously.

[36] "An Extract out of Josephus's Discourse to the Greeks, concerning Hades ... ," in Whiston, *Genuine Works of Flavius Josephus*, dissertation 5, 1:cxcii.

argues that Christianity as a whole took on Jewish characteristics – echoing Newton and fitting into Christian Hebraist scholarship that sought to use Jewish sources to understand the rituals of early Christians.[37] Jesus and the disciples, after all, "acted then as Persons subject to the Jewish Laws, and to the Jewish Priesthood, Sacrifices, and Ceremonies; to all which they paid a due obedience."[38]

But this was not of mere historical interest to Whiston; nor was it only a matter of noting what the future would bring. Whiston, as Snobelen has forcefully argued, viewed his life's work as ongoing public activity aimed at the reformation of the Christian Church to restore it to its primitive origins.[39] Whiston took this extremely seriously and emphasized the importance of understanding the Jewish practices of the primitive Christians. The eucharist, for example, was itself a "holy Oblation,"

as were the Oblations under the Law of Moses; and this without the least indication that the word was used in any other acceptation than it had been used among the Jews under that Law.[40]

In other words, the Eucharist as ordained by Jesus was nothing less than the ordination of a mitzvah. We should not be surprised then that Whiston turned to the halakhic authority most revered by Christian Hebraists for guidance on how the ritual ought to be performed in the revived primitive church:

Maimonides, from the Jewish Mischna and Gemara, inform[s] us, that by the fruit of the vine, they mean wine mixed with water: and that the Jews cups at the Passover were wine and water, and it was not lawful to use wine alone therein.[41]

Thus, Whiston tells us, he uses both wine and water in Communion.[42]

---

[37] See Goldish, *Judaism in the Theology*, chap. 6, "Judaism in Newton's Church History." For examples from Whiston, see his *Second Letter to the Right Reverend the Lord Bishop of London, concerning the Primitive Doxologies* (1719), 33.

[38] *Scripture Politicks*, 76.

[39] See Snobelen, "Caution, Conscience, and the Newtonian Reformation."

[40] *The Primitive Eucharist Revived* (1736), 89.

[41] Ibid., 99. Whiston is apparently referring to Maimonides' discussion of the four cups of wine at the Passover seder in the *Mishneh Torah* (Book of Seasons, Laws of Leavened and Unleavened Bread, chap. 7, no. 11). Whiston does not cite Maimonides directly but rather reports of Maimonides' views in the works of three Christian scholars: John Hooper, a Zwingli-influenced bishop in the early Anglican Church; John Lightfoot, one of the most renowned Christian Hebraists of the seventeenth century and a recognized authority on Maimonides; and Johann Ernst Grabe, one of the leading biblical scholars of early eighteenth-century England. Whiston's reliance on these English and Latin works is an indication of his membership in what might be called the second tier of Christian Hebraists: those whose primary sources for knowledge of Judaism were those of Christian scholars and who rarely made recourse to original Hebrew texts; cf. Goldish, *Judaism in the Theology*, 18; in Goldish's schema, Whiston along with Newton belongs in the "3rd-order" of Christian Hebraists.)

[42] Ibid., 101.

Despite his criticism of the rabbis, Talmudic and post-Talmudic, for their corruption of the Old Testament text and for their creation of new "laws of men" – not to mention their fundamental mistake in not accepting Jesus as Messiah – Whiston was apparently willing to look to rabbinic Judaism for guidance on the conduct of ceremonial practices when he found a practice common to the primitive church and to rabbinic Judaism. Although Whiston was sympathetic to the Baptists, he criticized them for not reading scripture every week as Jesus did each week in synagogue (and as Jews continued to do).[43] The Jewishness of true, or primitive, Christianity was not, therefore, a thing of the past, but an important guide in determining how Christianity should be practiced in Whiston's own time.

In his five-volume *Primitive Christianity Reviv'd*, Whiston lays out a carefully drawn distinction between two kinds of Jewish laws: those given prior to the golden calf incident, which were "natural" and "highly reasonable in themselves," and those given afterward, which were "ceremonial, positive, burdensome and rigorous."[44] The New Testament freed Christians entirely from the second kind but only from some of the first. Again, this sort of distinction between natural law and ceremonial law is not new to Whiston. But Whiston's notion of what falls into the first category includes two Jewish practices that most Christians believed to fall into the second, the Sabbath and the dietary laws of *kashruth*.

In his 1730 work *The Horeb Covenant Revived*, Whiston describes those Jewish laws that are still binding on Christians as a result of this distinction. The first of these is the Sabbath, which had been a concern of his since his undergraduate days, when he drafted an essay "Of the Neglect of the Sabbath." This first draft, written in 1686, makes the standard Christian argument that the observance of the Sabbath had shifted to Sunday. When he published it in his *Memoirs* in 1749, however, he added: "When I wrote this, I was not appriz'd that the Sabbath was never changed: But was ever to be observed in a lesser Degree, as the Lord's Day in a greater, by all Christians."[45] He suggests following the practice of the earliest Christians, who observed the Sabbath as a "rest for the meditation of the law, not for idleness of the hands."[46] Passages like this led David Katz to conclude that Whiston "was himself a Seventh Day Man."[47] While it is difficult to find direct evidence that Whiston actually observed a Saturday Sabbath, he was certainly friendly with some who did.[48] In either case, it is clear

---

[43] *Friendly Address to the Baptists* (Stamford, 1748), 16. See also Whiston's *Memoirs* (1749), 2:480.

[44] 1711, 3:54, and quoted by Whiston later in *The Horeb Covenant Revived; or an Account of those Laws of Moses Which Oblige Christians* (1730), 1.

[45] *Memoirs*, 1:53.

[46] *Horeb Covenant Revived*, 40.

[47] Katz, *Sabbath and Sectarianism in Seventeenth-Century England* (Leiden: E. J. Brill, 1988), 198.

[48] Ibid.

that Whiston considered the Jewish Sabbath an important concept for Christians even at an abstract level.

In his view of the Sabbath, Whiston removed the "negative" command-ments, which he found "burdensome," and retained what he believed to have been the positive core of the institution. But elsewhere in *Horeb Covenant Revived*, Whiston argued that Christians must obey a Jewish pro-hibition – that of not eating blood.[49] Richard Westfall notes that

Whiston spread it about that Newton refused to eat rabbits because they were stran-gled and black puddings because they were made of blood. Catherine Conduitt [Newton's niece] told her husband that this was a matter of ethics rather than taste.[50]

Could "ethics" be a euphemism for Newton and Whiston keeping a form of *kashruth*?

WHISTON'S CHRISTIAN ZIONISM

In light of the preceding discussion it is reasonable to describe Whiston's "Primitive Christianity," both conceptually and in some practical matters, as a Judeo-centric Christianity. He advocated a similarly "Judeo-centric mil-lenarianism," as Richard Cogley has defined it. Cogley makes a convincing case for the importance of this form of millenarianism in the modern world, and for a close connection between it and primitivist notions of Christianity.[51] Nowhere is this more evident than in Whiston's "Christian Zionism."

Whiston was not alone in his belief that the Jews would be restored to their ancient homeland. Indeed, the debate over the restoration of the Jews had been a constant in English Protestant thought since the Reformation, as Nabil Matar has shown, and remained an important issue well into the nineteenth century, as Mayir Vreté and others have demonstrated.[52] Three major events figured in most restorationist millenarian scenarios: (1) the return of the Jews to Palestine, (2) Jewish conversion to Christianity, and (3) the Second Coming. But these elements were put together in any num-ber of combinations and were the focus of ongoing discussion among mil-lenarian thinkers across this extended period of English restorationist millenarianism. Would the Jews establish a state with Jewish law? Would Christ's return to earth precede or succeed the conversion of the Jews? Would that conversion precede or succeed the restoration?

[49] *Horeb Covenant Revived*, 23–4.
[50] Westfall, *Never at Rest*, 850.
[51] See Cogley, "Fall of the Ottoman Empire and the Restoration of Israel," 311, 321, and the bibliography cited there.
[52] See the works of Matar, cited previously; and Mayir Vreté, "The Restoration of the Jews in English Protestant Thought 1796–1840," *Middle Eastern Studies* 8 (1972): 3–50.

Whiston's millenarian scenario largely fits the paradigm shared by Increase Mather, Thomas Brightman, and other seventeenth-century Puritans in England and New England, described in detail by Cogley. And as with those figures, Whiston's millenarian hopes for the restoration of the Jews are indeed linked to his hopes for a revival of primitive Christianity, since Whiston gives us many indications that his definition of the millennium consists of the universal establishment of primitive Christianity. But Whiston's restorationist scheme was nearly unique in providing for a complete restoration of the Jewish Temple and, for a "considerable" period of time, of the authority of Jewish law (both ceremonial and "natural"), before the restored Jews would eventually be converted to Christianity.

In his earliest treatises on restoration from the first decade of the eighteenth century (at a time when Matar notes a dip in support for the notion),[53] Whiston argued that the sequence of millennial events would begin with the "Restoration of the Jews to their own land in general" and the "Rebuilding of their Temple, with the Restoration of their Sacrifices." Following this would be Armageddon. Only after Armageddon would the Jews convert, simultaneously with the Second Coming, which would consist of "the exaltation and advancement of the Kingdom of Christ Jesus over the Jews."[54] In 1717, Whiston continued the line of argument he had begun a decade earlier, explaining that the priesthood will be "restored when the Jews shall be resettled in their own Land, and thence is to continue to the very End of the Jewish Worship, and of that High Priesthood itself, when that Nation shall be converted to Christianity."[55] Whiston continued to hold to this scheme in the 1720s, when he had a model of the Temple built, and, in 1727 and 1728, lectured on Temple practice "preparatory to the Restoration of the Jews hereafter."[56]

Whiston realized early on that his conception of restoration was different from that of many of his contemporaries, in that he envisioned the revival of a Jewish state, governed by Jewish law, prior to the conversion of the Jews. Whiston knew that most restorationists tied the return of the Jews immediately with their conversion, acknowledging that "most Men are not yet convinced that the Restoration of the Jews is any considerable Time to precede their Conversion to the Christian Faith."[57] Here Whiston may also have been thinking of his own mentor Newton, who apparently saw restoration and conversion as linked closely in time.[58] Whiston not only envisions

[53] Matar, "Idea of the Restoration," 146.
[54] See "Of the Restoration of the Jews," 222, 225; and cf. *Accomplishment of Scripture Prophecies*, 4.
[55] *Scripture Politicks*, 74.
[56] *Memoirs*, 1: 333–4; and see n. 27.
[57] "Of the Restoration of the Jews," 225.
[58] See Steven Snobelen, "'The Mystery of this Restitution of All Things': Isaac Newton on the Return of the Jews," in Force and Popkin, eds., *Millenarian Turn*, 105, and Goldish, *Judaism in the Theology*, 71–3.

a return to Zion, but he argues that the Jews will "live securely in their own Land before the famous Battel at Harmageddon."[59] Here, he differs from the large number of scenarios in which Jewish armies would first defeat Muslims and Catholics in the battle(s) of Armageddon, thus clearing the way for their restoration.[60] Whiston also argued that the restoration of the Jewish state would have to take place miraculously and thus would be confirmation of prophesies and of a revival of the Jews' special relationship with God.[61]

Many restorationists of the period rejected the notion that a third Temple would be built.[62] But Whiston, agreeing with Newton, argued strongly that there will be a rebuilt Temple and moreover suggested that Jewish law would continue in Palestine up to the conversion of the Jews. Those who relied on the Book of Revelation believed that the "restored" Jews would not have a Temple. Whiston answered their objection by noting that John is describing "the state of Things after the Marriage of the Lamb, or the Conversion of the Jews."[63] Whiston then suggests that Jewish law will continue in Palestine even after the conversion of the Jews and the final disappearance of the Temple:

For that the Law of Moses has never yet been Properly and Formally Abolished, is agreed by all; and is plain from the Observance thereof by the first Jewish Christians, and even by St. Paul himself, at that very Time when he is so Express as to its Non-Obligation, not only as to the Christian Gentiles, for those indeed were never concerned with it; but to the Christian Jews also, who had before been subject to it.[64]

The same argument for why primitive Christianity must look more like Judaism is now employed to explain why even "Christian Jews" after the Second Coming might continue to obey Jewish law. His phrasing here suggests that despite the disappearance of the Temple and the priesthood following the conversion of the Jews to Christianity, Jewish law and ceremonial practice will continue. Earlier, many had opposed restoration because it seemed to imply the "reintroduction of Jewish law and ordinances."[65] For Whiston, this was exactly the point. Whiston's "Judeo-centrist" millennium included ongoing Jewish worship and practice in the spiritual hub of the world, just as the worship and practice of the earliest Christians were "Jewish."

---

[59] "Of the Restoration of the Jews," 225.

[60] See Cogley, "Fall of the Ottoman Empire."

[61] "Of the Restoration of the Jews," 233–4. On the importance of the restoration of Jews in confirming prophecy for Whiston and Newton, see Snobelen, "Mystery of the Restitution of All Things," 109.

[62] Matar, "Controversy over the Restoration of the Jews," 244–5.

[63] Ibid., 224.

[64] Ibid., 225.

[65] Matar, "Idea of the Restoration of the Jews in English Protestant Thought," 30.

WHISTON AND "REAL" JEWS

Goldish has argued that "for Newton, the Jews have a past and a future, but no present," pointing out that Newton, in contrast to many of his contemporaries, had seemingly no contact with living Jews.[66] There is some evidence that Whiston had more contact with living Jews than his teacher. He reports that he received a Latin document describing attempts to build a third Temple under Julian from a "Jewish Rabbi."[67] presumably David Nieto.[68] Second, Whiston served as a conduit for a donation of £100 when "the Jews in Duke's Place, by Aldgate, had a most dreadful Fire."[69] Another point of possible contact with Jews in London would have been Jewish members of the Royal Society. Although Whiston was not a member, he was in close contact with many who were and frequently attended meetings. Six Jews were admitted as members during Whiston's residence in London that ended in 1748.[70] In his notes to Josephus, Whiston cites "De Castro, a mathematician."[71] This is most likely Jacob de Castro Sarmento, who joined the Royal Society in 1729 and was known as a student of Newtonianism.[72] Finally, Steven and Henry Schwarzschild speculate that Raphael Levi of Hanover, a close associate of Leibniz, and an aged Whiston met each other when Levi visited London in 1748.[73] Levi was in London to present his solution to the longitude problem, a navigational challenge for which Whiston had proposed a solution some years before. Although these potential contacts need to be explored further, they may constitute additional evidence – along with his writings – that Jews had a present as well as a past and a future for Whiston. In any case, in Whiston's vision the future (which looked a lot like the past) was rapidly approaching, and perhaps even blurring with the present.[74] Working

---

[66] Goldish, *Judaism in the Theology*, 63; and see 32 for the discussion of a lack of contact between Newton and living Jews.

[67] *Memoirs*, 1:300.

[68] See David Ruderman, "Jewish Thought in Newtonian England: The Career and Writings of David Nieto," *Proceedings of the American Academy for Jewish Research* 58 (1992): 193–219. Ruderman traces the similarity in thought of Nieto and Samuel Clarke, Whiston's associate. We know, in addition, that Nieto made himself available to Christians to answer their questions about Judaism (D'Blossiers Tovey in *Anglia-Judaica* [London, 1738] mentions contacting Rabbi "Netto" for some information, 279.)

[69] *Memoirs*, 2:356–7. Duke's Place was the site of London's largest Ashkenazic synagogue.

[70] Paul Emden, *Jews of Britain: A Series of Biographies* (London: Sampson Low, 1943), 33.

[71] *Genuine Works of Flavius Josephus*, 1:407.

[72] Harry Friedenwald, *The Jews in Medicine* (Baltimore: Johns Hopkins University Press, 1944), 457.

[73] Steven Schwarzschild and Henry Schwarzschild, "Two Lives in the Jewish Früaufklärung: Raphael Levi Hannover and Moses Abraham Wolf," *Leo Baeck Institute Yearbook* 29 (1984): 245. They also suggest that an intermediary between Whiston and Levi may have been Jacob de Castro Sarmento.

[74] See Snobelen, "Caution, Conscience, and the Newtonian Reformation," on Whiston's belief in the imminence of the millennium.

to revive primitive Christianity required some knowledge of what Jews did and were still doing; the expectation of an imminent restoration meant that the future Jews to be restored were in fact the Jews of his own era.

WAS WHISTON A PHILOSEMITE?

For these reasons, Whiston would most likely have described himself as a friend to the Jews – he was working toward their restoration and redemption. At the same time, Whiston was neither an outspoken defender of Jewish rights and settlement nor a vigorous critic of persecution of Jews, although he describes the Inquisition's treatment of the "Jews" of Spain and Portugal as "sad"[75] and gives some other indications of a tolerant attitude and a preference for separating church and state.[76] Yet at least one of Whiston's contemporaries certainly did not see Whiston as a philosemite. Moses Marcus, the Jewish convert to Christianity who published his translation of Johann Carpzov's defense of the Masoretic text in 1729, accused Whiston of "slanderously" making charges against the Jews.[77] According to Marcus, despite his own conversion to Christianity, he felt it necessary to defend "the Jews, my own Brethren and Countrymen, from so heavy and heinous a Charge, as that of maliciously and sacrilegiously corrupting and depraving the sacred Text."[78] Whiston had aimed the charge of altering the biblical text at the "rabbis," but Marcus took this as an attack on all Jews. Marcus had a point: clearly, Whiston's view of Judaism owed a lot to a misconception that many Christians had held since the Middle Ages – that a distinction between "rabbinic Judaism" and "Judaism" *tout court* could make any sense to contemporary Jews.

From Whiston's perspective, however, an attack on the rabbis was no different from an attack on Christian scholars of the "fourth or fifth centuries" or those of the present whose reliability was in doubt and who manipulated the text for their own purposes. Just as Trinitarian Christians had suppressed proper understanding of primitive Christianity and led Christians astray, so too had rabbis led Jews astray from true religion.

Whiston certainly saw his millenarian scenario as one of benefit to the Jews. Although he believed that the restored Jews would eventually convert to true, that is, primitive, Christianity, his emphasis on the preconversion restoration of a Jewish commonwealth under Jewish law and featuring a rebuilt Temple led him to feel that he was making common cause with

---

[75] "Of the Restoration of the Jews," 227.
[76] See *Genuine Works of Flavius Josephus*, 3:138; *Scripture Politicks*, 119, 146; and *Memoirs*, 1:170–3.
[77] *A Defence of the Hebrew Bible in Answer to the Charge of Corruption Brought against It by Mr. Whiston …* (1729), translator's preface, x.
[78] Ibid., ix. For discussion of Marcus's views, see Ruderman, *Connecting the Covenants*, chap. 4.

contemporary Jews. In his essay "Of the Restoration of the Jews," he worries not only about Christians who "disbelieve, or once hesitate about this Point [the rebuilding of the Temple] in general," but also about Jews who have failed to make "careful and impartial Enquiries into the Sacred Writings."[79] In his notes to Josephus, Whiston refers to the work of Manasseh ben Israel, noting that the Jews also hope for and expect their return to Palestine.[80] By doing so, Whiston seems to suggest that Christian and Jewish advocacy of restoration constituted a common project. However much Whiston's "Christian Zionism" represented a Christian millenarian scenario, he certainly perceived it as friendly toward Jewish redemptive schemes as well.

Whiston also viewed the restoration of a non-Trinitarian Christianity, in which Jesus was regarded as a nondivine Messiah and worship was imbued with Jewish ceremonial practices, as making Christianity attractive to Jews. A return to primitive Christianity would facilitate Jewish conversion, just as the first century had seen many Jews become followers of the new religion. However, for Whiston's critics, such as Pierre Allix and Daniel Finch, Whiston was quite mistaken: Converting Jews to Unitarian Christianity would, they believed, be a terrible mistake, bringing converts to a false religion and leaving the unconverted Jews as the unwitting guardians of a key religious truth (i.e., that the Messiah was indeed divine).[81] Nonetheless, in highlighting Whiston's errors, Allix ironically accuses Whiston and other Arians of being a "Friend" to the (misguided) Jews who would celebrate the triumph of Arianism as a "matter of joy and triumph."[82] In addition, for Allix, Whiston's millenarian scenario (along with that of Joseph Mede) represents an acceptance of Jewish (indeed, rabbinic) exegesis.[83] Thus, to at least one of Whiston's Christian critics, Whiston was indeed a philosemite since he actually agreed with (false) Jewish views.

Is there a way out of this hall of mirrors? Whiston was neither the first nor the last to think that his reformed version of Christianity would be

---

[79] "Of the Restoration of the Jews," 222.

[80] *Genuine Works of Flavius Josephus*, 5:84.

[81] See especially Pierre Allix, *Remarks upon some places of Mr. Whiston's books* (1711), 17; Allix, *The Judgment of the Ancient Jewish Church, against the Unitarians* (1699), iii; Finch, *The Answer of the Earl of Nottingham to Mr. Whiston's Letter to Him ...* (2nd ed., 1721), 16–17. On Allix's alternate version of "Judeo-Christianity," see Matt Goldish, "The Battle for 'True' Jewish-Christianity: Pierre Allix's Polemics against the Unitarians and the Millenarians," in James Force and David Katz, eds., *Everything Connects: In Conference with Richard H. Popkin* (Leiden: E. J. Brill, 1999), 143–62. Goldish carefully analyzes Allix's response to Whiston's *Essay on the Revelation of St. John* (1707) in his *Answer to Mr. Whiston's Late Treatise on the Revelations*. What Goldish's analysis reveals is the extent to which Whiston and Allix were arguing not only over millenarianism but also over the correct understanding of primitive Christianity and of the relationship between Judaism and Christianity.

[82] *Remarks upon some places of Mr. Whiston's books*, 17.

[83] See Goldish, "Battle for 'True' Jewish-Christianity," 159–76.

attractive to Jews: this trope stretches back to Martin Luther and would gain renewed vigor as the eighteenth century went on.[84] But Whiston perhaps had a better case then others: to accept his version of Christianity, Jews need not accept Jesus as divine nor any loss of their own redemptive hopes. And Whiston's defense of Christianity and Judaism (as he understood them) against deism could be contrasted to more vigorous defenses of toleration of Jews that were far more critical of Judaism as a religious tradition.[85]

If being a friend to the Jews, however, requires an acceptance of Jewish aspirations and claims on their own terms, Whiston certainly fails the test. For Whiston, Jews remain largely of interest because of their future potential as Christians and Judaism for the role that it plays in his conception of Christianity. In this sense, Whiston's attitude toward Jews functions like that of almost all premodern Christians. Many recent historians have focused on the ways in which Christian views of Jews and Judaism have tended to be projections of Christian thinking rather than realistic perceptions of actual Jewish behavior or thought. Jeremy Cohen has recently used the formulation "hermeneutical Jew" to refer to medieval theological constructions of the image of the Jew.[86] And Gavin Langmuir has famously argued that "antisemitism" is best understood as hostility toward Jews that is distinguished by its "chimerical" basis.[87] For Langmuir, antisemitism is based on a set of beliefs about Jews that have no realistic basis, are attributed to the entire group, and cause holders of such beliefs to think abstractly about the behavior of the group. Thus, antisemitism, as it emerges in the Middle Ages, is no mere dislike of Jews but a dislike of Jews based on fantastic notions of what Jews do or might do to Christians. Whiston's positive evaluation of Judaism seems based on chimerical notions of a different sort. And as in many other examples of apparent philosemitism, it would be a severe oversimplification to conclude that Whiston's philosemitic attitudes reduced merely to a variant of antisemitism. Yet it is worth noting the extent to which much philosemitism has been built on expectations of Jewish behavior that Jews found difficult or even impossible to meet. Moreover, this type of philosemitism is often one in which Jews are expected to play a role to which living Jews might or might not acquiesce. Might it not be analytically useful to see Whiston's fantasies about what Jews will do for Christianity

---

[84] See, for example, the efforts to convert Moses Mendelssohn to an enlightened Christianity, discussed in Alexander Altmann, *Moses Mendelssohn* (Philadelphia: Jewish Publication Society, 1973), 203.

[85] See, for example, the prominent example of Voltaire, treated by Adam Sutcliffe, *Judaism and Enlightenment* (Cambridge: Cambridge University Press, 2003), chap. 12, "The Ambiguities of Enlightenment: Voltaire and the Jews."

[86] *Living Letters of the Law: Ideas of the Jews in Medieval Christianity* (Berkeley: University of California Press, 1999).

[87] *Toward a Definition of Antisemitism* (Berkeley: University of California Press, 1990), 328.

as a sort of Langmuirian "chimerical" philosemitism? In this sense, the type of philosemitism represented by Whiston's "Judeo-Christianity" is not the mere inversion of antisemitism, but it does represent the projection of a non-Jew's hopes and dreams onto unwitting, and perhaps unwilling, Jews.[88]

---

[88] In this regard, it is worth noting that Whiston's millenarian scenario bears a striking resemblance to a particular American Protestant millenarian scenario known as pre-millennial dispensationalism that Yaakov Ariel has pointed to as the basis for American fundamentalist support for Zionism (*Evangelizing the Chosen People: Missions to the Jews in America, 1886–2000* [Chapel Hill: University of North Carolina Press, 2000], 2–3); also see his essay in this volume. For a number of reasons, Whiston's "Judeo-centric" millenari-anism cannot be considered the *source* of American Christian support for Zionism and the state of Israel. But the similarities are useful analytically in considering the question of philosemitism. In the late twentieth century and the early twenty-first century, the American Jewish community has been divided over how to interpret and understand fundamentalist Christian support for Israel, deriving as it does from theological roots that are unappealing to many Jews. So, too, it would seem that the question of whether Whiston was a philosemite cannot be conceptually separated from the attitude of the observer toward the particular Christian theological claims that underlie Whiston's dis-cussions of Jews and Judaism.

5

A Friend of the Jews?

The Abbé Grégoire and Philosemitism in Revolutionary France

Alyssa Goldstein Sepinwall

> It is primarily to the abbé Grégoire that we owe the emancipation of the Israelites of France and the great example of tolerance given by our country to all civilized nations.
>
> *Univers Israélite*, 1882, 363[1]

The abbé Henri Grégoire, an eighteenth-century French priest and revolutionary, has long been called the great emancipator of the Jews of France. The author of an essay about Jews written on the eve of the French Revolution, Grégoire is the revolutionary most frequently credited with helping them obtain equal citizenship in 1791. Beginning in the nineteenth century, French Jews devoted what has been called a veritable cult to his memory, building statues in his honor and making him an icon of their patriotism. For many French Jews, this veneration of Grégoire continues today. However, other Jews in France have viewed Grégoire more critically. In 1928, the philosopher André Spire suggested that Grégoire and others had "tried to denationalize" Jews. Another French Zionist, Méïr Leviah, suggested in 1931 that Grégoire had been a missionary, and thus someone who had "hateful contempt" for the heritage of the Jewish people, even while reserving "loving pity" for individual Jews. Such critiques accelerated in the late twentieth century. During the Revolution's bicentennial in 1989, as the French state honored Grégoire as an emblem of tolerance, Pierre Birnbaum and other Jewish thinkers (including many younger Jews) revived such charges, while the former justice minister Robert Badinter and other prominent French Jews defended the abbé.[2]

I am grateful to Lisa Moses Leff for her comments on an earlier version of this essay.

[1] Quote from "Circulaire du Comité des Présidents des Sociétés de bienfaisance israélite," *Univers israélite* 37, no. 12 (March 1, 1882): 363.

[2] See Pierre Birnbaum ("One might almost say that the diagnoses offered by the abbé Grégoire, the emancipator, and Edouard Drumont, the indefatigable anti-Semite, were virtually identical"), "Sur l'étatisation révolutionnaire: L'abbé Grégoire et le destin de l'identité juive," *Le*

With such opposing views of a single figure, one might at first suppose that one of the camps in this debate is simply misguided. How else could both sets of claims be possible? In fact, the truth of Grégoire's actions is more complex. Indeed, the debate over how to remember the abbé today is a perfect illustration of the fact that the boundary between philosemitism and antisemitism is not as absolute as has often been assumed. Indeed, the two different versions of Grégoire suggest, as do other essays in this volume, that philosemitism and antisemitism are not mutually exclusive categories. In many ways, Grégoire fits the classic definition of a philosemite, summarized by William and Hilary Rubinstein as a non-Jew who expresses "support or admiration for the Jewish people."[3] In accordance with this definition, Grégoire was the most noted defender of Jews of his time, and the most famous proponent during the French Revolution of their equal citizenship rights. He first became interested in the cause of the Jews in the 1770s when he entered an essay contest in Strasbourg on the possibility of improving their status. In 1786 he gave a talk applauding the opening of a synagogue in the eastern city of Lunéville. Most importantly, in 1785–8, he entered an essay contest sponsored by the Academy of Metz on whether there were ways to make the Jews "more useful and more happy" in Europe. This contest, whose prize he would share with another entrant in 1788, brought him international fame, since it was unusual for a priest to speak out against the persecution of Jews. His prize entry, entitled "Essai sur la régénération physique, morale et politique des juifs" [Essay on the physical, moral and political regeneration of the Jews], was published in France in 1789 and in English translation in 1791.

Grégoire actively promoted his image as the Jews' greatest Catholic advocate. In 1788, shortly after he shared the prize in the Metz essay contest, he tried to win the patronage of an influential government minister by telling him that his essay had been "crowned ... at the head" of the three winners.[4] In the decades after the Jews received citizenship during the Revolution (with Sephardic Jews receiving equal rights on January 28, 1790, and all French Jews in September 1791), Grégoire often portrayed himself as having been the main champion of Jewish

Débat no. 53 (1989): 162; and Robert Badinter ("The abbé Grégoire defended, with more passion and consistency than anyone, the cause of the Jews") in *Libres et égaux: L'émancipation des Juifs sous la Révolution française (1789–1791)* (Paris: Fayard, 1989), 81.

3 W. D. Rubinstein and Hilary L. Rubinstein, *Philosemitism: Admiration and Support in the English-speaking World for Jews, 1840–1939* (New York: St. Martin's Press, 1999), ix.

4 See Grégoire to Guillaume-Chrétien de Lamoignon de Malesherbes, September 6, 1788, in Archives Nationales (AN) 154 AP II 136, Chartrier de Tocqueville Papers, fol. 1. In fact, the prize committee had not favored any of the three co-laureates over the others and had made critical comments on Grégoire's essay as it had for the others; see [P.-L. Roederer], *Prix proposés, en 1787, par la Société royale des sciences et des arts de Metz, pour les concours de 1788 et 1789* (Metz: Veuve Antoine & fils, 1788), AN 29 AP 6, Roederer Papers.

emancipation.[5] He also boasted about how much Jews of his time adored him. In his *Mémoires* (drafted in 1808), he included a letter from the Jews of Bordeaux expressing great enthusiasm for him and thanking him for the "dazzling kindnesses that you have lavished upon [our] unfortunate brothers."[6] He also reported in his *Mémoires* that, after the Jews received citizenship in 1790–1, "All the synagogues in France voted to thank me, and many made public prayers in my honor." He noted that he had been received in a similar way by Dutch and German Jews during his travels in the early nineteenth century. By 1806, he told a friend, "Letters from children of Israel from different countries are raining upon me."[7]

Many authors writing about Grégoire in the last two hundred years, especially within France, have accepted the abbé's depictions of his actions. The mythic image of him as the Jews' emancipator was already established by 1807, as a delegate to Napoleon's Assembly of Jewish Notables told the gathering that it was "on the report of [Grégoire] that the National Assembly passed the decree which put the Jews on a level with the rest of [the] citizens."[8] In 1931, the preeminent Jewish studies journal in France, the *Revue des études juives*, celebrated the centennial of Grégoire's death by calling him a "man who holds such a beautiful place in modern Jewish history, having been one of the most active and most generous artisans of emancipation, through his pen, word, and deeds."[9] Studies written later in the twentieth century called the abbé "the friend of men of all colors" and a "great friend of Jews."[10] This tradition continues in the work of scholars

[5] See for instance his comments on February 2, 1792, in Bibliothèque Abbé Grégoire (Blois), Ms. 677, "Procès verbaux des sociétés populaires, 1791–[1793]"; his remarks in *Mémoires de l'abbé Grégoire*, ed. J. M. Leniaud and preface by J. N. Jeanneney (Paris: Éditions de Santé, 1989; originally drafted in 1808), that when he was elected to the Estates-General in 1788 as a clerical deputy from Lorraine, his main goal in going to Versailles was to "plead the cause of the Jews" (53); Grégoire to Ruth Barlow, August 17, 1806, in Houghton Library, Harvard University (Cambridge, MA), Barlow Papers, hereafter Houghton-Barlow Papers, bMS AM 1448, fol. 606; and Grégoire to the abbé Jennat, October 14, 1816, in Henri Cosson, "Lettres de l'abbé Grégoire à l'abbé Jennat," *Révolution française* no. 3 (1935): 253.
[6] See letter of August 14, 1789, reprinted in *Mémoires*, 171. On Grégoire's "self-promotion," see also Frances Malino, "Jewish Enlightenment in Berlin and Paris," in Michael Brenner, Vicki Caron, and Uri R. Kaufmann, eds., *Jewish Emancipation Reconsidered: The French and German Models* (Tubingen: Mohr Siebeck, 2003), 32–3.
[7] Grégoire to Joel Barlow, September 1, 1806, in Houghton-Barlow Papers, bMS AM 1448, fol. 606, cited by permission of the Houghton Library, Harvard University.
[8] *Transactions of the Parisian Sanhedrim, or, Acts of the Assembly of Israelitish Deputies of France and Italy, convoked at Paris by an Imperial and Royal Decree, dated May 30, 1806*, trans. Diogene Tama (Lanham, MD: University Press of America, 1985), 330.
[9] "Centenaire de l'abbé Grégoire," *Revue des Études Juives* 91, no. 182 (1931): 220–1.
[10] Paul Grunebaum-Ballin, *Henri Grégoire: L'ami des hommes de toutes les couleurs. La lutte pour la suppression de la traite et l'abolition de l'esclavage. 1789–1831* (Paris: Collection de la Société des Amis de l'Abbé Grégoire, 1948); and Paul Catrice, "L'abbé Henri Grégoire (1750–1831), 'ami de tous les hommes,' et la régénération des Juifs," *Mélanges de sciences religieuses* 36 (1979): 139.

like Rita Hermon-Belot, who has said of Grégoire that "one of his most beautiful claims to fame" was his attitude toward Jews, and Josiane Boulad-Ayoub, who has called him "the most beautiful figure in the Revolution," on account of his treatment of Jews and other oppressed groups.[11]

Grégoire's *Essai* on the Jews was consistent with this reputation in several ways and contains a number of positive assessments of Jews. The ostensible goal of the essay was to convince Christians not to discriminate against Jews – to recognize that it was possible to improve them. To persuade his readers of this point, one of Grégoire's textual strategies was to highlight Jews' positive virtues. He placed particularly positive emphasis on Jewish family life. As a Catholic priest, who was concerned about promiscuity and immorality among Christians, he noted that these behaviors were highly unusual among Jews: "Nothing is more rare among them than adultery. Their conjugal unions are truly edifying; they are good husbands and fathers." He particularly praised their marriage laws as "wisely harmonized, equally in keeping with the needs of the flesh and with decency." He also praised Jews (at least in France) for not having a dowry system that prevented the poor from marrying, unlike Christians of the time.[12]

For Grégoire, other good qualities of the Jews were their charitable instincts and their respect for elders. He applauded Jews' feelings of charity toward each other, noting that he detected among them "a nearly universal ... tenderness for their indigent brothers." He also praised the respect Jews gave to educators, the "tender veneration" they accorded the elderly (a trait "nearly unknown in our own customs"), and their overall disinterest in luxury. Moreover, he applauded Jews' "profound esteem for their ancestors," as evidenced by their eleven-month mourning period and the daily recitation of the Kaddish (memorial prayer).[13] Finally, the abbé held Jewish women up for special praise. Implying that Christian women were deficient in this regard, he commented that "after childbirth, Jewish women deign still to remember that they are mothers." He also lauded Jewish women's tendency to breast-feed their own children, as opposed to the common eighteenth-century practice of using wet nurses.[14]

Grégoire repeated these philosemitic assertions and made others once the Revolution started. In his *Motion en faveur des juifs*, published in fall 1789, he added that moral decency was "nearly innate" among the Jews.

[11] Rita Hermon-Belot, *L'abbé Grégoire, la politique, et la vérité* (Paris: Seuil, 2000), 254; and Josiane Boulad-Ayoub, *L'abbé Grégoire, apologète de la république* (Paris: Champion, 2005), 17.
[12] Grégoire, *Essai sur la régénération physique, morale et politique des Juifs; ouvrage couronné par la Société royale des Sciences et des Arts de Metz, le 23 août 1788* (Metz: Claude Lamort, 1789), 36, 57, 58. Grégoire would adopt a similar strategy of making positive generalizations about blacks in order to support abolitionist ideas in his work *De la littérature des nègres* (Paris: Maradan, 1808).
[13] *Essai sur la régénération*, 36, 58.
[14] Ibid., 57.

Moreover, he intimated, Jewish women knew how to be good housewives better than most Christian women: "One never sees them neglecting their housework or squandering household funds. They are not possessed with a passion for gambling, nor do they let themselves be affected by revolutions in fashion."[15]

Given his reputation as the greatest philosemite of his time, one might expect that the abbé's two most famous writings on the Jews would be full of positive stereotypes such as the ones presented above.[16] The idea of these texts as essentially pro-Jewish has also been advanced by claims that Grégoire's *Essai* was actually cowritten with Jewish friends. However, as I have shown elsewhere, the contributions of Jews to the text were of a limited nature and were primarily incorporated by Grégoire to give the *Essai*'s final version a greater claim to authenticity.[17] More notably, the passages praising Jews' good qualities constitute but a tiny portion of the *Essai* on regeneration, no more than 5 of the text's 194 printed pages. Much more common in the text are discussions of the Jews' alleged degeneracy, in chapters with titles such as "Dangers of Tolerating the Jews as They Are, Because of Their Aversion for Other Peoples and Their Lapsed Morality" and "Danger of Tolerating the Jews as They Are, Because of Their Commerce and Usury."

Why would a text ostensibly defending the Jews talk about their great danger to society? The text is more comprehensible if we understand that Grégoire's interest in alleviating Jews' plight was only one goal of the *Essai*, and hardly its major one. Certainly, the text was in part motivated by compassion for a people who had, in Grégoire's words, been "persecuted endlessly" and made the object of innumerable "bloody tragedies." Grégoire's empathy for Jews increased after he befriended local Jews such as Isaiah Berr-Bing and Simon von Geldern in the course of his revisions for the essay contest.[18] However, the *Essai* had several purposes that were of greater importance to Grégoire than defending Jews. Perhaps most basically, like another famous eighteenth-century writer on the Jews, Christian Wilhelm Dohm, the young priest had a motive for entering the contest that was quite apart from the issue of the Jews themselves. Like many aspiring authors from humble backgrounds in the eighteenth century, Grégoire saw winning a prestigious essay contest as an opportunity to gain a reputation on the national intellectual scene. The Metz contest on the Jews was at least

[15] Grégoire, *Motion en faveur des juifs* (Paris: Belin, 1789), 24.
[16] On positive stereotypes of Jews as a hallmark of philosemitism, see Alan Edelstein, *An Unacknowledged Harmony: Philo-Semitism and the Survival of European Jewry* (Westport, CT: Greenwood Press, 1982), 1 and passim.
[17] Sepinwall, "Strategic Friendships: Jewish Intellectuals, the Abbé Grégoire and the French Revolution," in Ross Brann and Adam Sutcliffe, eds., *Renewing the Past, Reconfiguring Jewish Culture: From al-Andalus to the Haskalah* (Philadelphia: University of Pennsylvania Press, 2004), 195.
[18] *Essai sur la régénération*, 6, 1; Sepinwall, "Strategic Friendships," 195–200.

the fourth essay contest Grégoire had entered in hopes of making a name for himself in Enlightenment literary circles.[19]

Grégoire was also anxious to protect his parishioners from what he saw as Jewish rapacity. The 1779 Strasbourg contest he had entered on the Jews had suggested that change in their status was desirable, since their usury was ravaging the lives of hardworking Christians in Alsace. Through usury – which, that contest's call for entries admitted, Jews practiced because they had few other options – Jews had made themselves "onerous to the common people." The call for entries cited (without contesting) arguments that "their industry has been ruinous and calculated on fraud; that in the cities they have received stolen goods and consume life savings with usury ...; that in the countryside they have devoured the assets of farmers with easy advances [and] extorted reimbursements at the wrong moment."[20] Jewish usury, the society's program hinted, posed terrible dangers for the social, economic, and moral order of the French countryside.

To what extent Grégoire shared the sentiments of the Strasbourg contest organizers is hard to know, since his original entry from this contest is lost. Nevertheless, his Metz contest entry (which Grégoire later claimed was simply a revision of his Strasbourg entry) echoed many of the ideas put forward in the Strasbourg contest's call for entries. In it, Grégoire seemed concerned that many peasants were being "ruined by the Jews," both economically and morally.[21] Though he did not believe that the Jews were essentially defective, he did believe that they had *become* degenerate; without reform, they would continue to "oppress" peasants.

It may seem ironic that an essay purporting to defend the Jews was actually more about protecting others from them. But the text bears another incongruity. Even as it professed to support the Jews, the *Essai* functioned as Catholic apologetic, aiming to prove the truth of Christianity to readers. In the nineteenth century Grégoire would write a series of texts on oppressed peoples around the world, which were less about the groups themselves than about Christianity's generosity in alleviating their burdens

---

[19] In addition to the 1785–8 Metz Academy contest, the other contests that l'abbé Grégoire entered include the 1773 Nancy Academy contest on the importance of poetry (which he won), the same academy's 1774 contest on poetry (in which his anonymous entry was ridiculed), and the Société des Philantropes de Strasbourg's 1779 contest on the Jews (which he later wrote prompted him to be interested in their status). On the eve of the French Revolution, he was also engaged in projects on the training of clerics, the education of peasants, and the history of Gypsies. For more on Grégoire's authorial ambitions, see Sepinwall, *The Abbé Grégoire and the French Revolution: The Making of Modern Universalism* (Berkeley: University of California Press, 2005), esp. 23–5 and 75–7; on those of Dohm, see Robert Liberles, "Dohm's Treatise on the Jews: A Defence of the Enlightenment," *Leo Baeck Institute Yearbook* 33 (1988): 37, 39.

[20] *Programmes de la Société des Philantropes*, at Bibliothèque de la Société de Port-Royal, Collection Grégoire (BSPR-G), Rév. 86/6.

[21] *Essai sur la régénération*, 96, also 48.

and its superiority over other faiths. The roots of this agenda were present in the *Essai*, as Grégoire highlighted the enduring benevolence of the Catholic clergy toward Jews even while insisting that the Jews' unhappy fate confirmed the truth of Christianity. He here battled both Enlightenment philosophes and Protestants who had accused the Catholic Church of intolerance.[22]

The positive stereotypes in the *Essai* had two other purposes. One concerned Grégoire's belief in human perfectability. As a priest involved in Enlightenment circles, Grégoire was caught between emphasizing original sin and believing in the possibility of progress and human improvement. Later in life, Grégoire would reassert the primacy of original sin, but at the time of his *Essai* he accepted the Metz contest organizers' premise that the Jews could be improved via human, not divine, intervention.[23] The positive remarks about Jews in the essay aimed to show that Jews already had some good traits and could be further improved if approached properly. In this regard, the abbé differed from antisemitic figures of his time such as Johann David Michaelis, who argued that "the Jews are incapable of being regenerated, because they are absolutely perverse."[24] For Grégoire, improving the Jews was part of a larger plan that involved improving peasants and, later, the entire kingdom.

[22] Grégoire was particularly keen to correct criticisms made of the Catholic Church by the Protestant writer Jacques Basnage (see Grégoire to Dubois de Fosseux, December 8, 1788, in Léon-Noël Berthe, "Deux illustres correspondants de l'Académie d'Arras: Lamourette et Grégoire," in *Arras à la veille de la Révolution* [*Mémoires de l'Académie des sciences, lettres et arts d'Arras*, 6e sér., T. I] [Arras: Imprimerie Mordacq, 1990], 199), in Basnage's book *Histoire des Juifs, depuis Jésus-Christ jusqu'à présent pour servir de continuation à l'histoire de Joseph: Nouvelle édition augmentée*, 9 vols. (The Hague: Henri Scheurleer, 1716). Though Basnage had criticized the Catholic clergy for persecuting Jews, he was no great admirer of Jews, ridiculing rabbis in the bitterest of terms and seeking to encourage Jews to convert. For him, speaking of the Catholic clergy's persecution of Jews was a way to evoke Catholic persecution of Protestants. On Grégoire's nineteenth-century corpus on oppressed groups, see Sepinwall, *The Abbé Grégoire and the French Revolution*, chap. 9. For an example of another Enlightenment era Catholic who employed philosemitic tropes in order to battle unbelievers, see the work of the abbé Antoine Guénée, discussed in Paul Benhamou, "Antiphilosophes éclairés et les Juifs," in Ilana Zinguer and Sam W. Bloom, eds., *L'antisémitisme éclairé: Inclusion and Exclusion: Perspectives on Jews from the Enlightenment to the Dreyfus Affair* (Leiden: E. J. Brill, 2003), 61–75.
[23] In a footnote in his *Mémoires* (drafted in 1808), l'abbé Grégoire acknowledged that his hopes for a social regeneration of the Jews had been more consistent with Jean-Jacques Rousseau's writings than with traditional Christian theology. He now declared, "It is an error to say *man is good*, because original sin corrupted him. I must correct this error [which I made] in my work on the Jews" (*Mémoires*, 110).
[24] *Essai sur la régénération*, 107. For a sample of Michaelis's views on Jews, see Johann David Michaelis, "Arguments against Dohm," in Paul Mendes-Flohr and Jehuda Reinharz, eds., *The Jew in the Modern World: A Documentary History*, (New York: Oxford University Press, 1995), 42–4.

A final reason for the philosemitic stereotypes in the *Essai* relates to Grégoire's agenda with regard to gender. The eighteenth century witnessed a good deal of debate about proper gender roles. At a time when many mothers hired wet nurses, Jean-Jacques Rousseau caused a stir by suggesting that women needed to breast-feed their own children. Priests like Grégoire were also concerned by what they saw as the growing independence of late eighteenth-century urban women, an anxiety he voiced often during his career.[25] In the *Essai*, Grégoire seems to have been using the behavior of Jewish women to try to shame their non-Jewish counterparts. In many ways, the abbé shared the tendency of many contemporary gentiles to look down on Jews; here, however, was an area in which he felt that many gentile women had reason to feel inferior. Unlike you, he seemed to tell them, Jewish women know how to act as modest wives and good mothers.

Given Grégoire's multiple purposes in entering the Metz contest, his text placed less emphasis on complimenting the Jews than on arguing that they were deficient and needed to be changed, in order to thwart their "danger" to the Christians around them. He focused on the necessity of educating Jews, inducing them to intermarry, moving them along the road to conversion, and eliminating their usury. Even while he expressed sympathy for Jews' plight, his distaste for their religion – and his low opinion of most Jews' character – was manifest.

The *Essai* included an extended critique of Judaism – something unsurprising coming from a man who had devoted his life to a church that considered Jews to have rejected the son of God. He blasted the "ridiculous" teachings of rabbis and the Talmud; maligned Jews' "exclusive religion," "obstinate adhesion to their dogmas," and "hatred for the nations"; and declared that God's fury had dispersed Jews across the globe. He dismissed the idea that Jews and Christians venerated the same books, asserting that the vast majority of Jews had replaced the morality of the Bible with "Talmudic reveries." He also argued that Jewish holy books were filled with "an infinity of inanities that are beyond ridiculous." Finally, even as he noted that "I do not want ... to blame today's Jews for the death of the Savior," elsewhere in his text he seemed to say the opposite: "The blood of J[esus] C[hrist] has fallen on the Jews just as they wished."[26]

---

[25] See Sepinwall, *The abbé Grégoire and the French Revolution*, 97–101, 121–3 and passim.

[26] *Essai sur la régénération*, 25, 29, 65, 177, 219n8, 23. For other critical readings of Grégoire's *Essai*, see Arthur Hertzberg, *The French Enlightenment and the Jews* (New York: Columbia University Press, 1968), 335–8; Pierre Birnbaum, "Sur l'étatisation révolutionnaire" [translated as chap. 1 of Birnbaum, *Jewish Destinies: Citizenship, State, and community in Modern France* (New York: Hill & Wang, 2000)]; Shmuel Trigano, "The French Revolution and the Jews," *Modern Judaism* 10 (1990): 171–90; Gil Tzarefaty, "Une relecture de l'*Essai* de l'abbé Grégoire," in Bernhard Blumenkranz, ed., *Juifs en France au XVIIIe siècle* (Paris: Collection Franco-judaïca, 1994), 213–21; and Ronald Schechter, *Obstinate Hebrews: Representations of*

However, Grégoire did not only deride Jews' religious beliefs: despite his philosemitic reputation, his text was full of negative generalizations about Jews themselves. Some of these were cultural; some related to Jews' economic activity; others were physical in nature. For instance, notwithstanding his comments about Jews' positive qualities within family life, Grégoire had little respect for the intellectual achievements of the Jewish people. He disparaged authors who suggested that Jews had made important contributions to European culture: "when in a work printed twenty years ago, one reads that Europe is indebted to the Jews for the renaissance of Letters and Fine Arts, one is tempted to believe that one's eyes are failing, instead of trusting the author." He also mocked Jews' attempts at poetry, calling David the only true poet that Jews had ever produced. Aside from some learned exceptions, he saw Jews as a "nation sunk in a lake of vulgar credulity, and submerged in an ocean of idiotic opinions."[27]

Grégoire further rebuked Jews for their usury, saying it had driven peasants to immorality. He went out of his way in the *Essai* to defend François Hell, the most notorious antisemite of the time in France. Hell had charged the Jews with killing children and incited violence against them in Alsace because of their moneylending. Even as he disagreed with Hell on some issues, Grégoire asked provocatively, "has it really been proven that everything he said was false?" In his *Motion en faveur des juifs*, Grégoire described the Jewish people as having a "financial genius" [*génie calculateur*], even as it was balanced by their "rapacity, ... a vice which has long gangrened the Hebrew people."[28]

Grégoire also criticized Jewish gender relations. In contrast to his use of gender discourse to praise Jewish women, he deployed gender to vilify Jewish men. In the nineteenth century, he would write about the comparative treatment of women worldwide as a means to assert that European Christian norms were superior to those of other groups. Similarly, in the *Essai*, he suggested that Christian men were more chivalrous in their treatment of women than were Jewish men, and that this was another proof of the superiority of Christian civilization. The abbé accused Jewish men of

Jews in France, 1715–1815 (Berkeley: University of California Press, 2003), 87–95. On the centrality of Catholic theology in the way Grégoire viewed the Jews, see esp. Rita Hermon-Belot, "L'abbé Grégoire et la conversion des Juifs," in Evelyne Oliel-Grausz and Mireille Hadas-Lebel, eds., *Les Juifs et la Révolution française: Histoire et mentalités ...* (Louvain: E. Peeters, 1992), 21–7.

[27] *Essai sur la régénération*, 176, 182, 175. Grégoire's reference was to J. B. D. V. S. J. D. R. [Israël Bernard Valabrègue], *Lettre, ou Réflexions d'un milord à son correspondant à Paris; au sujet de la requête des marchands des six-corps, contre l'admission des Juifs aux Brevets &c.* (London: N.p., 1767). Valabrègue was himself an Avignonais Jew living in Paris, but he wrote this text as if he were a Christian in England writing to a French friend.

[28] Ibid., 219n8; *Motion en faveur des juifs*, 28.

having always had "scanty esteem for the opposite sex [*personnes du sexe*]." To him, the institution of divorce among Jews (outlawed in French Catholic society) allowed women to be cast aside, viewed by men as no more than "base objects of pleasure."[29]

Beyond speaking of Jews' social faults, Grégoire depicted Jews as sexually and physically degenerate. He criticized their "precocity" with regard to puberty, argued that "solitary libertinage is extremely common among them," and intimated that "Jewish women would be strongly subject to nymphomania" if they did not marry early. The abbé also agreed with antisemites such as Michaelis about the negative physical features of the Jews. He noted with pride his having met the famed Swiss writer Johann Caspar Lavater, who had taught him that "in general, Jews have a pallid face, hooked nose, sunk-in eyes, prominent chin, and strongly pronounced muscles constricting the mouth." As a believer in eighteenth-century physiognomic theories, Grégoire felt that these physical flaws reflected Jews' deficient moral character.[30] To remedy these physical defects, Grégoire urged various measures to help "elevate their souls" and "give them energy," such as "crossing" them with other "races" through intermarriage.[31]

Because of these physical flaws, Grégoire warned specifically of the "danger" of Jews' growing population. While he felt that, in general, a large population could make a society more prosperous, the Jews were an exception. He warned his readers of the "alarming" speed at which Jews were "multiplying" and invoked a time when "the Jews, having become too numerous, will inundate and infest our country."[32] Only if they were reformed and their status ameliorated – through measures ranging from physical regeneration to the revocation of the discriminatory laws that distanced them from gentiles and forced them into moneylending – could this danger be averted.

Grégoire did not simply want Jewish usury to be eliminated, however; he made clear his hope that granting civic toleration to the Jews would foster their voluntary conversion to Christianity. Noting that "persecuting a religion is a sure means of making it even dearer to its adherents," he argued that more tolerant laws would help ensure that Jews did not cling to their backward faith. "If we encourage the Jews," he added, "they will insensibly adopt our way of thinking and acting, our laws, our customs, and our morals." Though he sincerely denounced forced conversions, he had no objection to requiring Jews to attend mandatory lectures on Christianity.[33]

---

[29] *Essai sur la régénération*, 180. On Grégoire's writings about women in the 1820s, see
       Sepinwall, *The Abbé Grégoire and the French Revolution*, 215–16.
[30] *Essai sur la régénération*, 50, 35, 52–3.
[31] Ibid., 49, 161, 164, 141.
[32] Ibid., 214n8, 59, 63, 257–62.
[33] Ibid., 31, 132, 139, 152.

He also recommended using humor and sarcasm to push Jews along this path. He commented that the Talmud was "not funny enough to excuse its stupidity" and that only irony could induce Jews to see this.[34]

While acknowledging Grégoire's derogatory remarks about Jews, it is important to recognize that he was hardly their severest eighteenth-century critic. Voltaire was in fact a greater critic of Jews than was Grégoire. Moreover, neither Grégoire's nor Voltaire's assessments of Jews were at the level of blood libel or denouncing Jews as Christ killers (common enough charges in Alsace, especially during the anti-Jewish pogroms of the 1770s). Indeed, many Christians of the time believed it was impossible to incorporate Jews into society; they saw Jews as inherently corrupt and believed that Jewish "devils" could not be reformed.[35]

That Grégoire made positive comments about the Jews thus made him atypical for a priest of the time. He argued zealously against anti-Jewish violence, insisting that justice should only be exacted by God; moreover, he protested against the crushing tax burden that Jews were forced to bear, particularly in Metz. In that sense, he represents a much more progressive position for his time than those who considered Jewish integration impossible. He ultimately believed that Jews were members of the same "human family" as their Christian brothers, and that they *could* be incorporated into society if steps were taken to reverse their degenerate condition.

During the first months of the Revolution, while he was a deputy in the National Assembly, Grégoire emphasized the positive half of his message. He subordinated his critique of Jewish beliefs to his hope that giving Jews equal citizenship would help change them and improve the social order as a whole. He pressed the issue of Jewish citizenship enthusiastically, not only introducing Jewish petitioners to important revolutionaries, but also denouncing on the floor of the Assembly anti-Jewish persecution. His *Motion en faveur des juifs* was published in October 1789 after other deputies, who regarded his position on Jewish citizenship as too radical in a society pervaded with antisemitism, prevented him from speaking in the Assembly on the matter.

However, despite his early interest in the Jewish issue and his image as the key proponent of Jewish emancipation, Grégoire turned his attentions elsewhere after 1789. When the Assembly voted to make Jews equal citizens in 1790–1, other revolutionaries were more involved than he. After fall 1789 he remained silent on the Jews in order to avoid jeopardizing his

---

[34] Ibid., 183.

[35] On eighteenth-century antisemitism, see also Léon Poliakov, *The History of Anti-Semitism*, vol. 3, *From Voltaire to Wagner* (Philadelphia: University of Pennsylvania Press, 2003); on "impossibilism," see Sepinwall, *The Abbé Grégoire and the French Revolution*, 62–4, 102–3. For an overview of the large literature on Voltaire and the Jews, see Sepinwall, "François-Marie-Arouet de Voltaire," in Richard S. Levy, ed., *Antisemitism: A Historical Encyclopedia of Prejudice and Persecution* (Santa Barbara, CA: ABC-CLIO, 2005), 2:746–8.

other projects, especially his efforts to combat monarchist clerics and to establish that Catholic and revolutionary values were consistent.[36] His correspondence also reveals his doubts about how much Askhenazi Jews were ready to change themselves in order to be citizens.[37]

In the years after the Revolution, when he felt Jews had not done enough to prove their gratitude for the gift of citizenship, he seems to have become more frustrated with them. His later writings more explicitly expressed his distaste for Judaism and his desire to prompt Jews' conversion to Christianity. Many of his remarks to this end were made in private, such as a 1796 letter he wrote to an Italian priest, showing his interest in Jews' adopting Christian beliefs and customs:

> The newspapers here report an astonishing piece of news: they assure us that the Jews of Livorno, following a kind of assembly of rabbis from different regions of Italy, have presented to the government of Tuscany a memorandum in which they declare that they will move the Sabbath to Sunday, that Jews will be permitted to eat pork, etc. I have written much about this people, whose dispersion is one of the proofs of the Christian religion.

Grégoire continued, "It is thus extremely important to me to know whether these newspaper reports are true; this would perhaps be a key step in the return of these people into the bosom of the Church."[38]

The abbé's conversionism is also revealed in his letters to figures such as Hannah Adams, a Protestant Massachusetts writer with similar interests. In an 1810 letter, the abbé reported to Adams that while he had served as an emissary of the French Revolution in Nice he had made sure to apply there the decree granting equality to the Jews. At the same time, he conveyed to Adams his longtime hope that "one day the Jews, recognizing the divinity of Jesus Christ, whom their fathers crucified, will enter into the bosom of the Catholic Church." He also told Adams of his personal experience with converted Jews, especially in his home region of Lorraine, where there was a special institution offering lodging to Jews who embraced Christianity.

---

[36] Ruth Necheles, *The Abbé Grégoire 1787–1831: The Odyssey of an Egalitarian* (Westport, CT: Greenwood, 1971), 27–33.

[37] Grégoire to J. A. Balthasar, July 2, 1791, Lucerne, Zentralbibliothek, Abt. Bürgerbibliothek, Nachlass Balthasar, no. 70, reprinted in Hans W. Debrunner, *Grégoire l'Européen: Kontinentale Beziehungen eines französischen Patrioten. Henri Grégoire 1750–1831* (Anif/Salzburg: Verlag Müller-Speiser, 1997), 27–30.

[38] See Grégoire to Scipione de Ricci, May 31, 1796, in Maurice Vaussard, *Correspondance, Scipione de' Ricci, Henri Grégoire (1796–1807)* (Florence: Edizioni Sansoni Antiquariato, 1963), 15. Ricci responded that the report that Grégoire had heard was erroneous; the rabbis had said only that Jewish women no longer needed to wear wigs or observe marital purity laws (*niddah*). He assured Grégoire, however, that aside from some "bigoted old women," progress was being made in moving Italian Jews away from their traditions; "in general, Jewish youth and the most educated Jews hardly worry about observing their religious practices and rabbinic dictates" (June 30, 1796, 20).

Finally, he was eager that she read a book on the conversion of the Jews by his friend Pierre-Jean Agier, a Jansenist thinker.[39] Other letters show Grégoire's personal friendships with leading figures in the French effort to convert Jews, such as the abbé Labouderie.[40] By the last decade of his life, Grégoire's interest in conversion had intensified. He told Adams in 1823, "The cause of the Jews has been won for them in France; they are equal there to other citizens. Religious people occupy themselves now more than ever with their conversion."[41]

Grégoire's nineteenth-century comments criticizing Judaism and promoting conversion were not uttered only in private; as he had before the Revolution, the abbé expressed the same sentiments frequently in print. In two essays from 1806–7 (concerning Napoleon's convoking of a "Sanhedrin" of Jewish leaders), Grégoire blasted "persecutors of all ranks and of all nations" and praised the progress of German Jews in regenerating themselves. Nevertheless, he also argued that Jews' own prejudices accounted for much of their failure to integrate, and he made several offhand jabs at Judaism. Mystified that Jews were still attached to the Talmud (a collection "which recalls what Horace said about a few pearls stuck in Eunius's excrement"), the abbé strongly denounced the "despotism" of French rabbis and community leaders." He encouraged Jews to "courageously escape the yoke of Rabbinism" and insisted that their continued usury "perpetuates the hate directed against them."[42]

---

[39] Grégoire to Hannah Adams, September 7, 1810, in New England Historic Genealogical Society (NEHGS), Thomas and Hannah Adams Papers, hereafter Adams Papers (Mss. 665), unnumbered fols. In a later work, Agier would analyze biblical prophecies to forecast that in 1849, all the Jews of the world would convert together and move to Israel; they would rebuild Jerusalem, and it would become the new seat of the Catholic Church (see Grégoire, *Histoire des sectes religieuses ... Nouvelle édition, corrigée et considérablement augmentée*, 6 vols. [Paris: Baudouin, 1828–45], 2:362–6).

[40] See the sermons given by Labouderie to congratulate converted Jews who renounced other Jews, thereby cleansing themselves of the "horrible crime that [Jews] committed against the person of their liberator,"and of the "blasphemy that they vomit against *le Saint de Dieu*" [Jesus], in Abbé Labouderie, *Discours prononcés à Notre-Dame, le 7 mars 1817, à l'occasion du baptême, du mariage, de la première communion du sieur Alphonse-Jean-Sébastien-Louis Jacob, Juif Converti* (Paris: Demonville, 1817); Abbé Labouderie, *Discours pour le baptême de Joseph-Marie-Louis-Jean Wolf, Juif Converti, prononcé à Saint-Eustache, le 23 mai 1818* (Paris: Demonville, 1818). Grégoire owned a number of Labouderie's conversion discourses (see BSPR-G, Rév. 141/9 and 141/9bis); the intensity of his admiration for Labouderie is also shown in his letters to the latter (Archives départementales de Loir-et-Cher, F 592, fols. 27, 28, and 66).

[41] Grégoire to Adams, May 20, 1823, in NEHGS, Adams Papers. Cf. Rita Hermon-Belot, who acknowledges Grégoire's interest in Jews' converting in the future but insists that this was something he actively opposed helping others achieve during his lifetime (Hermon-Belot, "L'abbé Grégoire et la conversion des Juifs," esp. 27 and *L'abbé Grégoire, la politique, et la vérité*, 259).

[42] See Grégoire, *Observations nouvelles sur les Juifs, et spécialement sur ceux d'Amsterdam et de Francfort* (N.p., 1807), 4, 18; and Grégoire, *Observations nouvelles sur les Juifs, et spécialement*

In his *Histoire des sectes religieuses* he voiced similar criticisms of Judaism. This text was not a straightforward history of various religious groups; it aimed to highlight the errors of non-Catholic believers in order to draw them back into the church. The *Histoire* was Grégoire's greatest opus, something he spent much of his last decades researching. A two-volume edition was published in 1810, and a six-volume edition appeared beginning in 1828.[43]

On the one hand, the *Histoire des sectes* retained some of the defense of Jews from the 1788 *Essai*. As in that text, Grégoire pointed out that Jews had turned to moneylending only because of Christian persecution. He stressed the unity of the human species and argued, "If the Hebrews are a degenerate race," it was not because they were inherently debased, but because of the "crimes of our ancestors." To him, the existence of at least some "good" Jews showed the potential of the Jewish people, and "good education and good laws" could help improve others; he singled out exceptional Jews from Maimonides to Moses Ensheim. Grégoire also reprinted his earlier philosemitic admiration of the Jews' family values. He even added some praise for the humanitarian logic behind the laws of *kashrut*, which prevented unnecessary suffering by animals. Moreover, he observed that, if Jewish men had treated their women badly in the past, this was starting to change in certain cities.[44]

Nevertheless, the abbé now argued even more vehemently than in the past that Jews perpetuated their own degeneracy. Even as some portions of the *Histoire des sectes* empathized with Jews, other sections mocked them. Grégoire depicted a nation deliberately setting itself apart from all others: "the Jew has his eyes constantly turned towards Jerusalem, desiring only it for his patrie.... All nations have tried in vain to annihilate this people who exist among them, without resembling any, nor identifying themselves with any." He also continued to criticize the Talmud and the Parnassim (lay leaders of Jewish communities), as well as the "tyranny" of

sur ceux d'Allemagne (N.p., 1806), 6, 7, 9, and passim. On the Sanhedrin, see esp. Simon Schwarzfuchs, *Napoleon, the Jews, and the Sanhedrin* (London: Routledge/Littman Library of Jewish Civilization, 1979).

43 Grégoire, *Histoire des sectes religieuses*..., 2 vols. (Paris: Potey, 1810); and *Histoire des sectes religieuses...Nouvelle édition, corrigée et considérablement augmentée*, 6 vols. (Paris: Baudouin, 1828–45). The 1810 edition is more commonly called the 1814 edition because it was banned in France shortly after publication and later reissued with an 1814 title page. However, many of the copies of this book preserved in North America have the original 1810 title page, from having been sent abroad before the ban. For a fuller analysis of the *Histoire des sectes religieuses*, see Sepinwall, *The Abbé Grégoire and the French Revolution*, chap. 9.

44 *Histoire* 1810, 2:351, 353–5, 394–7; and *Histoire* 1828, 3:354–8, 397–400, 407, 416–17, 419–21.

the rabbis. He derided the former as written in "Babylonian patois, with no taste, no method, no accuracy," and said it "interprets the Holy Scripture absurdly [and] is filled with puerile fables, obscure precepts, explicit obscenities and even blasphemies." As for the Parnassim, Grégoire called them aristocratic tyrants, from whom ordinary Jews needed Christian protection.[45]

In the *Histoire des sectes* Grégoire also portrayed contemporary Jews as afflicted by a misery that stemmed from their rejection of Jesus. The unhappy fate of the "wandering Jew" only confirmed the predictions of Christianity, "a religion he abhors." Jews had betrayed Jesus and had received their just deserts; sounding much like Hell and other prerevolutionary antisemites, Grégoire repeated his comments from the *Essai* about Jesus's blood "fall[ing] back on the Jews just as they wished."[46] In addition to these comments, Grégoire ridiculed other recent currents in Judaism. Like many contemporaries, he mocked the Jews who had continued to follow the self-proclaimed Messiah Shabbatai Zvi even after his conversion to Islam. Citing an account by German-Jewish reformers, Grégoire also gave a disparaging portrayal of Hasidism.[47]

Underlying these remarks was Grégoire's refusal to see rabbinic Judaism as normative; for him, the true principles of Judaism should have led Jews to embrace Jesus. He was fascinated by the Karaites and the Samaritans, both of whom rejected oral tradition and followed only the Pentateuch. Rabbinists (by which he meant adherents of mainstream Judaism, which he defined as a tyranny of the rabbis with little connection to scripture) were only one kind of Jew; it was Karaites, Samaritans, and Rabbinists together who would, through their conversion, "console the Church for the ingratitude and the apostasy of the Gentiles." Grégoire was delighted by reports he interpreted as suggesting that east European and Dutch Jews were beginning to embrace Christianity.[48] As he noted in another work from the 1820s, he remained certain that "the Jews will return to He whom their ancestors *pierced.*"[49]

In addition to writing to gentile audiences about his hopes for the conversion of the Jews, Grégoire made similar comments to Jews face to face. For instance, while visiting the synagogue in Amsterdam in 1803, a scene he later described with bemusement because of the "harangues" of the rabbis, he told his Jewish hosts that "the Catholic Church imagines with

[45] *Histoire* 1810, 2:349–50, 357, 358, 366–8.
[46] *Histoire* 1810, 2:349–50. Cf. comments by Hell cited in Hertzberg, *French Enlightenment and the Jews*, 288.
[47] *Histoire* 1810, 2:309, 338–9, 348.
[48] *Histoire* 1828, 3:302, 303, 401, 312, 426; *Histoire* 1810, 2:309, 314.
[49] Grégoire, *De la liberté de conscience et de culte à Haïti* (Paris: Baudouin Frères, 1824), 30; and also *Histoire* 1828, 5:314–15. Italics in original.

a tender impatience the future moment which must bring the scattered remnants of Israel under the standard of the cross."[50]

While scholars such as Hermon-Belot have suggested that Grégoire's comments appear negative only in retrospect, some of Grégoire's contemporaries indeed read them as harsh. In 1791, a London newspaper, reviewing the English translation of the *Essai*, called Grégoire's attitude hypocritical: "How easy it is, to point out follies and fancies, of a ridiculous nature, in the customs of others, while we neglect those which are equally so in our own. A Roman Catholic priest must have been witness to, or engaged in, several practices, which can hardly be exceeded, for folly and absurdity, by any that prevail among Jews, or even Heathens." While these comments reflected English Protestants' views about Catholics, French newspapers also understood the *Essai* as having both positive and negative views of Jews. The *Journal encyclopédique* praised the abbé for "devoting himself to defending the cause of the Hebraic sect" while also "blaming it when necessary"; its reviewer particularly welcomed Grégoire's discussions of Jewish usury and of the "causes of Jews' contempt for women." Similarly, the *Mercure de France*, while focusing on Grégoire's positive remarks on Jews, acknowledged that he spoke of the dangers of integrating them without advance preparation, based on his "local knowledge" of Jews in the east.[51] Grégoire's friends also recognized the negative aspects of his various writings on Jews; after his 1806 essay on them, for instance, an old friend told him: "You do not flatter the Jews of our country. But what you say about them is very true."[52]

Jews who read Grégoire's essays also recognized their critical aspects. Though the abbé cited the complimentary part of the Bordeaux Jews' letter to him to show how much Jews adored him, his *Mémoires* omitted the heart of the letter, in which they implored him to stop both generalizing about Jews and suggesting that they needed a regeneration different from that of other Frenchmen. Correspondence between Grégoire and other Jews – and evidence in the footnotes of the *Essai* – reveals the discomfort that even Grégoire's closest Jewish friends had with some of his ideas.[53]

---

[50] *Mémoires*, 54. Grégoire in fact made similar remarks to Protestants such as Hannah Adams, telling her of his hope that she and other Protestants would soon reembrace Catholicism (Grégoire to Adams, January 19, 1811, in NEHGS, Adams Papers).

[51] *Monthly Review* (1791), 2nd ser., 5:174; *Mercure de France* (January 2, 1790), 29–42; *L'Esprit des Journaux* (July 1789): 85–102, quote from 99 (reprinted from *Journal encyclopédique*); see also *Journal de Paris* 2, no. 187 (July 1789): 840–1.

[52] Frédéric-Rodolphe Saltzmann to Grégoire, March 21, 1806, BSPR-G, dossier "Bas-Rhin."

[53] Abraham Furtado, Azevedo, David Gradis, and Salomon Lopes du Bec, *Lettre adressée à M. Grégoire ... par les Députés de la Nation Juive Portugaise de Bordeaux* (Versailles: Baudouin, 1789), 2–3; and Sepinwall, "Strategic Friendships." Most Jews, of course, did not have access to Grégoire's texts for reasons of their cost and because Jews' literacy in French was limited; they knew Grégoire only in terms of his general image as the Jews' great defender.

A prime example of Jews' ambivalence about Grégoire is that of Berr-Isaac Berr, a prominent Lorraine Jew who was disturbed by the abbé's early nineteenth-century writings on Jews. Having worked with Grégoire on the citizenship campaign during the early months of the Revolution, Berr emphasized his "gratitude and profound esteem" for the priest. Yet he could barely restrain his anger over Grégoire's comments in 1806. He protested that to attack sacred books "is to attack the very religion to which they belong. ... It would be extremely easy to ridicule the majority of books which the various Christian sects admit as sacred." But, he asked, "what would be the point?" Berr further complained:

[when] invitations to renounce totally the yoke of Rabbinism are repeated to the Jews by respectable men like you, *Monsieur*, soon confusion will ensue. These individuals, forgetting the religion of their ancestors, will be neither Jews nor Catholics nor Protestants. They will only augment the number of atheists, or men without solid moral principles.[54]

Berr's response demonstrated the Jewish community's quandary in dealing with Grégoire. They disagreed vigorously with his portrayal of the essential bankruptcy of their religion. Nevertheless, they were grateful for his attacks on violence against Jews and knew that he was very different from the most obdurate antisemites of the time. Unlike them, Grégoire denounced those who persecuted Jews; moreover, he believed that Jews could ultimately be improved.

Nevertheless, we cannot simply deem Grégoire a "defender of the Jews." If philosemitism implies, following the Rubensteins' definition, *support*, *admiration*, and *friendship* toward Jews, many of his comments cannot be classified under that label. The abbé's support for Jews was premised on the hope that they would eventually relinquish their religious and cultural particularities; he admired certain parts of their character but disparaged many others; and he extended friendship toward individual Jews, but primarily in the hope that if he better understood them he could better help lead them toward conversion. Just as today's "philosemites" (notably the American evangelical Christians who declare their love for the Jewish people and the state of Israel) are hardly equivalent to Holocaust deniers, one must be careful not to assert that gentile philosemitism is no different from antisemitism. Yet it is still worth remembering the way in which philosemitism can have multiple motives and sometimes rely uncomfortably on ideas that disparage both individual Jews and Judaism as a whole.

[54] Berr-Isaac Berr, *Lettre ... à M. Grégoire, Sénateur, à Paris* (Nancy: Imprimerie de P. Barbier, 1806), 5, 6, 9.

6

Ordinary People, Ordinary Jews

Mór Jókai as Magyar Philosemite

Howard Lupovitch

German Jews could not find a friend in Schiller; in Goethe they found a steadfast adversary. As long as we had Kazinczy the Jewish school supervisor, Bajza rallying and laboring for a Jewish teacher training institute, Vörösmarty watching with a heavy heart already during the 40s that equality and brotherhood have left the eternal Jews untouched in their suffering, Petőfi scolding the German burghers with all his might for daring to persecute the Jews, justice and love regulating Kossuth's behavior toward us, Pal Szemere and Ferencz Pulszky rushing to acknowledge our worth with great skill – we could envision a bright future; but among all of these our most sincere friend was none other than Mór Jókai.

Béla Vajda, "Jókai," 1904, 246[1]

When he wrote these words in 1904, Béla Vajda, a late nineteenth-century Hungarian Jewish historian, captured the love affair between Hungarian Jewry and the great Hungarian romantic novelist Mór Jókai (YO-kah-ee). For more than a century, Jókai has been singled out as the Magyar philosemite par excellence. Jókai himself reinforced this view by extolling his own camaraderie with Jews, whom he regarded as fellow Magyars.

In the larger context of European philosemitism, however, Jókai is somewhat of an anomaly. His attitude toward Jews betrays little or none of the allosemitic tone that pervades the outlook of other philosemites, and nothing whatsoever of the missionary tone evinced by many English millenarians and comparably minded philosemities.[2] In other words, Jókai's portrayal of Jews lacks what Alan Edelstein and others have described as an "anti-antisemitic" demeanor. Rather than lauding Jews as the bearers of particular virtues or explaining away their alleged foibles, as other defenders of and apologists for Jews commonly did, Jókai described

---

[1] Béla Vajda, "Jókai," *Magyar Zsidó Szemle* [Hungarian Jewish review] 9 (1904): 246.

[2] William D. Rubinstein and Hilary L. Rubinstein, *Philosemitism: Admiration and Support in the English-Speaking World for Jews* (London: St. Martin's Press, 1999), 3ff.

Jews as ordinary people with the virtues and foibles of other ordinary people.[3]

This was no small task. Philosemitic writers often stumbled in their attempt to portray Jews realistically without affirming positive or negative stereotypes. The simple fact is, there were characteristics and tendencies commonly associated with Jews – a commercial or capitalist mentality, for example – that were true of many though certainly not all Jews. To his credit, Jókai sidestepped this pitfall by distinguishing Jews' external appearance and behavior, on the one hand, from their internal character and mentality. On the outside, Jókai's Jewish characters were typically composites of pervading Jewish stereotypes – caftan-clad tavern keepers, with earlocks and oddly styled beards; on the inside, these Jews experienced the same corpus of emotions as were experienced by non-Jews: love, angst, despair, sorrow, devotion, loyalty, gratitude, fear, remorse. In the multiethnic, multiconfessional world of pre–World War I Hungary, distinguishing inner humanity from external peculiarity resonated clearly.

Jókai's ability to make this distinction was facilitated in no small part by his personal odyssey during his childhood and teenage years from Judeophobe to Judeophile. His personal transformation prefigured not only a bifurcated portrayal of Jewish characters, but the satirical and often caustic renderings of his fictional characters, who were unable to overcome their disdain for Jews. Jókai rooted the latter's attitude in an inability to divest themselves of the principal sources of Jew-hatred: heterophobia, the fear of Jews as different; and proteophobia, the fear of Jews as agents of uncertainty and change.[4]

Jókai's personal transformation, in this regard, provided him with a blueprint with which to invest his seemingly unappealing Jewish characters with ordinary emotional characteristics, while exposing the mindlessness of anti-Jewish sentiments. Jókai's Jewish characters provide a venue for the author to present antagonism toward Jews as an intellectual and moral failure on the part of Magyar culture and nationalism, and camaraderie with Jews as a telling step toward maturing as a culture and as a nation. In this sense, Jókai's change in attitude toward Jews resembled a conversion experience. Sociologists have shown that converts from one religious or political ideology to another will often reinterpret the preconversion period of their life as inherently flawed and as inevitably leading up to the moment of conversion.[5]

---

[3] Alan Edelstein, *An Unacknowledged Harmony: Philosemitism and the Survival of European Jewry* (Westport, CT: Greenwood Press, 1982), 5.

[4] Zygmunt Bauman, "Allosemitism: Premodern, Modern, Postmodern," in Bryan Cheyette and Laura Marcus, eds., *Modernity, Culture, and "the Jew"* (Stanford, CA: Stanford University Press, 1998), 144.

[5] Alan F. Segal, *Paul the Convert: The Apostolate and Apostasy of Saul the Pharisee* (New Haven and London: Yale University Press, 1990), 287–8. As Anna Fábri notes, Jókai later republished

As will be discussed presently, prior to his "conversion" Jókai embraced many. of the stereotypes concerning Hungarian Jews, regarding Jews as inherently foreign, menacing, and less than civilized. Likewise, as a young man in his late teens Jókai came to see his disdain for Jews as the product of youthful immoderation, ignorance, unenlightenment, and a young nobleman's arrogance, and his ability to overcome this disdain as an intellectual, spiritual, and moral triumph. He thus wove into his anti-Jewish literary characters the elements of his own erstwhile anti-Jewish outlook that he had since repudiated. Foremost among these was the intense disdain for Jews that resulted from a sense of being inferior to Jews.

A CHILDHOOD METAMORPHOSIS AND ITS LITERARY LEGACY

Mór Jókai was born on February 18, 1825, in Rév-Komárom, a small town near Pozsony in the Transdanubia region of Hungary, into a Calvinist noble family. He was the youngest of three children. His father, a lawyer, had acquired an affinity for art and belles lettres while traveling abroad as a young man. Though he died when Mór was twelve, his romantic embrace of universal brotherhood left a lasting imprint on his son. Jókai regarded his artistic and literary talents as a legacy from his father; his affinity for enlightenment and liberalism he inherited from his mother, to whom he was equally devoted. His mother was instrumental in steeling his sensitive personality to a host of fears born of a child's active imagination: being buried alive, stray dogs, and, as he would recall later, "old, long-bearded Jews."

In this regard, the noble-born Jókai's disposition toward Jews echoed a broader tendency within the complex relationship between Jews and the Hungarian nobility. This relationship began during the eighteenth century as a series of commercial arrangements between individual Jews and a magnate benefactor. Magnates, particularly in the developing areas of central and northeastern Hungary, granted their Jewish commercial agents and other Jews – whom they regarded as a lucrative source of revenue from taxes and bribes – an expanding array of residential and travel privileges.

This economic relationship expanded during the early nineteenth century into a political alliance between Jewry and nobility against the Habsburg dynasty and its protégé, the German Burghertum. By the mid-nineteenth century, liberal-minded nobles, in particular, came to regard Hungarian Jewry as a useful ally in their campaign against Habsburg rule, and the Magyarization of Hungarian Jewry as an indispensible element in

in 1894 as "Én és a zsidók" [The Jews and me] in a collection of essays called *Életemből* [From my life]. This essay was in a recent collection of Jókai's works edited by Fábri, *Jókai Mór* (Budapest: Új Mandátum Könyvkiadó, 1998), 162–3. All quotations are from this last version of the essay.

the struggle between Magyars and rival nationalist movements. This laid the basis for a cultural alliance between Jewry and nobility.

For Jókai, as for other nobles who embraced such enlightened notions as the universal brotherhood and perfectibility of humanity, applying such principles to Jews often tested these beliefs, particularly for those who hailed from the northeast, where most of the Jews were unacculturated Ostjuden. Lajos Kossuth, a native of Zemplen County, personified the Hungarian Jew as the tavern keeper who causes the local peasants to squander their hard-earned money on liquor, thus remaining in a state of drunken poverty. Kossuth, while endorsing emancipation, regarded the vast majority of Hungarian Jews as so vastly different and foreign that any attempt to assimilate them into mainstream Magyar society would cause the latter's demise.

Jókai, though, was among those nobles who, in the spirit of the Enlightenment, managed to see past the external, foreign appearance of Hungarian Jews and recognize the persons underneath. In this sense, he was much like his contemporary Baron József Eötvös, the architect of Jewish emancipation in 1868, who already acknowledged the humanity of Hungarian Jews by the 1830s.

Whereas Eötvös's positive disposition toward Jews resulted initially from his encounters with English Jews while traveling abroad, Jókai's shift in attitude began when he was a child. It was as an impressionable child that Jókai first experienced fear of and disdain for Jews. Decades later, he reconstructed this early attitude and his subsequent change of heart in an essay that he published in the Budapest weekly *Pesti Hírlap* in 1884, "Hogyan lettem én filoszemitává? [How did I become a philosemite?]."[6] In this essay, he described his initial, impersonal encounter with Jews; his confrontation with Koricsaner, the first Jew he knew personally; his mother's ecumenical intervention; and his reinvention as a nonhater of Jews.

Jókai attributed his initial disdain for Jews to the uneducated and unenlightened household servants, who smuggled in retrograde ideas under his parents' enlightened radar:

I was certainly an anti-semite during my youth, like many unenlightened people. Our servants put stories in my head that Jews used the blood of Christian children on their Passover holiday. And between our house and school was the Baranyay Hall, where Jews were allowed to live. The ritual slaughterer lived there too. Daily I saw when Jewish women would bring throat-slitted geese through the doorway: my imagination filled in the rest. … How are these people permitted to go freely, who kill so mercilessly?

Lest his readers harbor any doubt that Jókai ascribed Jew-hatred to the unenlightened and ignorant, Jókai sardonically added one additional

---

[6] Vajda, "Jókai," 246–7.

"unenlightened" childhood influence: "It was our dog Cicke who gal-
vanized my views most thoroughly; if ever something so oddly bearded
came into our courtyard, I urged my dog: get him, pooch, bite him. And I
laughed grandly as the Jew clacked at his pursuer until he reached the gate
to the street."

While he was attending Calvinist schools in Pozsony and Komárom,
Jókai's disdain for Jews was reinforced by a pervading fear of even minimal
contact with them: "Later when I had grown older, I was sent to Pozsony, a
German diaspora. There I later learned that at the edge of the city there is
a damned place called the Schlossberg, the abode of Jews ... if it became
known that a student was in the Schlossberg, he would quickly be expelled."
The concern among the school administrators lest young Christian students like Jókai have even the slightest contact with Jews reflected, in Jókai's
mind, not only a sense of contempt for Jews but an underlying fear of Jews.
Later, Jókai would root this fear in parochial ignorance.

KORICSANER: DISLODGING A STEREOTYPE

Prior to the age of fourteen, it is doubtful that Jókai knew any Jews personally. His perception of Jews to this point reflected what Zygmunt Bauman
described as the "unbridgeable gap between the Jew as such and the Jew
next door."[7] This situation changed abruptly while he was a student at the
Calvinist gymnasium in Komárom. His tutor and future brother in-law,
Ferenc Vály, challenged Jókai's negative view of Jews by admitting a Jewish
student to his class: "Once when they offered a class in poetry, it happened miraculously that a Jewish student named Koricsaner enrolled in
our class. He was no longer a lad; he was over forty. He had been a callig-
rapher until this point, and taught penmanship. Reproducing celebrated
manuscripts in the form of metal engravings. The other students and I
mocked him."[8]

Yet this episode took a dramatic turn when, to Jókai's surprise and horror, he watched as his revered teacher treated Koricsaner with the same
respect due any student:

Once [Koricsaner] missed class; following class, he offered as an excuse: "pardon
me Professor sir, I truly could not come, because my wife bore a son yesterday."
Only the teacher did not laugh at this odd excuse. He was entirely solemn, and
wished his student best wishes on his new child, excused him for the day to take
care of his wife, and cancelled for him the following lesson. The good Koricsaner
himself was equally solemn.

[7] Bauman, "Allosemitism," 143.
[8] Jókai, "Én és a Zsidók." In Mór Jókai, *Összes Müvei* [Complete works], 100 vols. (Budapest: Réva
testvérek kiadasa, 1894–1898, 66:296ff. All references to *Összes Müvei* [Complete works]
are to this edition.

Horrified and confused by the respect Koricsaner received from Vály, Jókai continued to confront his Jewish classmate, even to the point of violence:

Once the Jew and I got into an argument before school over whether Hungarian metric poetry has the consonant sound "h." I maintained yes, he said no. I assailed him saying "what do you know of it, you are a Jew."He retorted "but you are only a child."Such a horrible slight, telling a 14 year-old boy that he is a child. Nowadays the offender would be called to a duel.... He was 41 and I only 14, but I was Magyar and he only a Jew. It was just cause and pretense to grab him by the collar and strike his back with my fist.

Looking back on this moment, Jókai attributed this outburst to a sense of inferiority. Koricsaner the Jew, in addition to demonstrating a superior knowledge of Magyar grammar – the heart and soul of Jókai's emerging Magyar identity – thrust into the boy's face the insurmountable disadvantage of youth in matters of knowledge and wisdom. As will be discussed presently, Jókai would regard a sense of inferiority among Christians with respect to Jews – manifest in a variety of forms – as a driving force behind negative views of Jews.

For the moment, though, Jókai's violent outburst quickly became a watershed moment in his attitude toward Jews. He arrived at home and, convinced that he had finally overcome the timidity of his youth by acting in a way befitting a nobleman coming of age, began to boast of his "honorable" behavior. His mother, by this point Jókai's sole living parent and the focal point of Jókai's sense of authority and wisdom, wholeheartedly disagreed with her son's appraisal of this event. As Jókai recalled, she lashed out at him with utter disappointment and disapproval:

"What" she exclaimed, "you say he is only a Jew. Is the Jew not a person like another? You despise another person because of his religion? Have you forgotten that 'our' co-religionists were persecuted in this city only fifty years ago, just as you now persecute the Jew? This you did not learn from me or from your father. You shall arise and seek out the Jew whom you drubbed, ask for his pardon, and bring me a letter saying that he forgives you." I was in horror beside this draconian harshness. "I should humble myself before a Jew?" "Humble yourself before God, who created the Jews equal to you."[9]

As he set out to find Koricsaner in order to tender an apology, as per his mother's instructions, he found Koricsaner already waiting on the doorstep of the Jókais' domicile, preparing himself to apologize to Jókai. Jókai, moved to remorse by the force of maternal consternation, discovered a certain respect for the Jew's honorable behavior and embraced Koricsaner.

---

[9] Jókai described his relationship with his mother in "Az Anyám" [My mother], in *Összes Művei*, 32:101.

In retrospect, his mother's rationale for treating Koricsaner with respect reflected an ecumenical current within the mentality of Hungarian nobility that resulted from the nobility's historical development from the sixteenth through the eighteenth century. Since the sixteenth century, the Magyar nobility had divided along confessional lines between Catholicism and two Protestant denominations – Lutheranism and Calvinism; for the nobility to forge any sense of unity, it was necessary for nobles to divest themselves of religious-based antagonism toward rival Christian sects. Alongside this religious division, moreover, much of the nobility had been subjected during the sixteenth and seventeenth centuries to Ottoman rule. Ottoman law and its administrators regarded the confessional differences among Catholics, Lutherans, and Calivinists as secondary to the overriding fact that the members of all three churches were Christian and hence equally second-class in the eyes of the state. The need to set aside religious divisions for the sake of unity, coupled with the common experience of Islamic rule, bred a sense of ecumenicism within the Hungarian nobility. For some nobles, expanding this Christian ecumenicism into a broader ecumenicism that included Jews proved too great a step until well into the nineteenth century. Jókai's mother, however, was among those nobles who were able to take this step far earlier.[10]

Following his altercation with Koricsaner, Jókai attributed the animus toward Jews of the unenlightened to a fear born of ignorance, a fear that prompted them to perceive Jews not only as different but also as powerful and dangerous people. This notion accompanied him to the world of higher education and liberal thought. At the age of sixteen, Jókai entered the Calvinist university in Pápá, where he met, among others, Sándor Petőfi, who would later emerge as the poet laureate of the Hungarian Revolution of 1848. The two frequently critiqued one another's works, the first installment of an extended friendship marked both by camaraderie and by conflict.

Two years later, in 1843, Jókai entered law school in Kecskemét, an early center of the Magyar national and cultural awakening. One of Jókai's biographers described this key period in his development as an intellectual and as an advocate on behalf of Jews as follows: "It was here in the fine, bracing air of the *Alföld*, amidst miles of orchards and vineyards, that Jókai ... was first brought into contact with the true Magyar folk-life and folk-humor; here, he became a man and a Hungarian writer.... It was at Kecskemét, that he wrote his first play, *A Zsidó Fiu* [The Jew boy].[11] This play placed

[10] On the ecumenical mentality of the Hungarian nobility and its seventeenth-century roots, see Ferenc Szekály, "A Magyar Nemesség a török hódoltságban" [The Hungarian nobility during the Turkish occupation], *Századok* 125, nos. 5–6 (1992): 565–6.
[11] "Jókai életraza" [A biography of Jókai], in *Összes Művei*, vol. C (Budapest, 1898), 106ff.; an abridged English translation is Jókai, *Tales from Jókai*, trans. R. Nisbet Bain (1904; repr., New York: Books for Libraries Press, 1971); Bain, "Biography of Jókai," in Bain, ed., *Tales of Jókai* (Freeport, NY, 1904).

second in a national competition and launched Jókai into the public eye as an up-and-coming Hungarian writer.

That his entrée into the realm of Magyar culture and politics coincided with his first piece of literature dealing with Jews was no coincidence. On the contrary, by the 1840s the prospect of Jewish emancipation in Hungary was emerging as a leading issue in public life and politics. From the outset, supporters of citizenship for Jews entertained competing visions of Jewish emancipation. At the heart of this disagreement was the burning question of whether in its current condition Hungarian Jewry could be assimilated into contemporary Magyar society.

This question illustrates the notion that, in the words of one twentieth-century historian, nineteenth-century Europeans envisioned Jews as the "eponymous weed in an Age of Gardening."[12] This claim resonates deeply within the debate over Jewish emancipation in nineteenth-century Hungarian politics. István Széchenyi, the father of Hungarian political reform, articulated a culinary equivalent to Baumen's horticultural metaphor by equating the perils of emancipating and assimilating Hungarian Jews with a bottle of Jewish ink ruining the Hungarian soup. While conceding the important role that Jews played in stimulating commerce and providing credit and in the development of urban life, Széchenyi did not believe Hungarian society was ready to withstand a sudden onslaught of Jewish entrepreneurs freed of the shackles of second-class citizens.[13]

Széchenyi, in other words, regarded Jewish otherness – in this case, the overwhelmingly commercial tendencies of Hungarian Jewry – as inherently incompatible with and destructive to the arduous task of state and nation building in Hungary. His successors, especially Lajos Kossuth, carried this concern a step further by insisting that Jews shed their distinctiveness as a precondition to emancipation. This would remain the prevailing contractual term between Hungarian Jews in search of civic equality and social acceptance, on the one hand, and the Hungarian state and Magyar nation, on the other.[14]

Jókai, however, took strong issue with the position of Széchenyi and Kossuth. To paraphrase E. M. Cioran, Jókai did not fear the dynamism that Jewish yeast would inject into the flour of Magyar society.[15] Instead, Jókai joined ranks with those statesmen and literati, notably Baron József Eötvös and Bertalan Szemere, who rejected the notion that emancipation

---

[12] Bauman, "Allosemitism," 152–3.
[13] On Széchenyi see Nathaniel Katzburg, "The Public Debate over Jewish Emancipation in Hungary during the 1840s" [in Hebrew], *Bar Ilan Annual* 1 (1973): 293.
[14] On Kossuth's view of and contributions to the debate over the Jewish question, see Michael Silber, "Roots of the Schism in Hungarian Jewry: Cultural and Social Change from Joseph II to the Eve of the 1848 Revolution" (PhD diss., Hebrew University, 1985), 232–6.
[15] Quoted in Bauman, "Allosemitism," 146.

could only be extended to Jews quid pro quo in exchange for total assimilation. While Jókai concurred with the expectation that Jews embrace the
Magyar language and Magyar culture, he did not see this expectation as
necessarily requiring Jews to shed all distinct forms of Jewishness, including religious distinctness.[16] He already agreed with Eötvös and Szemere
that insofar as Jews played a vital role in the ongoing development of commercial and urban development, their economic concentration in commerce did not preclude their emancipation.

   This point of view is an important subtext in *A Zsidó Fiu*. The play begins
by depicting the Jews as outsiders: "I am a Jew, homeless in your land /
not like God's other people because I am scorned between the eyes / and
whither I look down, my land is not there. / You exclude us from the convenience of existence / Honor, esteem, and respect is not a blooming flower
to us."[17] During the course of the play, it becomes apparent that Jews need
not necessarily be outsiders, if they simply abandon their faith. Solomon,
the title character and appropriately the Jewish voice of wisdom in the play,
faces ongoing pressure to convert in exchange for a better life. He refuses
and defends his right to remain true to his religion. When his friend Kajan
prods him yet again to convert, Solomon replies:

No, it is not possible. My father, whom I should curse, my good father, on whose
knees I once nestled, and the bosom from which I suckled milk, my mother and
her harness; and the faith in which I was born and my ancestors died – how could
I abandon them, how could I part from them? What good does the destruction
of my spirit do you? Plant a palm tree in the sand by a cliff, and you will not pick
fruit.[18]

Subsequently, Jókai carried a step further the notion that Jews, though
ostensibly different, posed no real threat to Magyar society, by satirizing the
Christian sense of inferiority to Jews as an explanation of Jew-hatred. In one
of Jókai's many stories set during the Ottoman occupation of Hungary,[19]
two beautiful women – Rebecca the Jew and Lizza the Muslim – vie for the
patronage of Suleiman Bey, a high-ranking official in the Ottoman court:

In every song, in every dance, Mukhtar Bey's beautiful Jewish damsel Rebecca and
the blue-eyed dancer Lizza, who was Suleiman Bey's favorite, equally excelled.
It was impossible to decide which of the pair deserved the palm [i.e., the token
of his greatest affection]. ... With that he beckoned to the two odalisks. Rebecca,
the lovely Jewish damsel, sank with full amorous languor onto Suleiman's breast

[16] Howard Lupovitch, *Jews at the Crossroads: Tradition and Accommodation during the Golden Age of the Hungarian Nobility* (Budapest: CEU Press, 2006), 189ff.
[17] Jókai, "A Zsidó Fiu," in *Összes Művei*, 36, 4.
[18] Ibid., 26.
[19] See Paul Coles, *The Ottoman Impact on Europe* (New York: Harcourt, Brace & World, 1968); Illiko Beller-Hahn, "The Turks in Nineteenth-Century Hungarian Literature," *Journal of Mediterranean Studies* 5/2 (1995): 222–38.

while Lizza, with sylph-like agility, sat down upon his knee, and the intoxicated Bey, in an access of rapture, kissed first one and then the other.[20]

At this point, a crass, unenlightened member of the court notes a key difference between the affectations of the two women: "Rebecca's lips are more ardent, but the kisses of Lizza are sweeter. The kiss of Rebecca is like the poppy *that lulls you into sweet unconsciousness*, but Lizza's kiss is like sweet wine which makes you merry." For this observer, the Jewess had the power not only to entice powerful statesmen but also to manipulate them by lulling them into a stupor. In response, Mukhtar, whom the author characterized as a more enlightened observer, described Rebecca's allure differently: "Lizza's kiss may perchance be like sweet wine … but Rebecca's kiss is like heavenly musk of which only the blessed may partake, and those who partake thereof *are* blessed." Through the enlightened Mukhtar, Jókai dismissed the notion that Jews such as Rebecca exerted undue influence, directing his readers' attention to her moral fiber and biblical roots.[21]

That Jókai set this scene in the Ottoman Empire, moreover, is especially important in this regard. As they were for other nineteenth-century Hungarian writers, the early stages of Jókai's literary career were marked by the impediments imposed by Habsburg censorship. The latter often forced Hungarian writers to mask their subject matter by setting it in a different time or place. For Jókai, this meant, inter alia, disguising comments regarding the intrusiveness of Habsburg politics in Hungary as narratives regarding the Ottoman Turks, who intruded into Hungarian politics two centuries earlier. In this case, one might suggest that the perceived influence of "Jewish damsels" like Rebecca on the Ottoman court may have been a masked allusion to the putative influence of Salon Jewesses in Vienna on the members of the Habsburg regime. By repudiating the claim that Rebecca exerted undue influence, therefore, Jókai challenged the assertion of undue Jewish influence in Vienna.[22]

Jókai observed, moreover, that narrow-minded Christians, while acknowledging the Jews' indispensable role in city life, blamed the Jews for taking advantage of good Christian burghers. In one novel, set in seventeenth-century Hamburg, Jókai engaged claims regarding the deleterious impact that Jewish businessmen, the archetypical transformers of urban and commercial life, had on ordinary individuals.[23] Jókai described a conversation between Herr Mayer, the "stodgy, narrow-minded" Christian burgher, and

[20] Jókai, *Janicsárok végnapjai* [The last days of the Janissaries], trans. R. Nisbet Bain (London: Jarrold & Sons, 1897), 20.
[21] Ibid. (italics added).
[22] On the Salon Jewesses and their putative influence on Habsburg politics, see Salo Baron, *Die Judenfrage auf der Wiener Kongress* (Vienna: Löwit, 1920), 117ff.
[23] *Egy Hirdetett Kalandar a XVII Században* [A published calender in the seventeenth century] (Budapest, 1879).

his more progressively minded son. Upon hearing of his son's interest in cultivating a commercial relationship with Jews in Hamburg, the simple-minded Herr Mayer attempts to dissuade him by claiming that the Jews take unfair advantage of the Christian denizens of the city. Not realizing that he is professing his own simplemindedness and gullibility, Herr Mayer explains that Jews naturally take advantage of less sophisticated Christians: "As a rule, calves appear in towns where power is monopolized by Jews.... As everyone knows, the calf is the tamest and most innocent of creatures in the world so it never seemed plausible for someone to assail them, let alone the entire city to maltreat them." In particular, Herr Mayer attributes the rising Jewish presence in Hamburg to the influx of unusually skilled and crafty Jews from Spain:

"Jews are immigrating to Hamburg in droves from Spain ... and once here ruin every respectable merchant by acquiring goods for a trifle in a mysterious way and then trading in clipped gold.... my dear boy, must you enter the Jewish quarter.... You don't know, my son, what a calf is. It is a dreadful beast that wreaks havoc since the Jews arrived. Calves are animals and so are Jews. But these Spanish Jews are well-versed in all sorts of art, and have figured out how to make a cruel beast out of a little calf by giving it milk with human blood to drink."[24]

Nonetheless, Herr Mayer's son is undeterred. He proceeds to the Jewish quarter and ultimately flourishes. Herr Mayer, trapped by his outmoded fear of Jews, stagnates. Thus Jókai lampoons how a a fear of difference and of change precludes the elder Herr Mayer from recognizing in the Jews anything other than a menace – even in the face of the clear benefits that he himself could reap from welcoming Jews.

Yet Jókai's perhaps most profound satirizing of a Christian sense of inferiority to Jews appears in his *Red Starosta*. Set in eighteenth-century Poland, this story of intrigue among Polish nobles begins with two nobles recalling a tale widely believed by the Polish populace and even by much of the Polish nobility. This tale begins in conventional fashion, describing the commercial relationship between Jews and their magnate benefactors:

In the days of the Red Starosta, the Jews had great influence in the Grodno District; indeed, it would be difficult to imagine Poland without them. Bialystok was their headquarters and there they had their synagogue. The Starostas allowed them to multiply and get rich, just as a highly practical agriculturist allows the bees to collect their stores throughout the summer, and when the autumn winds begin to blow does not treat them after the manner of ungrateful and unreasonable bee-keepers, who smoke out the industrious insects with sulphur; no, but in the most approved modern fashion he subtracts the honey, leaves the bees just enough to live on, and then puts back the empty cells into the hive that the bees may fill them

---

[24] Jókai, *Egy Hirdetett Kalandar a XVII Században*, 141.

again. The bees themselves regard this method as perfectly normal, for otherwise
they would leave the hive and go into the forest and fill the stumps of trees with
honey. But then the bears would eat them and so, after all, it is much better for the
bees to have to contend with the bee-keepers.

By comparing the relationship between Polish magnates and their Jewish
commercial partners to a symbiosis between bees and a beekeeper, Jókai
underlines the equally useful relationship between Jewry and nobility in
Hungary. The bear, moreover, can be seen as representing how the auto-
cratic rule of the tsarist regime disrupted what had been a functional
relationship between Jewry and aristocracy in Poland. By holding the
Habsburgs' similar intentions at bay, Hungarian magnates and Jews preserved their healthy symbiosis.

At this point, the tale caricatures what some Poles believed to be the
political implications of this commercial relationship, namely, the belief
that Polish Jews used magical silver coins, which were among those Judas
received to betray Jesus, to manipulate the succession of the Red Starostsa,
a princely dynasty whose capital was in Bialystok.[25]

THE JEW AS ORDINARY PERSON

For Jókai, then, the willingness of non-Jews to grant Jews influence engendered a contempt for them born of fear and a sense of inferiority. Not
surprisingly, Jókai regarded the antidote to this contempt to be the notion
that Jews were, external appearances notwithstanding, part of the universal brotherhood of man. This ecumenical view, powerfully instilled in
him by his mother, had quelled the young Jókai's fear of Koricsaner. His
newfound friendship with Koricsaner, though, had opened his eyes to the
possibility that Jews were not fundamentally different from Christians.
Jókai believed that a similar understanding of Jews would quell this fear in
others. He even voiced this outlook using a literary version of his mother.
Szomoru Napok [Sorrowful days] is set during the surge of animosity against
Jewish tavern keepers that swept across northeastern Hungary during the
cholera epidemic of 1831. At that time, there was a prevailing suspicion
among peasants that the epidemic had been caused, among other things,
by Jewish distillers, who were dispensing "elixirs of madness" to unsuspect-
ing peasants.[26] Jókai's literary account of this episode includes a description of this anti-Jewish animus:

Some hundreds of peasants, the dregs of the agricultural population, were swarm-
ing in and out of the tavern door, savagely singing and shouting. ... A white-bearded
Jew had been tied to the leg of a chair placed between two casks. The drunken mob

[25] Jókai, "*Starosta*," *Összes Művei*, 81, 26ff.
[26] Lupovitch, *Jews at the Crossroads*, 114ff.

was paying attention mainly to him, and pulling out his beard hair by hair as they interrogated him.[27]

Jókai contrasts the chivalry of the Jewish victim with the depravity of the mob: "The tortured victim … would not answer his assayers, except with a periodic plea to spare his innocent daughter." From his own venomous assault on an innocent Jew as a child, Jókai describes the Jewish tavern keeper's daughter, "a childish shape … lying across the doorway, being kicked by all who exited or entered. Fortunately, she felt nothing now."[28]

Appropriately, perhaps, the author contrasts the fanatical behavior of the mob with the sympathy for the Jew evinced by Maria, a Polish noblewoman on horseback disguised as a nobleman, who happened to be riding by. Reminiscent of his mother's intervention on behalf of Koricsaner, Jókai describes Maria's courageous attempt to check the cruel actions of the mob: "Maria, full of indignation, spurred her horse right into the midst of the mob that was tormenting the old innkeeper, and exclaimed in a voice of virile assurance, 'What are you all doing here?'" In response to a young lout who claimed, seemingly by rote, that "the gentry got the Jews to put poison in the brandy," Maria notes how the same peasants who presumed the brandy was poison "went on drinking out of the barrel as if they had made up their minds to discover what poison really tasted like." Jókai thus inverted the negative image of the Jewish tavern keeper, stereotypically presented as the bane of the peasantry, into an innocent and honorable victim of the peasantry's destructive behavior. At the same time, Jókai refashioned the alliance between Jew and noble from a conspiracy against the best interests of ordinary peasants into a conflict between human decency and the vulgarity of a Hungarian mob.

In this sense, Jókai built on a foundation that Eötvös had already laid in humanizing the Jews. In *A Falu Jegyzője* [The village notary] Eötvös had created an unforgivably despicable Jewish character named Jancsi the Glazier – a composite of seemingly every pejorative Jewish stereotype. In addition, Jancsi is the main accomplice of the novels's antagonist and winds up in prison. Toward the end of the novel, however, Eötvös exonerates Jancsi by attributing his depraved character and hostility to the protagonist to the corruption of the Hungarian nobility:

He was a Jew; that one word tells his whole history. Born to be a sharer in the distress of his family, brought up to suffer from the injustice of the masses, cast loose upon the world, not to be free but abandoned; struggling for his daily bread, not by honest labor, for that is forbidden to a Jew, but by trickery and cunning; crawling on the earth like a worm which any body may tread upon and crush; hated,

[27] *Szomurú Napok* (Budapest: Akadémiai Kiadó, 1963), 19.
[28] Ibid., 20.

hunted, persecuted, scouted; such was his past. Such are the sufferings common to the Jews in Hungary.[29]

Jancsi, therefore, winds up not as a villain but as a sympathetic victim of a crime he was powerless to prevent or avoid. In this way, Eötvös contrasts the contemptible characteristics of Hungarian Jews with the corrupt character of the Hungarian nobility and finds the nobility to be far more in need of reform than the Jews.

Jókai echoed Eötvös's condemnation of noble corruption and its deleterious effects on Hungarian Jews. In *Nincsen ördög* [There is no devil] Jókai described an impoverished Jew in the throes of death during a local election. As the man lay dying, a local noble locked in a very close race offers him a large bribe in exchange for his ill-gotten vote and has the man taken to the voting booth literally on his deathbed:

This poor fellow had a fortune at his call, for he could bequeath to his family 1,000 forints which they were willing to pay for his vote. All his life he had been as honest as he was poor. … He stared vacantly into their faces when they offered him this enormous sum of ready money, while his wife and children broke into a howl of despair that the offer had not come earlier, for how could a dying man leave his bed to vote? But my drummers were not to be beaten. They hastened the bed with the sufferer in it to the voting tent. … With a last look of sorrow and affection at his wife, he sighed with his dying breath "you, my love" and died.[30]

Like Eötvös's Jancsi, Jókai allows this Jew to die honorably while lampooning the dishonorable behavior of the nobles.

Jókai, though, added a measure of effectiveness and subtlety to Eötvös' humanizing of the Jews. He portrayed Jews not only as human beings but as ordinary human beings, that is, neither heroic nor tragic. This was apparent in two of his characters: Solomon the proprietor of a novelty store in *A Kőszivű ember fiai* [The sons of the hard-hearted man] and the unnamed Polish Jew in *Nincsen ördög*.

Solomon encounters the protagonist – one of the title characters, Richard Baradlay – who enters his shop to reclaim a portrait that had inadvertently been sold to the Jewish proprietor. From the outset of this scene, Jókai upends the stereotype of the Jewish shopkeeper by contrasting the Jew's external appearance with his inner character. "But the most ancient and curious object in the whole shop was its owner, who sat in a big leather armchair, wrapped in a long caftan, fur shoes on his feet and a fur cap tilted over his eyes." Solomon looks like a typical Jew of nineteenth-century Hungary.

[29] József Eötvös, *The Village Notary; a Romance of Hungarian Life*, trans. Otto Wenckstern (London, 1850), 145.
[30] Jókai, *Nincsen Ördög* [There is no devil] (Budapest: Adakémiai Kiadó, 1967), 23.

As the conversation between Solomon and the young noble unfolds, it is clear that the Jew is not only selling novelties, but dispensing wisdom. When Baradlay asks how Solomon knew his customer had come in to sell his former fiancé's portrait, Solomon proceeds to advise the young man in the delicate matters of love and romance: "You see, young people have a way of falling in love and then falling out again. They hang a portrait over their bed, and presently their taste changes and another takes its place. Then when a young gentleman wishes to marry, he finds it inadvisable to keep a lot of strange portraits in his house." When Baradlay asks him to be discreet about their transaction, Solomon then leaves no doubt as to his honorable character. "Oh captain, Solomon never does that sort of thing; he always does what is right and just.... He is no extortioner.... Solomon knows the history of all these things, but he never breathes a word to any mortal soul." Jókai thus refashioned the biblical Solomon the wise as an equally wise and honorable caftan-clad Jewish shopkeeper.

In *Nincsen ördög*, Jókai juxtaposes the seemingly superstitious and unusual image of religious behavior of Jews with the very human character of Jews in the face of tragedy. An early scene in this novel takes place at the site of a train wreck in which most of the passengers were killed or unaccounted for. Among those on the station platform who had been awaiting passengers was a Polish Jew. Jókai's description of this man begins with a caricature of traditional Jewish prayer: "An aged Polish Jew lay across the barricade wall. His two hands were stretched downward, and there he muttered the prayers and invocations of his ancient liturgy, which no one there understood but himself and his God. The ritual prayer-bands were upon his thumbs and wrists, and encircling his forehead. His forked beard and greasy side-locks dangled as he chanted his hymns."[31]

Abruptly, Jókai makes it clear that beneath an odd ritual is a man desperately concerned for the welfare of his family: "His eyes, almost popping out of their sockets, were fixed upon one of the carriages. What did that car contain? His wife? His children? Or his worldly goods, the fortune hoarded up through a lifetime of cunning and privation?" Here again, Jókai juxtaposes the outward character of a Jew's life – cunning and privation – with the Jew's very human inner emotional universe. Suddenly the Jew's prayers do not seem so foreign or out of place. His worries are shared by everyone else on the platform: "He chants his prayers, yelling loudly, or muttering low as the ghastly scene before him vanishes in smoke and darkness, or glows out again in dreadful distinctness.... All those frightened, maddened, running, crouching, creeping men and women around, with the chanting Jew, in his long silken caftan and dangling locks in the midst of them, made a picture of terrible sublimity." Amidst a frantic crowd of people, each reacting in his own way to a tragic event, the Jew is hardly distinct.

[31] Ibid., 20.

In the end, the Jew's prayers to rescue his family are no less futile than the desperate actions of the others on the platform:

> No one remained but the Polish Jew. He did not move away. He had risen to his knees on the barricade wall, and his hands, with their prayer-bands, were uplifted to heaven. Louder and louder he chanted his hymns, raising his voice above the thundering roar of the crackling fire, the rolling stones and the last despairing cries of the doomed ones. The fur cap on his head, his forked beard and dangling locks were singed by the falling cinders … yet he chanted on. But when he saw at last that his prayer was in vain, all at once he sprang up, and seemed to strike at the flames with both palms then, spitting into the fire "psha" he fell down senseless. … Who and where is that awful deity into whose altarfire that conjuring Jew had spat, because he would not listen to his invocation?[32]

By emphasizing the ordinariness of Jews, Jókai freed himself from having to explain away the foibles of Jews as the result of some other group's depravity or folly, as Eötvös had. Rather, Jókai embraced these foibles as part of the Jews' character. This allowed him to underline the plain human virtue of his Jewish characters, by downgrading what others regarded as the overriding importance of Jewish particularism.

Having differentiated between the external and internal dimensions of Jewish identity, Jókai envisioned a Jew who exemplified the seamless interplay between Jewishness and humanness: Bar Noémi. Along with Solomon in *Zsidó fiu*, Bar Noémi was exceptional among Jókai's Jewish characters insofar as he was the main character and not a supporting character who helps the main character find resolution. Indeed, in tandem Solomon and Bar Noémi delineate bookends in Jókai's attitude toward Jews. In Solomon, Jókai took a first step toward positing that Jews could be included in the larger camaraderie of humanity and Hungarianness (Magyarság) without ceding Jewish identity or distinctness. In *Bar Noémi*, Jókai argued that the virtues of Jewish Magyars, and the challenges they faced, were virtually identical to those faced by all Magyars.

Jókai's Bar Noémi lived during the biblical age of the Judges. As Jókai describes at the beginning of *City of the Beast*, Bar Noémi was "one of the few survivors of those Benjaminites who had been extirpated together with their city by the men of the other eleven tribes to avenge the dishonor done to a single woman."[33] He lived "in the days when Tyre still stood in all her glory and her merchant vessels left not even the East Indies unexplored." Bar Noémi was thus the biblical antecedent of nineteenth-century Hungarian Jews: the primordial wandering Jewish merchant in exile.

In Bar Noémi, Jókai refashioned this widely disparaged image of nineteenth-century Jews in a heroic form. Bar Noémi was an amalgam of the strongest virtues of Odysseus and the Rothschilds, woven together with

[32] Ibid., 26.
[33] A reference to Judges 19.

the faith of Job in the face of persecution. While living in the heart of the cosmopolitan world of international trade, Bar Noémi "cleaved strictly to the traditions of Holy Zion even in the midst of the city of delights." As he and his maritime entourage embark on a commercial venture to a distant heretofore-unexplored land, Bar Noémi encounters a series of challenges and adversaries. Like Solomon in *Zsidó fiu*, Bar Noémi refuses to abandon his faith. As with Jókai's other Jewish characters, the fact that Bar Noémi is a wandering merchant is incidental to the story. Instead, his unwavering commitment to his faith and his origins is what defines him. This was the virtue that Jókai regarded as the common heritage of Jews and Magyars, and an incontrovertible illustration of the compatibility between Jewish and Magyar identity. As Béla Bernstein noted more than eighty years ago: "Unbelief reduces people to dust and makes them spiritless slaves to material things; [Bar Noémi's] belief elevates mortals to heaven and sanctifies the unsuccessful into heroes."[34]

Given Bar Noémi's steadfast devotion to his Jewish faith, one might assume that Bar Noémi embodied Jewish separateness and particularism, living apart from other peoples. Perhaps anticipating this conclusion, Jókai provided Bar Noémi with a non-Jewish wife, Bessenia. Not only does she accompany Bar Noémi on all of his adventures, she provides him with wisdom at key moments of indecision, and strength at moments when his fortitude wavers. Thus Jókai reconfigures the wisdom that travels from Solomon to Richard Baradlay into a two-way flow of wisdom between Magyars who are Jews and those who are non-Jews. By the end of the novella, Jókai has fashioned the archtypical Magyar of the Jewish faith. Bar Noémi is fully and equally committed to his Jewish faith and to his non-Jewish wife and fellow travelers. Jókai regarded Hungarian Jews as fully and equally committed to the needs – individual and collective – of Jews and Magyars. Moreover, Jókai regarded this mentality not simply as an ideal that should eventually be cultivated among the Magyars and non-Magyars, but as an aim that the Hungarian state was well on its way toward achieving. In this sense, Hungarian Jews were no different from other Magyars – on the contrary, they typified the way that the ethnic and religious diversity of Hungarian society did not preclude the possibility of the members of these various faiths and ethnicities sharing a common Magyar culture.

Within a generation after Jókai's death, the rapprochement he envisioned and advocated during his career as novelist and political activist began to unravel. The radical transformation of Hungary after World War I and the concomitant rapid rise of antisemitism rendered Jókai's camaraderie with Jews a vestige of a bygone age. At the same time, however, Jókai's legacy persevered through the decades of systemic antisemitism in

[34] Béla Bernstein, *Jókai és a zsidók* [Jókai and the Jews] (Budapest, 1925), 14.

interwar Hungary, and, perhaps more remarkably, through the limitations placed on Jewish expression in communist Hungary.

In this sense, the dramatic resurgence of Hungarian Jewry since the 1990s following the collapse of communism marked a return to the pre–World War I world that Jókai lauded. This resurgence reflected not only the repressed vitality of Hungarian Jewry's Jewish identity, but also its strong affinity for Magyar culture. Rather than abandon their country and culture for Israel or the United States, thousands of Hungarian Jews opted to remain in Hungary and to help reinvigorate the seamlessly hyphenated Magyar-Jewish identity of their grandparents and great-grandparents. Jókai's belief in the inexorable and intimate link between and *Zsidóság* (Jewishness) and *Magyarság* (Magyarness) perhaps found its way from the pre–World War past into the twenty-first century.

PART III

THE CULTURAL POLITICS OF PHILOSEMITISM IN VICTORIAN BRITAIN AND IMPERIAL GERMANY

7

Bad Jew/Good Jewess

Gender and Semitic Discourse in Nineteenth-Century England

Nadia Valman

Nineteenth-century literary culture has, in recent years, proved a rich resource for antisemitism studies. From the satanic imagery with which Dickens surrounds his Jewish archcriminal Fagin to Trollope's suspicion of assimilated arrivistes to the racial terror invoked by Bram Stoker's Dracula at the fin de siècle, research has uncovered the persistent threads of hostility to Jews that found expression in novels.[1] And thanks to the work of Sander Gilman, we also know how widely discourses of the diseased and degenerate Jewish body were disseminated through medical and sociological as well as literary texts in the period.[2] What is equally striking about this scholarship, however, is its almost universal assumption that "the Jew" in the text is male. When Todd Endelman writes, for example, that the

---

[1] Juliet Steyn, "The Figuration of a Type: Fagin as Sign," in *The Jew: Assumptions of Identity* (London: Cassell, 1999), 42–58; Bryan Cheyette, *Constructions of "the Jew" in English Literature and Society: Racial Representations, 1875–1945* (Cambridge: Cambridge University Press, 1993), 23–42; Michael Ragussis, *Figures of Conversion: "The Jewish Question" and English National Identity* (Durham, NC: Duke University Press, 1995), 234–60; Judith Halberstam, "Technologies of Monstrosity: Bram Stoker's *Dracula*," in Sally Ledger and Scott McCracken, eds., *Cultural Politics at the Fin de Siècle* (Cambridge: Cambridge University Press, 1995), 248–66; H. L. Malchow, "Vampire Gothic and Late-Victorian Identity," in *Gothic Images of Race in Nineteenth-Century Britain* (Stanford, CA: Stanford University Press, 1996), 124–66; Jonathan Freedman, "The Temple of Culture and the Market for Letters: The Jew and the Way We Write Now," in *The Temple of Culture: Assimilation and Anti-Semitism in Literary Anglo-America* (Oxford: Oxford University Press, 2000), 55–88; Carol Margaret Davison, "Britain, Vampire Empire: Fin-de-Siècle Fears and Bram Stoker's *Dracula*," in *Anti-Semitism and British Gothic Literature* (Basingstoke, UK: Palgrave Macmillan, 2004), 120–57; Diane Long Hoeveler, "Charlotte Dacre's Zofloya: The Gothic Demonization of the Jew," in Sheila A. Spector, ed., *The Jews and British Romanticism: Politics, Religion, Culture* (New York: Palgrave Macmillan, 2005), 165–78.

[2] Sander L. Gilman, *The Jew's Body* (New York and London: Routledge, 1991); also see Gilman's *Freud, Race and Gender* (Princeton, NJ: Princeton University Press, 1993), and *Jewish Self-Hatred: Anti-Semitism and the Hidden Language of the Jews* (Baltimore: Johns Hopkins University Press, 1986).

intellectual arsenal of European antisemitism can be reduced to "a handful of accusations about Jewish character and behavior: Jews are malevolent, aggressive, sinister, self-seeking, avaricious, destructive, socially clannish, spiritually retrograde, physically disagreeable, and sexually overcharged,"[3] the Jew in such descriptions is implicitly masculine. Perceptions of Jews, indeed, are frequently seen as projections of anxieties about masculinity. As Gilman writes in *The Jew's Body*, his focus is on "an image crucial to the very understanding of the Western image of the Jew at least since the advent of Christianity": "the male Jew, the body with the circumcised penis."[4] Where the Jewish woman *has* been the object of study, masculinity has still been the focus. Recent studies of Sarah Bernhardt, for example, have been interested in the ways that her business acumen and her Jewishness were linked to cast her as a masculinised figure.[5] In a different context, Riv-Ellen Prell's work on the image of the Jewish mother in modern American popular and literary culture argues that male anxieties about affluence and consumption in postwar America were projected onto the demonized figure of the domineering, emasculating Jewish mother.[6] In reiterating the link between antisemitism and various historical crises of masculinity in this way, Jewish cultural studies has tended not only to occlude relationships between femininity and Jewishness but also to elide the various and specific cultural contexts in which representations of Jews were produced.

Looking more closely at the case of England in the period, however, a different picture emerges. While it is certainly the case that a number of literary texts include or even center on figures of male Jews who are racially repellent, socially intrusive, or politically subversive, these figures

[3] Todd Endelman, "Comparative Perspectives on Modern Anti-Semitism in the West," in David Berger, ed., *History and Hate: The Dimensions of Anti-Semitism* (Philadelphia: Jewish Publication Society, 1986), 95–114 (95).

[4] Gilman, *Jew's Body*, 5. On discourses surrounding male Jews in nineteenth-century culture see also Daniel Pick, *Svengali's Web: The Alien Enchanter in Modern Culture* (New Haven, CT, and London: Yale University Press, 2000). On the figure of the male Jew in the long eighteenth century, see Frank Felsenstein, *Anti-Semitic Stereotypes: A Paradigm of Otherness in English Popular Culture, 1660–1830* (Baltimore and London: Johns Hopkins University Press, 1995). Work in queer Jewish studies is also predominantly focused on Jewish masculinity; see, for example, Daniel Boyarin, Daniel Itzkovitz, and Ann Pellegrini, eds, *Queer Theory and the Jewish Question* (New York: Columbia University Press, 2004), and Marjorie Garber, *Vested Interests: Cross-Dressing and Cultural Anxiety* (London: Penguin, 1993), 224–33.

[5] Sander L. Gilman, "Salome, Syphilis, Sarah Bernhardt, and the 'Modern Jewess,'" in *Love + Marriage = Death* (Stanford, CA: Stanford University Press, 1998), 65–90; Ann Pellegrini, *Performance Anxieties: Staging Psychoanalysis, Staging Race* (New York: Routledge, 1997), 17–47.

[6] Riv-Ellen Prell, *Fighting to Become Americans: Jews, Gender, and the Anxiety of Assimilation* (Boston: Beacon Press, 1999), 142–76; see also Joyce Antler, *You Never Call! You Never Write! A History of the Jewish Mother* (Oxford: Oxford University Press, 2007), 73–147.

are repeatedly shadowed by images of Jewish women that are in every way the opposite. Sander Gilman's analysis of the European culture of anti-semitism does not account for this more complex configuration. Closer, perhaps, are studies of the dangerously alluring *belle juive*, the stereotype of exotic sensuality and tragic self-sacrifice that haunted nineteenth-century French and German literature. This figure has invariably been read through the lens of Saidian Orientalism as an allegory that naturalizes the political subjugation or social exclusion of Jews.[7] But in English literary culture the Jewess was idealized rather than exoticized, a model for rather than a foil to bourgeois femininity. Yet scholars have been so eager to uncover instances of antisemitism in English culture that they have all but ignored this crucial aspect of semitic representation. What I want to explore here is the flourishing in nineteenth-century middle-class culture of the figure of the virtuous Jewess and in particular to account for her presence in two of the most critically acclaimed and influential novels of the mid-Victorian period.[8]

REASON AND SPIRIT

The origins of the representation of the Jewish woman in English culture have recently been explored in Michelle Ephraim's work on early modern drama, which links the Jewess to the assertion of Protestant identity in Elizabethan England. The Jewess on the Elizabethan stage, argues Ephraim, was a figure for the Hebrew Bible, newly being claimed as the authentic foundation of Protestant meaning although also, at the same time, perceived as an ambiguous, unstable text.[9] The ambivalent philosemitism that is central to Protestantism was also the source for the emergence in the literary culture of early Victorian evangelicalism of the image of the good Jewess. In evangelical theology, the Jews were accorded a uniquely privileged status, and evangelical approaches to the Jews were marked with a peculiar intensity and ambivalence.[10] Reviving the ideology of

7 On German literature, see Florian Krobb, "'La Belle Juive': 'Cunning in the Men and Beauty in the Women,'" *Jewish Quarterly* 147 (Autumn 1992): 5–11; Jefferson Chase, "The Wandering Court Jew and the Hand of God: Wilhelm Hauff's *Jud Süss* as Historical Fiction," *Modern Language Review* 93, no. 3 (July 1998): 724–40, esp. 731–4; on French literature, see Carole Ockman, "'Two Eyebrows à l'Orientale': Ethnic Stereotyping in Ingres's *Baronne de Rothschild*," *Art History* 14, no. 4 (1991): 521–39.
8 For an extended study, see Nadia Valman, *The Jewess in Nineteenth-Century British Literary Culture* (Cambridge: Cambridge University Press, 2007).
9 Michelle Ephraim, *Reading the Jewish Woman on the Elizabethan Stage* (Aldershot, UK: Ashgate, 2008), 4–5.
10 Mel Scult, *Millennial Expectations and Jewish Liberties: A Study of the Efforts to Convert the Jews in Britain, up to the Mid Nineteenth Century* (Leiden: E. J. Brill, 1978); Michael Ragussis, *Figures of Conversion: "The Jewish Question" and English National Identity* (Durham, NC, and London: Duke University Press, 1995).

seventeenth-century millennialism, English evangelicals stressed not the rupture between Christianity and Judaism, but their identification with God's Chosen People and especially its Bible. Writers often invoked the familial relationship between Christians and Jews, who, it was said, were "kindred, 'as concerning the flesh' of the Saviour himself" or "God's peculiar family."[11] This affection, however, coincided with a severe critique of Judaism as archaic, law-bound, and materialist. Rapprochement with Jews was sought, then, with a view to their conversion, which evangelicals pursued with indefatigable vigor. Increasingly preoccupied with eschatological studies, evangelicals also saw the conversion of the Jews as a crucial step in hastening the Second Coming of Christ; England, with its history of tolerance rather than persecution, had a special role to play in this project. An often explicit anti-Catholic subtext to evangelical discussion of Jews sought to ascribe the advent of an expansive Christianity to the Protestant Reformation, and a uniquely tolerant atmosphere to modern England.

Evangelical ambivalence with regard to the Jews had a rhetorical analog in their ideology of gender. While men were regarded as inherently sinful and sullied by their contact with the world of work, the figure of the domestic woman was highly venerated. The evangelical emphasis on the humanity of Christ, his sacrifice in the atonement, his meekness and humility brought women into closer identification with his mission. Women, who must needs submit to duty, could thereby emulate Christ's sacrifice and wield his redemptive power.[12] Evangelicalism prescribed an exalted role for women through their influence on the public sphere; the emotionalism attributed to women brought them closer to God and to a more powerful embodiment of the evangelical appeal, and their inherent moral superiority conferred on them a key position in the crusade for national regeneration.[13] The evangelical notion of the "religion of the heart" – that is, easily accessible to the theologically unsophisticated – was also implicitly a feminized religion.

In the 1830s and 1840s writing on the Jews, especially by evangelical women, proliferated, aimed at a female readership and often focused on the figure of the Jewess. In countless narrative fantasies about the Jews' desire for conversion, the Jewess appeared as inherently spiritual and ardent, and also particularly oppressed by the archaic Jewish legal code – calling out for aid to her Christian sisters. In these texts, therefore, the

---

[11] Unsigned review of "The Spirit of Judaism" by Grace Aguilar, *Jewish Herald* 2 (February 1847): 31; Charlotte Elizabeth [Tonna], "The Jewish Press," *Christian Lady's Magazine* 18 (August 1842): 143.

[12] Jane Rendall, *The Origins of Modern Feminism: Women in Britain, France and the United States 1780–1860* (Basingstoke, UK: Macmillan, 1985), 76–7.

[13] Ibid., 74; Catherine Hall, "The Early Formation of Victorian Domestic Ideology," in *White, Male and Middle Class* (Cambridge: Polity Press, 1992), 75–93.

theological problem posed by the Jews' simultaneous proximity to and distinctiveness from Christianity is metonymically resolved by the figure of the Jewess who longs for conversion. In this example from the conversion novel *The Orphans of Lissau* (1830), the Jews' double potential for obduracy and salvation is explicitly projected onto gender difference. The author clearly differentiates the physical and psychological characteristics of two Jewish children:

> Seldom had two lovelier infants been seen, though in person and disposition entirely dissimilar. The strongly marked, animated features, and sparkling black eyes of Raphael, were indicative of that spirit and energy which afterwards characterised him, and had already begun to develope [*sic*] itself. Gertrude was unusually fair and delicate, with pale auburn hair, and soft blue eyes; contrasting strongly with the dark and vivacious character usual to Jewish female beauty. In manner, she was gentle, retiring, and thoughtful, even to melancholy; and her light and noiseless step, as she glided about the house, seemed to make the wild, riotous, bounding of Raphael more conspicuous.[14]

Here, the Jewish male is energetic and disruptive while the female is submissive and introspective. She blends in with her environment rather than standing out from it. The blue eyes of the Jewess are contrasted with the impenetrable black eyes of the Jewish boy; Gertrude's body and temperament (and Teutonic rather than Hebrew name) anticipate her destiny as a Christian proselyte. This gendered bifurcation of the figure of the Jew characteristically structures conversion literature. While the texts point repeatedly to the Jews as a troublesome and resistant presence, at the same time they also invariably draw on the virtues ascribed to women to insist on the redeemable nature of the Jews.

Conversion narratives also mapped the distinction between false and true piety onto gender. In a letter from a converted male Jew published in the evangelical periodical the *Christian Lady's Friend and Family Repository* in 1832 the narrator describes how his religious doubt was inaugurated by contemplating the irrational pedantry of Jewish law. When he began to read the New Testament, he "compared it with Moses and the prophets, and found that they corresponded in every respect"; eventually he came to the logical decision "that the Christian religion must be the best, because it is generally professed by all civilized nations." The rest of the letter labors to disprove this motive for conversion: "I found afterwards that it is not by philosophy and reasoning that a man is converted, or that water baptizes him; it is the grace of God which converts a sinner, and the Holy Ghost which baptizes him." The narrator describes how, in a moment of

---

[14] [Amelia Bristow], *The Orphans of Lissau, and Other Interesting Narratives, Immediately Concerned with Jewish Customs, Domestic and Religious, with Explanatory Notes. By the author of "Sophia de Lissau," "Emma de Lissau," &c.* (London: T. Gardiner and Son, 1830), 24–5.

destitution and despair, "involuntarily as it seemed, I called on the name of the Redeemer, to strengthen me by his example of humility and patience, which he gave us while he walked in this world." It was only through a spontaneous, nonrational, and submissive need that the narrator realized his conversion had been confirmed.[15]

The unhealthy masculine reasoning that had impeded the ascent of this Jew's soul is absent in evangelical accounts of the proselytizing of Jewish women. Such accounts emphasize the spiritual and affective components of religion that persuade unencumbered by argumentative proofs. A typical narrative tells of a Jewish banker's daughter, who converts to Christianity after her mother dies, when the words of the New Testament are the only "consolation" for her.[16] A letter to the *Jewish Herald* in 1849 contained the narrative of "Mrs D.," a woman who had been brought up in the Jewish religion. Later in life she "became the subject of many great and sore troubles, and being ignorant of the only way to access to God, I was bowed down with continued sorrow." Her emotional yearning was only relieved on her meeting with "two young ladies" who "conversed with me on the all-important concerns of my never-dying soul."[17] Here, as in many other narratives, religion is shared between women and fulfills needs ascribed to them as women.

The trials of conversion, moreover, supplied an inherently novelistic narrative. Jewish conversion autobiographies supposedly authored by Jewish women were a particularly popular subgenre. The texts follow a strict formula, relating the spiritual rebellion of a Jewish daughter against her patriarchal family, her resistance to their attempts to force her into marriage, the persecutions she suffers as she courageously clings to her new-found faith, and ultimately her martyrdom. The story of "Leila Ada," for example, published posthumously in the 1850s in a series of books by her "editor," the Reverend Osborn W. Trenery Heighway, describe the heroine's disillusion with her religious education, which had been based on the Talmud, "an impure, stupid fabrication, composed by fallen and sinful man"; her increasingly "strong opinion that the advent of the Messiah is probably near"; and her instinctively "simple, devout reading, and study of Thy Holy Word, the New Testament."[18] In this narrative we see the typical evangelical emphasis on the authority of the individual in scripture reading and the high value placed on female suffering as a religious virtue. In conversion texts, the Jewish woman is represented as not only particularly susceptible

[15] J.L., "Letter from a Converted Jew to his Brethren in Prussian Poland," *Christian Lady's Friend and Family Repository* 1 (June 1832): 443–6.
[16] Unsigned review of "Thirza, or the Attractive Power of the Cross: From the German by Elizabeth Maria Lloyd," *Jewish Herald* 1 (March 1846): 54–9.
[17] "Intelligence: Letter from the Rev. T. Craig of Bocking," *Jewish Herald* 4 (July 1849): 182–3.
[18] Osborn W. Trenery Heighway, *Leila Ada, the Jewish Convert: An Authentic Memoir*, 3rd ed. (London: Partridge & Oakey, 1853), 14.

to conversion, but also particularly responsive to it. In Madame Brendlah's *Tales of a Jewess* (1838) the heroine reflects on her love for the Christian hero that "a time will come when William shall see that a despised Jewess can love with all the fervour of a Christian! Ah, far more sincere and devoted is the love of a Jewess!"[19] The exceptional ardor – and exceptional suffering – of the Jewess make her, in these texts, the more enthusiastic, and more authentic, Christian.

Conversion texts, like the voluntary societies from which they emanated, never achieved the goals of evangelization for which they ostensibly aimed. What they undoubtedly did effect, however, through their extraordinarily wide dissemination, was a deep and lasting influence on literary constructions of Jews, an influence that was to endure throughout the century in the writing of non-Jews and Jews alike. Moreover, by the mid-Victorian period the figure of the beautiful, virtuous, and self-sacrificing Jewess, and all that she symbolized, had entered the literary mainstream.

COMMERCE AND CULTURE

Although the evangelicals endowed them with enormous theological and rhetorical importance, Jews remained a tiny and materially insignificant fraction of the British population in the early Victorian years. By the 1860s and 1870s, by contrast, newly emancipated, they had become highly visible in public life. The dominant new figure in semitic discourse of the mid-Victorian period was the Jewish man of commerce. In the rapidly expanding London finance market of the 1860s and 1870s, the startling success of Jewish banking and stockbroking firms appeared to T. H. S. Escott, editor of the *Fortnightly Review*, as a barometer of social change: "English society once ruled by an aristocracy is now dominated by a plutocracy," he wrote. "And this plutocracy is to a large extent Hebraic in its composition. There is no phenomenon more noticeable in society than the ascendancy of the Jews."

Efforts to explain this ascendancy invoked the "essentially speculative" nature of the Jew and the "corporate cohesion that distinguishes his race"; both could be seen as antipathetic to the moral conduct of business.[20] This view was underlined by the government investigation into foreign loan schemes in the early 1870s, which reserved particular criticism for Bishoffsheim and Goldschmidt, the Jewish firm behind the notorious failed Honduras Inter-Oceanic Railway loan. Jewish commerce provides

[19] Madame Brendlah, *Tales of a Jewess: Illustrating the Domestic Manners and Customs of the Jews: Interspersed with Original Anecdotes of Napoleon* (London: Simpkin, Marshall and Co., 1838), 44.
[20] A Foreign Resident [T. H. S. Escott], *Society in London* (London, 1885), and *Truth*, March 21, 1878, 33, both cited in David Feldman, *Englishmen and Jews: Social Relations and Political Culture 1840–1914* (New Haven, CT: Yale University Press, 1994), 81.

a narrative for several key mid-Victorian novels, including Anthony
Trollope's *The Way We Live Now* (1875), which centers on a fraudulent
probably-Jewish railway loan-monger; it also lurks in the background of
George Eliot's *Daniel Deronda* (1876), the plot of which is precipitated by
a bank collapse, more specifically a (presumably Jewish) "Mr Lassman's
wicked recklessness, which they say was the cause of the failure."[21] For the
cultural critic Matthew Arnold, meanwhile, Judaism functioned in more
metaphorical terms, albeit invested with similar meanings. "Hebraism,"
according to his *Culture and Anarchy* (1868), the Puritan, individualistic, and pharisaical strain in British culture, had led, in the nineteenth
century, to "the growth of commercial immorality in our serious middle
class."[22] Rooted in Christian theology, the critique of Judaism as materialist and of the Jews as materialistic was reinvented for the age of rampant
capitalism.

Yet, insisted Arnold, there was hope. "The remedy is the same as that
which St. Paul employed" with the Jews who had lost sight of the spirit
of the law: "an importation of what we have called Hellenism into his
Hebraism, a making his consciousness flow freely round his petrified rule
of life and renew it."[23] Culture, or "Hellenism," could be a redemptive or
transformative force. The *Economist* employed similar terms in a leader
published in June 1875, which suggested that "by far the best check on
this intense vitality and recklessness of the commercial intelligence would
result from such wider culture as would give these men other keen intellectual interests as well as those which are identified with their occupations."[24]
The same dualism is also strikingly visible in novels of the period, in which
"these men" – figures of enterprising self-interest, frequently Jews – are
invariably shadowed by a Jewess. Texts cast the Hellenistic Jewess against
the Jew as a force of redemption, highlighting her persecution by her family, her affinity for culture rather than wealth, and her critique of Jewish
social and financial transgressions. This familiar story of the Jewess forms
a crucial narrative strand both in Trollope's tragedy of speculation and
(twice) in Eliot's meditation on the rival claims of art and nation. These
texts revitalize the philosemitic element in narratives about Jews and retell
in secular terms the conversion stories of the 1830s.

Suffused with nostalgia for the stability of feudal England, *The Way We
Live Now* is a sustained critique of the "newer and worse sort of world" in
which the power and property of the traditional aristocracy and gentry are

---

[21] George Eliot, *Daniel Deronda* (1876; repr., London: Penguin, 1995), 15–16. Further references to this edition will appear in the text.

[22] Matthew Arnold, *Culture and Anarchy* (1868; repr., Cambridge: Cambridge University Press,
1935), 159.

[23] Ibid., 160.

[24] *Economist,* June 19, 1875, 722–3.

increasingly reliant on the commercial class.[25] Trollope's irony lays bare the system that cynically benefits both: upper-class profligates have come to understand the marrying of an heiress as "an institution, like primogeniture … almost as serviceable for maintaining the proper order of things. Rank squanders money; trade makes it; – and then trade purchases rank by re-gilding its splendour" (2:59). As the ultimate source of stability – inherited land – is increasingly undermined, "an atmosphere … burdened with falsehood" prevails (1:132–3). Instead of inhabiting their appointed roles as the sons of the ruling class, Trollope's young aristocratic males talk their way into unlimited credit and then spend it philandering and gambling. The grotesque avatar of this way of living is Augustus Melmotte, the "Great Financier," a cosmopolitan parvenu whose rise and fall furnish the novel's plot. Melmotte is a supreme performer, whose ostentatious spending of wealth he does not possess is the sure route to further credit. Such speculation is frequently linked in Victorian fiction not only with undesirable social mobility but also with the threat of economic disorder that haunted the 1870s.[26] These concerns were particularly acute at the time of the novel's composition during the financial crisis of 1873, two years after the death of the "Railway Napoleon" and Conservative MP George Hudson and in the midst of the House of Commons Select Committee investigation into fraudulent loan schemes.

Symptomatic of the social disorder of *The Way We Live Now* is the perversion of feudal patriarchy in London society. The wife and daughters of the debt-ridden Mr. Longestaffe regard him as "their natural adversary," failing in his duty of protection (1:193). The novel is full of sisters and daughters rendered vulnerable by the reckless spending of their menfolk. This theme is emphasized with even greater force in the story of Marie, Melmotte's daughter. Marie is first seen dancing at her mother's ball with the reluctant Lord Buntingford, a potent symbol of the "bargain" between the impoverished aristocracy and Melmotte that guarantees their debts and his social entrée. Referred to throughout the novel by both her father and her suitors as "the girl" rather than by her name, Marie is relentlessly "trafficked for" by the avaricious young lords (1:107). Marrying Marie with an uncertain knowledge of her fortune becomes the key gamble of the novel; Sir Felix Carbury is considered "the favourite for the race," but he regards his suit as even more risky than a very dangerous game of cards, and when Melmotte demands his credentials feels himself "checkmated"

---

[25] Anthony Trollope, *The Way We Live Now*, 2 vols (1875; repr., Oxford: Oxford University Press, 1982), 1:71. Further references to this edition will appear in the text.

[26] J. Jeffrey Franklin, "The Victorian Discourse of Gambling: Speculations on *Middlemarch* and *The Duke's Children*," *ELH* 61 (1994): 899–921. For a comprehensive account of fictional representations of financial speculation see John R. Reed, "A Friend to Mammon: Speculation in Victorian Literature," *Victorian Studies* 42 (1999): 227–55.

and concludes that "the game was over" (1:87, 223, 223). While the traffic
in women is a theme in Trollope's other novels,[27] here it also has a particular resonance and provenance from earlier nineteenth-century literary
representations of the Jewess. If Melmotte's Jewish identity is uncertain,
it is nonetheless strongly suggested by his relationship with his daughter,
whose "destiny had no doubt been explained to her" – Marie's miserable
subjection suggesting the by-now-commonplace narrative of the Jewish
woman's helpless suffering (1:33).

As critics have noted, Marie Melmotte's willingness to elope with the
fortune that Melmotte has settled on her for safekeeping places her in the
role of Shakespeare's Jessica ruthlessly robbing her father of his ducats.[28]
Another intertext, however, is the evangelical novel. In her repeated insistence on her capacity for suffering, Marie is conceived within the terms
of early Victorian representations of the Jewess. Beginning her life poor
and illegitimate, she is long inured to "alternately capricious and indifferent" treatment by her father (1:107). Marie's acceptance of the suit of
the impoverished Sir Felix, however, liberates her from Melmotte's world
of material "magnificence," opening her mind to fantasies "which were
bright with art and love, rather than with gems and gold. The books
she read, poor though they generally were, left something bright on her
imagination" (1:107, 164). As with the heroine of conversion narrative,
Marie's liberation begins with texts. Similarly, if Marie's romance reading
has given her the means to oppose the prevailing ethos of acquisitiveness,
she expresses that "identity of her own" as an embattled devotion to her
lover: "She would be true to him! They might chop her in pieces! Yes; –
she had said it before, and she would say it again" (1:233, 473). Frequently
reiterating this signature refrain, Marie imagines self-assertion as bodily
martyrdom.

Yet Marie's enthusiasm for self-sacrifice becomes the crucial motor of
the novel's plot. At the height of his ascendancy, when "the world worshipped Mr. Melmotte," Marie alone expresses her dissent, disrupting
her father's power by refusing his arrangement to marry her to Lord
Nidderdale (1:331). In determining that "nobody shall manage this matter for me ... I know what I'm about now, and I won't marry anybody just
because it will suit papa" she is the only character in the novel to resist
Melmotte's control (1:382). In contrast to Longestaffe and Nidderdale,
who, on the brink of Melmotte's bankruptcy, are still persuaded by
the eloquence of his "false confessions" (2:239), Marie, clear-sightedly,
is unmoved by his rhetoric. As Robert Tracy argues, Melmotte's fall
occurs when he lays sacrilegious hands on the property that, throughout

[27] Franklin, "Victorian Discourse of Gambling," 906–7.
[28] Edgar Rosenberg, *From Shylock to Svengali: Jewish Stereotypes in English Fiction* (London: Peter
     Owen, 1961), 148–9.

Trollope's writing, stabilizes society.[29] But the novel also orchestrates the downfall of Melmotte as spiraling from Marie's climactic refusal to sign over her own fortune to honor the purchase, and thus save him from prosecution for fraud. Despite a cruel beating that leaves her wishing for death, she continues to defy the man her mother sees as "an awful being, powerful as Satan" (2:258). Not only does Marie reveal that, far from being "an absolutely passive instrument" of her father's will, "she had a will of her own," but, by disobeying Melmotte, she becomes the novel's only agent of virtue (1:275).

In the role of the rebellious Jewish daughter, then, Marie not only resists Jewish ambition, but redeems it. In contrast to her father's self-interested obfuscation of language, Marie's tenacious love for Felix is characterized by "a certain brightness of truth" (1:166). Yet Marie ultimately comes to accept her place in a preordained hierarchy and in doing so plays an important role in the novel's final restoration of social and sexual order. At the end of the novel, she humbly renounces her claim on the English aristocracy, thus both enacting the self-denying virtues associated with the traditional gentry and atoning for the excesses of her father. If, as Jonathan Freedman insightfully argues, Melmotte's "bulky Jewish body … metonymically symbolizes speculation – the swelling of money by illegitimate means,"[30] Marie's "little" body is its nemesis (1:32). Thus, Melmotte's hypermasculine appetency is counterbalanced by his daughter's feminine continence. As his former clerk comments: "He vas passionate, and did lose his 'ead; and vas blow'd up vid bigness.… 'E vas a great man; but the greater he grew he vas always less and less vise. 'E ate so much that he became too fat to see to eat his vittels.… But Ma'me'selle, – ah, she is different. She vill never eat too moch, but vill see to eat alvays" (2:449). In her future career as a "woman of business" with a perspicacious "strength in discovering truth and falsehood," the Jewess represents a redemptive, because restrained, Protestant kind of commerce (2:448).

Trollope's literary reinforcement of the values of feudal England in *The Way We Live Now*, then, is dependent on the figure of the Jewess. Marie Melmotte's willingness to be chopped into pieces by her father exposes the full horror of his violence against the domestic and social order and at the same time undermines it. Marie's romantic imagination combats Melmotte's amoral pragmatism; her ardor stands against his artifice. In the novel's conclusion, moreover, Marie directs her sacrificial inclinations toward England, recognizing her position as an "impostor" and voluntarily removing herself. (2:341) Redeeming Melmotte's cosmopolitan treachery, Marie, like her converting literary forebears, symbolically resolves the problem of the Jews.

---

[29] Robert Tracy, *Trollope's Later Novels* (Berkeley: University of California Press, 1978), 176.
[30] Freedman, *Temple of Culture*, 85.

COSMOPOLITANISM AND NATIONALITY

The imagination, resolution, and masochism of Trollope's Jewess are revived in another, more complex meditation on the corruptions of the 1870s, George Eliot's last novel, *Daniel Deronda* (1876). Here, Eliot brings into unexpected dialogue the parochial concerns of the privileged gentry with the nationalist aspirations of a group of poor East End Jews inspired by the rise of Italian nationalism. Moving between these two worlds in the course of the novel is the protagonist Deronda, a baronet's adoptee, whose shame about his unknown parentage has led to an inclination to sympathize with the suffering, and thence to an interest in the history of the Jews. Eliot's novel, like Trollope's, diagnoses decadence, anomie, and moral hypocrisy at the heart of the mid-Victorian ruling class. Unlike Trollope, however, Eliot posits Judaism as a corrective to these ills – "a noncombative, spiritually oriented nationhood," as Katherine Bailey Linehan describes it, "founded on racial separateness."[31] In the novel, this proposition is most explicitly articulated in a series of discussions between working men at the "Philosophers' Club" in a London tavern, and between Deronda and Mordecai Cohen, the consumptive mystic he encounters in Whitechapel. But it is also advanced, I will argue, through the contrasting life narratives of two Jewesses, the assimilated cosmopolitan Alcharisi and the religious nationalist Mirah Lapidoth. Eliot's philosemitism in *Daniel Deronda* was well recognised and much derided (from the 1876 *Saturday Review* to F. R. Leavis in 1948), but its theological and literary genealogy has been less well explored.[32] In her version of the story of the Jewess, Eliot, who famously scorned popular pious fiction as "Silly Novels by Lady Novelists," demonstrates striking debts to, as well as radical departures from, the tropes of evangelical writing.[33]

One of the key turning points in Deronda's Bildungsroman is his encounter with his previously unknown mother, who summons him to Genoa to tell him the story of her life and, to his astonishment, his true identity as a Jew. Now in the grip of terminal illness, Deronda's mother reveals herself as the Princess Halm-Eberstein, formerly the opera singer Leonora

[31] Katherine Bailey Linehan, "Mixed Politics: The Critique of Imperialism in *Daniel Deronda*," *Texas Studies in Literature and Language* 34, no. 3 (1992), 323–46 (325). See also Marc E. Wohlfarth, "*Daniel Deronda* and the Politics of Nationalism," *Nineteenth-Century Literature* 53, no. 2 (1998): 188–210, and Carolyn Lesjak, "Labours of a Modern Storyteller: George Eliot and the Cultural Project of 'Nationhood' in *Daniel Deronda*," in Ruth Robbins and Julian Wolfreys, eds., *Victorian Identities: Social and Cultural Formations in Nineteenth-Century Literature* (Basingstoke, UK: Macmillan, 1996), 25–42.
[32] See Nadia Valman, "'A Fresh-Made Garment of Citizenship': Representing Jewish Identities in Victorian Britain," *Nineteeth Century Studies* 17 (2003): 35–45.
[33] George Eliot, "Silly Novels by Lady Novelists," *Westminster Review* 66 (old ser.), 10 (new ser.) (October 1856): 442–61.

Alcharisi, who fled her restrictive family to devote her life to art. Alcharisi's narrative has been thoroughly mined by critics for the bitter protest that Eliot articulates against the suppression of female vocation.[34] Alcharisi recalls the intractable clash of wills between herself and her father: "He never comprehended me, or if he did, he only thought of fettering me into obedience. I was to be what he called 'the Jewish woman' under pain of his curse. … you can never imagine what it is to have a man's force of genius in you, and yet to suffer the slavery of being a girl" (630–1). But it was in this context that she first learned to dissemble so well: "when a woman's will is as strong as the man's who wants to govern her, half her strength must be concealment. I meant to have my will in the end, but I could only have it by seeming to obey" (632). Fostered, paradoxically, by the constraint of patriarchal law, Alcharisi's capacity for deliberate self-representation became the basis of her dramatic brilliance – what the narrator calls her "double consciousness" (629).

In Alcharisi's story, Arnold's Hebraism and Hellenism are given narrative incarnation. Thus, it is not simply a universal patriarchal tradition under which she suffered, but her father's religion in particular. Judaism is experienced by her as a system of narrow restraints, a reverence for law and the Jewish past, whereas she desired "a large life, with freedom to do what every one else did, and be carried along in a great current" (630). Transcending the insular life of the Jewess, acting gave Alcharisi the expansive existence of the cosmopolitan: "Men followed me from one country to another. I was living a myriad lives in one" (626). This key tension between the Jewish separatism of Alcharisi's father and the universal humanism of her own artistic ambition structures Eliot's novel as a whole. As Amanda Anderson has shown, this frame of reference also locates *Daniel Deronda* within the wider current of nineteenth-century philosophical constructions of Judaism. In the Hegelian tradition, Jews were understood as incapable of becoming modern – which required having a reflective relation to one's cultural heritage rather than adhering unthinkingly to a fixed legal code. The Jews, in this view, "are fundamentally unfree insofar as they fail to develop the dimension of interiority that characterizes Protestant Christianity and the capacity for self-authorization of beliefs that forms the core of the Enlightenment conception of autonomy."[35] Alcharisi's inner life, yearning toward both self-realization and self-dissolution, then, points to the incompatibility not only of Judaism and art, but also of Judaism and modernity.

In the figure of Alcharisi, Eliot meshes this Enlightenment polemic against Judaism with the gendered terms of the evangelical conversion

[34] For example, Nancy Pell, "The Fathers' Daughters in *Daniel Deronda*," *Nineteenth-Century Fiction* 36, no. 4 (1982): 424–52.
[35] Amanda Anderson, "George Eliot and the Jewish Question," *Yale Journal of Criticism* 10, no. 1 (1997): 39–61, esp. 42.

narrative to produce a feminist critique. Judaism, in Alcharisi's account, is masculinized, and her rebellion against the archaic patriarchal law is abetted by the instruction and encouragement of a woman, her aunt Leonora. For holding ambitions outside her father's destiny for her as a Jewish wife and mother, Alcharisi says, "I was to be put in a frame and tortured" – identifying Judaism with the inquisitorial methods of forced conversion (662). Invoking the Christian image of the yoke of Jewish law – "things that were thrust on my mind that I might feel them like a wall around my life" – she elides it with the ghetto of Jewish persecution (637). With this figurative language, Alcharisi's story recalls that of the Jewish daughter in conversion literature, whose greater capacity for Christian faith was grounded in the elevating suffering to which she was subjected within the Jewish family. In Eliot's secularized conversion narrative, the Jewess finds her salvation not in Christianity but in the alternative religion of culture. A life in theater, for her, is "a chance of escaping from [the] bondage" of Judaism, and her Jewish "double consciousness," formed under the strain of that bondage, is what transforms her life into great art (631). The Jewess once again liberates herself from the narrow material world of Judaism into a life of the spirit.

Despite the emotional power of Alcharisi's rhetoric, however, this argument – that a legalistic Judaism can be transcended by the universalism of art – is not endorsed by the novel as a whole. For in striking contrast to Arnold, Eliot does not regard "culture" as necessarily redemptive. The art of the stage, in particular, as a number of critics have argued, forms part of a nexus of associations among gambling, usury, and prostitution that constitutes the moral framework encompassing the text's various narratives.[36] Rather than redeeming the ruthless individualism and cosmopolitanism associated with "Jewish" commerce, then, the figure of the assimilated Jewish actress in *Daniel Deronda* is its female avatar. In responding to Alcharisi, Deronda reads her devotion to art over racial inheritance in precisely these terms, warning that it is ultimately futile since "the effects prepared by generations are likely to triumph over a contrivance which would bend them all to the satisfaction of self" (663). Deronda, and the novel as a whole, cast the Jewess's claim to autonomy as a modern and misguided effort to replace collective obligations with individual will.

In contrast, the novel offers an alternative Jewess, the child actress Mirah Lapidoth. Mirah enters the narrative when she is rescued by Deronda from

[36] Catherine Gallagher, "George Eliot and *Daniel Deronda*: The Prostitute and the Jewish Question," in Ruth Bernard Yeazell, ed., *Sex, Politics and Science in the Nineteenth-Century Novel* (Baltimore: Johns Hopkins University Press, 1986), 39–62; Gail Marshall, "George Eliot, *Daniel Deronda* and the Sculptural Aesthetic," in *Actresses on the Victorian Stage: Feminine Performance and the Galatea Myth* (Cambridge: Cambridge University Press, 1998), 64–90; Joseph Litvak, "Poetry and Theatricality in *Daniel Deronda*," in *Caught in the Act: Theatricality in the Nineteenth-Century English Novel* (Berkeley: University of California Press, 1991), 147–94.

a suicide attempt, having journeyed across Europe in a fruitless search
for her lost mother. Mirah, as Deronda reluctantly informs his mother, "is
not given to make great claims" for herself (664). Her body is repeatedly
described in diminutives, and her smallness and delicacy make her a kind
of purified Jew.[37] Indeed, she resembles the idealized Jewess of evangelical
fiction, whose "exquisite refinement" points to her elevation above Jewish
degradation (206). While Mirah's story begins from the opposite premise
to Alcharisi's – "I did not want to be an artist; but this was what my father
expected of me" (213) – their narratives have a noticeably similar structure: both are stories of female rebellion in which Judaism and art are
counterposed against one another. Like Alcharisi, Mirah learns the means
of her opposition to paternal domination from another woman, a landlady
in one of their many lodgings, and harbors a secret life with her Bible and
prayer books. Like Alcharisi, Mirah learns to counterfeit her feelings in
resistance to her father: "whatever I felt most I took the most care to hide
from him" (216). Whereas Alcharisi abandons her father because of his
narrow orthodoxy, Mirah flees the cosmopolitan commercialism of hers.
The representation of Mirah, like that of Alcharisi, draws on these tropes
of conversion writing but directs them toward different ends.

Mirah's narrative of her life also offers an alternative account of Judaism,
casting it not as a system of law but in the feminized language of affect. She
associates both Judaism and music with early childhood memories of hearing "chanting and singing" at the synagogue and her mother murmuring
Hebrew hymns; in the absence of her understanding the meaning of the
words "they seemed full of nothing but our love and happiness" (214, 210).
In her later, sadder life, Jewish history figured similarly: "it comforted me
to believe that my suffering was part of the affliction of my people, my part
in the long song of mourning that has been going on through ages and
ages" (215). Mirah's Judaism is mystified and prerational; it is "of one fibre
with her affections, and had never presented itself to her as a set of propo-
sitions" (362). Her own uncontrived performance style, moreover, is a version of this kind of unmediated emotion. She has nothing of Alcharisi's
"double consciousness"; she has "no notion of being anybody but herself,"
and to her the artifice of the theater, where she was forced to earn her living, is anathema (213). While the narrative links transparency and affection with the figure of the mother, a different story is told of the Jewish
father. The prime cause of his daughter's suffering, Lapidoth parades her
before sneering antisemites, panders her, and finally abducts her to subject
her to his will. Physically as well as morally they are opposites: when she is
seen with him later in the novel Mirah appears in the "quiet, careful dress

---

[37] Susan Meyer, "'Safely to Their Own Borders': Proto-Zionism, Feminism, and Nationalism
in *Daniel Deronda*," in *Imperialism at Home: Race and Victorian Women's Fiction* (Ithaca,
NY: Cornell University Press, 1996), 157–94, esp. 181.

of an English lady," in contrast to "this shabby, foreign-looking, eager, and gesticulating man" (738). In this respect also, her story, like Alcharisi's, invokes the narrative of Jewish conversion, in which the suffering of Jews is invariably ascribed to the Jewish father.

In contrast, Mirah's progress toward martyrdom, suggested in her description of the final agony of abandonment that preceded her suicide attempt, is a Calvary that renders her a type of Christ: "I wandered and wandered, inwardly crying to the Most High, from whom I should not flee in death more than in life – though I had no strong faith that He cared for me. The strength seemed departing from my soul: deep below all my cries was the feeling that I was alone and forsaken" (222). Redeemed, not only by the messianic Deronda but also by the Christian Mrs. Meyrick and her daughters, Mirah has an appropriately submissive attitude: "I want nothing; I can wait; because I hope and believe and am grateful – oh, so grateful!" (211). In this she cannot but jar strikingly with Alcharisi, whose proud declaration "I cannot bear to be seen when I am in pain" is also a refusal to be pitied (639). These elements of the conversion genre, which emphasize the suffering and submission of the Jewess – by which she is ennobled and made worthy of redemption – are linked, I will now argue, to the novel's conceptualizing of Jewish history and crucial to its broader political vision.

This vision is elaborated in the scene in which Deronda and Mordecai attend a meeting of the workingmen's Philosophers' Club at the Hand and Banner tavern, where Mordecai puts forward an argument for the revival of Jewish national consciousness. Against the charge made by Lilly that the Jews "are a stand-still people" incapable of modernization, Mordecai contends that theirs is a heroic tenacity: "They struggled to keep their place among the nations like heroes – yea, when the hand was hacked off, they clung with the teeth" (531). In Mordecai's vision, the restoration of Jewish nationality "shall be a worthy fruit of the long anguish whereby our fathers maintained their separateness, refusing the ease of falsehood" (535). The emotional power of this argument, however, has already made itself felt to Deronda, when he witnesses Mirah affirm her devotion to her religion in response to her fear of the conversionist inclinations of the Meyrick women:

As Mirah had gone on speaking she had become possessed with a sorrowful passion – fervent, not violent. Holding her little hands tightly clasped and looking at Mrs Meyrick with beseeching, she seemed to Deronda a personification of that spirit which impelled men after a long inheritance of professed Catholicism to leave wealth and high place, and risk their lives in flight, that they might join their own people and say, "I am a Jew." (376)

Just as his immediate thought on first meeting Mordecai is to imagine him in "some past prison of the Inquisition," Deronda's identification of Mirah with the figure of the Iberian *converso* enduring deprivation in order to return to the faith underlines the version of Jewish identity to which he is attached: that of the Jew elevated by suffering (386).

The meaning of Mirah becomes clearest to Deronda, however, when she performs Leopardi's "Ode to Italy." The first time she sings it, we are given the opening lines of the song: "O patria mia, vedo le mura e gli archi / E le collonne e i simulacri e l'erme / Torri degli avi nostri.... Ma la Gloria non vedo [O my fatherland, I see the walls and arches and columns and statues and lonely towers of our ancestors; but their glory I cannot see]" (483–4). The second time, Mirah performs in public at a musical party. The text is glossed by the narrator: "when Italy sat like a disconsolate mother in chains, hiding her face on her knees and weeping," words that link the lyric to the Lamentations of Jeremiah. Now, hearing Mirah sing, Deronda is deeply moved at the thought of the "heroic passion" for nation that is also "the godlike end of ... unselfish love" (559). In Mirah's performance, the self is subsumed rather than asserted. Her singing stirs emotional depths precisely because, rather than being a contrived "representation" of the grief of exile, it is a direct expression of it. Mirah's submission to persecution and her self-identification with Jewish history now merge with and are given meaning by the political debate that Deronda has just witnessed at the Philosophers' Club. As his own comment in that debate had tentatively suggested, the image of Italy mourned in Mirah's song but reenvisioned by Mazzini provides a model for the national restoration of the Jews too: "As long as there is a remnant of national consciousness ... there may be a new stirring of memories and hopes which may inspire arduous action" (536). Mirah is Leopardi's weeping Italy in chains, Jeremiah's exiled daughter of Jerusalem, and the Iberian crypto-Jew. Her own redemption by Daniel Deronda, then, stands emblematically and prophetically for the future redemption of the Jewish nation. By orchestrating images of Mirah in this way, *Daniel Deronda* provides an affective narrative of the development of "national consciousness."

As Bernard Semmel has commented, George Eliot was, in the 1870s, turning away from her earlier commitment to a Comtian religion of humanity and toward the "idea of Nationality" and the protection of "distinctive national characteristics." Her thinking resonated with Disraeli's pronouncements in the 1860s and 1870s on the need "to preserve the British national inheritance from both a divisive and alienating individualism and a cosmopolitanism that denied the bonds of a shared past." Despite her earlier disdain for Disraeli's Jewish chauvinism, Eliot was increasingly aligning herself not with Gladstone's liberal cosmopolitanism but with Disraeli's nationalism.[38] In the stories of the two Jewesses, then, Eliot illustrates the

---

[38] Bernard Semmel, *George Eliot and the Politics of National Inheritance* (New York and Oxford: Oxford University Press, 1994), 132, 127.

alternative routes of "cosmopolitanism" and "nationality" for the Jews. Alcharisi is arrested in an attitude of strife, reenacting the irreconcilable conflict between individual ambition and collective destiny, between assimilation and racial loyalty, between universalism and particularism. The self-abnegating Mirah with her "unselfish love," on the other hand, inspires the resolution of this conflict. Alcharisi stands for the discontents of the Diaspora Jew, Mirah for submission to the higher ideal of nationhood. As I have argued, these stories of the oppression, rebellion, and suffering of the Jewess read like striking echoes of the tropes of evangelical fiction. In Eliot's hands, however, they become a complex political allegory, suggesting the route to national renewal for the English as well as the Jews.

In other ways, *Daniel Deronda* draws together elements of the Jewish conversion narrative in a radically new configuration. The much-analyzed project of the Jews' restoration to Zion suggested at the conclusion of the novel can be read, for example, not only as a recasting of Mazzinian romantic nationalism but also as specifically Protestant aspiration inherited from earlier philosemitic millennialist discourse.[39] More audaciously, in the novel's endorsement of Mirah's version of Judaism as a religion of affect over Alcharisi's legalistic patriarchalism, Eliot casts Judaism itself as feminine rather than masculine. "Israel," declares Mordecai, "is the heart of mankind, if we mean by heart the core of affection which binds a race and its families in dutiful love" (530). This metaphor of humanity as an organism, in which the different races are organs, each with its "own work" to do but linked together in sympathetic affection by the Jews, is taken from the theory of Jewish nationalism proposed by the Young Hegelian German Jewish radical Moses Hess, whom Eliot had read.[40] In the context of Eliot's oeuvre, however, it is being used as much for a gendered as a political vision. In the novel, Judaism is associated with the female capacity for domestic tenderness that, as Katherine Bailey Linehan has argued, Eliot regards as the linchpin of civilization.[41] Mirah's ideally feminine "unselfish love" is thus also an expression of Judaism itself. In characterizing Judaism as the supreme religion of the heart, Eliot boldly challenges the symbolic economy of evangelicalism.

CONCLUSION

In *Philosemitism: Admiration and Support in the English-Speaking World for Jews, 1840–1939*, William D Rubinstein and Hilary L Rubinstein seek to overturn

[39] The imperial dimension of the notion of Jewish national restoration is also considered at length in Meyer, "'Safely to Their Own Borders,'" 183–7.
[40] Moses Hess, *The Revival of Israel: Rome and Jerusalem, the Last Nationalist Question*, trans. Meyer Waxman (1862; repr., Lincoln and London: University of Nebraska Press, 1995), 123–6.
[41] Linehan, "Mixed Politics," 340.

the dominant historiography of Jewish–non-Jewish relations in the century leading up to World War II. Alongside the disabilities and discriminations, the outbreaks of violence and ideological antisemitism that assailed Jews in eastern Europe and the Afro-Asian world, the "English-speaking world," they assert, was "different" because it "almost entirely lacked the tradition of venomous popular antisemitism found in Central and Eastern Europe," and there Christian advocates of Jewish rights "gave their support unconditionally. They championed Jews as Jews." Philosemitism "often more than balanced whatever religious antisemitism remained in the English-speaking world after the early nineteenth century."[42]

The Rubinsteins' corrective to a lachrymose teleology that seeks precursors to genocide in the nineteenth and early twentieth century; their wish to distinguish the particular religious culture that promoted an identification with rather than a denigration of Judaism in England, its colonies, and its ex-colonies; and their insistence that instances of antisemitic persecution in this period, as indeed in our own time, consistently generated swift and strong expressions of outrage from across the social spectrum, is important. Nonetheless, they strikingly fail to account for the phenomenon of philosemitism beyond the surface of the statements of the enthusiasts themselves. What they do, in effect, is to replicate rather than analyze the Anglocentric triumphalism of Victorian philosemitism. In contrast, I have sought here, by considering the gendered rhetoric of nineteenth-century philosemitism, to examine the relationship *between* antisemitism and philosemitism and the ideological uses to which this rhetoric was put.

The fundamentally contradictory place occupied by Judaism and Jews in both Christian and secular culture, I have argued, was inscribed into nineteenth-century narratives in gendered terms. Repeatedly, the figure of the Jewess marked the bifurcation between the discursive denigration and idealization of Judaism. The Jew was represented as archaic, legalistic, materialistic, intolerant, superstitious, and primitive; Judaism itself was masculinized. The Jewess, by contrast, was spiritual, cultured, patriotic, emotional, and modern. While the Jew was irredeemable, the Jewess represented the capacity of the Jews to transcend their spiritual and social narrowness. Persisting across the nineteenth century, this rhetorical figure appeared at the crux of discursive contestations over religious, national, and gendered identities.

Writing about Jews encompassed not only the projection of otherness on to male Jews, but also the figuring of the Jewess as an ideal self. As the broader political and cultural questions represented by the Jews changed, however, so did the terms in which the Jewess was idealized. In the first half of the century, ecclesiastical controversy defined the public debate

[42] William D. Rubinstein and Hilary L. Rubinstein, *Philosemitism: Admiration and Support in the English-Speaking World for Jews, 1840–1939* (Basingstoke, UK: Macmillan, 1999), 4, 137, 127.

about Jews. For evangelicals, anti-Catholicism provided the conceptual model for understanding Jewish difference, but, at the same time, they enthusiastically reclaimed the Old Testament and Jewish textuality. In this context, evangelical writers regarded the Jewess as the most desirable kind of convert, because she was both a link to the roots of Christianity and an emblem of its supersessionary power. By the 1860s, the economic and social success of middle-class Jewry had become a symbol both for the ascendancy of liberalism and for the apparent determinism of "race." The ubiquitous, racialized figure of the Jewish man of commerce, however, was frequently shadowed by the artistic Jewess, whose position between Jewish and gentile cultures was seen to produce a peculiarly alienated and eclectic intellect. Here, the exceptional spiritual potential ascribed to the Jewess in evangelical culture was secularized. Deeply indebted to the literature of conversion, novelists dynamically reshaped semitic discourse by accommodating the existing narrative of the redemptive Jewess to the changing circumstances of the mid-Victorian period.

Ambivalent responses to the Jews were embedded in political, theological, scientific, and philosophical texts in the nineteenth century. The medium of fiction, however, had unique rhetorical capabilities. In particular, writers used the image of the passionate and tormented Jewess to elicit a sentimental emotive response from readers. The spectacle of suffering exhibited in the "Jewish" autobiographers beloved of evangelical readers powerfully demanded sympathy from their audience. The sympathetic imagination, a cornerstone of Romantic politics and creativity, was equally central to the feminized theology of evangelicalism. It was, therefore, evangelical writers who developed the trope of the suffering Jewess most insistently of all, regarding her as particularly afflicted and hence particularly susceptible to the "conversion of the heart" with which women readers could especially identify. Later in the century, the Jewess continued to be linked with "feeling": in the work of Trollope, her refined sensitivity was pitted against the cold, calculating, and masculinized force of Jewish commerce. By the late nineteenth century the Jewess was admired above all for her resistance to the instrumentalizing and excessive rationality of the Jews. All these texts produced in the reader simultaneously and symbiotically an aversion to Jewish male figures and an identification with the Jewess.

In Eliot's intricately juxtaposed portrayal of the two Jewesses in *Daniel Deronda*, we see the most nuanced articulation of the gendered structure of Victorian philosemitism. The Jewess was invariably seen as exceptional: torn between the most fundamentally incompatible allegiances and therefore subjected to exceptional suffering. However, it was precisely this suffering that generated her unique relationship to religion, nation, or art. The Jewess was not simply redeemable where the Jew was beyond salvation; she was an *ideal* version of the Christian, the patriot, or the artist.

The Jewess was valuable as a convert not in spite of but because of her Jewishness, which gave her conversion miraculous and portentous meaning. Similarly, national loyalty in the face of intolerance gave the Jewess's patriotism a particularly poignant and durable quality. In struggling as an artist against a narrow world of religion or commerce, moreover, the Jewess's imaginative and performative propensities were heightened and honed. The Christian value of the virtue of suffering underpinned the story of the Jewish woman both within and beyond Christian narratives. Equally, Judaism as an absent presence haunted the representation of the religious or secular convert.

8

Anti-"Philosemitism" and Anti-Antisemitism in Imperial Germany

Lars Fischer

To the uninitiated, the imperial German era might well seem like the Golden Age of philosemitism. Rarely have the very terms "philosemitism," "philosemite," and "philosemitic" featured so prominently, pervasively, and persistently in public discourse as they did in Germany in the four decades or so leading up to the First World War. Yet this almost obsessive interest in "philosemitism" by no means bears testimony to a deep yearning for relations between non-Jews and Jews that are based on genuine solidarity, mutual respect, and constructive engagement. For the terms "philosemitism," "philosemite," and "philosemitic" were used well nigh universally not in an affirmative sense but rather with a pejorative intent. In imperial Germany, to be called a "philosemite" was a bad thing, an accusation against which even many avowed "anti-antisemites" (i.e., opponents of antisemitism) felt the need to defend themselves.

In a number of respects, imperial Germany confronts us with a highly complex constellation when it comes to the study of relations between Jews and non-Jews and notions of "philosemitism." With the emergence of modern political antisemitism proper in the 1870s begins the comparatively short era of self-avowed, overt, and proud antisemitism. Since the Shoah antisemitism generally no longer dares speak its name. Even those who nurture a strong conscious enmity toward "the Jews" and would condone or actively participate in measures designed to do them serious harm would today almost invariably deny in public that they are antisemites. Seen from this vantage point, imperial Germany is well and truly a strange land. Among its inhabitants we find a significant and vocal minority that publicly identified itself as antisemitic. Yet far from offering us a clear-cut means of identifying who stood where, this in fact raises more questions than it answers. For the majority who presumably thought of themselves as not being antisemitic, and the rather less significant and less vocal minority who thought of themselves as being expressly anti-antisemitic, *both* generally subscribed to most of the anti-Jewish stereotypes of the day.

Few anti-antisemites would have denied that the antisemites had a point. The problem with the antisemites, as they saw it, was that they took matters too far. In short, it is entirely possible that someone who would be considered an antisemite today would have been regarded as an outspoken anti-antisemite in imperial Germany.

In imperial Germany many sentiments and stereotypes that we today would regard as anti-Jewish would have been considered unproblematic or even legitimate – that is, unless at least one of two additional conditions were fulfilled. First, those who *explicitly* argued that "the Jews" were ultimately responsible for all that was wrong in society and *explicitly* suggested that all social maladies could be rectified by curtailing the Jews' rights or removing them altogether were generally perceived of as antisemites. In this regard, the crucial issue was not what people thought about Jews but what they thought should happen to them. It was not people's perceptions of "the Jewish question," in other words, but their prescriptions for its resolution that were considered crucial when distinguishing between antisemites and non-antisemites.[1]

The second means of drawing this distinction hinged not on the content of remarks about "the Jews." Instead, the question was, Who was making the remark about whom and with what intent? As a rule of thumb, anti-Jewish remarks made by one's political opponents were considered antisemitic. If one made essentially the same remark oneself, on the other hand, this was obviously a different matter altogether. One person's self-evidently non-antisemitic, perfectly legitimate critique of actual "Jewish" transgressions could well be another person's antisemitic attempt to exploit that legitimate critique for illegitimate political ends. Socialists, for instance, argued that popular anti-Jewish sentiment was essentially anticapitalist in motivation. Left to its own devices, it would serve as an eye opener, allowing people to recognize that they needed to combat capitalism as a whole and "not just" individual Jewish capitalists. Yet the antisemites, so the Socialists' argument went, sought to disguise this fact and instead harnessed popular anti-Jewish sentiment for policies that in fact consolidated the capitalist status quo. To acknowledge the justification of popular anti-Jewish sentiment as far as it went, as the Socialists did, was perfectly legitimate; to enlist it for counterrevolutionary purposes, as the organized political antisemites did, was not.

Problematic as these two criteria were, they did at least hinge on the antisemites' attitudes toward "the Jews." Probably more often than not, the terms "antisemite" and "antisemitic" were in fact used simply to denote an individual's affiliation or connection with the self-avowed antisemitic movement.

---

[1] I have discussed and demonstrated this at length in Lars Fischer, *The Socialist Response to Antisemitism in Imperial Germany* (Cambridge: Cambridge University Press, 2007). Hereafter Fischer, *Socialist Response*.

A deputy elected to the Reichstag on an antisemitic ticket was obviously an antisemite. Consequently, so the logic went, everything he said or did was antisemitic. Needless to say, however, not all his words and actions hinged exclusively or even primarily on his stance vis-à-vis "the Jews." He might give speeches in the Reichstag or publish articles on any number of topics or engage in all sorts of activities that did not involve an expression of his position regarding "the Jews." Yet among imperial German Socialists at least, the odds were that all those utterances and activities (including private issues such as adultery or shady business dealings) would automatically be characterized – and denounced – as "antisemitic." I have cited a paradigmatic example illustrating this issue elsewhere.[2] In October 1898, the Socialist *Sächsische Arbeiter-Zeitung* (Dresden), then under the editorship of Rosa Luxemburg (1871–1919), published a short piece on the recent congress of the antisemitic Deutschsoziale Reformpartei. It criticized the antisemites' veneration of Bismarck and the kaiser, the fact that they were unable to agree among themselves on an issue as important as the naval bill, and their prescriptions in defense of small to medium-sized enterprises (*Mittelstandspolitik*). While these were indeed all considered standard anti-antisemitic arguments at the time because they questioned the antisemites' integrity and credibility, not a single word uttered by the antisemites regarding "the Jews" was mentioned in the article.[3] The antisemitic Deutschsoziale Reformpartei nevertheless promptly shot back, its paper, the *Deutsche Wacht*, concluding its rant against the Socialist *Sächsische Arbeiter-Zeitung* with the statement that one could have no serious dealings with "a Jewish madam [i.e., Luxemburg] who churns out such tasteful clichés."[4] Luxemburg, who generally responded whenever her Jewish background was used against her in public, immediately published a rejoinder in which she clarified that in this case the article in question had been not by her but "by my perfectly Christian colleague."[5] This rejoinder by Luxemburg, in turn, was included in the edition of her collected works published in the GDR in the early 1970s. There, in the editors' explanation of the background to Luxemburg's rejoinder, they claim that the initial criticism formulated in the *Sächsische Arbeiter-Zeitung* was "directed especially against the antisemitic stance of the party as well as its support for the imperialist armament policies."[6] In short, in keeping with a widespread practice, the editors automatically *assume* that any critique of an antisemitic organization would inevitably include a criticism of the antisemites' stance vis-à-vis "the Jews," even though the critique in question failed to touch on this issue.

[2] Cf. ibid., 1, 13–15.
[3] "Die Antisemiten," *Sächsische Arbeiter-Zeitung* 9, no. 237 (October 12, 1898): 2.
[4] Quoted in Rosa Luxemburg, "Die 'Deutsche Wacht,'" *Sächsische Arbeiter-Zeitung* 9, no. 242 (October 18, 1898): 3.
[5] Ibid.
[6] Rosa Luxemburg, *Gesammelte Werke* (Berlin: Dietz, 1970–5): 1–I: 256n2.

Or take some of the formulations in the publications of the Zentralverband der Handlungsgehilfen und -gehilfinnen Deutschlands that I will discuss in more detail toward the end of this essay. Surely with our contemporary sensitivities we would expect an article with the title "Antisemitic Forgers and Fraudsters" to show how antisemites falsify information about Jews to arrive at their bizarre claims. Yet in the two articles published under this heading in the *Handlungsgehülfen-Blatt* in spring 1904,[7] the emphasis lay on the fact that the Zentralverein's antisemitic rival organization (the Deutschnationale Handlungsgehilfen-Verband, DHV) had publicly misquoted a statement in Hamburg's Socialist paper, the *Hamburger Echo*, about the displacement of small shops by large department stores. Apparently, the DHV's misrepresentation of the paper's stance was an *antisemitic* forgery simply because it was a forgery undertaken by self-avowed antisemites. On another occasion the *Handlungsgehülfen-Blatt* accused one of the leaders of the DHV of being an antisemitic chameleon because he regularly presented himself to different audiences in different guises, sometimes as a small entrepreneur, sometimes as an artisan, sometimes as a "Christiannational worker," and so on.[8] This made him an "*antisemitic* chameleon" simply because he was also an antisemite.

In many instances, then, Socialists criticized antisemites without actually taking issue with their antisemitism. Consequently, it was perfectly possible to be an outspoken anti-antisemite in imperial Germany while concurring with a variety of anti-Jewish sentiments and stereotypes proudly held by outspoken antisemites.

It is against this backdrop that we need to understand the manifold references to "philosemitism" and "philosemites" in imperial German public discourse regarding Jewish–non-Jewish relations. Virtually in tandem with the emergence of modern political antisemitism, the term "philosemitism" was introduced by the antisemites to denounce their opponents. Wolfram Kinzig specifically credits the supporters of the godfather of respectable antisemitism, imperial Germany's most prestigious historian of the day, Heinrich von Treitschke (1834–96), with coining the term, which most likely first appeared in print in an article by Treitschke, published in December 1880, in which he speaks of the "philosemitic zealotry of the Fortschrittspartei."[9]

---

[7] "Antisemitische Fälscher und Schwindler," *Handlungsgehülfen-Blatt* 8, no. 164 (April 15, 1904): 59–60, and 8, no. 165 (May 1, 1904): 68.

[8] "Ein antisemitischer Verwandlungskünstler," *Handlungsgehülfen-Blatt* 8, no. 176 (October 15, 1904): 159.

[9] Wolfram Kinzig, "Philosemitismus. Teil I: Zur Geschichte des Begriffs," in *Zeitschrift für Kirchengeschichte* 105, no. 2 (1994): 202–28, here 211–13. Hereafter Kinzig, "Philosemitismus." The text in question is Heinrich von Treitschke, "Zur inneren Lage am Jahresschlusse," *Preußische Jahrbücher* 46, no. 6 (1880): 639–45; partly reprinted in Karsten Krieger, ed., *Der "Berliner Antisemitismusstreit": 1879–1881* (Munich: K. G. Sauer, 2003), 711–15, here 712.

Although not equally popular with all antisemites,[10] the term very quickly
established itself as a shorthand denoting various forms of opposition to
antisemitism. As Kinzig points out, the proper etymological counterpart to
antisemitism would have been "prosemitism."[11] The term "philosemitism" is
even more charged, of course. Its obvious implication was that anybody who
could be bothered to oppose antisemitism actively must be in cahoots with
"the Jews." There could be no neutral ground, no nonexceptionalist discourse on this issue: one could only be the Jews' foe or their "friend." The
onus to demonstrate the validity of this contention by no means lay with the
antisemites, and most (non-Jewish) anti-antisemites vigorously objected to
being labeled philosemites quite of their own accord.

One might be tempted to assume that imperial Germany – in a direct
reversal of the current state of play – was characterized by conditions in
which antisemitism dared speak its name while "philosemitism" did not.
However, the vehemence with which non-Jewish anti-antisemites sought to
assure their readers or listeners that they did not oppose the antisemites
because they liked "the Jews" or wanted to whitewash their many admittedly ghastly characteristics makes this an implausible suggestion. They
appear to have genuinely felt profoundly embarrassed by their own anti-
antisemitism.[12] This embarrassment instilled in them the urge to make
clear that they too considered "the Jews," at least in some respects, a problematic other and that what worried them was not antisemitism's effect on
Jewry but its potential effect on society as a whole.

This is not to deny that there were, of course, non-Jews in imperial
Germany whose relationships with Jews were based on genuine solidarity,
mutual respect, and constructive engagement. Nor, to my knowledge, has
anybody ever tried to deny this. Yet mutual respect and constructive engagement were never the norm and always the exception.[13] Of course these

---

[10] Kinzig, "Philosemitismus," 214. Kinzig too inclines toward the notion that anti-philosem-
itism soon became a preserve of the socialists.

[11] Ibid., 211. The term "prosemitism" does also occur and is occasionally used, for instance,
by Treitschke's most outspoken non-Jewish opponent in matters Jewish, the liberal ancient
historian Theodor Mommsen (1817–1903).

[12] Cf. Fischer, *Socialist Response*, 13, 35–6, 209.

[13] Take the example of the prominent (non-Jewish) German philosopher Karl Jaspers (1883–
1969) and his wife, Gertrud Mayer-Jaspers (1879–1974). Their marriage undoubtedly
bears moving testimony to the level of mutual respect and constructive engagement that
could be achieved between non-Jews and Jews on an individual basis. Looking back over
her life during the Second World War, Gertrud Mayer-Jaspers recalled the beginnings of
her relationship with Jaspers in 1907. Although he later changed his mind, Jaspers initially
intended to tell his parents right away that he had become involved with Gertrud. As he
left to visit his parents, she recalled, "I said to him: write immediately what your parents
say about the fact that I am a Jewess. I will never forget his answer. 'Among us that word will
not feature as relevant. That is not a problem.'" How easily might one take this for a touch-
ing indicator of social acceptance. Yet needless to say, the very fact that Gertrud Mayer
(as she then was) considered her Jewishness an issue that would need to be raised already

exceptions deserve our attention, and they deserve to be remembered not least because they can help us nuance the bigger picture. But whenever we make them our focal point we are brushing against the grain; we are examining the subtext and not the main plot, exploring what might have been had the exception constituted the norm and what it might take to make the exception of the past the norm of the future. Yet none of this can change the actual historical record.[14]

In any case, whatever may or may not have been the norm or the exception in imperial Germany, one point is beyond doubt. Even to those who did aspire to relations based on mutual respect and constructive engagement between German Jews and non-Jews it would have seemed virtually inconceivable to think of themselves, let alone publicly present themselves, as "philosemites." To be sure, the fact that anti-"philosemitic" rhetoric played a role not only in antisemitic but also in anti-antisemitic discourse in imperial Germany is, in itself, hardly news. Its significance, however, has been massively underrated. Far from being considered integral to anti-antisemitic discourse in imperial Germany, the anti-"philosemitic" trope has often been portrayed as a marginal, not to say obscure, curiosity. Supposedly,

---

indicates the opposite. What can or cannot be inferred from her recollections becomes immediately clear from her subsequent remark: "I hadn't known that this could be possible. This experience made me very happy." DLA Marbach, A: Jaspers, Box 12, undated autobiographical manuscript by Gertrud Jaspers, 9–10. In fact, then, it is precisely its exceptionality that throws the apparent open-mindedness of the Jaspers family so sharply into relief. And it would seem that this open-mindedness was in any case not without its ambivalences. Writing to Jaspers on May 19, 1910, shortly before their marriage, Gertrud Mayer concluded by querying a previous remark by Jaspers. "Your mother is interested in everything Jewish?" she asked and then added: "As something that is strange/alien for her [Als etwas ihr fremdes]?" DLA Marbach, Jaspers Familienarchiv, Box 132 [1910]. I am extremely grateful to the Deutsches Literaturarchiv and the University of London Central Research Fund for awarding me the grants that have allowed me to undertake archival research in Marbach.

[14] In this respect, if I understand it correctly, Alan Levenson and I are in full agreement. However, a point of radical disagreement between Levenson and me is his affirmation of the "contact hypothesis." I remain convinced by Adorno's conclusion that "one cannot 'correct' stereotyping by experience" and that antisemitism cannot be remedied "merely by taking a real look." Instead, one "has to reconstitute the capacity for having experiences" (Theodor W. Adorno, *Gesammelte Schriften* 9 [Darmstadt: Wissenschaftliche Buchgesellschaft, 1998]: 303). I obviously do not deny that a number of former antisemites subjectively felt they owed their ability to move on to direct experiences with Jews. Yet it seems self-evident to me that knowing a number of "nice" Jews can obviously, in and of itself, no more disprove the antisemites' claims than knowing a number of less attractive Jews can prove them. Hence the willingness to change one's attitudes toward "the Jews" is in fact a prerequisite for the ability to consider "nice" Jews anything other than just the exception that confirms the rule. On this issue cf. Fischer, *Socialist Response*, 6–11, and review article in *East European Jewish Affairs* 37, no. 2 (2007): 249–55; I intend to discuss the case of Hellmut von Gerlach elsewhere; for an initial discussion cf. Lars Fischer, "Social Democratic Responses to Antisemitism and the 'Judenfrage' in Imperial Germany: Franz Mehring (A Case Study)" (PhD diss., UCL, 2003), 141–9.

anti-"philosemitism" was a preserve of the Socialists, and even among them it was not generally accepted but really only an obsession shared by a few exceptionally problematic individuals, foremost among them the prominent party journalist and historian, Franz Mehring (1846–1919).[15]

If we take the social democratic[16] rhetoric at its face value, Socialist anti-"philosemitism" hinged on the notion that the "philosemites," while claiming to oppose antisemitism out of concern for the Jews, were in fact opposed to antisemitism's anticapitalist thrust. In the minds of many Social Democrats, the philosemites' ostensible defense of Jewry against antisemitism, in other words, was in fact no more than a pretext for the defense of capitalism. To cite one of Mehring's classic formulations: "The brutalities committed against the Jews by antisemitism, in words rather than deeds, should not lead us to lose sight of the brutalities philosemitism commits, in deeds rather than words, against anyone, be he Jew or Turk, Christian or Pagan, who resists capitalism." For "philosemitism opposes antisemitism only to the extent that antisemitism opposes capitalism."[17]

The notion that Mehring was a special case whose obsession with "philosemitism" was not shared and was at times even publicly criticized by his peers is based in large measure on a single proof text, a review article published by Eduard Bernstein (1850–1932) in the party's theoretical journal, the *Neue Zeit*, in May 1893 under the title "Das Schlagwort und der Antisemitismus [The catchphrase and antisemitism]."[18] The suggestion that Mehring, who would die a founding member of the German Communist Party (KPD), and Bernstein, the conceptual founding father of revisionism,[19] locked horns over the issue of anti-"philosemitism" has intriguing implications. Many would doubtless feel deeply satisfied if it could be shown that the future stalwart of "democratic Socialism" was the one who saw through the anti-"philosemitic" discourse while a man with

---

[15] For a longer and more contextualized discussion of some of the following issues cf. Fischer, *Socialist Response.*

[16] Prior to the split between socialists/social democrats and communists during and after the First World War, mainstream socialism was generally referred to as social democracy, and in imperial Germany this term was used to denote not just the Socialist Party but the entire spectrum of political, social, and cultural organizations affiliated with the socialist movement.

[17] Franz Mehring, "Anti- und Philosemitisches," *Neue Zeit* 9-II, no. 45 (July 27, 1891): 585–8, here 587.

[18] Eduard Bernstein, "Das Schlagwort und der Antisemitismus," *Neue Zeit* 11-II, no. 35 (May 17, 1893): 228–37. Hereafter Bernstein, "Schlagwort."

[19] On the basis of the notion that recent economic, social, and political developments had not conformed to Marx's prognoses and utilizing certain remarks that Engels had made toward the end of his life, the revisionists called for a radical revision of the Marxist program implying not least that socialism would ultimately be the product of a steady evolutionary process rather than violent revolutionary change.

protototalitarian predilections like Mehring subscribed to it hook, line, and sinker. Intriguing though this suggestion may be, it is not borne out by the evidence.

To be sure, in "Das Schlagwort und der Antisemitismus" Bernstein did indeed voice his concern that Socialists might grant the antisemites "a certain legitimacy"[20] by subscribing to the critique of "philosemitism." Yet as ever, the devil is in the details. First, Bernstein made it clear at the very beginning of his review article that the "terminology" he was taking issue with, that is, the juxtaposition of antisemitism and "philosemitism," far from being a personal obsession of Mehring's, was "widely accepted in the Socialist press."[21] Second, it really was very much the "terminology" that Bernstein was concerned about and not the logic of the underlying argument.

He directed his critical remarks in particular measure against those who were the "most frequent" critics of "philosemitism," "namely the comrades of Jewish descent who, precisely because they are of Jewish extraction, consider it their special duty to spare the party any suspicion of aiding and abetting Jewish interests." Bernstein's focus at this point is not without irony for he was, of course, himself a "comrade of Jewish descent," and he too felt the desire to "spare the party any suspicion of aiding and abetting Jewish interests." He expressly called this a "very commendable" intention; his point was merely that it could be "better and more effectively underscored" by other means. Instead of using the term "philosemitism," Bernstein suggested, Socialists should refer to the genuine "other extreme" opposed to antisemitism, which was "pansemitism." Antisemitism and pansemitism were polar opposites, Bernstein went on to explain, in just the same way "as slavophobia and panslavism" were.[22]

What makes this suggestion so remarkable is the fact that it not only leaves unchallenged the bizarre assumption that "philosemitism" is a socially harmful tendency on a par with antisemitism: it in fact reinforces it. For panslavism was, after all, an actually existing, self-avowed political and ideological movement that ever since 1848 had been firmly established in the minds of virtually all progressives, radicals, and Socialists in Europe as a particularly lethal enemy. Bernstein quite clearly analogized the amorphous collection of anti-antisemitic trends commonly identified with the blanket term "philosemitism" with a recognizably "reactionary" movement like panslavism. And yet, despite the evident analogy Bernstein drew here, this very same article of his has generally been interpreted by historians as a "warning against the use of the catchword of philo-Semitism,"[23] one that

---

[20] Bernstein, "Schlagwort," 233.
[21] Ibid., 228.
[22] Ibid., 234.
[23] Paul Massing, *Rehearsal for Destruction* (New York: Harper Brothers, 1949), 188.

supposedly "cautioned the Social Democratic Party against ambiguity of language and attitude in the Jewish question."[24]

This assessment seems even more remarkable if we take the line of Bernstein's argument in this review article as a whole into consideration. For Bernstein concludes "Das Schlagwort und der Antisemitismus" by tackling what he considers antisemitism's worst quality. Far from pressuring Jews into assimilation antisemitism would provoke them into renewed Jewish separatism, "and it is here, above all," Bernstein explained, "that the critique of antisemitism has to begin."[25] Against this background one cannot help wondering about the timing of Bernstein's review article. It was published in mid-May 1893, six weeks after an event of considerable significance for Jewish–non-Jewish relations in imperial Germany. The Centralverein deutscher Staatsbürger jüdischen Glaubens [Central Association of German Citizens of the Jewish Faith], which soon consolidated itself as the dominant representative of mainstream Jewry in Germany, was established on March 26, 1893. Perhaps it was this event that convinced Bernstein that the amorphous phantom "philosemitism" had now become an institutionalized and self-avowed movement analogous to panslavism and needed to be tackled accordingly. Far from being concerned that the thrust of his peers' anti-"philosemitism" was misdirected or went too far, his real concern was that it did not go far enough, and his suggestion that they should focus their justified ire not on "philosemitism" but on "pansemitism" was meant to heighten their vigilance.

At no point did Bernstein mention Mehring in all this. As we saw, he initially noted the, to his mind, widespread but problematic usage of the term "philosemitism" in the Socialist press but then went on to single out specifically "the comrades of Jewish descent" as those who were most guilty of this sin. Somewhat ironically, this did not prevent Mehring himself from suspecting what historians have claimed ever since, all the evidence notwithstanding, namely, that Bernstein's critique was in fact directed against him. He raised this issue on June 7, 1893, in a letter to Karl Kautsky (1854–1938),[26] the de facto editor in chief of the *Neue Zeit*, who would finally emerge as the uncontested chief ideologue of the Second International after the death of Friedrich Engels in 1895.

Yet Kautsky, responding on June 12, assured Mehring that "Bernstein's articles are not directed against you." In their previous discussions of the matter, Kautsky reported, Bernstein had mentioned not Mehring but the leader of the Austrian party, Victor Adler (1852–1918), who was himself of Jewish extraction and "who indeed propagates a stance similar to yours."

---

[24] Ibid., 267n15.

[25] Bernstein, "Schlagwort," 237.

[26] International Institute of Social History (IISH, Amsterdam), Collection Karl Kautsky D XVII: 43.

In fact, Adler was perhaps even more emphatic in his notions about "philosemitism." Why would this be the case? Kautsky apparently did not consider the possibility that Adler might simply be yet another of those "comrades of Jewish descent" singled out by Bernstein, "who, precisely because they are of Jewish extraction, consider it their special duty to spare the party any suspicion of aiding and abetting Jewish interests." Adler's vehemence, Kautsky suggested, resulted from the fact that the Austrian party was faced with even more virulent forms of antisemitism than the German party, and the strength of Austrian antisemitism had generated a form of "philosemitism" to match. "Nowhere," Kautsky explained, "has 'philosemitism'emerged in such force as a natural response to anti-semitism," as it had in Vienna. He then went on to give a definition of "philosemitism." He characterized it as "that school of thought that regards every event and every phenomenon exclusively from the vantage point of whether it will benefit or harm the Jews." Kautsky expressly confirmed that "philosemitism in this sense exists" but also suggested that "the antisemites use the word in a different sense than we do." He concluded by reassuring Mehring that the differences between Bernstein's and Mehring's take on "philosemitism" "strike me as being primarily of a formal nature."[27]

Kautsky neither discerned a substantial difference between the positions of Bernstein and Mehring when it came to their anti-"philosemitism" nor himself expressed any misgivings about what he considered their essentially identical stance on this matter. To the extent that Bernstein took issue with the terminology involved (and not with the logic of the underlying argument), he did so precisely because what he considered to be the wrong terminology was "widely accepted in the Socialist press."[28] In short, the suggestion that anti-"philosemitism" was one of Mehring's private obsessions, let alone one that he was publicly taken to task for, is simply untenable. Instead not only was this opposition to "philosemitism" quite evidently considered acceptable by his peers, but they in fact subscribed to it themselves.

Not that this anti-"philosemitism" was the sole preserve of the German Socialists, of course. Few episodes illustrate this as dramatically as the well-known debate about antisemitism and "philosemitism" at the International Socialist Congress in Brussels in 1891. Abraham Cahan (1860–1951), who would later emerge as one of the most renowned Yiddish-language Socialist publicists in the United States, attended the congress as the representative of the United Hebrew Trades, a New York–based Jewish trade union organization. Rather naively, he hoped that the congress would move a strongly worded anti-antisemitic statement and express its support

[27] Russian Centre for Preservation and Research of Modern Historical Documents (RCChIDNI, former IML/CPA), Fonds 201: Mehring: 50.
[28] Bernstein, "Schlagwort," 228.

for his organization. Victor Adler, along with the leading German Social
Democrat and long-standing leader of the parliamentary party Paul Singer
(1844–1911) – one of the few Socialist leaders who maintained his affiliation with the Jewish community throughout his life – bombarded Cahan
with passionate pleas to withdraw his motion. They argued it would make
the Second International vulnerable to the accusation that it had sided with
"the Jews" and would thus do it untold harm. Cahan would not relent, and
in the debate that eventually ensued French and Belgian Socialists alike
articulated their anti-"philosemitism" with verve and abandon. Indeed, in
the light of the debate it seems almost remarkable that the congress eventually moved a motion condemning antisemitic and "philosemitic" "incite-
ment" in equal measure rather than directing its ire exclusively against
"philosemitism."[29]

Singer's involvement in this episode barely seems to have registered
among historians working on the attitudes of German Socialists toward
antisemitism and "the Jews." Against the backdrop of the conventional
assumption that Mehring's anti-"philosemitism" was exceptional among
German Socialists, it has perhaps seemed more plausible to surmise that
Singer's behavior on this occasion, rather than being born of genuine conviction, was merely tactical. That he proceeded in tandem with Adler in
any case makes this seem highly unlikely, though, since Adler's heartfelt
anti-"philosemitism" is well documented. Yet as we saw, Mehring's anti-
"philosemitism" was in fact by no means exceptional within the German
party, and this renders the suggestion that Singer's attempts to make
Cahan withdraw his motion might have been of a purely tactical nature
even more implausible. Since the likes of Mehring, Bernstein, and Kautsky
all subscribed to this anti-"philosemitism" and Bernstein, as we saw, felt
compelled to single out "the comrades of Jewish descent" as the most
ardent anti-"philosemites," it is hardly surprising that Singer too should
have been one of them. Even so, his case is perhaps particularly disconcerting because he was arguably the most self-confidently Jewish member of
the party leadership.

On two later occasions (in 1898 and 1899) Bernstein did in fact make
affirmative references explicitly to "philosemitism."[30] This is by any standards so rare an occurrence that it definitely merits closer attention. Are
these references to "philosemitism" indicative of a serious attempt on
Bernstein's part to reclaim the term/concept "philosemitism" for the anti-
antisemitic cause? To gauge the extent to which these later utterances

[29] Abraham Cahan, *bleter fun mayn lebn* 3 (New York: Forverts, 1926): 149–85; Edmund
Silberner, "Anti-Semitism and Philo-Semitism in the Socialist International," *Judaism* 2,
no. 2 (1953): 117–22.
[30] Cf. Jack Jacobs, *On Socialists and "the Jewish Question" after Marx* (New York: New York
University Press, 1992), 60.

signify a genuine change vis-à-vis his earlier position, we need to revisit Bernstein's line of argument in "Das Schlagwort und der Antisemitismus" for a moment. There Bernstein had in fact drawn a distinction between two different types of "philosemitism." One of them, he explained, implied "merely a certain sympathy for the Jews that rules out neither a condemnation of notorious mistakes nor a repudiation of their presumptuousness where it shows itself." This form of "philosemitism" Bernstein considered legitimate. The other, illegitimate type that Bernstein thought ought to be referred to as "pansemitism" amounted to "obsequiousness towards capitalist money-Jewry, support of Jewish chauvinism, glossing over injustices perpetrated by Jews and loathsome characteristics developed by Jews."[31]

The fact that he was so defensive in explaining the nature of the legitimate form of "philosemitism" (*"merely* a certain sympathy") clearly demonstrates that Bernstein by no means perceived of these two forms of "philosemitism" as being on a par. The illegitimate form that ought really to be called "pansemitism" emerges as the obvious and easily recognizable reality. The legitimate form of "philosemitism" that does not fall into the trap of becoming "pansemitic," on the other hand, would seem to amount to a veritable tightrope act requiring all manner of safeguards to remain viable and avoid collapsing into "pansemitism." Bernstein's line of argument clearly accepts and indeed underscores the basic assumption that the burden of proof lies not with those who subscribe to the prevalent anti-"philosemitism" but with those who claim that there can be an alternative and legitimate form of non-"pansemitic" "philosemitism." In other words, even Bernstein's very insistence that such a legitimate form of "philosemitism" is conceivable, far from questioning the prevalent critique of "philosemitism" in fact presupposed and merely complemented it. This could, of course, be no other way since Bernstein's line of argument, as we saw, by presenting "pansemitism" as a phenomenon analogous to "panslavism," in any case did more to reinforce than subvert the logic underlying the prevalent anti-"philosemitic" discourse.

It is against this background that we need to understand his two affirmative references to "philosemitism" in 1898 and 1899.[32] The first of these references was made in the context of Bernstein's fairly protracted feud with the English Socialist Ernest Belfort Bax (1854–1925). In substantive terms, the controversy between them sprang from the fact that they interpreted the implications of imperialism differently. Consequently they also evaluated the role and status of the Armenians in the Ottoman Empire very differently, and it was this issue that brought matters to a head between them. Their exchanges were unusually vicious, even by the harsh standards that characterized much of the ideological debate among German Social

---

[31] Bernstein, "Schlagwort," 233.
[32] For a more detailed discussion of the following cf. Fischer, *Socialist Response*, 179–86.

Democrats and within the Second International more generally, and there
was clearly no love lost between the two men. Bax's critique of Bernstein
repeatedly included remarks that it would be hard not to interpret as
allusions to Bernstein's Jewish origin. On more than one occasion, Bax
referred to the Armenians as "usurers" and "moneylenders." Although
anti-Armenian sentiment was rife among nineteenth-century European
Socialists, Bax's insinuation that Bernstein supported the Armenians
because they were "usurers" and "moneylenders"[33] does suggest that these
remarks were indeed meant to draw attention to Bernstein's Jewish background. Bernstein initially kept his cool. Bax eventually proceeded to
throw the risk of Anglo-Saxon world domination into particularly sharp
relief by contrasting it to the imagined threat of Jewish world domination.
On the one hand, Bax clearly meant to poke fun at the antisemites for
their unfounded obsession with the threat the Jews supposedly posed. On
the other hand, to declare that "in the Anglo-Saxon you are up against ten
Jews" obviously only makes sense if there is an actual Jewish threat as well.
(Ten times zero, after all, would only be zero.) Nor is there really any rational explanation for Bax's remark that "I for my part cannot find the idea
terribly gratifying that control of the world should be divided between two
strongly superior ethnic groups like, for instance, the Anglo-Saxons and
the Jews."[34] Why introduce a tricky analogy like this – between a threat he
considers real and one he supposedly considers purely hypothetical – if not
in order to draw Bernstein's Jewish background into the debate in no matter how tenuous a fashion? Even at this point Bernstein merely mentioned
in passing that Bax had embellished his most recent comments "so very
tastefully with moderately antisemitic remarks."[35] Bax was outraged. "*I am
no antisemite and hate the antisemites*," he explained, and then added: "It goes
without saying that I would have thought twice about making these, to my
mind, perfectly harmless remarks had I known that Herr Bernstein was …
so damn touchy."[36] Although Bax had not spelled it out, the thrust of this
argument was surely clear enough. Bernstein's response to Bax's "perfectly
harmless remarks" had been "so damn touchy" because he was a Jew.

Strangely enough, Bernstein now felt himself to be on the defensive. He
explained that he had "made the accusation of moderate antisemitism"

[33] Cf. Ernest Belfort Bax, "Our German Fabian Convert: Or Socialism According to
Bernstein," *Justice* 13, no. 669 (November 7, 1896): 6; "Letters to Editor: The Socialism of
Bernstein," *Justice* 13, no. 671 (November 21, 1896): 6.
[34] Ernest Belfort Bax, "Kolonialpolitik und Chauvinismus," *Neue Zeit* 16-I, no. 14 (December
21, 1897): 420–7, here 426–7.
[35] Eduard Bernstein, "Der Kampf der Sozialdemokratie und die Revolution der Gesellschaft,"
Neue Zeit 16-I, no. 16 (January 5, 1898): 494–7, here 493.
[36] Ernest Belfort Bax, "Der Sozialismus eines gewöhnlichen Menschenkindes gegenüber
dem Sozialismus des Herrn Bernstein," *Neue Zeit* 16-II, no. 34 (May 11, 1898): 824–9, here
826.

because Bax had repeatedly drawn "Jewry into the debate in a manner that was not merited by the matter at hand." Bernstein had therefore felt compelled to interpret this "as an inappropriate attempt to utilize against me the fact that I am of Jewish extraction." There is a strange discrepancy here, though. While the thrust of Bax's earlier remarks remained ambiguous in this respect, it was precisely his most recent remark about Bernstein's "touchiness" that in fact represented his most obvious attempt to allude to Bernstein's Jewishness. It ought therefore to have vindicated Bernstein in his assumption that he had been right all along in interpreting the earlier, more ambiguous remarks in this vein too. Yet in actual fact Bernstein now beat a hasty retreat and conceded that he had been wrong in accusing Bax of "moderate antisemitism." It would seem that for all the weird anti-Jewish ruminations he was willing to take lying down, being accused of that wretched "Jewish" quality of "touchiness" was the one thing Bernstein could not stomach. He therefore clarified that, wrong as he might have been in this particular instance, touchiness did not come into it. "Those who are more intimately familiar with me know that I am by no means touchy in this respect," he explained. And it was at this juncture that he added, "but I consider it a categorical imperative to be a 'philosemite' in the face of any antisemitism."[37]

It is hard to imagine a more defensive backdrop for this remark. Bernstein was retracting his accusation of "moderate antisemitism," and his overriding interest was to dispel the suspicion that he had overreacted with excessive "touchiness" born of his Jewish origin. Grasping at straws he came up with the one alternative to excessive "touchiness" he could think of as a motive explaining his behavior: reasoned anti-antisemitism or, to put a recognizable label on it, "philosemitism" of the sort that does not fall into the trap of "pansemitism." Even then it was a term Bernstein did not feel confident using without placing it in inverted commas. This whole discussion, we might add, took place in a footnote appended to a text discussing an entirely different issue. Few readers are likely to have bothered with the footnote at all, and even if they did the odds that they considered it anything other than an expression of personally motivated petty bickering are slim to say the least. That any reader of the *Neue Zeit* could conceivably have understood Bernstein's remark as an invitation to fundamentally reconsider the prevalent anti-"philosemitic" discourse is surely an entirely implausible suggestion.

Bernstein's second affirmative reference to "philosemitism" was in fact a direct reiteration of this very remark that had been tucked away in a footnote in the *Neue Zeit*. It transpired in an interview that Bernstein gave to the

37 Eduard Bernstein, "Das realistische und das ideologische Moment im Sozialismus. Probleme des Sozialismus, 2 Serie II," *Neue Zeit* 16-II, no. 34 (May 11, 1898): 225–32, here 232n2.

London *Jewish Chronicle*. The interviewer concluded their discussion with the following "parting question": "'What do you think of the anti-Jewish attacks of some Socialists?'" Bernstein's response ran as follows: "Apart from any agitation in this country, where my opinion might be resented, I have stated a year ago in the *Neue Zeit*, that, *although in no way connected with any Jewish movement as such,* I think it is my duty to be a 'philo-Semite' in all cases where I meet anti-Semitism. As a Social Democrat I fight for all political reforms Jews can reasonably demand."[38]

This reiteration of Bernstein's previous affirmative reference to "philosemitism" is effectively buried under a succession of disclaimers. It was not this remark but the preceding disclaimer clarifying Bernstein's Jewish disaffiliation that appeared italicized in print: the emphasis thus lay on the disclaimer, not on the affirmative statement itself. The final sentence was then presumably supposed to clarify what he meant when he called himself a "philo-Semite," and it too required yet another disclaimer. "As a Social Democrat" he supported "all political reforms" that Jews "can reasonably demand." In other words, provided one did not fall into the trap of Jewish separatism and maintained a clear distinction between Jewish demands that were reasonable and those that were not one could just about be a reasoned anti-antisemite or what we might, for lack of an alternative label, call a "philo-Semite." That all this should have constituted a brave attempt to rescue "philosemitism" from the claws of the prevalent anti-"philosemitic" discourse and reclaim it for anti-antisemitism is surely not a plausible suggestion.

How representative of broader attitudes in imperial German society more generally was the Socialist response to antisemitism in imperial Gemany? Did the liberal spectrum, for instance, take an altogether different or more sophisticated stand on these matters? I readily concede that more research needs to be undertaken in this direction. Even so, there is significant evidence that much of the relevant discourse among imperial German Social Democrats was indeed indicative of societal trends more generally.

Mehring himself is an interesting case in point, for we have Mehring's own word for it that his anti-"philosemitism" predates his affiliation with Social Democracy and that his defection to the Socialists did not require him to review or adapt his position on the matter. In other words, he was no less prone to indulge in anti-"philosemitic" rants while writing for liberal papers as a staunch anti-Socialist in the early 1880s than he was when writing for Socialist publications in the 1890s. Moreover, he caused Jewish boycott calls against two of the liberal papers for which he worked in the 1880s, once directly with a text he authored, in the other instance

---

[38] "Evolutionary Socialism: Interview with Herr Eduard Bernstein," *Jewish Chronicle* 1,599 (November 24, 1899): 21. Emphasis in the original.

as the editor responsible for publishing a contentious text by one of his colleagues. Yet in neither case does this seem to have had negative repercussions for him.[39]

Or take, as another interesting example for the compatibility of Socialist and liberal anti-antisemitic discourse, the pamphlet that the erstwhile Social Democratic Party leader, Wilhelm Hasenclever (1837–89), published under a pseudonym (*Wilhelm Revel*) early in 1881: *Der Wahrheit die Ehre. Ein Beitrag zur Judenfrage in Deutschland* [Calling a spade a spade: A contribution on the Jewish question in Germany]. As Hasenclever saw it, "the Jews" had only themselves to blame for the recent upsurge in antisemitic activity, and the way in which they and their "friends" (i.e., the "philosemites") responded to it only made matters worse. He made repeated references to the "touchiness" of "the Jews," which he qualified alternatively as "almost laughable" and "effectively malicious" and considered "one of the worst characteristics of the Jews."[40] The pamphlet is replete with anti-Jewish stereotypes presented in a deft and vicious manner. Why did Hasenclever publish this pamphlet under a pseudonym? We might hope and assume he did so because he feared that he was not being anti-antisemitic enough to pass muster with his comrades. Yet Ludger Heid, the scholar currently on most intimate terms with Hasenclever, suggests that he used the pseudonym because he feared he was being *too* anti-antisemitic for his comrades' liking.[41] Hasenclever not only did not publish the pamphlet under his own name, though. The pamphlet in fact consists of a series of slightly revised articles that had previously been published, in December 1880, not in a Socialist paper but "*in einer freisinnigen Zeitung*,"[42] that is, a Left-liberal paper. This does not automatically imply, of course, that the editors of the Left-liberal paper in question shared all or indeed any of Hasenclever's views. It certainly rules out, however, that they were seriously disquieted by the sort of anti-Jewish and anti-"philosemitic" mockery and ranting that characterized Hasenclever's *Der Wahrheit die Ehre*.[43]

The book *Friede der Judenfrage!* [Peace to the Jewish question!] offers another instructive example. Hans Schmidkunz, a progressive theoretician of art and pioneering campaigner for the application of pedagogical principles in university education, published it under a pseudonym (Johannes Menzinger) in 1896. Schmidkunz was no Social Democrat, to be sure, but his book is of interest here because none other than Eduard

[39] Cf. Fischer, *Socialist Response*, 22–5.

[40] Wilhelm Revel, *Der Wahrheit die Ehre* (Nuremberg: Wörlein, 1881), 21, 29. Hereafter Revel, *Wahrheit*.

[41] Ludger Heid, "… gehört notorisch zu den hervorragenden Leitern der Sozialdemokratischen Partei," in Ludger Heid, Klaus-Dieter Vinschen, and Elisabeth Heid, eds., *Wilhelm Hasenclever: Reden und Schriften* (Bonn: J. H. W. Dietz Nachf., 1989), 15–68, here 55.

[42] Revel, *Wahrheit*, iii.

[43] Cf. Fischer, *Socialist Response*, 46–53.

Bernstein warmly recommended it to the readers of the *Neue Zeit* in 1898, calling it "very perceptive."[44] Not only is this book replete with anti-Jewish stereotypes, but Menzinger/Schmidkunz also emphasized how important it was to insist on the negative qualities of "the Jews," "especially *vis-à-vis* the blindness of philosemitic rhetoric."[45]

As Alan T. Levenson rightly points out, my reseach on this topic has focused (and consciously so) in the first instance not on "the bottom up" or on "middlebrow actors" but on members of the intellectual party elite who were firmly grounded (at least at some point in their political biography) in Marxism: most significantly Franz Mehring, Eduard Bernstein, and Karl Kautsky. One might well ask how representative these leading intellectuals are of the state of mind that prevailed in the party more generally. The debates that Mehring, Bernstein, and Kautsky became involved in inevitably drew in theoretically far less sophisticated leaders like August Bebel (1840–1913) and Wilhelm Liebknecht (1826–1900), but also altogether less illustrious "middlebrow actors" such as Edmund Fischer (1864–1925) or Hans Leuß (1861–1920). Hasenclever too is an interesting case in point, for despite holding high office in the party he was ideologically rather plain and has rightly been considered a good indicator of the way matters were seen at the bottom rather than the top of the party. Even so, in order to understand prevalent Socialist attitudes to Jews and antisemitism it makes sense to focus on the Marxist elite. The likes of Kautsky, Bernstein, and Mehring prided themselves on their ability to deploy Marxist analysis to see beyond mere appearances and grasp how things "really" worked. Time and again they insisted on the ideological and mythological nature of social constructs that had taken on the appearance of natural facts of life but were in fact man-made and resulted from conflicts of interest between competing social groups. The fact that their myth-busting dynamism seems to have faltered in the face of two of the crudest and most rampant myths of the day, nationalism and antisemitism, is obviously indicative of a failure on their part. I would argue, though, that it is also indicative of just how strong these myths were and how widely anti-Jewish sentiments and stereotypes pervaded imperial German society.

In an important sense one could perhaps say that the sway these sentiments and stereotypes held over society as a whole can be gauged rather well by looking both at those Socialists who had distanced themselves the most and those who had distanced themselves the least from mainstream society. The case of the former is instructive because it tells us how strong

44 Eduard Bernstein, "Eleanor Marx: Erinnerungen,"*Neue Zeit* 16-II, no. 30 (April 13, 1898): 118–23, here 122.
45 Johannes Menzinger, *Friede der Judenfrage!* (Berlin: Schuster & Loeffler, 1896), 71; cf. Fischer, *Socialist Response*, 188–93.

the hold of widespread perceptions regarding "the Jews" remained even on those who made a systematic and sustained effort to transcend the outlook and values that the society into which they had been socialized had instilled in them. The case of the latter is telling because it offers us a glimpse of the sort of mind-set that prevailed where Socialist ideology had barely made inroads and can therefore hardly be responsible for problematic attitudes toward "the Jews" that we may come across. I have begun to extend my research more in this second direction, toward "the bottom up," in other words, by examining the anti-antisemitism articulated between the turn of the century and the First World War in the publications of the Zentralverband der Handlungsgehilfen und -gehilfinnen Deutschlands, the Social Democratic union of shop assistants and commercial employees (*Handlungsgehilfen*).[46]

As is well known, by far the single largest Handlungsgehilfen organization was the Deutschnationale Handlungsgehilfen-Verband (DHV), an openly *völkisch* and antisemitic organization that propagated the exclusion of both Jewish and female *Handlungsgehilfen* from the profession and admitted neither as members.[47] Although "the Jews" were not its only concern, antisemitism was far from incidental to the DHV's success in organizing the *Handlungsgehilfen* and formed an integral part of its attraction. Needless to say, its antifeminist and antiproletarian profile were also important in securing wide support among the *Handlungsgehilfen*, and on all three counts the Zentralverband stood no chance of competing: it wanted the *Handlungsgehilfen* to consider themselves workers, propagated equal rights for women, and considered itself an anti-antisemitic organization.

By the turn of the century, and especially after 1903, party-political and especially parliamentary party-political antisemitism was in decline. Party-political opposition to party-political antisemitism thus moved down the list of Social Democratic priorities. The Zentralverband, by contrast, presents us with an organization in the Social Democratic orbit that never ceased to stand on a daily basis in direct opposition to a superior antisemitic organization. Yet contrary to what one might expect, this exceptional situation and constant confrontation with the DHV do not seem to have rendered the Zentralverband any more sensitive to the antisemitic threat

---

[46] For a more detailed discussion, cf. my article, "The Social Democratic Response to Antisemitism in Imperial Germany: The Case of the *Handlungsgehilfen*," *Leo Baeck Institute Yearbook* 54 (2009): 151–70. I acknowledge with gratitude the grants awarded by the School of Humanities at King's College London and the University of London Central Research Fund that funded my stays at the IISH, during which I was able to gather the material underpinning this discussion.

[47] On the DHV cf. Iris Hamel, *Völkischer Verband und nationale Gewerkschaft: Der Deutschnationale Handlungsgehilfen-Verband, 1893–1933*, Veröffentlichungen der Forschungsstelle für die Geschichte des Nationalsozialismus in Hamburg 6 (Frankfurt/Main: EVA, 1967).

or any more acute and inventive in its response to it than the rest of the
Socialist movement.

The Zentralverband was indeed vehemently anti-antisemitic. Yet while
this anti-antisemitism took issue with virtually everything under the sun,
the one thing it focused on less and less was the DHV's actual stance vis-
à-vis the Jews. The three most persistently raised issues were, first, that
the DHV claimed to represent the employees when in fact all its policies
favored the employers; second, the DHV claimed to be a union when in
fact it used the members' contributions to shore up the party-political antisemitic movement; third, the personal integrity of many of the DHV's leaders was questionable. Indeed, arguably the single greatest anti-antisemitic
success the Zentralverband ever achieved involved exposing an antisemitic
leader who had placed an advertisement for a female travel companion
and then apparently suggested to a respondent that she should join him
and his wife in a ménage à trois. In short, the Zentralverband's main issue
with the DHV was simply that it was its leading (and much stronger) non-
Socialist competitor. That the DHV's specific brand of non-Socialism was
völkisch and antisemitic was neither here nor there in this context. To be
sure, the DHV was routinely referred to as "antisemitic," but it was called
that simply because it was part of the antisemitic movement. This was a
useful shorthand not least because it placed the DHV squarely in the camp
of Social Democracy's sworn enemies. Yet none of this implies that the
Zentralverband actually considered the DHV's stance vis-à-vis "the Jews"
the reason why one should reject it.

Around the turn of the century the publications of the Zentralverband
did still occasionally make critical references to the DHV's anti-Jewish orientation, but even then they were few and far between. At the same time
the few remarks that did explicitly refer to Jews or Jewish concerns (real
or imagined) were generally anti-Jewish and did not feature in the context of arguments that even claimed to be anti-antisemitic. Subsequently,
while the DHV and its associates were still referred to with some regularity
as "antisemites," the label "antisemitic" was used less and less frequently
(especially after 1908) to describe their activities and qualities, and by
1914 the antisemites' stance vis-à-vis "the Jews" had more or less ceased to
feature in the publications of the Zentralverband altogether.

Two concerns were conspicuously absent from the Zentralverband's anti-
antisemitic rhetoric. In keeping with the larger picture I have drawn so far,
the first was genuine concern regarding the antisemites' anti-Jewish orientation and its impact on Jewry. Rather more surprising, given my strong emphasis on the centrality of anti-"philosemitism" to anti-antisemitic discourse in
imperial Germany, is the almost total absence of anti-"philosemitic" rhetoric. It might seem only logical that as party-political antisemitism went into
decline around the turn of the century, anti-antisemitism would generally
become a less pressing issue and with it the need for anti-"philosemitic"

vigilance. Yet what makes the case of the Zentralverband so interesting is the fact that, as mentioned, it was competing on a daily basis with an anti-semitic organization much stronger than itself. Yet despite this it does not seem to have been dogged by the strong anti-"philosemitic" urge to which so many other anti-antisemites had previously succumbed. From where did the anti-antisemites of the Zentralverband draw the self-confidence required to avoid the embarrassment of anti-antisemitism without resorting to aggressive anti-"philosemitism"? I would suggest that the source of their self-assuredness lay in the fact that they had developed the fine art of non-"philosemitic" anti-antisemitism – that is, anti-antisemitism that simply never concerned itself, critically or otherwise, with the antisemites' stance vis-à-vis "the Jews" in the first place – to such perfection that they were well and truly beyond all suspicion of being "philosemites."

That the publicists of the Zentralverband no longer felt the need to make a song and dance about the dangers of "philosemitism," in other words, by no means indicates that "philosemitism" was now considered a less serious threat when and if it reared its ugly head. Instead it demonstrates just how confident they were that they had succeeded in comprehensively immunizing their constituency – including indeed many who were themselves of Jewish extraction – against the pitfalls of "philosemitism." For them, as for most Socialists and many liberals in imperial Germany, the suggestion that the term "philosemitism" could be used in a positive rather than a pejorative sense would have seemed as inconceivable as ever.

9

From Recognition to Consensus

The Nature of Philosemitism in Germany, 1871–1932

Alan T. Levenson

In its December 1931 issue the Prague publication *Der Philosemit* quoted the novelist Stefan Zweig to the effect that by its very nature philosemitism contains a "program." "Philosemitism is a program," Zweig insisted "if it constitutes the antithesis to antisemitism. Everything that is not destructive, uprooting, thoughtless should find a place here."[1] Featuring mainly non-Jewish contributors, *Der Philosemit* lauded the Jewish contribution to culture, praised the religious teachings of Judaism, exposed the lies of antisemites, and appealed to German-speaking Europe to acknowledge the Jews as part of the modern mosaic. We can hardly stop ourselves from looking up from this journal and glancing forward to 1933, when the Nazis seized power; to 1935, when the Nuremburg Laws made *Judenfreundlichkeit* a punishable crime; to Kristallnacht and to the crematoria. But with a concerted effort at side shadowing – at reading the past as more than a prologue to the present – we can look backward and try to explain how individuals and organizations in an antisemitic society came to champion the cause of Jews and Judaism.[2] That is fundamentally what I tried to do in *Between Philosemitism and Antisemitism: Defenses of Jews and Judaism in Germany, 1871–1932*. In this essay I will put forward five broad observations that I drew from my research on philosemitism from the 1870s to the 1930s. I will also put forward a defense of philosemitism as a coherent category and attempt to meet Jacques Berlinerblau's recent challenge, to "suggest what the deeper relevance of the discussion [regarding philosemitism] might be."[3]

[1] M.H.J., "Appel an Hirn und Herz," *Der Philosemit* (Prague, 1931).
[2] I borrow the term "side shadowing" from Michael Andre Bernstein, *Foregone Conclusions: Against Apocalyptic History* (Berkeley: University of California Press, 1994).
[3] Jacques Berlinerblau, "On Philosemitism," Occasional Papers on Jewish Civilization, Jewish Thought and Philosophy (Washington, DC: Georgetown University, Winter 2007), 8–19; Alan T. Levenson, *Between Philosemitism and Antisemitism: Defenses of Jews and Judaism in Germany, 1871–1932* (Lincoln: University of Nebraska Press, 2004).

German philosemitism might seem a surprising research focus for a teacher in a small Jewish college; it certainly has surprised my students. The questions that drew me into this inquiry may be summarized as follows: Were there groups or individuals who fundamentally rejected the antisemitic stereotypes so widespread, some would say ubiquitous, in imperial and Weimar Germany? Much research had been devoted to showing the level of antisemitic hostility was not uniform.[4] Even earlier, Marrus and Paxton's *The Jews of Vichy France*, in the course of addressing why the Holocaust was carried out in France with so little opposition, posited three levels of antisemitic hostility.[5] Were there, I wondered, groups and individuals who simply did not fit within their schema? That is, did anyone have generally positive rather than negative associations with German Jewry? From yet another angle, I had long been interested in the problem of why some German Jews had a negative self-image. I did not think that the term "Jewish self-hatred," popularized by Theodor Lessing and resurrected by Sander Gilman, was an overstatement.[6] Yet surely most Jews could easily identify the ranting of Marr or Stoecker or Ahlwardt as having little to do with the realities of Jewish existence. It seemed that an investigation of Istvan Deak's claim, that "Jewishness indeed was determined not so much by one's enemies as by one's friends,"[7] would shed some light on this phenomenon. Finally, intangibly, my own upbringing as a suburban American in a liberal time and an integrated space probably drove a skepticism that any modernized society could be wholly illiberal.

WAS THERE A PHILOSEMITIC TRADITION IN GERMANY?

Two books published in the 1980s deserve credit for raising the subject of philosemitism in English. Alan Edelstein, a sociologist, felt that the survival of Jews as a beleaguered minority logically dictated a countervailing force to discrimination. Solomon Rappaport, although essentially without a method, pointed to pockets of sympathy and/or interest toward Jews in the course of European history. The complaint lodged by Edelstein and Rappaport that the presence of philosemitism has simply been neglected

[4] Among the seminal studies in English demonstrating the variegated nature of antisemitism in Nazi Germany: Sarah Gordon, *Hitler, Germans and the Jewish Question* (Princeton, NJ: Princeton University Press, 1984); Ian Kershaw, *Popular Opinion and Political Dissent in the Third Reich* (New York: Oxford University Press, 1984); David Bankier, *The Germans and the Final Solution* (Oxford: Basil Blackwell, 1992).
[5] Michael Marrus and Robert Paxton, *The Jews of Vichy France* (New York: Basic Books, 1981), suggest a three-tiered level of hatred: ideological-proactive antisemites, defense-reactive antisemites, and passive-latent antisemites.
[6] Theodor Lessing, *Der jüdische Selbsthass* (Berlin, Jüdischer Verlag, 1930); Sander Gilman, *Jewish Self-Hatred* (Baltimore: Johns Hopkins University Press, 1986).
[7] Istvan Deak, *Germany's Left-Wing Intellectuals* (Berkeley: University of California Press, 1968), 25.

by historians was true in the 1980s, but not today.[8] The present volume, sessions at the 2006 and 2007 Association of Jewish Studies, and an international conference held in Potsdam, Germany, in June 2007 belie that claim.[9] Still, the gap between scholarly recognition of a phenomenon and consensus about what it signifies is a large one. Some scholars, including Paul Lawrence Rose, Daniel Goldhagen, and (in this volume) Lars Fischer, would keep "philosemitism" strictly within quotation marks. For Rose, philosemitism" is simply a "false category."[10] For Fischer philosemitism was a shorthand dismissal of party-political antisemitism, but simultaneously, an endorsement of the idea that there was a Judenfrage, which elided any actual enthusiasm for Jews, Judaism, or Jewishness. (All three English meanings are covered by the single German word *Judentum* – which must be translated into English according to the referent.)[11]

What should we conclude about the presence of philosemitic sentiment in imperial and Weimar Germany? If it is understood as pro-Jewish tendencies existing in discrete individuals or groups, I remain convinced that philosemitism was widespread. Germans – prominent and otherwise – proved willing to reject antisemitism and willing to speak out in favor of positive Jewish qualities, albeit often stereotypical ones. I do not claim, as did *Der Philosemit*, that philosemitism was a program. I do not claim, as Rappaport and Edelstein implicitly do, that there was a philosemitic *movement* or *tradition* in modern Germany. In Germany, as elsewhere, antisemitism was obviously the regnant attitude, and even the episodes of philosemitism (in the baroque era, in the Berlin salons before 1806, in left-wing circles in Berlin in 1920s) involved small minorities. I am not even convinced that these terms are justified for the friendlier atmosphere of the Anglo-American milieu, as William and Hilary Rubinstein have argued.[12] One cannot write the history of philosemitism in modern Germany: one can only explore, episodically, a minority outlook that deserves recognition and contemporary cultivation.

My investigation began with the world of imperial era Left-liberalism. Bismarck's "second *Reichsgründing*" of 1877–9 split German liberalism into the national and Left-liberal wings. How different German history would have been had Bismarck maintained the alliance with national liberals that served him so well from 1866 to 1877 is, of course, an unanswerable

---

[8] Salomon Rappaport and Alan Edelstein shared a blatantly apologetic agenda. Nevertheless, they were correct in the assertion that the issue of philosemitism had been ignored; see Berlinerblau, "On Philosemitism," 8–9.

[9] See Adam Sutcliffe and Jonathan Karp's introduction to this volume.

[10] Paul Lawrence Rose, *German Question/Jewish Question* (Princeton, NJ: Princeton University Press, 1990), index, "philosemitism, false category," 392.

[11] Lars Fischer, *The Socialist Response to Antisemitism in Imperial Germany* (Cambridge: Cambridge University Press, 2007).

[12] William Rubinstein and Hilary Rubinstein, *Philosemitism: Admiration and Support in the English-Speaking World for Jews, 1840–1939* (New York: St. Martin's Press, 1999).

question. In any event, an ever-present factor in the liberal defense of
Jewish emancipation was their steadily decreasing political power. As
James Sheehan put it, "By the 1890s, their dreams emptied by frustration,
dissension and defeat, the liberals receded to the fringes of political life."[13]
One product of the German liberal mind-set that mirrored more successful special interest groups such as the Pan-German League was the Verein
zur Abwehr des Antisemitismus (Society to defend against antisemitism),
founded in 1891 by German liberals (mainly Left-liberals). The well-heeled
Abwehrverein, as it was commonly known, counted many prominent politicians, authors, and public figures and even spawned a Viennese branch. It
would seem like a logical place to find philosemitic expression. However,
as Barbara Suchy and Erik Lindner have shown, the Abwehrverein hewed
closely to its defensive title. The Abwehrverein defended Jews against
attacks, but it did not, as a rule, promote German Jewry as an inherently
valuable asset to society. One revealing reflection of mainstream liberal
ambivalence may be taken from the Abwehrverein stalwart and novelist Gustav Freytag. In a blistering attack on Richard Wagner, whose "Das
Judentum in der Musik" did much to promote cultural antisemitism,
Freytag opined, "In the sense of his brochure, Wagner seems himself to
be most Jewish."[14] Since Freytag's own *Soll und Haben* contained arguably
the most famous antisemitic stereotype in nineteenth-century German
literature (Itzig Veitel), one might be inclined to travel even further left
in search of unambiguous philosemitism.[15] Yet even the German peace
movement [Deutsche Friedensgesellschaft] stopped short of taking an official stand on a "Jewish" issue. Bertha von Suttner, one of the movement's
founders, condemned the Russian pogroms, ardently admired Theodor
Herzl and supported his version of Zionism, and collaborated closely with
Hermann Fried, a Hungarian Jew and her organizational right-hand man.
Like other left-wing movements, pacifists included Jews in their ranks without explicit reference to their Jewishness. Socially and culturally, the world
of German Left-liberalism provided a comfort zone for Jews; politically,
the German Left-liberal rhetoric stuck mainly to anti-antisemitism, while
certain individuals independent of particular political groupings – artists,
novelists, members of the German avant garde – advocated elements of
German Jewry in a more explicitly philosemitic vein.[16]

---

[13] James J. Sheehan, *German Liberalism in the Nineteenth Century* (Chicago: University of
Chicago Press, 1978), 273.

[14] Gustav Freytag, "Der Streit über *Das Judentum in der Musik*," *Neue Freie Presse* (Wien, May 21,
1893): 325.

[15] It is worth noting that Freytag's second wife was Jewish and that they agreed to raise their
child as a Jew – this was "cutting edge" liberalism for the Kaiserreich.

[16] Sheehan, *German Liberalism in the Nineteenth Century*, remains the best overview of Left-
liberalism; see also Peter Pulzer, *Jews and the German State: The Political History of a Minority,
1844–1933* (Oxford and Cambridge: Blackwell, 1992).

That Jewish-Christian relations display a problematic history is gross understatement. Any investigator should expect Jewish-Christian tensions, especially when the society in question has only partially secularized. A recent volume confirms Thomas Nipperdey's contention in *Religion im Umbruch* (Munich, 1988) that interreligious tensions remained high: Protestant versus Catholics, but also Calvinist Hohenzollerns and their Lutheran citizens, ultramontane Catholics and German Catholics, rural and urban churches, central hierarchy and local clergy.[17] Given that base-level animosity, one may be all the more impressed that Judaism (the religion) found defenders at all. Franz Delitzsch (1812–90) and Hermann Strack (1848–1922), knowledgeable scholars of Judaism, both widely published authors, university men, and missionaries, took the lead in responding to the antisemitic slanders that began to get a wide hearing in the 1870s. Strack appeared numerous times in German courts as an expert witness on behalf of Judaism, wrote a scholarly expose of the blood libel, and was an indefatigable defender in the German press. To my mind, the linkage of their Judaic scholarship and their advocacy of Jewish civil rights is especially impressive when compared to earlier examples of intellectual philosemitism. The Victorine monks in medieval Paris,[18] the millenarian British,[19] and the German-Christian Kabbalists, while interested in Judaism, drew no favorable political conclusions regarding actual Jews from their investigations.[20] Delitzsch and Strack did, their Christian supersessionism notwithstanding. I do not intend to overstate my case: some missionary Protestants loved certain aspects of Judaism, but others did not. While Delitzsch and Strack pass muster as proponents of German Jewry, many missionaries (e.g., Gustaf Dahlmann/Johann De Le Roi) were more hostile than friendly to Jewish interests. Liberal Protestants like Michael Baumgarten of Rostock in the 1880s or Eduard Lamparter in the 1920s were mainly out of step with their counterparts.[21] As scholars from Uriel Tal to Susannah Heschel have demonstrated, liberal Protestantism was illiberal regarding Judaism.[22] Ignaz Döllinger was the most prominent

---

[17] Hellmut Wälser Smith, ed., *Protestants, Catholics and Jews in Germany, 1800–1914* (Oxford and New York: Berg Books, 2001).

[18] Beryl Smalley, *The Study of the Bible in the Middle Ages* (South Bend, IN: Notre Dame University Press, 1964).

[19] David Katz, *Philosemitism and the Readmission of the Jews into England* (Oxford: Clarendon Press, 1982).

[20] Hans Joachim Schoeps, *Philosemitimus im Barock* (Tübingen, J. C. B. Mohr, 1952).

[21] Eduard Lamparter, an activist in the Stuttgart branch of the Abwehrverein (there was no contradiction between being both a pastor and a political liberal or a socialist), wrote extensively on behalf of Jewry, as did Paul Fiebig, Max Löhr, and Otto Baumgarten. They were exceptions to the rule of liberal Protestant animosity toward Judaism.

[22] Susannah Heschel, *Abraham Geiger and the Jewish Jesus* (Chicago: University of Chicago Press, 1998).

Catholic theologian to mount a principled, ideological attack on antisemitism in the Kaiserreich. For Döllinger, as Jacques Kornberg has argued, this anti-antisemitism was linked to his reformist views and opposition to the church in Rome.[23] The anti-antisemitic parliamentary positions of Catholic center politicians such as Windhorst and Leber, though admirable, were mainly the product of pragmatic considerations. The latter were only what Professor Wolfram Kinzig has aptly termed "secondary philosemitism."[24]

Donald Niewyck helpfully divided all solutions to the "Jewish question" into three: integrationist, segregationist, annihilationist.[25] German liberals, however one parses the degree of their pro-Jewishness, fall into Niewyck's first category. For missionary Protestants, obviously, conversion also stands as a form of radical integration. But one could opt for Niewyck's second option, segregationist, and still espouse views that were more philo- than anti-semitic. After all, Zionism – a national liberation movement that started in eastern Europe – gained ground when Theodor Herzl staged an international congress in Basle in 1897, highlighting the international plight of the Jewish people. Precisely because integration had failed, Herzl argued against his liberal friends, both Jewish and non-Jewish, a Jews' state was a necessity. Through the Zionist congresses, the Zionist newspaper *Die Welt*, and his many contacts in the literary world, Herzl (and others) won over a number of gentile enthusiasts. "You ancient people! You wonderful people! Just see how strong your blood is even in the worst of you, and how it will rise up again despite your will.... How I love you people of sorrow! How strong your heart is and how young it has remained! No you shall not go under in the confusion of alien peoples. In being different lies all your beauty, all happiness and joy of earth remain your own.... How I love you people of people, how I bless you!"[26] With its references to the Bible and to Jewish blood, as well as its essentialist and glamorizing tones, this passage might suggest an author fairly detached from her subject – except that in this case the author is the avant-garde writer Paula (Winkler) Buber, who would go on to marry the most famous Jewish thinker in twentieth-century Judaism and move to Israel. Her language may be offputting; the depth of her commitment is borne out by subsequent events. Naturally, the Bubers traveled in a circle that was not representative – I have no desire

[23] Jacques Kornberg, "Ignaz von Döllinger's *Die Juden in Europa*: A Catholic Polemic against Antisemitism," *Journal of the History of Modern Theology* 6 (1990): 233–45.

[24] Wolfram Kinzig, "Philosemitismus: Zur Geschichte des Begriffs," *Zeitschrift für Kirchengeschihcte* 105, nos. 2–3 (1994): 202–28.

[25] Donald Niewyck, "Solving the 'Jewish Problem,' 1871–1945," *Leo Baeck Institute Yearbook* 35 (1990): 335–70.

[26] Paula Winkler, "Betrachtungen einer Philozionistin," *Die Welt* 36, no. 6 (September 6, 1901).

to overstate the significance of this support. The aristocratic, racialist, romantic, and chiliastic gentile supporters of Herzlian Zionism had little leverage – they were an atomized group without significant impact on German political life.

If understood merely as pro-Jewish or pro-Judaic tendencies in individuals or groups, actual philosemitism certainly existed in imperial Germany; however, if understood as a potent political or religious movement, philosemitism remained without significant impact in the Kaiserreich. The loci of philosemitic sentiment were too diverse, mutually incompatible, internally divided, and fundamentally ambivalent to make a political difference. German philosemites never succeeded in raising their banner in any way comparable to the successful deployment of antisemitism as a "cultural code," a catch-all of general disaffection.[27] The fact that pro-Jewish sentiment never coalesced into "a program," as the editors of *Der Philosemit* hoped, is powerful testimony to the German desire for an *Einheitskultur*.[28] And yet, it would be unjust to this minority to say that the hostility toward Jews was unbroken, or that any attitude other than a purely antisemitic one was even conceivable.

HOW EXTRAORDINARY GERMANS BECAME PHILOSEMITIC: THE "CONTACT HYPOTHESIS"

One response to Berlinerblau's challenge to limn "the deeper relevance" of this discussion is as follows: the making of a philosemite is not shrouded in mystery but, rather, contains some frequently observed components. A number of individuals offer us a glimpse into the process by which positive feeling for a minority group gradually eclipsed negative feelings. Nothing suggests that these people were immune to antisemitic feeling. (Quite the contrary, for many testified that they considered themselves antisemitic by inclination and upbringing.) Little evidence supports a dramatic conversion to philosemitism, although there were cases of sudden disenchantment with antisemitism.[29] The path to philosemitism was more often a gradual

---

[27] Shulamit Volkov, "Antisemitism as Cultural Code," *Leo Baeck Institute Yearbook* 23 (1978): 25–46.

[28] John Gager writes of Greco-Roman sympathizers with Jewry, "These authors are utterly heterogeneous; with few exceptions, they reveal no ties of kinship, social status, place of origin or education. It is precisely this heterogeneity that gives them their value as witnesses against the traditional picture of Romans as overwhelmingly hostile toward Judaism": *The Origins of Anti-Semitism* (New York and Oxford: Oxford University Press, 1985), 67. In modern Germany, I would describe the presence of philosemitism as heterogeneous, but not random. There were surely more philosemites in peace clubs and Goethe societies than in Prussian officers' clubs, in free student fraternities than in Volkshochschüle faculties.

[29] See, for an example, Wilhelm Georg, *Hinter den Coulissen der Antisemiten! Mein Austritt aus der antisemitischen Partei* (Hannover, 1895).

process than a conversionary experience.[30] No doubt, some people are more disposed to throw off prejudice than others. Moreover, the famous cases of Voltaire, Wagner, and Marr indicate that contact alone did not guarantee a philosemitic outcome – all three had extensive Jewish contacts and all three played a major role in formulating modern antisemitism.[31]

Nevertheless, what may be documented is that encounters with a member (or members) of German Jewry in this era were often pivotal to the process of becoming philosemitic. Personal relationships often served as the catalyst to a reevaluation of the group as a whole: Nahida Ruth Lazarus, Paula Buber, Thomas Mann, Hellmut von Gerlach, Bertha von Suttner, and Ludwig Quidde are some specific examples. I am certain that investigations of scientific institutes, literary societies, and Socialist Party cells would yield many more. To put it bluntly, the contact hypothesis regarding racial prejudice finds strong support in my research.[32] Some of the elements of this hypothesis are the importance of participatory (as opposed to "sightseeing") contact, collaboration in cooperative (as opposed to competitive) activities, the importance of intimate (as opposed to merely casual) contact. A glance at the German peace movement alone, I maintain, offers a point-by-point confirmation of the application of this hypothesis to German-Jewish reality.[33]

At less than 2 percent of the general population, there is something quixotic in Rabbi Leo Baeck's famous pronouncement that if every German family had had a Jewish member there would have been no Holocaust. But Baeck seems closer to the mark than Professor Michael Brenner, a brilliant scholar but I think quite mistaken when he concludes that a glamorization of Jews and Judaism among its defenders precluded true dialogue. In a short article titled "God Protect Us from Our Friends" Brenner writes: "None of the philosemites of the Kaiserreich considered here had an accurate recognition of Jews as Jews; rather, they all constructed an idealized Jewish cross-section as a fictive partner in conversation. An actual dialogue did not transpire."[34] Did not Hermann Strack, who wrote an introduction to the Talmud and Midrash still widely used, understand the

---

[30] Hellmut Von Gerlach, *Von Rechts Nach Links* (Zürich: Europa-Verlag, 1937), esp. 108–18, offers a virtual point-by-point illustration of the details of this "contact hypothesis": 1) Von Gerlach's were "participatory contacts"; he encountered Jews of equal or social status (Von Gerlach was a Junker, but Charles Hallgarten was a millionaire); he experienced collaborative activities (the peace movement); he dwelled in a supportive social atmosphere.

[31] Von Gerlach, *Von Rechts Nach Links*, 118.

[32] Yehuda Amir, "Contact Hypothesis in Ethnic Relations," *The Handbook of Interethnic Coexistence* (New York: Continuum, 1998), 162–81; Levenson, *Between Philosemitism and Antisemitism*, esp. 21–9.

[33] Alan Levenson, "The German Peace Movement and the Jews: An Unexplored Nexus," *Leo Baeck Institute Yearbook* 46 (2001), 277–304.

[34] Michael Brenner, "Gott schütze uns vor unseren Freunden," *Jahrbuch für Antisemitismusforschung* 2, nos. 174–99 (1993): 191.

teachings of Judaism? Did he not publish many tracts meticulously refuting the blood libel and other spurious charges against Jewry? Did Strack not consult a wide range of rabbis regarding contemporary Jewish practice? And, to take a secular example, did not the historian Ludwig Quidde (son-in-law of a Jewish ophthalmologist) strategize with fellow pacifists? Was Quidde wrong when he praised Jews as being overrepresented in the progressive movements of his era? Did Quidde not correspond with Albert Einstein regarding the pros and cons of enlisting Oscar Wasserman, a Jew who headed the Deutsche Bank, for the Deutsche Friedensgesellschaft? Were not the post–World War I offshoots of the peace movement (e.g., Bund neues Vaterland; Liga für Menschenrechte) populated by Jewish and non-Jewish members connected by beliefs, politics, and sometimes family? To invoke the famous phrase of the great historian Jacob Katz, there were "neutral societies" in imperial and Weimar Germany. Socially speaking, the recent works of Kirstin Meiring and Till von Rahden support the notion that pockets of structural integration existed before the National Socialists.[35] There were real dialogues and real partners – marital, social, and organizational.

WHAT WAS THE CONNECTION BETWEEN PHILOSEMITISM AND JEWISH LEARNING?

A striking feature of German philosemites in the Kaiserreich and Weimar is their determination to acquire information about Jews and Judaism. For missionary Protestants this development is not surprising and needs little commentary – for Delitzsch and Strack their learning largely expressed their philosemitic inclinations. In the novels of Heinrich Johann Siemer (1886–1936) and Emil Felden (1871–1959), two socialists, not only do the authors evince a considerable immersion in Jewish studies, they give their Christian characters a similar impulse. Felden, the better known of the pair, was an evangelical pastor from Metz who became an Abwehrverein member and wrote a parody of Artur Dinter's racist best sellers. Felden's "hero," a thinly veiled stand-in for himself, becomes a professor of Semitics and attacks Stoecker's Berlin movement as a national cancer. In the text and in thirty-two dense pages of endnotes, Felden shows himself to be an impressive Judaic autodidact. Nahida Remy/Ruth Lazarus's *Das jüdische Weib* (1891), a work translated into many languages, served as a vehicle for reading herself into the Jewish tradition. Nahida Remy, a best-selling author who addressed audiences numbering in the hundreds, eventually

35 Kerstin Meiring, *Die Christlich-Jüdische Mischehe in Deutschland* (Hamburg: Dölling und Galitz, 1998); Till van Rahden, "Unity, Diversity and Difference," in Hellmut Smith, ed., *Protestants, Catholics and Jews in Germany, 1800–1914* (Oxford and New York: Oxford University Press, 2001), 217–44.

converted to Judaism and changed her name when she married the philosopher Moritz Lazarus. The process that drew her toward Judaism, at least as she portrayed it in her autobiographical *Ich süchte Dich*, lasted decades. Thomas Mann's use of Jewish sources constitutes an important – and only recently appreciated – dimension of his biblically based novel *Joseph and His Brothers* (1935–45). Mann corresponded with Rabbi Jacob Horvitz in the 1920s and frequently deployed the German translation of Micha Bin-Gorion's *Mimekor Yisrael [Die Sagen der Juden]*. Anyone familiar with traditional Jewish exegesis will find well-known rabbinic dicta strategically placed in all four volumes. Since Mann stands as such a central figure in twentieth-century German culture, I trust readers will excuse the following lengthy citation:

> One might be inclined to see in *Joseph und seine Brüder* a Jewish novel only for Jews. Well, the choice of Old Testament material was certainly no accident.... To write a novel with Jewish spirit was certainly timely, especially because it seems untimely. And it is true, my story holds fast with half-joking earnestness about the dates in Genesis and often reads like a Torah-Exegesis and Torah-expansion, like a rabbinic Midrash. And yet the Jewish is overall in the work only the foreground, only one style among others, only one layer.[36]

Mann's attitude toward German Jewry was not a simple one. He was, after all, the product of a typical upper-class North German Lutheran upbringing. One can find comments and literary characters (even as late as Doctor Faustus) that display a strain of negativism. But Mann's attacks on antisemitism, his admiration for the European spirit of Jewry (he and brother Heinrich were accused of the same), his support of Zionism, and his *Joseph* novel are consistent with his gravitation from Right to Left politically – and the role he played in an émigré community in America. Although he never eliminated every element of prejudice, I contend that Mann should be considered philosemite at age seventy – though not at age seven or seventeen.

Mann was the most famous author who displayed philosemitic tendencies, but there were others who surpassed him for erudition and advocacy. The educational philosopher Friedrich Wilhelm Förster (1869–1966), whose father, Wilhelm, was an astronomer and a left-wing peace activist,

---

[36] Thomas Mann, "Joseph und seine Brüde: Ein Vortrag," in *Gesammelte Werke*, Bd. 11 (Berlin, S. Fischer Verlag, 1960). I have rendered this rather freely. Here is the original: "Man hat in Joseph und seiner Brüder einen Judenroman, wohl gar einen Roman für Juden sehen wollen. Nun, die alttestamentliche Stoffwahl war gewiss kein Zufall. Ganz gewiss stand sie in geheimen, trotzig-polemischen Zusammenhang mit Zeit-Tendenzen, die mir von Grund aus zuwider waren, mit dem in Deutschland besonders unerlaubten Rassewahn, der einen Hauptbestandteil des faschistischen Poebel-Mythos bildet. Einen Roman des jüdischen Geistes zu schreiben war zeit gemäss, gerade weil es unzeitgemäss schien. Und es ist wahr, meine Erzählung hält sich mit immer halb scherzhafter Treulichkeit an die Dates der Genesis und liest sich oft wie eine Thora-Exegesis und -Amplifikation, *wie ein rabbinischer Midrash*" (my italics).

influenced his son's politics. But the son's interest in Jewry emerged from a combination of his many encounters with German Jews and his spiritual seeking – unlike Wilhelm, who was a convinced secularist. A typical letter from Albert Einstein, who helped secure Förster's entry into the United States, chided the latter's glamorization of Christianity: "Christianity – taken as an abstract notion – may rightly be considered as the principle of moral good, of real human progress. The churches, however, in the name of Christian principles, have served apocalyptic darkness more than the eternal goals of humanity." As Einstein recognized, Förster's philosemitism came with a strong dose of traditional Christian superiority; politically, intellectually, and socially, however, he was far removed from the missionary mind-set of Delitzsch or Strack.

Possibly the strangest Germanic defender of the early twentieth century, the Austrian aristocrat Heinrich Coudenhove Kalergi (1859–1906) wrote a massive indictment of antisemitism which originated as a doctoral thesis at the University of Prague. First published in 1901, *The Essence of Antisemitism* was reissued by his son Richard (also a peace activist) in 1923, translated into English in 1935, and reissued with his granddaughter's preface in 1992. The aristocratic right-wing Junker turned left-wing activist, Hellmut Von Gerlach, may not have been so studious, but he did bother to acquaint himself with the basic facts of Jewish history.[37] Von Gerlach devoted a number of chapters in his autobiography *From Right to Left* chronicling his disenchantment with antisemites and his growing appreciation of German Jewry. These figures bolstered their sentiments with learning, tacitly equating antisemitism with ignorance and sensing that their positive inclinations toward a despised minority needed intellectual scaffolding. The persistence of this tendency provides evidence against overstating the degree to which gentile sympathizers did no more than construe fictional Jewish partners with whom to dialogue (*pace* Michael Brenner). Possibly because it was a minority viewpoint, philosemitism in imperial Germany entailed (required?) a sincere interest in the Jewish condition. Berlinerblau regards this sort of intellectual philosemitism, "the project that studies Jewish texts and interpretations of those texts," as legitimate, arguing, "Such an approach invariably recognizes that Jews are not one thing. Indeed, their extreme heterogeneity makes the irrationality of liking or hating all of them easy to discern."[38] But Berlinerblau's respect for intellectual philosemitism requires contextual application. In the Graeco-Roman world, as amply documented by Louis Feldman and the late Menachem Stern, there were pro-Jewish authors in Greek and Latin, but their interest appears to have been primarily academic-antiquarian. Moreover, from the thirteenth-century friars' orders to the

[37] Von Gerlach, *Von Rechts Nach Links*; cf. n. 24.
[38] Berlinerblau, "On Philo-Semitism," 15.

late seventeenth-century author Johann Andreas Eisenmenger, erudition about Judaism could be detached from any engagement with Jews, or even drive anti-Jewish sentiments and policies. Imperial-era philosemites sought information about Jews and Judaism in order to strengthen a particular, politically unpopular pro-Jewish position. Theirs was not idle curiosity.

WHY SOME PHILOSEMITIC SENTIMENTS BLOSSOMED AND OTHERS WITHERED: THE IMPORTANCE OF SOCIAL CONTEXT

The survival of philosemitic sentiments in a hostile environment required a social circle. Often, this social search corresponded to a political move. Von Gerlach's autobiographical *From Right to Left* offers one example. So does the story of the Nobel Prize–winning physicist James Franck, who resigned and emigrated in 1933 in protest against the Nazi regime. The final positions of right-wing figures such as the authors Walter Bloem, Wilhelm von Scholz, and Werner Sombart, all of whom wound up in the Nazi camp, suggest that without the reinforcement of social support, philosemitic sentiments withered. (It should be recalled that Sombart, the most famous of this trio, was lauded as pro-Jewish in many quarters, especially student youth groups, when *The Jews and Modern Capitalism* first appeared in 1911.) Franz Delitzsch's complaint to Moritz Lazarus that some Christian friends found his efforts on behalf of Judaism objectionable – a letter I found in Lazarus's files in Jerusalem – indicates the former's sense of isolation.[39] Jewish contacts played an important role in fostering otherwise unappreciated efforts. Within the world of Left-liberalism, free student fraternities, *Heimat*-clubs, peace societies, scientific institutes, and editorial boards, a mixed social circle of Christian and Jew offered the philosemitically inclined confirmation that the antisemites had it wrong and that Jews were worthy colleagues.[40] The cases of Thomas Mann and Nahida Remy/Ruth Lazarus indicate that traveling in Jewish worlds could not only dilute hostile attitudes, but strengthen positive ones. Mann had a wife with a Jewish connection (Katya Pringsheim Mann had a Jewish father and a Christian mother), a Jewish publisher (Simon Fisher), a Jewish translator (Helen Löwe-Porter), and many Jewish supporters. Nahida Remy/ Ruth Lazarus enjoyed the acclaim of the Jewish world, a chance encounter with a young Jewish nanny whose simple faith she found inspiring, and

[39] Franz Delitzsch to Moritz Lazarus (January 5, 1883), Moritz Lazarus Archive, National and University Library (Jerusalem) VAR 298/94.
[40] On the nature of antisemitism and philosemitism in the German scientific community, see Alan Rocke, *The Quiet Revolution: Hermann Kolbe and the Science of Organic Chemistry* (Berkeley: University of California Press, 1993), esp. 34–5; Fritz Stern, *Einstein's German World* (Princeton, NJ: Princeton University Press, 1999).

a close friendship with a woman (Zerline Meyer) who introduced her to Jewish circles in Berlin. In addition to the general support that the case of German philosemitism offers the contact hypothesis regarding the diminution of out-group prejudice, one can specify that a philosemitic social or political milieu often had a discernible impact over time on given individuals.

A HISTORIOGRAPHIC LOGJAM: SOCIALISM BETWEEN ANTISEMITISM AND PHILOSEMITISM

The target of hostile legislation in 1878–90, socialism gradually emerged in the imperial era as the most attractive alternative to Bismarckian conservatism. While German socialism varied widely, from the rather straight-line Marxism of Karl Kautsky to the revisionist socialism of Eduard Bernstein, all socialists were viewed with suspicion by the ruling Hohenzollerns. In the post–World War I era, the SPD became a leading party in the Weimar coalition. Scholars of German socialism disagree over its record on antisemitism.[41] On the one hand, there are those who stress the antisemitism of its founding thinkers (especially the Jewish renegade Ferdinand Lassalle and the Jewish-born Karl Marx), the willingness to excuse antisemitic excesses as misplaced class-consciousness (epitomized in Bebel's famous dismissal, "antisemitism is the socialism of fools"), the refusal of orthodox socialism to allow any special Jewish dimension within the movement (seen especially in the fate of the Jewish Bund after the Russian Revolution), and the occasional outbursts by the intellectual leadership condemning Jews as bourgeois (for instance, Franz Mehring's "Philosemitismus").[42] On the other hand, there are those who stress the successful inoculation of the movement against electoral antisemitism by the 1890s (Austrian socialism fares less well on this score than German socialism), the openness of the SPD at the highest levels to Jews, the clear opposition to antisemitic proposals regarding the Jews, and the aggressive anti-antisemitism of the KPD until its destruction by Hitler.[43]

---

[41] For an excellent historiographic overview of socialism and antisemitism, see Robert Wistrich, "Socialism and Judeophobia – Antisemitism in Europe before 1914," *Leo Baeck Institute Yearbook* 37 (1992): 111–46; see also Philip Mendes, "Left Attitudes towards Jews: Antisemitism and Philosemitism," *Australian Journal of Jewish Studies* 9, nos. 1–2 (1995): 7–44.

[42] The group that tends to evaluate socialism's record unfavorably would include Edmund Silberner, *Kommunisten zur Judenfrage* (Opladen: Arbeiter Verlag, 1983); Richard Lichtheim, *Ruckkehr: Lebenserinnerungen* (Stuttgart: Deutsch Verlags-Anstalt, 1970); and, with qualifications, Robert Wistrich, *Revolutionary Jews from Marx to Wagner* (New York: Barnes & Noble, 1976); and Jack Jacobs, *On Socialists and the Jewish Question after Marx* (New York: New York University Press, 1992).

[43] The group that tends to evaluate socialism's record favorably would include Paul Massing, *Rehearsal for Destruction* (New York: Harper, 1949); Donald Niewyck, *The Jews in Weimar*

Lars Fischer's *The Socialist Response to Antisemitism in Imperial Germany* (see also Fischer's essay in this volume) is a bold attempt to break the stand-off described in the preceding paragraph. Fischer clearly sides with those who take a dim view of the record of the SPD, especially its leadership. He claims that much Social Democratic discourse hinged on a critique of philosemitism. By leaving the premises of antisemitism and "the Jewish question" unchallenged, socialists, with the notable exception of Rosa Luxemburg, played a role in allowing antisemitic prejudices to fester.[44] Fischer's goal is laudable: not letting any element of Germany (specifically the German Left) off the hook for its failure to champion minority rights is, surely, an inducement for further reflection on what leftist politics should now include.[45] Fischer has made his case that the socialist leadership harbored antisemitic views, and I am persuaded that my own reading of Franz Mehring was too generous.[46] But I would contend that when one studies antisemitism and philosemitism, most is never all. I believe Fischer has neither proven that the cultural milieu of socialism was antisemitic, nor proven that there were no important exceptions to socialist ambivalence. Such a demonstration would require much more focus from the bottom up (such as Volkov, Niewyck, Massing, et al., engaged in) and on middlebrow actors whose presentations tended to be more straightforwardly pro- or anti- than Mehring, Kautsky, or Bernstein. On the whole, it seems difficult to dispute Donald Niewyck's judgment that by the Weimar era socialists were avid defenders of Jewish civil rights.[47] Yet, if this is so, does it not follow that the seeds of this defense were planted in the imperial era socialism that Fischer regards as fundamentally antisemitic?

German socialism, in my view, offered a breeding ground for sympathy toward other "deviants." The novelists Emil Felden and Heinrich Siemer, discussed earlier, were socialists. Rudolf Schay was a socialist: his 1922 doctoral dissertation became a well-known book, *Juden in der Deutschen Politik*.[48] The privileged academicians known as "Kathedersozialisten," among them Karl Lamprecht, Gustav Schmoller, and Hajo Holborn, were socialists and were among the university professors prepared to condemn antisemitism. The writers of the *Weltbühne*, though unaffiliated with the SPD, were left-wingers who consistently opposed antisemitism. True, many *Weltbühne* writers were Jewish and thus fall outside the rubric of philosemitism. Nevertheless, one may assume some affinity of ideas between the journal's authors and its

Germany (Baton Rouge: Louisiana State University Press, 1980); and Shulamit Volkov, *Antisemitism as Explanation* (Chicago: University of Chicago Press, 2003).
44 Fischer, *Socialist Response to Antisemitism in Imperial Germany*, 17.
45 Ibid., 228.
46 Levenson, *Between Philosemitism and Antisemitism*, xiii.
47 Donald Niewyck, *Socialist, Anti-Semite and Jew* (Baton Rouge: Louisiana State University Press, 1971), 215–22; see also Deak, *Germany's Left-Wing Intellectuals*.
48 Rudolf Schay, *Juden in der Deutschen Politik* (Berlin: Welt Verlag, 1929).

readership. Socialism was no guarantee of philosemitism, but it was often a point of departure. Although I consider Professor Kinzig's distinction between "primary" and "secondary" philosemitism very useful, Professor Todd Weir has argued that in the case of religious dissidents, the decision to dissent preceded the move toward philosemitism.[49] One suspects that Weir's judgment applies also to the world of German socialism: that commitment to socialism made one a likely candidate for pro-Jewish attitudes rather than those attitudes drawing one toward socialism. Whatever the process, I think one is entitled to conclude that in any given situation, philosemitism, like antisemitism, will not be spread evenly over the political spectrum. If not by the imperial period, then certainly by the Weimar Republic, the socialist camp housed many figures sympathetic to the Jewish community – even if they underrated the antisemitic threat to its existence.[50]

CONCLUSION

Philosemitism in imperial and Weimar Germany was ambivalent, defensive, compromised by residual antisemitic prejudices, the by-product of conflicting agendas, and based on certain misunderstandings about the nature of Jews and/or Judaism. That German philosemites were ambivalent seems so obvious that no investigation ought to be needed to demonstrate it. German liberals, possessing no concept of twentieth-century cultural pluralism or even a nineteenth-century concept of national identity as the product of political loyalty, regarded the disappearance of the Jews through conversion and intermarriage as the ultimate resolution of the "Jewish question." Missionary Protestants saw the acceptance of Jesus as the savior as the ultimate end of German Jewry. This inability to see religious pluralism as positive or even neutral remained a stumbling block to forming more than a tactical alliance with Jewry – a reality that Jews then and now well appreciate. Sympathetic "segregationists" saw Zionism as the natural response for those Jews possessed of a self-respecting concept of nationhood. Despite these qualifications, a conscientious attempt to defend Jews and Judaism did take place in imperial and Weimar Germany.

One objection remains, however, to the term "philosemitism," and it is a critical one that transcends the particular period and place under discussion – namely, that philosemitism is an inherently problematic posture for a non-Jew.[51] (That Jews ought to have a positive relationship to their own

[49] Todd Weir, "Religious Dissidence as a Pathway to Philosemitism," lecture delivered at *Geliebter Feind/Gehasster Freund* (International Conference on Philosemitism in History and in the Present), Potsdam, June 12, 2007.

[50] Niewyck, *Socialist, Anti-Semite, Jew*, 215–22.

[51] As the epigraph to Michael Brenner's article indicates, he considers the dialogue between Jews and philosemites for imperial Germany a failure. It is by no means obvious, however, that successful intergroup dialogue necessitates the abandonment of all preconceptions.

culture is – I hope – beyond dispute.) Ernst Bloch's bitter and sarcastic "The So-Called Jewish Question" first appeared in the *Frankfurter Allgemeine Zeitung* in 1963. Years before Frank Stern's seminal study *Im Anfang War Auschwitz* (1991), Bloch pointed to the hollow sound of the mandatory affirmations by gentiles of the Jews' humanity and good citizenship in the modern era. While Bloch conceded that the philosemitism in the salon period was indeed "a spiritual discovery," its post–World War II counterpart was only "a patronizing way of making amends."[52] Bloch's initial distinction, which recognizes that the content of terms depends on their historical context, is abandoned in the rest of this essay. Relying exclusively on his reading of immediate post-Holocaust Germany, Bloch issued a blanket condemnation of philosemitism as inherently antisemitic: "Finally, to state the entire issue clearly and sharply: even to speak of 'A Jewish Question' ['Die sogenannte juedische Frage'] verges upon and perpetuates, an antisemitic element that, while vanquished, remains immanent."[53]

Thus philosemitism, in Bloch's view, is not only insincere, a matter that can be supported or refuted by investigation, it is also fundamentally dangerous. The second step of this argument can be phrased, as Christopher Clark's approving summary of Bloch's view does, "A philosemite is an antisemite that loves Jews."[54] Clark's admirable work on the Prussian missionary societies takes Bloch's verdict as a truism. But Clark is hardly the only one to do so. More strident is the German Jewish journalist Fritz Sänger's "Philosemitism – Useless and Dangerous," which opposes all generalizations of any people whatsoever.[55] This approach has one advantage over Bloch's more refined one: it demonstrates through a reductio ad absurdum just how impossible it is to avoid generalization and stereotype. This seems especially true when the people under consideration are as weighted with baggage as Jewry – baggage that in European lands before the Holocaust was presumed to be filled with old clothes.

Yet Bloch's verdict was similar to the one broached in the period under discussion in this essay – by Jews and friendly non-Jews alike. An article in the *Israelitische Wochenschrift* in 1890 pronounced itself satisfied with the minister of religion's declaration, "I am neither inclined nor disinclined toward the Jews. I will protect their rights and guard against injustice done to them." Writing as if one could maintain a cordon sanitaire

---

[52] Ernst Bloch, "The So-Called Jewish Question," in *Literary Essays* (Stanford, CA: Stanford University Press, 1998), 490. Bloch uses the terms "judeophilia" and "philosemitism" interchangeably.

[53] Ibid., 488–91.

[54] Christopher Clark, *The Politics of Conversion* (Oxford: Clarendon Press, 1995), an excellent monograph on the conversionary movements in Prussia, takes Bloch's dictum too much to heart.

[55] Fritz Sänger, "Philosemitismus – nutzlos und gefährlich," in Axel Silenius, ed., *Antisemitismus, Antizionismus – Analyze, Funktionen, Wirkung* (Frankfurt aM: Tribüne, 1973).

between what one thinks about a group and how one acts toward them, the *Israelitische Wochenschrift* loftily proclaimed itself indifferent to German public opinion.[56] Similarly, the Left-liberal stalwart Heinrich Rickert, in an 1880 Prussian Landtag debate, needed to say, "The Jewish Question is not a question of sympathy or antipathy."[57] Most anti-antisemitic activists of the era recognized that attitudes influenced actions, but they shared the presumption that society sought an undifferentiated humanity as its legitimate goal. The overall thrust of liberal apologetic was to minimize Jewish difference, a position the philosopher Michel Foucault called annihilating sympathy. This was exactly the point of Gershom Scholem's famous complaint that non-Jews failed to accept what Jews had to offer qua Jews rather than qua Germans.[58]

Bloch's celebration of working-class socialists and left-wing intellectuals as being indifferent to the distinction between Jew and non-Jew embodies one limitation of his modernist goal. For the enemies of these two groups – despite their wildly inflated and essentialist assertions about "Jewish socialism" or the "Jewish press" – correctly recognized that Jews played a disproportionately large role in both groups. Tactically, socialists and left-wingers placed themselves at a considerable disadvantage by proclaiming as irrelevant a blatant reality, by saying that Jewishness did not matter, when it did. Strategically, the inability to affirm *any* Jewish role in political movements shows the limits of leftist politics in imperial and Weimar Germany. The "idea" of taking this approach existed: the socialist Rudolf Schay wrote an entire book celebrating the role of Jews in German politics. The historian Bruce Frye cites a letter in which a non-Jewish DDP activist proudly championed his party as a *Judenpartei*. This posture was, of course, rejected.[59]

For the Polish-Jewish sociologist Zygmunt Bauman, the true culprit is not the claim that Jewishness does not matter (the liberal posture), but rather, the fact that Jewishness is constructed:

The area delineated and separated by the notion of anti-Semitism (the cutting criteria being hostility to Jews and hostility to the Jews) is too narrow to account fully for the phenomenon the notion intends to grasp; it leaves aside quite a few socio-psychological realities without which the understanding must remain inconclusive if not faulty. I propose that what must be explained first – what indeed must stand in the focus of explanatory effort, is rather the phenomenon of allosemitism, of

---

[56] Dr. Fritz Rothschild, "Unsere Freunde und Feinde," *Israelitische Wochenschrift* (24) Beilage (1890).

[57] Heinrich Rickert, cited in *Die Antisemitismus im Lichte des Christentums, des Rechtes und der Moral* (Danzig, 1890), 8–9.

[58] Geshom Scholem, "Against the Myth of the German-Jewish Dialogue," in Werner Dannhauser, ed., *On Jews and Judaism in Crisis* (New York: Schocken Books, 1976), 63.

[59] Bruce Frye, "The German Socialist Party and the Jewish Problem," *Leo Baeck Institute Yearbook* 21 (1976): 151.

which anti-Semitism (alongside philosemitism, as it were) is but an offshoot or a variety.[60]

For Bauman, the medieval/modern appraisal of Jewishness is best called allosemitism – the supercharging of the construct "Jew" or "Semite" with too many and too often contradictory significations. Bauman posits that Jews in the Christian West occupied a special place as not pagan, yet somehow more pagan than the pagans. Medieval people perceived Jews as "an awkward and unpleasant yet indispensable part of the Divine Chain of Being."[61] Resolving the ambivalence of the Jew became more critical in the modern world with its desire to weed out of the garden any growth disturbing class, nation, or society. "To summarize, modern anti-Semitism was a constant yield of the modern ordering flurry.... The Holocaust was but the most extreme, wanton and unbridled – indeed, the most literal expression of that tendency to burn ambivalence and uncertainty in effigy."[62]

Although the evidence of the Enlightenment's limitations continue to mount, Bauman's prediction that in our postmodern era allosemitism will lose the unique position it occupied in premodern and modern history has yet to come true.[63] Both Diaspora Jewry and the state of Israel continue to exert a fascination out of proportion to numbers or influence. The Holocaust, while discrediting some kinds of antisemitism, has become a new signifier of Jewish uniqueness, and in the views of some – Harvard's Ruth Wisse, for instance – an inducement for Jewry's enemies to try it again.[64] This view, which seemed ludicrous a decade ago, seems less so in light of the recent Holocaust Denial Conference in Iran, the repeated proposals for academic boycotts of Israel, and the role the state of Israel plays as a lightning rod of hatred for much of the Arab and Islamic world.[65]

I would like to conclude on a parochial and pragmatic note. As long as the world insists on constructing meanings of "Jewishness" or "Semitism," prudence dictates that positive constructions of Jewishness or Semitism be encouraged, not condemned. Antisemitism, demonstrably, constitutes a real danger to the Jewish people; philosemitism does not, whatever its efficacy as an antidote to the former.[66] In a 2003 edition of a New York

[60] Bauman, "Allosemitism: Premodern, Modern, Postmodern," 143.

[61] Ibid., 152.

[62] Ibid., 154.

[63] Ibid., 155.

[64] Ruth Wisse, "On Ignoring Antisemitism," in Ron Rosenbaum, ed., *Those Who Forget the Past* (New York: Random House, 2004).

[65] Anyone doubting the vitality of contemporary antisemitism should consult Rosenbaum, ed., *Those Who Forget.*

[66] The various messianic, conversionary movements (e.g., Jews for Jesus) may constitute an exception to my claim that philosemitism poses no danger to Jews. In my view, Jews for Jesus is mainly a challenge to provide better Jewish education.

newspaper (once Yiddish, now English) called the *Forward*,[67] Melvin Bukiet, a novelist and professor of literature, wrote, "We must stamp out philosemitism, wherever it rears its ugly head." Admittedly, philosemitic sentiment is not immune to insincerity or kitsch. I am not so naïve as to think Poland's discovery of the joys of klezmer music will have a real impact on the Jewish future, or that Madonna will inaugurate an era of serious study of the Kabbalah. Like most American Jews, I can appreciate the support of the evangelical Right for Israel without agreeing with their social program. But Bukiet's reversion to Bloch-like rejection of any acknowledgment of Jewish difference is bound to fail – I would argue that the case of Israel proves that it already has. Now that the scholarly world is shedding its dismissive attitude toward the phenomenon of philosemitism, perhaps it is time for cautious cultivation of this sentiment – as the editors of the ill-fated *Der Philosemit* wished.

---

[67] Melvin Jules Bunkiet, "Quick Crush This Philosemitism Before It Gets Out of Hand," *Forward*, January 31, 2003, 12.

PART IV

AMERICAN PHILOSEMITISMS

10

Ethnic Role Models and Chosen Peoples

Philosemitism in African American Culture

Jonathan Karp

During the twentieth century, African Americans drew upon a variety of philosemitic traditions to devise strategies (sometimes religious or idealistic, sometimes hardheaded and pragmatic) for their collective advancement. Idealizing the Jews offered blacks the comforting knowledge that another oppressed minority had triumphed over seemingly insuperable odds by employing imitable means. The Jewish example of group advancement in America was particularly potent because of the Jews' identification with the chosen people of the Old Testament, especially compelling to a black population seeking to complete its own journey from slavery to freedom. But religious associations did not crowd out pragmatic evaluations. Just as Jews have historically sought to induce philosemitism (and avoid inflaming antisemitism) as a matter of practical policy, many black leaders recognized that making pro-Jewish pronouncements and currying favor with the Jewish community could yield concrete rewards. If philosemitism is a form of ethnic seduction, we should not be surprised to find an isolated group like blacks keen to win Jewish partners.[1]

The evidence for a black philosemitism is abundant. Up until the late 1960s polls suggested that American blacks were less antisemitic than whites.[2] Popular attitudes fed off and back into policies on the ground. Black civil rights organizations like the NAACP and National Urban League sought out Jewish professionals and philanthropists to provide assistance, while black writers and artists exhibited a marked interest in

---

[1] For some examples, see Hasia Diner, *In the Almost Promised Land: American Jews and Blacks, 1915–1935* (Baltimore and London: Johns Hopkins University Press, 1995), 125–8; Steven Hertzberg, "Blacks and Jews," in Maurianne Adams and John Bracey, eds., *Strangers and Neighbors: Relations between Blacks and Jews in the United States* (Amherst: University of Massachusetts Press, 1999), 258.

[2] See Fred Ferretti, "New York's Black Anti-Semitism Scare," in Adams and Bracey, eds., *Strangers and Neighbors*, 648.

and appreciation of Jewish topics.[3] But black philosemitism can also be gauged in comparison with its antithesis. The apparent rise of black antagonism toward Jews in the last third of the twentieth century brought the philosemitism of earlier decades into sharper relief. When by the 1970s evidence of black hostility toward Jews unmistakably began to mount, Jewish organizations sponsored a host of studies to find out why. Jews *expected* blacks to approve of them and expressed dismay to discover otherwise.[4] They assumed that comity was normal and sought ways to restore the relationship to its earlier "golden age."[5]

Many recent examinations of the "black-Jewish alliance" have shown that this golden age was in reality far from unalloyed. Tensions between the two groups were palpable even during the period of their presumed greatest affinity, from the 1940s through the early 1960s. But while occasionally exaggerated and idealized, the black-Jewish alliance was quite real during these years (and even more broadly in the period 1910 to 1970). An alliance of civil rights and advocacy organizations at the elite level, it enlisted the sympathies of countless individuals on the ground: union members, religious congregants, community organizers, educators, and the like.[6] Black philosemitism helped promote the alliance by rationalizing the desirability of Jewish assistance and symbiosis. It was part of the romantic superstructure, one might say, of a marriage of convenience.

This chapter attempts to outline and introduce the topic of black philosemitism by focusing on the writings of three prominent figures: Booker T. Washington (1856–1915), the preeminent "race leader" of his day; Zora Neale Hurston (1891–1960), the novelist and folklorist; and the singer and political activist Paul Robeson (1898–1976). While these three cannot stand in for African Americans as a whole, they do reflect important strands within elite black opinion. They also exhibit a variety of positions and perspectives that renders their collective philosemitism

---

[3] In addition to the cases of Hurston and Robeson explored in this essay, see also Milly Heyd, *Mutual Reflections: Jews and Blacks in American Art* (New Brunswick, NJ: Rutgers University Press, 1999); Diner, *In the Almost Promised Land*, 118–63.

[4] Murray Friedman, *What Went Wrong: The Creation and Collapse of the Black-Jewish Alliance* (New York: Free Press, 1995).

[5] For example, the study published by the Reform movement rabbinical seminary, Hebrew Union College, by Nicholas C. Polos, *Black Anti-Semitism in Twentieth-Century America: Historical Myth or Reality* (Cincinnati: Hebrew Union College, 1975); Ben Halpern, *Jews and Blacks: The Classic American Minorities* (New York: Herder and Herder, 1971); Earl Raab, *The Black Revolution and the Jewish Question* (New York: Commentary, 1969).

[6] Of course, the "black-Jewish alliance" never possessed a mass appeal. It is likely that most African Americans and American Jews in the twentieth century gave relatively little attention to one another. Nevertheless, to describe the relationship as lacking a grassroots dimension would be incorrect. See most recently Cheryl Lynn Greenberg, *Troubling the Waters: Black-Jewish Relations in the American Century* (Princeton, NJ: Princeton University Press, 2006).

a valuable composite: a range of age (Washington a product more of the nineteenth than the twentieth century), of geography (a Virginian, Floridian, and New Jerseyan, respectively), and of politics (Washington was a conservative, Hurston a freethinker, and Robeson a radical). That all three manifested philosemitism of quite distinct varieties suggests that the black "love of Jews" possessed genuine complexity and depth.

BOOKER T. WASHINGTON

Booker T. Washington came to prominence during the period of the so-called nadir in postemancipation African American history, an era marked by a racist retrenchment after the advances of the Reconstruction years, institutionalized through exclusionary "Black Codes" and Jim Crow segregation laws. Washington, who had been born a slave, found his salvation in the vocational education offered him at Hampton Normal and Agricultural Institute, founded by the white missionary Samuel Armstrong. Vocational education, particularly agronomy, became Washington's gospel for black group advancement and the basis of his own school in Tuskegee, Alabama, which he helped create in 1872 and which he built into a vast educational complex with a multimillion-dollar endowment by 1900. The Tuskegee Institute became the nucleus of a network of schools, philanthropic organizations, and newspapers that Washington controlled, with the backing of Republican Party politicians and funds initially supplied by New England patrician backers but after 1900 increasingly by Jewish bankers and businessmen, such as Paul Warburg, Jacob Schiff, and later the Sears, Roebuck and Company mogul, Julius Rosenwald.[7]

Yet Washington's interest in Jews predated and transcended his indebtedness to the largesse of these philanthropists. "Ever since I can remember I have had a special and peculiar interest in the history and the progress of the Jewish race," he recalled.[8] While this comment referred specifically to Washington's early intimacy with the Old Testament, religion alone cannot account for his brand of philosemitism (and though a proponent of the "social gospel" Washington was relatively cool to organized religion). Equally crucial were his cultural and economic diagnoses of the disease afflicting black America and his prescription for its cure, which he linked to the Jews.

---

[7] For general background, see Louis Harlan, *Booker T. Washington, the Wizard of Tuskegee* (Oxford: Oxford University Press, 1983); Kevern Verney, *The Art of the Possible: Booker T. Washington and Black Leadership in the United States, 1881–1925* (New York: Routledge, 2001); on Washington and Jewish philanthropy, see Louis Harlan, "Booker T. Washington's Discovery of Jews," in Adams and Bracey, eds., *Strangers and Neighbors*, 290–1.

[8] Quoted in St. Clair Drake, introduction to Booker T. Washington and Robert E. Park, *The Man Farthest Down* (New Brunswick, NJ: Transaction, 1984), xxxiv. See also Harlan, "Booker T. Washington's Discovery of Jews," 292.

The root cause of black poverty, Washington insisted, was the legacy of slavery, specifically chattel slavery's devastating impact on the black work ethic and occupational structure. On the one hand, argued Washington, slavery had trained the Negro in "every trade, every industry, that constitutes the foundation for making a living." Yet, on the other, it had the unfortunate effect of stigmatizing physical labor. Slavery did so, first, by associating labor with servitude, and, second, by unnaturally segregating physical labor from intellectual and managerial operations, what Washington called "headwork."[9] The consequence of both these tendencies, according to Washington, was that slaves came to devalue physical labor and craft skills while overvaluing the leisure associated with the aristocratic ethos of the white masters.[10] Once slavery ended, moreover, the abstraction of physical from mental labor impelled the freedmen to overcompensate for what they had been previously denied by urging their children to acquire a purely humanistic education. Consequently, the postemancipation Negro economy was characterized by a massive deskilled peasant class on the bottom and a small educated middle class of professionals above (what Washington's rival, W. E. B. DuBois, would later call the "Talented Tenth"). Notably lacking was a black entrepreneurial class buttressed by a sizable yeomanry and a healthy body of skilled artisans, necessary strata, in Washington's estimation, for a healthy black economy.[11] The only cure for this enervated condition, according to Washington, would be vocational education on a massive scale (albeit built on the "positive" dimension of slavery's legacy) and a psychological reorientation of blacks toward skilled labor.[12]

All of this will sound oddly familiar to anyone conversant with the economic themes of modern Jewish history. This is because, starting in

[9] Booker T. Washington, *The Future of the American Negro* (New York: Haskell House, 1968), 221.
[10] According to Washington, slavery distorted the work ethic of both blacks and whites: "Slavery taught both the white man and the Negro to dread labor, – to look upon it as something to be escaped, something fit only for poor people." Quoted in Robert J. Norrell, *Up from History: The Life of Booker T. Washington* (Cambridge, MA: Harvard University Press, 2009), 157.
[11] Ibid., 56 and passim. According to his most recent biographer, deep down Washington favored black agriculture above all. Washington assigned greatest intrinsic value to the "improving farmer," whose independence as a freeholder anchored his political virtue. Thus Washington's core political orientation was akin to that of Jefferson. But in the face of agricultural contraction, growing industrialization, and intensifying southern white hostility, Washington concluded that artisanry and entrepreneurship would be the surest routes to white acceptance. See Norrell, *Up from History*, 97.
[12] Washington's assessment appears to have been motivated as much by practical as by ideological considerations. His emphasis on vocational at the expense of humanistic education reflected a keen awareness of the desperate situation of African Americans and the intense hostility even of many sympathetic white supporters to contributing funds for anything other than industrial education. Indeed, many of Tuskegee's donors were captains of industry and potential employers of its graduates. See Norrell, *Up from History*, 96.

the late eighteenth century, occupational transformation and the so-called productivization of Jews became the focus of a great many Jewish reform efforts: the endeavor to channel poor Jews into agriculture and the crafts, to make the Jewish occupational structure conform proportionately to the general one, to inculcate discipline, regimen, and respect for physical work and thereby reconstitute a presumably normal and healthy relationship between Jews and work life that centuries of persecution had destroyed. In Washington's ridicule of the pretensions of the Talented Tenth one can hear echoes of the criticism voiced by countless reformers that Jews were producing far too many rabbis and too few farmers and smiths.[13] As Washington wrote, "We [have] had scores of young men learned in Greek, but few in carpentry or mechanical or architectural drawing. We ... [have] trained many in Latin, but almost none as engineers, bridge-builders, and machinists."[14] But in the Jewish case, the crucial incapacitating experience had not been the slavery or debt peonage suffered by blacks, but rather a millennial engagement in petty commerce: in middleman occupations, peddling, usury, pawnbroking, "huckstering," and the like. Jewish reformers insisted that petty commerce had distorted the Jews' value system and undermined their physical well-being by estranging them from labor and land. The contrast here is simply that Jewish reformers wanted Jews to return to the land while Washington aimed to prevent blacks from leaving it.[15]

Curiously, in demanding vocational education for blacks, Washington did not demonstrate any awareness that during his own lifetime tens of thousands of Jews were the targets of similar productivization schemes devised by Jewish reformers and philanthropists, even though he became keenly aware of the poverty afflicting eastern European Jews.[16] This silence is especially striking since many of the same figures who funded Tuskegee, men such as Schiff and Rosenwald, were simultaneously pouring money into Jewish agricultural colonies in North and South America and Palestine.[17] But perhaps Washington, who was nobody's fool, chose to suppress his awareness of these efforts since it would have contradicted a key premise of his alliance with Jews. For Washington, blacks and Jews represented parallel lines moving in the same direction while not intersecting – at least for the immediate future. Jews occupied the business and commercial niche, while blacks remained rooted in primary production. Washington viewed Jews

[13] Jonathan Karp, *The Politics of Jewish Commerce: Economic Thought and Emancipation in Europe, 1638–1848* (Cambridge: Cambridge University Press, 2008), 204–5.
[14] Washington, *Future of the American Negro*, 56.
[15] On this theme see Karp, *Politics of Jewish Commerce*, chaps. 4 and 7.
[16] Washington observed and commented on the Jewish poor in Poland.
[17] The parallel, if not Washington's apparent ignorance of it, has been noted by David Levering Lewis, "Parallels and Divergences: Assimilationist Strategies of Afro-American and Jewish Elites from 1910 to the Early 1930s," reprinted in Adams and Bracey, eds., *Strangers and Neighbors*, 320–43.

as exemplars of successful economic adaptation to American ideals and
institutions that blacks must emulate, but he did not fear them as immediate competitors and rivals for the same positions (understandably, given
Jews' marginal role in American agriculture).[18] In his eyes, Jews provided
the best example of an oppressed minority, which, through concerted economic action anchored in individual self-discipline and group solidarity,
had "patiently struggled up to a position of power and preeminence in the
life and civilization in which all races are now beginning to share."

There is, perhaps, no race that has suffered so much, not so much in America as
in some of the countries in Europe. But these people have clung together. They
have had a certain amount of unity, pride, and love of race; and, as the years go
on, they will be more and more influential in this country, – a country where they
were once despised, and looked upon with scorn and derision. It is largely because
the Jewish race has had faith in itself. Unless the Negro learns more and more to
imitate the Jew in these matters, to have faith in himself, he cannot expect to have
any high degree of success.[19]

The "Jewish" virtue that blacks must emulate is not entrepreneurship in
itself, according to Washington, but more generally economic self-help and
mutual assistance. Here too, it should be noted, Washington's arguments
bear an uncanny resemblance to earlier Jewish ones. In the sixteenth and
seventeenth centuries, prior to the era of occupational productivization,
Jewish apologists argued that governments and states could greatly benefit
from the presence of Jews because they were the group best equipped to
perform specific essential commercial tasks. The best known of these apologetic works was the 1638 *Discourse on the Jews of Venice* by the Venetian rabbi
Simone Luzzatto. According to Luzzatto, in comparison with all other
commercial groups, Jewish merchants offered the surest guarantee of the
Serene Republic's prosperity because of the Jews' incapacity for political
participation (reflecting their own disinclination for politics as well as governmental prohibitions on Jews' capacity to own estates and hold public
office). This ensured that they would never seek to translate their wealth
into landed power and political offices. Thus the Venetian nobility, long
since graduated from the mercantile trade, could retire to their country estates at ease in the knowledge that the republic's fortunes lay in the
hands of a foreign minority that had no aspirations to political control.[20]

[18] Arnold Shankman, *Ambivalent Friends: Afro-Americans View the Immigrant* (Westport,
CT: Greenwood Press, 1983), 116–20.
[19] Washington, *Future of the American Negro*, 182–3.
[20] Simone Luzzatto, *Discorso circa il stato de gl'Hebrei in particolar dimoranti nell' inclita Citta di
Venetia, di Simone Luzzatto, Rabbino Hebreo* (Venice, 1638). A Hebrew translation by Dan
Lattes was published in Jerusalem in 1954 under the title *Ma'amar 'al Yehude Venetsiyah*.
For background, see Benjamin C. I. Ravid, *Economics and Toleration in Seventeenth-Century
Venice: The Background and Context of the "Discorso" of Simone Luzzatto* (Jerusalem: American
Academy for Jewish Research, 1978).

This, mutatis mutandis, was Booker T. Washington's argument too. As he wrote in 1899, "Almost the whole problem of the Negro in the South rests itself upon the fact as to whether the Negro can make himself of such indispensable service to his neighbour and the community that no one can fill his place better."[21] Like Luzzatto, Washington assured the white South that blacks would keep to their place. As he famously remarked in his 1895 speech at the Atlanta Cotton Exposition, "In all things that are purely social we can be as separate as the fingers, yet one as the hand in all things essential to mutual progress."[22] "Mutual progress," of course, meant the pursuit of economic improvement alone and not social integration or political equality. Unlike Luzzatto's Jews, however, Washington's Negroes would not, at least initially, seek to fill the mercantile niche but rather the agricultural and rural industrial ones. Given the South's desperate need for agricultural rationalization and increased productivity, it must look to its own unfortunate sons, black workers trained in the great industrial school of slavery and retrained in the latest agronomic and industrial methods, to aid in the region's modernization.

Washington was right not to fear Jewish competition in this mission, for despite the best efforts of Schiff and other philanthropists, Jewish agricultural colonies never gained a real foothold in the United States.[23] What Washington did fear, however, was immigration – not of Jewish middlemen but of Italian or Slavic peasants whose genuine caste and class likeness to blacks, Washington believed, directly threatened the Negro's claim to functional uniqueness. Washington penned repeated denunciations of eastern and southern European immigrants, condemning them as militantly nationalistic, contaminated by socialism and agricultural unionism, physically emaciated by disease, incorrigibly addicted to organized crime, so that their wholesale importation into the American South (as some southern whites claimed to favor) would create "a racial problem in the South more difficult and more dangerous than that which is caused by the presence of the Negro."[24] Not so the Jews, for in his account of a 1911 tour of eastern and southern Europe that he undertook with the sociologist Robert E. Park, Washington insisted that the Jews were different. Although

[21] Washington, *Future of the American Negro*, 98.
[22] The speech is quoted in full at http://historymatters.gmu.edu/d/39.html.
[23] See most recently, Tobias Brinkmann, "Between Vision and Reality: Reassessing Jewish Agricultural Colony Projects in Nineteenth-Century America," *Jewish History* 3–4 (2007): 305–24. Brinkmann's "reassessment," it should be noted, is of their underlying motivation and intention, not of their success, which he acknowledges as minimal. The entire issue of *Jewish History*, guest edited by Jonathan Dekel-Chen and Israel Bartal, is devoted to the topic of Jewish agriculture in modern Jewish history. See also Uri D. Herscher, *Jewish Agricultural Utopias in America, 1880–1910* (Detroit: Wayne State University Press, 1981).
[24] Washington and Park, *Man Farthest Down*, 85.

Washington visited Poland and observed in Galicia countless Jews who looked and behaved not at all like his northern philanthropic friends, he insisted that the Jews had long ceased to be peasants (implying that their immigration to the United States represented no threat whatsoever). Their social character and economic structure were sui generis. They were pure exemplars of race unity, thrift, hard work, perseverance, and adaptability, yet uprooted from direct material production. They thus constituted "the exception to everything."[25]

This quality of being the same in a variety of ways but different in some essential point is characteristic of much philosemitism. Jews are seen to possess qualities that make them compatible, useful, employable, and even exemplary, without, at the same time, being threatening. According to this image, they possess a chameleonic nature that allows them to be insiders and outsiders simultaneously, whether in the domain of faith (Christian-like but not Christian), economy (bourgeois but not identical to the bourgeoisie), race (off-white but not quite white), to name but the most relevant here. From Washington's perspective this quality made Jews an object of emulation for blacks but not of rivalry – thus the ideal group to serve as allies and exemplars. Yet despite Washington's best efforts, this balance in depicting Jews as exemplary and nonthreatening would prove difficult to maintain, as will become clear.

Washington was hardly alone in characterizing Jews as ethnic role models for black self-advancement. Washington's ally, the newspaperman T. Thomas Fortune, admired the Jews' capacity for "beating down opposition gradually by high character, great abilities in all directions, the accumulation of wealth and by sticking together."

The journalist Daniel Murray noted that Jews had historically been no less the targets of prejudice than are blacks today; yet today "by shrewdly seeking to control all handcrafts and manufacturing processes, the Jew has forced prejudice to be silent in this country."[26] According to the historian Arnold Shankman, Negro newspapers of the pre–World War II period listed perseverance, thrift, emphasis on family, reverence for education, and a willingness to cater to customers no matter how modest, even Negroes, as some of the qualities responsible for Jewish success in business.[27] Spokesmen of diverse perspectives, such as James Weldon Johnson, Kelly Miller, and W. E. B. DuBois, praised the Jew's sense of pride in his own identity. Writing in the *Atlanta Independent*, the journalist Benjamin Davis lauded the Jews' healthy sense of self-esteem: "The Jew is proud that he is a Jew, and he teaches his children to love the Jews and have more

[25] Ibid., 58.
[26] Quoted in Hertzberg, "Blacks and Jews," in Bracey and Adams, eds., *Strangers and Neighbors*," 255–7.
[27] Shankman, *Ambivalent Friends*, 119–20.

pride in a Jew's achievement, and points to Jewish history as the highest possibility of the human family."[28]

Such pride in membership, even in a group despised by the majority, was both admirable in its own right and conducive to high achievement, in the eyes of some blacks. The jazz pioneer Louis Armstrong spent some of his childhood years working for a Jewish immigrant family in New Orleans. To Armstrong the Karnofsky family epitomized the values of solidarity, sobriety, hard work, and self-discipline that he found sorely lacking in fellow blacks. In a chapter of his memoir, entitled "Louis Armstrong + the Jewish Family in New Orleans, LA., the Year of 1907," Armstrong harshly contrasts the virtues he discovered in his Jewish employers, despite their own poverty, with the self-destructive behavior he believed his own people evinced:

The Jewish people always managed to put away their Nickels and Dimes, Profits in which they *knew* would Accumulate into a *Nice* little Bundle some day. And from the way that *I* saw it, the Negroes which were handling *more* money than *those* people didn't do *anything* but *shoot* craps – played cards all night and all day until they would wind up *broke* – hungry – dirty and funky-smelling just like *first one thing* then *another*.[29]

While claiming that blacks often sought to undermine members of their own group (like Armstrong himself?) who through hard work had managed to achieve success, Armstrong insisted that "The Jewish people never betrayed their own people. 'Stick together' yes."[30]

Black admiration of the Jewish quality of "sticking together" could easily veer into hostility, however. The logic behind such a shift is not obscure. If the Jews are engaged in the relentless pursuit of their own group self-interest, then their presumed benevolence toward blacks must be a kind of stratagem. This would be exactly the charge leveled by the black nationalist and later black power advocates, such as Marcus Garvey, Sufi Abdul Hamid, Malcolm X, Harold Cruse, and Stokely Carmichael.[31] Most of these figures evinced a curious mixture of admiration for and resentment of Jewish achievement. And even Washington (who, despite some faux pas early in his career, never criticized Jews for exploiting blacks) anticipated

---

[28] Quoted in Hertzberg, "Blacks and Jews," in Bracey and Adams, eds., *Strangers and Neighbors*," 257.

[29] Louis Armstrong, *In His Own Words: Selected Writings* (Oxford: Oxford University Press, 1999), 14.

[30] Ibid., 17. It should be noted that Armstrong makes no mention of the Karnofskys in the autobiography he wrote in 1954 approximately ten years prior to these jottings. See Louis Armstrong, *Satchmo: My Life in New Orleans* (New York: Prentice Hall, 1954).

[31] On the early figures, see David J. Hellwig, "Black Images of Jews from Reconstruction to Depression," in Bracey and Adams, eds., *Strangers and Neighbors*, 309. See also Malcolm X, *The Autobiography of Malcolm X, as Told to Alex Haley* (New York: Doubleday, 1994), 283–4.

that blacks would eventually graduate from skilled labor into entrepreneurship. Someday, he forecast, they too would rise to the level of "owning stores, operating factories, owning bank stocks, loaning white people
money, manufacturing goods that the white man needs."[32] According to
this vision, blacks would eventually remake themselves in the stereotypical
economic image of Jews. The question is whether emulating the Jewish
"role model" meant superseding them as well.

ZORA NEALE HURSTON

Something similar could also occur in the religious sphere. If some blacks
revered Jews as descendants of the biblical Hebrews, other resented them
as imposter claimants to the title of *verus Israel*. This dynamic reflects
the peculiar legacy of Old Testament themes to the history of black
Christianity.[33] Most black Americans were slaves prior to emancipation
and exhibited a strong identification with biblical Hebrews, whose story
is one of liberation from bondage. The Old Testament heritage of slave
religion permeated Negro spirituals and continued to reverberate in the
postbellum period within black protest thought and social movements.[34]
Yet this pronounced biblical identification did not predetermine a singular attitude of blacks toward Jews. Rather, it set up the possibility of
a range of strong relations with them, of both a positive and a negative
kind. As noted, Jews could, for example, be depicted alternatively as fellow
Hebrews sharing a common legacy of slavery or as fierce competitors for
the role of chosen people.

But this obvious connection between the two groups has a built-in
complication: traditional Judaism itself is not fundamentally a biblical
religion. Since the early Middle Ages Judaism has viewed the Hebrew Bible
through the lens of a rabbinic sensibility, as expressed principally in the
voluminous Talmud of Babylonia. Rabbinic literature for Jews is roughly
analogous to patristic literature for Catholics: it provides a heavy layer of
mediation and interpretation that profoundly colors how the Bible is read
and understood. African American slave biblicism created the possibility of a literalist reading (or hearing, given its mostly oral transmission)
of the Old Testament that would have been fundamentally alien to most
contemporary Jews. In general, traditional Jews did not view themselves as

---

[32] Quoted in Norrell, *Up from History*, 158.
[33] See most recently Allen Dwight Callahan, *The Talking Book: African Americans and the Bible*
(New Haven, CT: Yale University Press, 2006). See also Eddie Glaude Jr., *Exodus! Religion,
Race, and Nation in Early Nineteenth-Century Black America* (Chicago: University of Chicago
Press, 2000), and Wilson Jeremiah Moses, *Black Messiahs and Uncle Toms: Social and Literary
Manipulations of a Religious Myth* (University Park: Penn State University Press, 1982).
[34] See Glaude, *Exodus*; Moses, *Black Messiahs and Uncle Toms*.

slaves or former slaves, even though the Passover Hagadah instructed them annually to do so.[35] They did not view Moses as a political leader, a liberator from tyranny, and a nation builder; they viewed him rather as Moshe Rabbenu, a rabbi. Jewish messianism partook less of biblical models than of aggadic and folkloric ones, drawn from apocalyptic and mystical traditions that were largely postbiblical.[36] For these reasons a black-Jewish symbiosis rooted in a common Old Testament orientation would seem to have been unlikely, except for one factor. Many of the forms taken by Jewish modernization entailed a "return" to the Bible, to biblical rather than rabbinic Hebrew, to biblical agriculture rather than medieval commerce and usury, to the relative simplicity (if not always the primitivity) of biblical religion in contrast with the baroque intricacy of Talmudic Judaism.[37] Modern Jewish reform movements of all kinds could see the Hebrew Bible as supplying a common ground with Christians (in Europe and America) in ways that the Talmud surely could not. And clearly, because of the special resonance of Hebrew slavery and exodus, few Christians anywhere felt as profoundly close to the Old Testament as African Americans.

Nevertheless, in the postbellum period blacks and Jews appeared to be moving in opposite directions with regard to the Old Testament. Just as Jews had been moving closer to it in an effort to integrate and acculturate, blacks were moving further away. As Lawrence Levine argued in his classic study *Black Culture and Black Consciousness*, in the post-Reconstruction period, during the "nadir" mentioned earlier, a concerted effort was made by northern white missionaries to reorient black Christianity toward a more orthodox, Augustinian worldview, emphasizing the values recommended by Booker T. Washington: patience, endurance, passivity, and inwardness – of delayed gratification and faith in a future better world.[38] Of course, it would be a mistake to overschematize the history of black American religion, positing that an "Old Testament," politicized, mythic, and nationalist slave creed was succeeded after Reconstruction by a passive, individualist, and "New Testament" outlook. In reality, both tendencies have coexisted in dynamic tension throughout modern American history. Nevertheless, the broad lines of development do appear to bear out Levine's general chronology. Many twentieth-century black political movements, ranging from the back-to-Africa ideals of Marcus Garvey to the freedom rides of the early 1960s, can be seen in part as efforts to throw off the political shackles

---

[35] On this theme, see Yosef Hayim Yerushalmi, *Zakhor: Jewish History and Jewish Memory* (Seattle: University of Washington Press, 1982).

[36] See, for instance, Moshe Idel, *Messianic Mystics* (New Haven, CT: Yale University Press, 1998).

[37] See Shmuel Feiner, *The Jewish Enlightenment* (Philadelphia: University of Pennsylvania Press, 2002).

[38] Lawrence Levine, *Black Culture and Black Consciousness* (Oxford: Oxford University Press, 1978), 158–79.

of otherwordly Christian devotion and reignite the old emancipatory spirit
of the antebellum Mosaic faith.

This yearning to revive "Old Testament" political activism in an era still
dominated by "New Testament" quietism was integral to the organizing
efforts of black and Jewish radicals between the 1930s and early 1960s. For
instance, the revival of slave spirituals within the mid-twentieth-century
leftist folk music movement sought to identify an "indigenous" American
cultural medium that could convey a militant protest message (a topic
explored in this essay's concluding section). But this same phenomenon
of Old Testament revival is also key to understanding the more ambiguous political message of Zora Neale Hurston's 1939 novel, *Moses, Man of the
Mountain.*

While highly idiosyncratic, Hurston's novel nevertheless offers a prob-
ing literary exploration of the black-Jewish biblical themes just discussed.
The novel is, among other things, 1) a retelling of the exodus story using
black folk dialect to highlight the historical analogy between Negro and
Hebrew slaves; 2) a compendium of folk legends from Africa and the
African Diaspora surrounding the figure of Moses the Magician, the wizard whose unsurpassed knowledge of nature's secrets has endowed him
with the majestic power to work miracles in God's name; 3) a striking meditation on the nature of freedom, power, and political manipulation; and
finally, 4) an evocation of the plight of contemporary Jews as disenfran-
chised and deemancipated victims of Nazi Germany, characterized in the
book as "Pharaoh's New Order."[39]

The author of this ambitious book remains a rather mysterious figure.
Half social scientist, half imaginative artist, retrospectively the most celebrated woman artist of the Harlem Renaissance but also a writer who
died long forgotten in 1961, Hurston by the final decades of her life had
become an outcast from the informal guild of African American writers,
often ridiculed as a failure and crank.[40] It was only in the early 1970s that
Alice Walker "rediscovered" Hurston both literally and literarily by locating Hurston's unmarked grave in Fort Pierce, Florida. Walker subsequently
celebrated Hurston's genius in a March 1975 essay in *Ms.* magazine, "In
Search of Zora Neale Hurston." That article helped to launch a Hurston
revival that continues to this day. The rediscovery, however, remains only
a partial one. The role that Hurston has come to play in current academic

[39] See Deborah McDowell, "Lines of Descent/Dissenting Lines," in Zora Neale Hurston,
Moses, Man of the Mountain (New York: Harper, 1991), vii–xxiv. It must be acknowledged
that this theme is broached but barely developed in the novel.
[40] The best biography remains Robert E. Hemenway, *Zora Neale Hurston: A Literary Biography*
(Urbana: University of Illinois Press, 1978). Hurston's letters provide an invaluable
source on her life and thought. See Carla Kaplan, ed., *Zora Neale Hurston: A Life in Letters*
(New York: Doubleday, 2002).

mythology is one that she herself would undoubtedly have scorned, that of a black feminist model and emblem of patriarchal and racial victimhood. Left out of this picture is the other side of Hurston: right-wing Republican (the Robert Taft wing), critic of the Supreme Court's 1954 *Brown v. Board of Education of Topeka* decision (from the Right!), and unabashed antivictim (as she wrote early in her career, "I do not belong to the sobbing school of Negrohood who hold that nature somehow has given them a lowdown dirty deal and whose feelings are all hurt about it"). Little wonder that Alice Walker labeled Hurston a "*cultural* Revolutionary," since she found Hurston's politics so unpalatable: "We are better off if we think of Zora Neale Hurston as an artist, period," Walker insisted, "rather than as the artist/politician most black writers have been required to be."[41] This is unfortunate, since there is a sense in which Zora Neale Hurston is the most political of all great black American writers. That is to say, she wrote about political ideas with a powerful awareness of their history within the canon of Western philosophy and republican theory.[42]

When and where Hurston acquired this particular body of knowledge remains uncertain, but other aspects of her political education can be pieced into a reasonably coherent whole.[43] Born in 1891, she grew up in the all-black community of Eatonville, Florida, the daughter of the town's charismatic preacher. As the product of a self-governing black community, Hurston saw questions of black politics as concretely practical and yet theoretically resonant. A student of folklore and anthropology at Barnard College under Franz Boas, she conducted extensive fieldwork on black cultures in her hometown, and later in Jamaica and Haiti. These studies afforded her an abiding appreciation for religion's central importance to the black folk as well as a deep indignation at its misuses.[44] Under Boas's tutelage, moreover, Hurston learned to view race as a cultural construction rather

---

[41] David Headon, "'Beginning to See Things Really': The Politics of Zora Neale Hurston," in Steve Glassman and Kathryn Lee Seidel, eds., *Zora in Florida* (Orlando: University of Central Florida Press, 1991), 28–9.

[42] On *Moses* as a pointedly *political* novel, see R. T. Sheffey, "Zora Neale Hurston's *Moses, Man of the Mountain*: A Fictionalized Manifesto on the Imperatives of Black Leadership," *C.L.A. Journal* 29 (1985), 206–20. Bruce Feiler's recent study of the image of Moses in American culture succumbs to the usual temptation to depict both Hurston and her novel *Moses* as straightforward liberal anticipations of the 1960s civil rights movement (he describes her Moses as "the first civil rights activist"). See his *America's Prophet: Moses and the American Story* (New York: William Morrow, 2009), 246–8.

[43] Hurston professes a deep familiarity with Spinoza in her autobiographical *Dust Tracks on the Road* (New York: Harper Collins, 1991) and was clearly familiar with the writings of Josephus and possibly with those of Philo. See, for instance, her September 12, 1944, letter to Carl Van Vechten in Kaplan, ed., *Zora Neale Hurston: A Life in Letters*, 528–32, 701, 732, discussed later in this chapter.

[44] Both of these features are abundantly clear from her first novel, originally published in 1934, *Jonah's Gourd Vine* (New York: Harper Collins, 1990), based on Eatonville and, at least loosely, on her parents' experiences.

than a biological reality. Her politics, a peculiar hybrid of ethnographic insight and radical individualism, reflected some of these influences. One might conclude that Hurston's childhood and formal education conspired to provide her with an orientation that was characterized neither by puffed up ethnic pride nor by a crippling sense of racial inadequacy.

Moses, Man of the Mountain combines folkloric images of Moses as a magician and conjurer that Hurston collected from her fieldwork in the South and in Haiti, with motifs derived from Western historical and philosophical literature, including Josephus, Machiavelli, and Spinoza. Hurston's Moses is an actual Egyptian prince, a conceit her novel shares not just with Freud's *Moses and Monotheism*, published in the same year, but with a body of ancient Egyptian traditions that are reported in the writings of Josephus and Eusebius.[45] Hurston's Egyptian Moses voluntarily throws in his lot with the deracinated Hebrew slaves in order to make of them a great and free nation. To accomplish these ends he employs deception and actual magic, both mastered under the tutelage of Egyptian priests. He is a Machiavellian manipulator, for whom reasons of state building justify almost any crime, including the murder of his "brother," Aaron, and the faking of his own death.

Hurston's portrait of Moses is ambiguous in the highest degree. The author appears both awed and repelled by her creation, leaving the reader uncertain about both his real nature and her own ultimate intentions. Is God a real divinity that chose Moses, or did Moses rather conjure God from his own imagination, as Spinoza had long before suggested?[46] Is the magic that Moses learns from the Egyptian priest, from his Midianite father-in-law, Jethro, and from the mysterious Book of Thoth efficacious because of its properties or because of its mystique? Finally, has Moses truly succeeded in liberating the Hebrews, or has he merely yoked them to a new tyranny, Yahwist instead of pharaonic? In a lengthy passage toward the book's conclusion, some of the questions are articulated if not resolved:

[Moses'] dreams had in no way been completely fulfilled. He had meant to make a perfect people, free and just, noble and strong, that should be a light for all the world and for time and eternity. And he wasn't sure he had succeeded. He had found out that no man may make another free. Freedom was something internal. The outside signs were just signs and symbols of the man inside. All you could do was to give the opportunity for freedom and the man himself must make his own emancipation. He remembered now how often he had had to fight Israel to halt

---

[45] Jan Assmann, *Moses the Egyptian: The Memory of Egypt in Western Monotheism* (Cambridge, MA: Harvard University Press, 1997); Flavius Josephus, *Against Apion*, in *The Works of Josephus: Complete and Unabridged*, trans. William Whiston (Peabody, MA: Hendrickson, 1980), pt. 1.

[46] Benedict Spinoza, *Theological-Political Treatise*, trans. Samuel Shirley (Indianapolis: Hackett, 1998), chap. 1.

a return to Egypt and slavery. Responsibility had seemed too awful to them time and time again. They had wanted to kill him several times for forcing them to be men. Only their awe and terror of his powers had saved his life. No man among the revolters had courage enough to touch his body or he would have died long ago. The few men, like Joshua who had courage, believed in his dream. So he had lived on and fought on through the wilderness and back again to the Jordan. And now he sat on Nebo's highest peak called Pisgah and gazed down on Israel and across at the Promised Land.

The passage is notable for its failure even once to mention God. Rather, the entire exodus reflects Moses' dream, which a "few men" shared. And even on that score Moses himself expresses doubts. There is, for instance, a clear contradiction between the bloody fight he wages against the backsliders and "revolters" and his eventual conclusion that freedom must be "something internal."

To understand Hurston's view of freedom we must consider her research into and speculation about the roots of monotheistic religion. Hurston's investigations into religious folklore, in her hometown of Eatonville and later in Haiti and elsewhere, taught her that what is elemental in pagan religion is the attribution of divinity to nature. In the novel, Moses' early lessons are learned from lizards and snakes. Hurston found surprising intellectual support for these notions in her study of Moses' image in Western literature. For instance, the first-century Greek geographer Strabo portrayed the God of Moses as a being "which encompasses us all, including earth and sea, that which we call the heavens, the world and the essence of things – this one thing only is God." In his *Origines Judicae* (1709), the British deist author John Toland, who originated the term "pantheism," cited Strabo's statement approvingly and even identified Moses as a pantheist and "Spinozist."[47]

It is unlikely that Hurston knew the work of Toland, but Hellenistic notions of the Mosaic God would have been familiar to her through Josephus's *Against Apion*. Josephus had described the Mosaic law as a "theocracy" (a term he coined), a perfect constitutional order whose justice and wisdom mirrored the mind of the divine legislator.[48] A conflicting depiction of Moses as shrewd *originator* of the Yahwist theocracy was also accessible to Hurston from Machiavelli's *Discourses* and especially Spinoza's *Theologico-Political Treatise*.[49] Spinoza is particularly relevant to Hurston,

---

[47] Karp, *Politics of Jewish Commerce*, 59–60.

[48] Josephus, *Against Apion*, 2:20. Melanie J. Wright, in her insightful study of the novel, claims that Hurston used Josephus very sparingly. This may be true of the plotline but not of the larger political themes she explores. See Melanie J. Wright, *Moses in America: The Cultural Uses of Biblical Narrative* (Oxford: Oxford University Press, 2003), 49–50.

[49] See Abraham Melamed, *The Philosopher-King in Medieval and Renaissance Jewish Thought* (Albany: State University of New York Press, 2003), 150–66; Spinoza, *Theological-Political Treatise*, 189–90.

not only because of his secular and psychological portrait of Moses, but also for his equation of "God or nature" (*Deus sive Natura*).[50] Hurston's own anthropological research had prepared her to entertain a notion of the original Mosaic religion as one built upon a pantheistic divinity that represented the substance of nature and its laws, the *to Hen* and *to pan*, or "one and all." It is precisely Moses' mastery of nature that enables him (like his priestly Egyptian mentors but far better) to perform magic and conjure divinity. Hurston tells us in her preface to the novel that African, Afro-Caribbean, and Afro-American folkloric notions of Moses all concur on this same point. Moses was divine because he mastered nature and recognized himself as a part of it:

The highest god in the Haitian pantheon is Damballa Ouedo Ouedo Tocan Freda Dahomey and he is identified as Moses, the serpent god [recall the above statement of Cudworth]. But this deity did not originate in Haiti. His home is in Dahomey and is worshipped there extensively. Moses had his rod of power, which was a living serpent. So that in every temple of Damballa there is a living snake, or the symbol [of it].[51]

This confluence of motifs from Hurston's wide reading and fieldwork helps to explain her critique of Mosaic politics. For Hurston, Moses is both a liberator and a tyrant. His protean biography and insatiable intellect make him an exemplar of human potentiality. But his politically motivated effort to depict God as a force over and above nature had the effect of subverting his original humanist aims. Moses invented Yahweh in order to inspire and discipline the liberated slaves. But this invention flew in the face of his own intimate knowledge of divinity as a force that pervades all being. Moses' politically motivated theological construction of a transcendent God, possessed of consciousness and authority, exerted a negative impact by opening the door to priestcraft and hierocracy. Starting with the Jews, priestly monotheism spread until it conquered and enslaved the world. It took perhaps cruelest advantage of American blacks, according to Hurston. Their history of servitude rendered them especially susceptible to the false promises and manipulations of con men and Messiahs, not to mention professional "race leaders" with a vested interest in perpetuating black chauvinism and separateness. These types of false liberators, suggested Hurston, feed blacks' psychic delusions regarding their race's unique suffering and future glory.

It was Hurston's rejection of both conformist integration and nationalist Afrocentrism that pushed her increasingly into the margins during her later years. Her 1948 novel *Seraph on the Swanee* was largely devoid of black

[50] On Hurston's pantheism, see Deborah G. Plant, *Every Tub Must Sit on Its Own Bottom: The Philosophy and Politics of Zora Neale Hurston* (Urbana: University of Illinois Press, 1995), 49–52.
[51] Hurston, *Moses*, xxiv.

characters and instead offered a sympathetic treatment of poor southern whites. She devoted much of the subsequent decade to composing an epic novel of Jewish history, that eventually resolved itself into a lengthy biography of the Judean King, Herod I. In fact there is evidence that this work, of which fragments remain, was merely to be a down payment on a far more extensive novel of Jewish history, detailing what she described as the "story of the 3000 year struggle of the Jewish people for democracy and the rights of man."[52] Hurston's aim in this eccentric and obsessive project was to provide a sequel to her Moses saga, to reveal the destination as well as the starting point of the story of mental bondage and enlightenment. As she explained in a 1945 letter to her friend the critic Carl Van Vechten, the nation that Moses left behind was fatally crippled. In attempting to force them to be free Moses had merely reenslaved the Hebrews, this time "to the arbitrary rule of the priesthood." Subsequent Jewish history, up to our own time, observes Hurston, is the story of the Jews' effort to emancipate themselves from the theocratic constitution that Moses had produced. The Jews or Jewish masses, excluding their rabbis and priests, thus represent the hard-won spirit of liberty. As Hurston puts it in her letter to Van Vechten, "They have fought the good fight longer than anyone else in the world."[53]

In regarding Jews as fundamentally nonconformist and antidogmatic, Hurston was likely thinking of such secularized and liberal Jews as her teacher, Franz Boas, and her patron, the novelist Fannie Hurst. These figures exhibited both mental acuity and broadmindedness, while their evident lack of chauvinism toward non-Jews did not appear to tempt them into a disdain of their own people. Perhaps Hurston had in mind "non-Jewish Jews" like these when she identified Jews as the vanguard of an individualistic millennium.[54]

As with other forms of philosemitism, here too the Jews' stature as the biblical chosen people requires that they be assigned a leading role (often *the* leading role) in the unfolding drama of man. Even when the vision of the future is entirely secularized the Jews continue to enjoy priority. One is reminded of Karl Marx's essay "On the Jewish Question," written in 1843, wherein the youthful author, in an early effort to formulate a socialist philosophy, identified the coming revolution with the "emancipation of the Jews." By this Marx meant that the Jews' abandonment of commerce and finance and transformation into productive workers would signify that history had come full circle; the very group that created the theological basis for money and capitalism ("Judaism") had finally renounced and relinquished it. As Marx wrote: "Jewish emancipation, in its final significance,

[52] See Deborah G. Plant, *Zora Neale Hurston: A Biography of the Spirit* (Westport, CT: Praeger, 2007), 159.
[53] Hurston to Van Vechten, September 12, 1944, in Kaplan, ed., *Life in Letters*, 528–32.
[54] Ibid.

is the emancipation of mankind from Judaism." As with Hurston, for Marx the Jews stand for both themselves and mankind as a whole (both the archetype and "the exception to all things"). True human liberation will occur only when there are no more Jews, that is, no more merchants, financiers, and capitalists, whether these "Jews" happen actually to be Jewish or Christian ones.[55]

Hurston's Jews have a similar world-historical mission. It will be fulfilled only when organized religion is finally dissolved through men's individual spiritual maturation. Yet unlike Marx Hurston can fairly be characterized as a philosemite. She is *sympathetically* engaged with the drama of Jewish history, viewing even the Jews' foibles as ultimately educative and self-correcting. More than that, Hurston's commitment to individualism cannot entirely efface her anthropological fascination with the *Volk* – with the speech, stories, illusions, rituals, conceits, and nobility embodied by group culture. In the case of the Jews what she admires most is the remarkable political drama of their saga, their longevity as seekers (from Moses to Spinoza and beyond), their questing nature and yearning for justice and transcendence.

In contrast to Washington's pragmatism, Hurston's idiosyncratic path to philosemitism was not likely to draw many fellow pilgrims. Yet in one important sense she has been typical: her interweaving of black and Jewish narratives through the medium of the Old Testament exhibits the sort of common ground through which blacks and Jews have continued, even now, to seek a sense of mutual heritage and purpose.[56]

PAUL ROBESON

Hurston's philosemitism can also be inferred from the fact that despite her intense hostility to communism, she did not identity Jews negatively with the political Left. In contrast, in the final case study offered here, that of Paul Robeson, the Left served as the principal locus of black philosemitism. Robeson's basically positive association between Jews and the Soviet Union and his belief that Jewish labor unions and left-wing artists had supplied some of the strongest support for black civil rights in the United States provide only the starting points for understanding

---

[55] On *Zur Judenfrage*, see Karp, *Politics of Jewish Commerce*, chap. 8 and the sources cited there.

[56] On this theme see, for instance, the best-selling memoir by James McBride, *The Color of Water* (New York: Riverhead, 1996), with its alternating Jewish-black/mother-son narratives designated "Old Testament" and "New Testament," respectively, as well as the essay by Susannah Heschel, "Theological Affinities in the Writings of Abraham Joshua Heschel and Martin Luther King," in Yvonne Chireau and Nathaniel Deutsch, eds., *Black Zion: African American Religious Encounter with Judaism* (Oxford: Oxford University Press, 2000), 168–86.

his deep attraction to Jewish culture. Like Hurston, Robeson was an avid student of folklore; he regarded blacks and Jews as sharing deep folk roots, especially musical ones. These cultural affinities, in his view, are what best explain the commitment of both blacks and Jews to achieving a just world order.

The prodigiously gifted Robeson was a football star in college ("Robeson of Rutgers"); a graduate of Columbia law school; a star of film, theater, and the concert stage; and an important activist in the civil rights movement in America and the anticolonialist struggle abroad. A man of brilliance and charm, and endowed with a beautiful if untrained baritone voice, Robeson possessed all the qualities necessary to break through to a mass white audience as no black performer, not even Marion Anderson or Roland Hayes, had before. At moments he appeared close to achieving such a position; in 1943, through his performance as Othello, he became the first black actor to star in a drama on Broadway. At this time Robeson was also an international sensation, who appeared on concert stages throughout Europe, the Soviet Union, and Latin America. In fact internationalism lay at the core of his artistic persona. Blessed with a great affinity for languages, he performed and recorded songs in Gaelic, Welsh, Finnish, Spanish, Hebrew, Yiddish, Russian, Yoruba, and numerous other tongues. Robeson used his musical and linguistic talents in the service of folk music, singing the "songs of many lands" at all of his concerts. The tonal and thematic commonalities of folk music everywhere, Robeson believed, would help the masses unite in a great antiimperialist and anticapitalist struggle. This struggle Robeson identified with the foreign policy of the Soviet Union. Although not a member of the Communist Party, he enjoyed close relations with the party leadership in Russia and elsewhere. His global popularity peaked in the immediate aftermath of the Second World War, just prior to the breakdown of the U.S.-Soviet alliance.

It was at that point that Robeson's career became an early casualty of the Cold War. In 1949 the State Department confiscated his passport, ostensibly for remarks he made suggesting that American Negroes, still deprived of basic rights at home, would not risk their lives in the service of an American imperialist attack on the Soviet Union. For almost a decade thereafter Robeson was blacklisted, deprived of physical access to his extensive audiences both at home and abroad. Unfortunately, his comeback, following the restoration of his passport in 1958, was short-lived. Robeson's mental health had begun to falter during the years of his confinement, and in the early 1960s he suffered a breakdown that led to his effective retirement from public life. He lived a reclusive existence in a modest home in Philadelphia until he died in 1976.[57]

[57] Martin Baumel Duberman, *Paul Robeson* (New York: Knopf, 1988).

Robeson's philosemitism, like Hurston's, was the by-product of an early immersion in biblical sources combined with later exposure, through a host of intimate relations, with actual Jews. Hurston had "discovered" the Jews partly through the intellectual and artistic patrons she acquired in 1920s New York. Robeson's own immersion in the worlds of theater, popular entertainment, folk music, and leftist politics ensured that his Jewish connections would be far more extensive. Yet like both Hurston and Washington, Robeson demonstrated a predisposition to philosemitism, so to speak, through his own inherited brand of black Christianity. Robeson's father, William, was a former slave who fled to the North during the Civil War and worked his way through college and divinity school in Philadelphia. William Robeson was ordained a Methodist minister, and for many years he held a pulpit at a prominent church in Princeton, New Jersey. As his son would later recall, "He knew Hebrew and Greek, and I remember one day he said: 'Now, these are the first words of the Bible ... "*bereshit bara' 'elohim et hashamayim ve et ha'aretz,*"' and since then I've learned to read at least in the [Hebrew] language."[58]

Paul did more than "learn to read" Hebrew. Throughout his life Robeson linked his paternal heritage – the culture and faith of his father – with the religious folk traditions of the Jewish people. The genesis of this linkage is too complicated to review fully here. Suffice it to say that Robeson's family exhibited all of the painful tensions that afflicted contemporary black life as a result of status distinctions in pigmentation and social class. His light-skinned mother died in a fire when Paul was six, some years after Robeson's father, as the consequence of a church controversy, had lost his Princeton pulpit, casting his family into a life of hardship. Paul's aristocratic maternal grandparents effectively disowned them, and Robeson may have unconsciously absorbed their snobbery (as well as their blame of his father for his mother's death). Although he performed slave spirituals from the early days of his career, he was not entirely reconciled with his father's humble legacy. Robeson aspired instead to an artistic respectability that he associated with classical music and operatic performance (skills he could not master despite his prodigious gifts). It was only with the advent of the Popular Front in the early 1930s, coinciding with Robeson's first visits to the Soviet Union, that he achieved a life-changing epiphany. Folk music, he came to understand, rooted in primal and universal sources, was as artistically valid as any high art. It was his discovery of the aesthetic validity of folk culture – most crucially including the spirituals that had long been a part of his repertoire – that enabled him to realize himself more fully as an artist and a man. As detailed later, Robeson attributed a key source of this discovery to his contacts with Jews and Jewish culture; in fact, he came

[58] "Robeson/Menuhin," *National Guardian*, February 15, 1960, 12.

to believe that Jewishness was integral to validating the spirituals that he had inherited from his father.[59]

This connection became especially pronounced in Robeson's performances of a Yiddish folk song, the "Hassidic Chant of Levi Isaac of Berditchev," that he featured in many of his concerts of the 1940s and 1950s. Rabbi Levi Isaac (1740–1810) was a remarkable spiritual figure within the early history of the Hasidic movement in eastern Europe, a leader around whom numerous legends arose, most emphasizing this tireless devotion to the welfare of impoverished and oppressed fellow Jews.[60] Robeson clearly felt a special attraction to this figure, in various ways linking Levi Isaac to his own father. The connection was both personal and tribal. In many of his performances of the song he indicated that Levi Isaac's Yiddish "Chant" had the capacity to exert "a profound impact on the *Negro* listener." The song's attraction to blacks, he insisted, lay not merely in its "protest" (against the oppression of God's people by wicked states and empires), but even in its very "phrasing and rhythm," which possess "counterparts in traditional Negro sermon-song."[61]

More than any other piece in Robeson's extensive performance repertoire, the "Hassidic Chant" became the occasion for the singer's lengthy spoken introductions and musicological digressions. In one such introduction in a June 16, 1956, performance at the First Unitarian Church in Los Angeles, Robeson made explicit the personal identification that he believed existed between the "Chant" – and Rabbi Levi Isaac himself – and own deceased father. As he explained, "I often heard my father minister preach, reminding me so much of one Levi Yitzhak of Berditchev, so much of the Hasidim." To illustrate the point that preaching "forms the basis of all of our [Negro] art," Robeson then recited the opening lines from the spiritual "Swing Low, Sweet Chariot," generating a rhythmic effect through spoken repetition of the lyrics before gliding into the song's familiar melody. At this point Robeson shifted seamlessly from the slave spiritual to a cadence from the "Hassidic Chant." Spelling out the point of his demonstration in an accompanying monologue, Robeson referenced Negro spirituals, Russian opera, and finally the first lines of the "Hassidic Chant's" Yiddish text:

And it just becomes a song where speech becomes – and Mussorgsky does it so much and so here I can imagine – "uh, uh, uh, *a gut morgen reboynoy shel'oylem, ich levi yitzhak[ben sarah] mi-barditchev, bin tzu dir gekummen [mit a din toyre fun] ... dayn*

[59] Jonathan Karp, "Performing Black-Jewish Symbiosis: The 'Hassidic Chant' of Paul Robeson," *American Jewish History* 91, no. 1 (2003), 54–81. On these aspects of Robeson's biography, see also Sheila Tully Boyle and Andrew Bunie, *Paul Robeson: The Years of Promise and Achievement* (Amherst: University of Massachusetts Press, 2001).
[60] See Samuel Dresner, *Levi Yitzhak of Berditchev* (New York: Hartmore House, 1974).
[61] Robeson, "Bonds of Brotherhood," *Jewish Life* (November 1954): 14 (my emphasis).

folk yisroel'" ("Good day, Master of the Universe, I Levi Yitzhak of Berditchev stand
before you to issue a complaint on behalf of my people, Israel").[62]

In a "pulpit editorial" that Robeson delivered to the same congregation the
following year (during his blacklisting, progressive churches were often the
only venues available to him), he explained how it happened that Africa
had derived its religious music from Judea:

> Who were the first Christians? They were the Hebrews. ... I remember once talking
> to my brother [Benjamin Robeson, pastor of the Mother A.M.E. Zion Church in
> Manhattan]; he went back and found it ... where the Rabbis called for Paul to come
> to Antioch to convince the Hebrews to let some goys be Christians. ... That's right;
> that's a fact! They had to fight to keep the Jewish people from becoming Christians
> for a long time. And some of this has been lost.[63]

According to Robeson, these "lost" traditions would reveal that the first
Christians (Jewish followers of Jesus) were "much darker than I am, or just
as dark." Robeson explained that these black Jews had conveyed, along
with the Ark of the Covenant, ancient bardic liturgical music from the
synagogues of Jerusalem and Babylonia to the young churches of Antioch
and then Abyssinia. This genealogy, in Robeson's estimation, accounts for
why the religious and folk music of many lands finds its common origins
in the pentatonic chants of ancient blacks and Jews.[64] Blacks and Jews had
together forged the Afro-Christian chant, whose patterns thence migrated
to churches and nationalities in all corners of the globe.

Elsewhere Robeson suggested that nearly two millennia after the birth
of Christianity, the same coalition of blacks and Jews had again joined
forces in the service of an equally momentous development: the birth of
the Soviet Union. Just as Jews like John the Baptist and St. Paul pointed
the way to Christianity, Jews later served as guideposts to Soviet socialism.
In a 1954 article published in the Communist-affiliated journal *Jewish Life*,
Robeson made a promise, albeit never fulfilled, to "some day soon ... write
at length, in the context of my life story, about the meaningful experiences
I have had with the Jewish people." As Robeson explained:

---

[62] Unreleased tape of Robeson's concert performance at the First Unitarian Church, Los
Angeles, June 16, 1957, Howard University, Moorland-Springarn Research Center, Paul
and Eslanda Robeson Collection, tape 4 of 4.

[63] Robeson is likely referring to Acts 11:19–30.

[64] Howard University, Moorland-Springarn Research Center, Paul and Eslanda Robeson
Collection, Writings by, 1953–1957: "Integration," typed transcript of a sermon delivered by Paul Robeson at the First Unitarian Church of Los Angeles, October 27, 1957,
6. Elsewhere, Robeson noted that the religious music of Ethiopians and Jews bore a
resemblance because "the first Bishop of Ethiopia was a Phoenician, that is a neighbor
of Palestinian Jews"; Howard University, Moorland-Springarn Research Center, Paul and
Eslanda Robeson Collection, Writings by, 1953–1957: "Thoughts about His Music," unpublished manuscript, December 1956, chaps. 2, 4.

In the early days of my singing career, the Jewish artists I came to know not only introduced me to the world of Sholem Aleichem through the Yiddish language and folksong; but since many of these friends were Russian Jews, I also came to know the language of Pushkin and the songs of Mussorgsky. And so it happened that, before I had any knowledge of the economic and political nature of the Soviet Union, I developed [via the medium of Jewish folk culture] an abiding love for the culture of the Russian people.[65]

In this admittedly convoluted progression, Robeson's formative contacts with Jewish leftists in the early 1930s helped him discover Yiddish and then Russian folk culture, a process that also enabled him fully to appreciate his own African American heritage (including especially the spirituals of his slave-born father). These developments in turn prepared Robeson to recognize Soviet communism as the avatar of the anticolonialist struggle and the global battle against racism and class exploitation. In this sense, Robeson seemed to believe that Jewishness lay behind the entire trajectory of his career as an artist and political activist and provided a historical genesis of the core values for which he fought.

CONCLUSION

Robeson held the Jews to be a special people, a prophetic nation as well as a primal *Volk*. As in most black philosemitism, such idealization would have been impossible without the legacy of biblical paradigms of Jewish chosenness. At the same time, each of the three cases examined here shows that the key philosemitic act is not to preserve an image of Jews drawn exclusively from scripture but to reconcile the biblical heritage with the disjunctive reality of modern Jewishness. Washington located chosenness in the sui generis class orientation of Jews, which invited emulation of virtuous Jewish economic behavior without requiring conflict over a particular sphere of economic functionality. Hurston powerfully reconstituted the Jews' sacred priority as both continuous with and in pointed contrast to their biblical heritage. Only the people that first introduced the notion of divine chosenness (and its theocratic corollary in the political sphere) could lead the struggle for an individualistic and pantheistic revolution. Finally, Robeson identified Jews as the biblical progenitors of black religious folk culture, a service that Jews now replicate by missionizing Soviet-led global liberation.

In each of the cases admiration of Jews evolved out of both religious and social contexts. Awareness of how Jewish patronage (including financial but also moral support, as well as providing access to networks that facilitated careers and causes) acted in the individual lives of Washington, Hurston, Robeson, and other black philosemites can help temper the sometimes grandiose character of their beliefs by tethering them to bread and

[65] Robeson, "Bonds of Brotherhood," 14.

butter realities. In the extensive history of black philosemitism Jews served as both material and spiritual benefactors for many blacks. Benevolence of such a concerted character could and did lead to charges of patronage and dependency. And here too philosemitism sometimes proved a double-edged sword. But it is important that we not lose sight of the larger picture. In the case of black philosemitism, Jews functioned as signposts marking the directionality of a long, arduous, but ultimately redemptive path. Yet while comparable, the course marked out for blacks is not identical to the one taken by the Jews. The utility of philosemitism demands that a degree of Jewish inimitability be preserved. In this sense, admiring the Jews serves paradoxically to open up the space in which others groups can discover themselves as chosen too.

11

Connoisseurs of Angst

The Jewish Mystique and Postwar American Literary Culture

Julian Levinson

"let's all be Jews bereft. ..."
    Berryman, *His Toy, His Dream, His Rest*, 1968, "151"

In October 1963, the scion of New England Puritans and nationally acclaimed poet Robert Lowell attended a symposium in New York City on Hannah Arendt's controversial new book *Eichmann in Jerusalem: A Report on the Banality of Evil*, which was published earlier that year. The symposium, sponsored by *Dissent* magazine, was attended by a number of the writers and critics known today as "the New York intellectuals," including Irving Howe, Daniel Bell, Lionel Abel, and Alfred Kazin; also present was a veteran of the Warsaw Ghetto uprising and a former leader of the revolutionary Jewish labor Bund (Arendt herself did not make an appearance). For many in attendance the symposium was a watershed event, one of the first public airings of long-suppressed emotions about the Nazi crimes against Europe's Jews.[1] For Lowell, a Boston Brahmin with a taste for the exotic, the event was noteworthy for other reasons. In a letter to his friend and fellow poet Elizabeth Bishop, he noted his delight at the vitality and passion of the speakers: "One was suddenly in a pure Jewish or Arabic world, people hardly speaking English, declaiming, confessing, orating in New Yorkese, in Yiddish, booing and clapping."[2] Having stumbled into an unfamiliar world where human speech flowed irrepressibly and where English had been transformed into "New Yorkese," Lowell was moved to reflect on the Jewish contribution to American culture more broadly: "There's nothing

[1] For a description of this event, see Irving Howe, *A Margin of Hope* (New York: Harcourt Brace Jovanovich, 1982), 273–5. For a number of responses to the event and to Arendt's book more broadly, see "Eichmann and the Jews," *Partisan Review* 31, no. 2 (Spring 1964): 253–83. See also Alexander Bloom, *Prodigal Sons: The New York Intellectuals and Their World* (Oxford: Oxford University Press, 1986), 329–31.
[2] Robert Lowell to Elizabeth Bishop, October 27, 1963, *The Letters of Robert Lowell*, ed. Saskia Hamilton (New York: Farrar, Straus & Giroux, 2005), 438.

like the New York Jews," he continued. "Odd that this is so, and that other American groups are so speechless and dead."[3] At a moment when Lowell feared that a generalized weariness had settled upon the nation, he discovered an uncanny strength and candor in the discourse of these "New York Jews" – all the more affecting since the source of all of this booing and clapping was the single most tragic event in modern Jewish history.

Lowell's letter to Bishop was hardly an isolated case of a non-Jewish writer expressing admiration for Jewish writers, thinkers, and debaters in postwar America. Indeed, whereas literary trendsetters from the previous generation such as T. S. Eliot and Ezra Pound were renowned for their antisemitic views, American literary culture in the post–World War II era was marked by an increasingly prevalent philosemitism. What emerged and soon became commonplace was a positive view of Jews as integral to the most daring and original developments in the national culture. This philosemitic enthusiasm reached its apogee, arguably, between the late 1950s and the early 1960s, a transitional moment in American cultural life when the buttoned-up conventions of the early Cold War had begun to lose their coherence, but the insurgent counterculture of the later 1960s had yet to assert itself. During these years, countless Jewish writers and critics rose to prominence, including Daniel Bell, Saul Bellow, Leslie Fiedler, Paul Goodman, Clement Greenberg, Joseph Heller, Sidney Hook, Irving Howe, Alfred Kazin, Norman Mailer, Bernard Malamud, Arthur Miller, Grace Paley, David Riesman, Norman Podhoretz, Harold Rosenberg, Philip Roth, Delmore Schwartz, Karl Shapiro, Meyer Shapiro, Susan Sontag, and Lionel Trilling.[4] These figures wrote some of the period's most influential works of fiction, sociology, political commentary, and literary and art criticism. More generally, they embodied an exciting new intellectual style marked by an admixture of cultural sophistication and ethnic vitality. Many observers came to see this "Jewish" style as exemplary. As Norman Podhoretz put it in his 1967 autobiographical work, suggestively titled *Making It*,

---

3 Ibid.
4 Much has been written about the "Jewish American Renaissance" in postwar America. On the one hand, there are innumerable essays and reviews by critics who are themselves part of this efflorescence. See inter alia Irving Howe, introduction to *Jewish-American Stories* (New York: Mentor, 1977); Alfred Kazin, "Introduction: The Jew as Modern Writer," in Norman Podhoretz, ed., *The Commentary Reader* (New York: American Jewish Committee, 1966); Alfred Kazin, *Book of Life* (New York: Delta Books, 1971), 125–61; Leslie Fiedler, *Waiting for the End: The Crisis in American Culture and a Portrait of Twentieth Century Literature* (New York: Delta Books, 1964), esp. chaps. 5 and 6. Among the most useful "secondary sources" (though I recognize that the boundaries separating these genres are permeable), I would include Mark Shechner, *After the Revolution* (Bloomington: Indiana University Press, 1987), and *The Conversion of the Jews* (New York: St. Martin's Press, 1990); Norman Finkelstein, *The Ritual of New Creation* (Albany: State University of New York Press, 1982); and Ruth Wisse, "The Jewish American Renaissance," in Hana Wirth-Nesher and Michael Kramer, eds., *The Cambridge Companion to Jewish American Literature* (Cambridge: Cambridge University Press, 2003).

"For the moment, Jews were culturally all the rage in America."[5] Alongside the actual contributions of Jewish writers and thinkers, then, what took shape was a distinct "Jewish mystique," an image of Jews as the embodiment of a unique mode of intellectual engagement, uniquely suited to the demands of the moment.

The philosemtic turn in postwar America raises numerous questions. What psychic and imaginative needs did non-Jews, particularly non-Jewish intellectuals, experience after World War II? How and why were these needs answered by Jews, whether actual Jewish individuals or the abstract notion of "the Jew"? And how did the lionization of Jews during this period relate to broader patterns of thinking about minority groups in American culture? To address these questions, I will explore responses to Jews among three representative midcentury, non-Jewish American poets: Robert Lowell, Sylvia Plath, and John Berryman. To approach American philosemitism via three poets runs the risk of obscuring the phenomenon in its broader manifestations, but I will claim that these poets articulated broadly felt impulses in the culture at large. Moreover, by studying selected poems that meditate on Jewishness or on specific Jewish individuals we gain a close-up view of the variable symbolic roles Jews played in the psyches and imaginative life of non-Jews.[6] Central to my argument will be two main points: first, that in dialectical opposition to the emergent culture of American triumphalism and suburban conformity, there arose a new valorization of vulnerability and marginality; and, second, that as American intellectuals made their détente with mainstream institutions, they came increasingly to admire forms of intellectual engagement that combined depth of insight with an ability to remain aloof from institutional norms. In both cases, Jews came to appear as exemplary figures. Their proximity to the worst terrors of the twentieth century made them emblems of suffering and survival, and their supposed ability to bridge the world of high culture and the ethnic street made them cultural heroes among those wary of the conformist sway of the institutions that increasingly defined their lives.

BACKGROUNDS

Before World War II, most American writers who mattered to the culture at large had treated Jews with disdain, if not downright hostility. In writings by prominent figures such as Henry Adams, Henry James, Theodore Dreiser, T. S. Eliot, Ezra Pound, Ernest Hemingway, and F. Scott Fitzgerald, the Jew

---

[5] Norman Podhoretz, *Making It* (New York: Random House, 1967).
[6] The first scholar to organize the poets I am considering around philosemitic motifs was Hilene Flanzbaum, "The Imaginery Jew and the American Poet," *ELH* 65, no. 1 (Spring 1998): 259–75. In my work here, I hope to build on and expand upon this excellent article.

typically appears as a force of *corruption*.[7] Jews are depicted as interlopers and imitators, damaging whatever is held to be precious, from the purity of language to the "natural" operations of the economy to the sanctity of social bonds. Adams, whose antisemitism was legion, blamed Jews for controlling the newspapers and for embodying the capitalist zeal that had eroded the core values of American life. As he wrote in a letter in 1914, "With communism I would exist tolerably well ... but in a society of Jews and brokers, a world made up of maniacs wild for gold, I have no place."[8] Adams's comment reflects the tenor of a period ripe with fears of a Jewish conspiracy to take over the world, epitomized by Henry Ford's *Dearborn Independent*, with its countless "revelations" of Jewish plots, culminating in the 1920 collection *The International Jew: The World's Foremost Problem*.[9] In Adams's discourse, Jews stand symbolically for the entanglement of forces responsible for disrupting the precious balance of nineteenth-century American society.[10]

The antisemitism of the conservative, nostalgic Adams was often matched by that of writers who championed the new experimental thrust of 1920s culture. In Hemingway's *The Sun Also Rises* (1925), a key text in the modernist revolution in the arts, the Jew is also maligned, though here the problem has less to do with imputed economic behavior than with an imagined failure to embody the new hedonism. The Jewish character Cohn is an unwanted interloper who suffers from an excess of self-consciousness

---

[7] A great deal has been written about the figure of the Jew in modernist writing. For useful recent discussions, see *Between "Race" and Culture: Representations of the Jew in English and American Literature*, ed. Bryan Cheyette (Stanford, CA: Stanford University Press, 1996), and Anthony Julius, *T. S. Eliot, Antisemitism, and Literary Form* (Cambridge: Cambridge University Press, 1995).

[8] Worthington Ford, ed., *Letters of Henry Adams, 1858–1918* (Boston: Houghton Mifflin, 1938), 2:33.

[9] See Henry L. Feingold, *A Time for Searching: Entering the Mainstream, 1920–1945* (Baltimore: Johns Hopkins University Press, 1992), 24–33; John Higham, *Strangers in the Land: Pattern of American Nativism, 1860–1925* (New Brunswick, NJ: Rutgers University Press, 1955), 300–30.

[10] There are important exceptions to this tendency, to be sure. Within nineteenth-century American religious thought in general, there was a tendency to valorize modern-day Jews as custodians of an original, unchanging biblical faith, supposedly untouched by the depredations and tumult of history. The influential novelist William Dean Howells expressed a version of this view in an article describing a trip to the Lower East Side in 1896 (Howells was accompanied by the novelist and Yiddish journalist Abraham Cahan, whose work Howells championed). Here Howells affirms the connection between New York's Jews and "that old Hebrew world which had the sense if not the knowledge of God when all the rest of us lay sunk in heathen darkness." As with other forms of Christian philosemitism throughout history, this view casts Jews as a noble relic from the ancient past. What is implied, however, is that the "old Hebrew world" is also essentially outmoded. While viewed in essentially sympathetic terms, the Jew also figures as a benighted figure whose purchase on the correct form of faith is tenuous indeed.

and refuses to get drunk. Just when a group of jolly American expatriates would find their new paradise in Paris and Pamplona, Cohn intrudes on the festivities, inducing one of the "hard-boiled" heroes to exclaim, "Go away, for God's sake. Take that sad Jewish face away."[11] The Jew simply cannot give himself over to spontaneous action and joy. As such, he provides a foil for the hero, Jake Barnes, whose easy familiarity with the ways of Parisian café society and Spanish bullfighting makes him the envy of the joyless Jew.

Yet another version of antisemitic discourse may be tracked in T. S. Eliot's work, most notoriously in *After Strange Gods*, originally delivered as a series of lectures at the University of Virginia in 1934. In the context of laying out a blueprint for a well-ordered society, he writes that "the population should be homogeneous … and reasons of race and religion combine to make any large number of free-thinking Jews undesirable."[12] Eliot explained that the commingling of different cultures at any given time leads to moral and political chaos, and while presumably any "alien" group might have stood for the offending interloper, "free-thinking Jews" represent the most offending, since they allegedly refuse to obey *any* authority. The linkage between Jews and cultural dissolution comes to the fore in Eliot's poem "Gerontion," which implicates the Jew in the decline of civilization, as we read in these lines: "My house is a decayed house / And the jew squats on the window sill, the owner, / Spawned in some estaminent of Antwerp, / Blistered in Brussels, patched and peeled in London."[13] The Jewish landlord is here a synonym for plague. He comes from everywhere and nowhere, leaving him without any allegiance beyond that of his own purse. Like Adams and Hemingway, then, Eliot imagines Jews as a mortal threat to community and cultural coherence; they must therefore be restrained or somehow kept out.[14]

To be sure, there were exceptions to these instances of pre–World War II antisemitism. A striking counterexample can be found in the writings of the Norwegian-born economist Thorstein Veblen, whose 1919 essay "The Intellectual Pre-eminence of Jews in Modern Europe" discovers the sources of Jewish genius in the very same cosmopolitanism that Eliot saw as a threat. Veblen imagines Jews along essentially the same lines as Eliot: once again we find a portrait of the cosmopolitan Jewish intellectual for whom skepticism follows as a response to homelessness. But for Veblen, whose concern was to identify the qualities necessary for original critical thought, these characteristics are charged with a positive valence:

[11] Ernest Hemingway, *The Sun Also Rises* (1926; repr., New York: Scribner, 2003), 181.
[12] T. S. Eliot, *After Strange Gods* (London: Faber, 1934), 19.
[13] T. S. Eliot, *The Complete Poems and Plays: 1909–1950* (New York: Harcourt Brace, 1971), 21.
[14] For a useful corrective to the now-standard view of Eliot as hostile to Jews, see Ranen Omer-Sherman, "Rethinking Eliot, Jewish Identity, and Cultural Pluralism," *Modernism/Modernity* 10, no. 3 (2003): 439–45.

It appears to be only when the gifted Jew escapes from the cultural environment created and fed by the particular genius of his own people, only when he falls into the alien lines of gentile inquiry and becomes a naturalised, though hyphenate, citizen in the gentile republic of learning, that he comes into his own as a creative leader in the world's intellectual enterprise. It is by loss of allegiance, or at the best by force of a divided allegiance to the people of his origin, that he finds himself in the vanguard of modern inquiry. He becomes a disturber of the intellectual peace, but only at the cost of becoming an intellectual wayfaring man, a wanderer in the intellectual no-man's-land, seeking another place to rest, farther along the road, somewhere over the horizon.[15]

The Jew who has been set free from Jewish traditions but has yet to find a new home becomes for Veblen the quintessential modern intellectual hero.[16] As Alfred Kazin has proposed, this portrait of the Jewish wanderer may be seen as a self-portrait: the foreign-born Veblen never became fully acculturated to America mores, and he clung to his outsider status as a safeguard for his own critical perspective.[17] It would take the sweeping social, cultural, and economic changes of the post–World War II years for Veblen's view, with its praise of marginality, to become much more prevalent.

POSTWAR DEVELOPMENTS

The aftermath of World War II witnessed a sea change in perceptions of Jews in American literary culture, largely displacing the paranoia of the Adams-Hemingway-Eliot group. On the level of society as a whole, this period witnessed a sharp decline in antisemitism. As the historian Edward Shapiro has shown, although antisemitic attitudes spiked in 1944, when Jews provided a ready scapegoat for frustrations and deprivations linked to the war, they declined steadily amid the economic expansion and triumphant Americanism that followed the war.[18] Among the signs of this new acceptance were that housing developments and country clubs increasingly dropped restrictions on Jews, fewer job listings excluded Jews, colleges and professional schools began eliminating quotas, and avowedly anti-Jewish organizations disappeared almost altogether. Public displays of antisemitism lost legitimacy for various reasons, including the association between antisemitism and Hitler; a renewed public commitment to the values of liberalism as the Cold War took shape; a rise in the popularity of religion,

---

[15] Thorsten Veblen, *Political Science Quarterly* 34, no. 1 (March 1919): 37.

[16] Many of the central ideas in Veblen's essay will resurface nearly fifty years later in Isaac Deutscher's famous essay "The Non-Jewish Jew"; see *The Non-Jewish Jew and Other Essays* (Oxford: Oxford University Press, 1968).

[17] For a discussion of Veblen as a European outsider, see Alfred Kazin, *On Native Grounds: An Interpretation of American Prose Literature* (New York: Reynal and Hitchcock, 1942).

[18] Edward Shapiro, *A Time of Healing* (Baltimore: Johns Hopkins University Press, 1992).

coupled with a new sense of the "Judeo-Christian" ethos underlying both Judaism and Christianity;[19] and the broadening of a white-collar labor force and the expansion of suburbia, which increasingly placed Jews and Christians side by side in places of work and residence.[20] All of these factors paved the way for Jews to enter the middle class on a more or less equal footing with Protestants and Catholics.

But while these developments suggest a gradual erasure of the idea of Jewish difference, the postwar years also proved to be a moment of heightened Jewish cultural vitality, including powerful reassertions of Jewish particularity. In the late 1940s and early 1950s, the New York Jewish intellectuals (the same group who would later gather to discuss the Hannah Arendt controversy we began with) began making their mark. Key organs for the dissemination of their ideas were the iconic journal of the anti-Stalinist Left, *Partisan Review*, and the newly established *Commentary*. By the early 1960s they could also be found in magazines of more popular appeal such as *Vogue, Saturday Evening Post*, and the *New Yorker*. While they generally affirmed the goals of American democracy, they also tended to adopt a critical stance vis-à-vis dominant social trends: one of Trilling's collections of essays was appropriately called *The Opposing Self*; the journal Howe founded in 1954 was called *Dissent*. This was also the period when Jewish novelists such as Saul Bellow, Bernard Malamud, and Philip Roth began winning prestigious literary awards and reshaping the terrain of American literature. In a period when many of the most acclaimed writers came from the South (e.g., Robert Penn Warren, James Agee, Allen Tate), these Jewish writers created a new literary discourse incorporating the accents of Yiddish and introducing a new stock of characters. Most commonly, their narratives centered around the misadventures of a humane but deeply suffering character, the newly ubiquitous schlemiel (consider Bellow's *Seize the Day* [1954], Malamud's *The Assistant* [1957], and Roth's *Goodbye, Columbus* [1959]).

Numerous explanations have been offered to account for this "Jewish American Renaissance." Some have seen it as part of a broad pattern of Jewish movement into mainstream American society, enabled by the decline in antisemitism.[21] Others have proposed that an impasse in socialism led those Jews who a generation earlier would have moved in radical

---

[19] Will Herberg's book *Protestant, Catholic, Jew: An Essay in Religious Sociology* (Chicago: University of Chicago Press, 1983) reflects the pervasive new sense of American as defined by religious, not ethnic identity. He proposes that Jews were one of what were essentially three denominations of an overarching monotheism.

[20] For a discussion linking the "whitening" of Jews in postwar society with the rise of the middle class, see Karen Brodkin, *How Jews Became White Folks and What It Says about Race in America* (New Brunswick, NJ: Rutgers University Press, 1998).

[21] See Jonathan Sarna, *American Judaism: A History* (New Haven, CT: Yale University Press, 2006); Shapiro, *Time of Healing*.

political circles towards intellectual work instead.[22] If young Jews in the
1930s might have thrown themselves into the struggles of the working
class, their heirs in the 1950s set to work before their typewriters, meditat-
ing on social and cultural questions that – without the ready aid of Marxist
dogma – had became endlessly complex and engaging. Still others have
attributed this cultural ferment to an existential situation characterized by
partial or incomplete assimilation.[23] Neither an integral part of the largely
religious, Yiddish-speaking immigrant milieu into which they were born,
nor of the mainstream American society they were entering, a generation
of American Jews turned inward and drew on untapped creative resources
to find their bearings. As an effect of this position of in-betweenness, the
argument goes, the generation of American Jews who came of age in the
1930s and 1940s were uniquely situated to create works of especially powerful insight. An added impetus to cultural work was given by the Holocaust,
which called for some type of reckoning and became a tacit point of reference for much of the Jewish writing during the period.[24]

To understand why the image of the outsider Jew gained broad appeal
among non-Jews at this time, it is useful to recall the set of new challenges
faced by American intellectuals in general after the war. As many have
noted, this was a time when the daunting complexity of social and political problems and unprecedented developments in science and other areas
lent new authority to the figure of the expert. With increased funding for
research and academia (thanks to factors such as the booming economy,
the G.I. Bill, and the Cold War), it became increasingly attractive for intellectuals to accept positions in institutions from think tanks to university
departments. Many American writers increasingly eschewed the lure of
expatriation, accepting instead positions teaching in English departments
or working in the expanding publishing industry. Indeed, whereas alienation from such institutions had once appeared the inevitable fate – and
perhaps the ideal condition – for innovative literary and cultural work,
American intellectuals of various kinds began to see some form of accommodation to institutional structures as their fate. But, as Richard Hofstadter
argues in *Anti-intellectualism in American Life* (1964), this rapprochement
between intellectuals and American institutions generated its own form
of anxiety. "Many of the most spirited younger intellectuals," he writes,
"are disturbed above all by the fear that, as they are increasingly recognized, incorporated, and used, they will begin merely to conform, and will

[22] See in particular Shechner, *After the Revolution*.
[23] See Howe, "New York Jewish Intellectuals," and Bloom, *Prodigal Sons*.
[24] The question about precisely when and to what extent American Jewish writers began
responding to the Holocaust remains the subject of some debate. For a useful survey of
this literature see S. Lilian Kremer, *Witness through the Imagination: Jewish American Holocaust
Literature* (Detroit: Wayne State University Press, 1989).

cease to be creative and critical and truly useful. This is the fundamental paradox in their position … that they are troubled and divided in a more profound way by their acceptance."[25] For many American writers caught between the old alienation and the new acceptance, the Jew became a new symbol for a mode of existence in the interstices of the culture. Insofar as Jews seemed to retain some measure of immunity to institutional pressures, they seemed to embody resistance to institutional conformity. This was not so much some atavistic escape from social pressures altogether, but a mode of inhabiting institutional structures while remaining essentially unaltered by them.

PHILOSEMITISM AMONG THE CONFESSIONAL POETS

This kind of view can be seen among poets associated with the school known as the "confessional poets." First used disapprovingly in a review of Lowell's *Life Studies* in 1959, the term "confessional poetry" is applied to a group of poets who emerged in the late 1950s and 1960s, including Lowell, Philip Berryman, Sylvia Plath, W. D. Snodgrass, and Anne Sexton.[26] All of them came of age during the 1930s under the shadow of high modernist masters such as Eliot and Pound but moved American poetry in decidedly different directions, introducing a candor and range of emotion absent from much prewar poetry.[27] In their focus on the pressures of middle-class family life and on the anxieties and emotional conflicts of the subjective ego, these poets created works that reflected the postwar zeitgeist. Their principal themes include divorce, sexual infidelity, childhood neglect, and the mental disorders that follow from psychic wounds received in early life.[28] Powerfully influenced by psychoanalysis, they often return in their poetry to traumatic and haunting experiences, making poetry serve as occasion for self-discovery and catharsis.

In the careers of many of these poets, a process of artistic development can be traced from an apprenticeship stage of working in formal, controlled

---

[25] Richard Hofstadter, *Anti-intellectualism in American Life* (New York: Alfred A. Knopf, 1964), 393.

[26] M. H. Rosenthal, "Poetry as Confession," *Nation*, September 19, 1959, 154–5.

[27] The use of the term "confessional" to refer to these poets has been widely and justifiably criticized, above all because the label suggests that the drive for personal catharsis overshadowed aesthetic criteria for these poets, and that was far from the case. See Adam Kirsch, *The Wounded Surgeon: Confession and Transformation in Six American Poets* (New York: Norton, 2005), x–xv. In this article, nevertheless, I will use the phrase "confessional poetry" because despite its inaccuracies it provides a useful shorthand to refer to the poets I am discussing.

[28] Diane Wood Middlebrook, "What Was Confessional Poetry?" in Jay Parini, ed., *Columbia History of American Poetry*, (New York: Columbia University Press, 1993), 632–49. See also Kirsch, *Wounded Surgeon*.

verse to a later stage when a palpably personal, expressive voice begins to emerge. With Lowell, this development occurs between *Lord Weary's Castle* (1946) and *Life Studies* (1959); with Plath between her first collection, *The Colossus and Other Poems* (1960), and her posthumous *Ariel* (1965); and with Berryman between *Homage to Mistress Bradstreet* (1956) and *77 Dream Songs* (1964). One of the striking aspects of this development in these three cases is that it coincides with a tendency to identify with Jews, who are imagined as emblematic victims and as independently minded intellectuals in a standardized world. That is, Jews become sympathetic figures precisely when these poets move toward their most personal and original work. It might then be argued that the Jew figures as a muse, or at least a symbolic figure of support, for the emergence of confessional poetry in its most distinctive forms.

ROBERT LOWELL

This fascination with Jews is evident at several moments in Lowell's *Life Studies* (1959). An example is "Memories of West Street and Lepke," a poem that fits into the volume's focus on the barely concealed conflicts haunting the complacency of middle-class life. The poem begins by describing the poet's routinized life as a part-time college teacher and a father during what Lowell calls the "tranquilized *Fifties.*" This period presents such a homogeneous aspect to the poet as he gazes out onto his Boston street that he imagines that "even the man scavenging filth in the back alley trash cans / has two children, a beach wagon, a helpmate, / and is 'a young Republican.'"[29] In order to escape this bland present, Lowell delves into memory, dwelling on the period of five months he served in jail in 1943 for being a conscientious objector to the war. In this decidedly more vital and principled period of his life, Lowell found himself in the company of an eccentric cast of characters, including "a Negro boy with curlicues / of Marijuana in his hair" (85) and the convicted Jewish mobster Louis "Lepke" Buchalter, who was executed in 1944. This is, as it were, a period of "slumming," and yet Lowell's partly ironic view of his youthful excesses cannot obscure a genuine feeling of comradeship he felt for his fellow inmates.

Among these inmates, Lowell recalls with distinct tenderness a figure marked by his name and overall bearing as a Jew:

> Strolling, I yammered metaphysics with Abramowitz,
> a jaundice-yellow ("it's really tan")

[29] Robert Lowell, *Life Studies and For the Union Dead* (New York: Farrar, Straus & Giroux, 2000), 85. For insight into Lowell's biography, see Paul Mariani, *Lost Puritan: A Life of Robert Lowell* (New York: Norton, 1996).

and fly-weight pacifist,
so vegetarian,
he wore rope shoes and preferred fallen fruit.
He tried to convert Bioff and Brown,
The Hollywood pimps, to his diet.
Hairy, muscular, suburban,
wearing chocolate double-breasted suits,
they blew their tops and beat him black and blue. (86)

Lowell sets up a dichotomy between the muscular, evidently non-Jewish brutes (Bioff and Brown) and the physically weak, intellectual, and morally pure Jew. Abramowitz's body is itself changeable, moving from "jaundice-yellow" to "black and blue" as the result of his afflictions. But this insubstantial body is merely the container for an exemplary mind, capable of moral discernment and metaphysical speculation. This figure makes an appropriate interlocutor for Lowell, the conscientious objector: both are pacifists; both have a penchant for "yammer[ing] metaphysics." The Jew here is thus a fellow inmate in a violent world, whose only crime, it would seem, is gentleness of spirit. The logic of reversal in the poem positions Abramowiz and Lowell, inmates in West Street Jail, as victims of an intolerant world. As for Lepke, even he becomes a strangely sympathetic figure, so beaten by the world (and his lobotomy) that he now drifts in a "sheepish calm."

The poem leaves us reflecting on two images of stasis: the opening image of the poet languishing at home as a part-time college professor in the "tranquilized fifties" and the final image of the lobotomized Lepke lingering in his cell, just before his execution. But the similarities between these images cannot distract the reader, nor presumably the poet himself, from the recognition that the Jewish mobster has been forcibly taken out of commission by the authorities while the poet/professor has willingly accepted *his* deadening life. The poem's indictment of 1950s America evinces a romance with criminality, which offers an image of temporary freedom in an ultimately crushing world.

In "To Delmore Schwartz" (1959), Lowell creates another portrait of an eccentric Jewish figure who, like Lowell's jail mate Abramowitz, offers friendship, conversation, and inspiration to the poet. Schwartz (1913–66) was widely considered one of the more brilliant of the New York Jewish intellectuals, whose short stories, poetry, and critical essays suggested a great potential that was never fully realized. From 1943 to 1955, Schwartz served as an editor for *Partisan Review*, and his writing frames a mode of experience that became associated with midcentury Jewish intellectuals. In his 1951 essay "The Vocation of the Poet in the Modern World," Schwartz posits an analogy between the essential identity of the modern poet and the modern Jew. The modern Jew, he writes, is "at once alienated and indestructible; he is an exile from his own country, exiled from

himself, yet he survives the annihilating fury of history."[30] Contemporary
poets, he adds, must be similarly willing to accept alienation as their lot;
in their devotion to what he calls the essentially affirmative art of poetry,
poets also resemble Jews in their tenacious powers of survival. Schwarz
was also associated with erratic behavior, including bouts of paranoia and
mania. Like Lowell, Schwartz was repeatedly hospitalized during the 1950s
for psychiatric problems. In a letter written to Elizabeth Bishop a few days
after Schwartz's death in 1966, Lowell summed up his impression of him as
a mad genius, exemplary though also terrifying in the reach of his mind.
"Delmore ... quickening with Jewish humor, and in-the-knowness, and his
own genius, every person, every book – motives for everything, Freud in
his blood, great webs of causation, then suspicion, then rushes of rage."[31]
In Schwartz's life and work, then, the themes of Jewishness, madness, and
creation join, a combination that made him an emblem of the modern artist in extremis and a hero to Lowell, among many others.

Lowell's poem conjures a visit he paid to the Jewish poet in his Cambridge
home in 1946. During a night of drinking, he and Schwartz are "underseas
fellows, nobly mad." Together they contemplate "the chicken-hearted shad-
ows of the world" and the "universal *Angst*." They also revel in the insights
of European cultural heroes: "'Let Joyce and Freud, / the Masters of Joy /
be our guests here,' you said" (53). The poem creates a contrast between
the intimacy and profundity of the poets' colloquy in Schwartz's house and
the frozen world of wintertime Cambridge that lies outside ("The Charles
/ River was turning silver" [54]). The only reminder of the proximity of
the Ivy League is, surprisingly, a stuffed duck from a hunting trip Schwartz
once took: "Your stuffed duck craned toward Harvard" (53). Schwartz's
duck is evidence of an absurd attempt to make it as an all-American out-
doorsman, and he has evidently returned to his books. As for Lowell, his
affinities are inside with the inspired Jewish poet in his garret rather than
outside in the more sedate quad, where his famous WASP heritage would
be more likely to place him.[32]

---

[30] Delmore Schwartz, "The Vocation of the Poet in the Modern World," in Reginald Gibbons,
ed., *The Poet's Work: 29 Poets on the Origins and Practice of Their Art* (Chicago: University of
Chicago Press, 1979), 91. A version of this essay was originally delivered as a lecture in
1949 at the Union Theological Seminary in New York.

[31] Lowell, letter to Bishop, July 16, 1966, in Hamilton, ed., *Letters of Robert Lowell*, 472.

[32] In a letter written to Lowell after the publication of *Life Studies*, Schwartz expresses tre-
mendous gratitude for this poem while also correcting one detail: "I liked all of your new
poems [*Life Studies*] very much and was quite touched and flattered by the poem to me,
and meant again and again to write and tell you so. The stuffed bird belonged to Bill Van
Keuren and he shot – I've never shot anything but pool." Letter to Lowell, April 12, 1959, in
Letters of Delmore Schwartz, selected and edited by Robert Phillips (Princeton, NJ: Ontario
Review Press, 1984), 353–4. Schwartz's point about shooting pool rather than ducks reinforces the point I am making about Lowell's poem, namely, that it hints at the absurdity in
considering duck hunting in relation to Schwartz, the urban Jewish poet.

Instructively, one of Schwartz's well-known poems, "Sonnet: The Ghosts of James and Peirce in Harvard Yard," which was published the same year as *Life Studies*, also evokes Harvard as a place of exile for the Jewish aspirant to high culture. As the poet walks through campus (Schwartz taught at Harvard in 1940–47) he hears the ringing of the Harvard bells and imagines that the sound they make is the repeating word: "Episcopalian! palian! the ringing soared."[33] The sonnet ends with the voices of the ghosts of William James and Charles Peirce, who warn the poet of the insufficiency of his own understanding: "'And you are ignorant, who hear the bell / Ignorant you walk between heaven and hell.'" The point would appear to be that the Jewish poet does not possess a deep enough knowledge to belong at Harvard, though the poem itself insinuates that the real problem is the WASP culture that does not want the Jew. Seen in relation to Schwartz's poem about self-consciousness and insecurity at Harvard, Lowell's "To Delmore Schwartz" points to a desire to decamp from the WASP world of his forbears and to join forces with the marginalized Jew at Harvard.

But Jewishness is not merely a symbolic identity for Lowell. He lays claim to an actual Jewishness – remote, to be sure, but biologically grounded nonetheless – in his prose memoir "91 Revere Street" (also in *Life Studies*). The text begins by reaching back to the Lowell family's early roots in America, and surprisingly the first member of his lineage the poet recalls is not one of the famous *Mayflower* descendants on his mother's side, but his great-great-grandfather on his paternal side, the venerable Major Mordecai Myers, whose portrait hung in his childhood home. "He was a dark man, a German Jew – no downright Yankee.... One of those Moorish-looking dons painted by his contemporary Goya" (12). This picturesque, orientalized ancestor turns out to have been a patriotic American from the time he arrived in the New World: he served in the War of 1812 and later became mayor of Schenectady. But Lowell makes clear that his Jewish ancestor fed his youthful fantasies of rebellion: "In the anarchy of my adolescent war on my parents, I tried to make him a true wolf, the wandering Jew!" (12). Though Lowell admits to distorting Myers's actual character, the point remains that Lowell identifies with a Jew in his need to find a model for himself. As with his portraits of Abramowitz and Schwartz, Lowell's memoir reveals a fascination with the Jew as a figure both inside and outside society, possessed of a rare insight gained from this kind of mobility.

SYLVIA PLATH

A onetime student of Lowell, Sylvia Plath also evokes Jewish figures in her efforts to name her own experience and aspirations. However, where Lowell

---

[33] Delmore Schwartz, *Selected Poems: Summer Knowledge* (1959; repr., New York: New Directions, 1967), 51.

recalls specific encounters with individual Jews who offer companionship and conversation, Plath evokes Jews more abstractly as symbols for bodily mutilation and persecution. In *The Bell Jar*, a harrowing narrative of the mental breakdown and hospitalization of a college girl, the opening passage evokes the Rosenbergs, whose trial and execution shadow the entire narrative. "I couldn't help wondering what it would be like, being burned alive all along your nerves.... I kept hearing about the Rosenbergs over the radio and at the office till I couldn't get them out of my mind."[34] While no one else in the novel seems to have any sympathy for the Rosenbergs, they haunt the protagonist, whose name seems vaguely Jewish (Esther Greenwood) and whose sensitivity to them reveals her affinity for victims in general. When she endures shock treatment after suffering a nervous breakdown, the ordeal appears to have been foreshadowed by the images of the electrocuted Rosenbergs. Though the protagonist survives, Plath's insistence on this analogy suggests that the narrative cannot be read in entirely triumphant terms.

In "Lady Lazarus," Plath evokes her own numerous failed attempts at suicide, and in the poem's opening lines she adduces the Jewish victims of the Holocaust as prototype and symbol for herself:

> A sort of walking miracle, my skin
> Bright as a Nazi lampshade,
> My right foot
> A paperweight,
> My face a featureless, fine
> Jew linen.
> Peel off the napkin
> O my enemy.
> Do I terrify?[35]

Plath identifies herself with the victims of the extermination camps, whose bodies have been transformed into lifeless objects. The poem affirms that Plath herself has survived, though this is far less a triumphant resurrection (as with the biblical Lazarus) than it is like an experience of continuously haunting of the world of living. Like the Freudian "uncanny object," which cannot be discerned as being living or inanimate, Plath herself seems to straddle life and death. The poem's confrontational tone ("Do I terrify?") is strengthened by Plath's identification with Jewish concentration camp victims. Having been singled out for the most brutal forms of dehumanization, the Jew comes to possess the authority of the witness of the deepest evil of which humanity is capable and indeed of death itself.

[34] Sylvia Plath, *The Bell Jar* (New York: Harper & Row, 1971), 1.

[35] Sylvia Plath, *The Collected Poems*, ed. Ted Hughes (New York: Harper & Row, 1981), 244. Subsequent citations from Plath's poetry refer to this edition.

By identifying with the slaughtered Jews, Plath lays claim to a *terrifying* discursive power.

Another set of allusions to Jewishness can be found in "Daddy" (1962), Plath's most anthologized work and a poem that announces the theme of female rage in more explicit terms than anything American poetry had witnessed to date. It is addressed to Plath's German father, whose early death has left the poet with a deeply ambivalent mixture of longing and resentment. On the one hand, she recalls how she used to pray to recover her father; on the other, she recalls the agony of trying to speak to him. As the poet recounts her difficulties communicating with her father, she moves associatively from the image of her tongue caught in the "barb wire snare" to an image of being a Jew carried off in a train: "A Jew to Dachau, Auswitz, Belsen" (223). Under the oppressive gaze of her father, the poet comes to see herself as a Jew: "I began to talk like a Jew / I think I may well be a Jew" (223).

Some readers have found Plath's leap from a personal experience of psychological pain to the theme of genocide to be unearned and troubling in its implications. "There is something monstrous, utterly disproportionate, when tangled emotions about one's father are deliberately compared with the historical fate of European Jews," writes Irving Howe.[36] On the other hand, Susan Gubar has argued that Plath's evocations of Jews can be read as an example of the technique of prosopopeia, speaking in the place of the other, which has a celebrated position in post-Holocaust poetry.[37] Rather than weighing in on this particular debate, I would call attention to the ways Plath's references to Jews fit in with a broader postwar tendency to imagine Jews as bearers of a particular kind of insight. In a more explicit way than "Lady Lazarus," the poem imagines Jews as representatives of a world of occult knowledge, as in the next stanza:

> The snows of the Tyrol, the clear beer of Vienna
> Are not very pure or true.
> With my gipsy ancestress and my weird luck
> And my Taroc pack and my Taroc pack
> I may be a bit of a Jew. (223)

Like Lowell, who lays claim through his great-great-grandfather to an alternate family history, Plath displaces her paternal heritage by laying claim to a secret affinity for her "gipsy ancestress." Associated with the figure of the Gypsy, the Jew here seems not so much an abject victim of persecution, but also a symbol for an exotic, mysterious figure in possession of occult

[36] Irving Howe, *Critical Point: On Literature and Culture* (New York: Horizon Press, 1973), 166.
[37] Susan Gubar, "Prosopopoeia and Holocaust Poetry in English: Sylvia Plath and Her Contemporaries," *Yale Journal of Criticism* 14, no. 1 (Spring 2001): 191–215.

knowledge. What her "Taroc pack" (a symbol also of Plath's own poems) enables her to see is the evil underside of Europe's mythic purity. If the snows of the Tyrol and the beer of Vienna are not "very pure or true," it is only the hated outsiders – the Gypsy and the Jew – who can glimpse this impurity and take its measure. And these figures seem to have gained a species of freedom through their insight. In the last line of this stanza, the tone takes on a whimsicality, as if the poet were regaining her own agency at the same moment that she identifies with the Jew. Plath's poem allows us to see, then, how a figure associated with subjugation could also be transformed into a figure of resistance. To "talk like a Jew" is not merely to talk as the shamed, incarcerated victim, but also to speak from a position of mysterious authority, freed from the straitjacket of conformity and her Oedipal enthrallment to her father. This is one way, perhaps, to read the phrase "weird luck": through the alchemy of her own imaginings, she has seen her weakness transformed into strength.

JOHN BERRYMAN

Born to Roman Catholic parents and raised in small towns in Oklahoma (Lamar, Sasakwa, and Wagoner), John Berryman (1914–72) served at Mass and attended Catholic schools from the age of five. After the death of his father, he moved with his mother and stepfather to New York; attended South Kent School, an Episcopal prep school in Connecticut; and got his B.A. at Columbia College. Over the course of his career, Berryman's work shows a development from a highly controlled, formally rigorous poetic style, modeled on the "academic" style of the 1940s, to an idiosyncratic, whimsical, and emotionally expressive voice. His fascination with Jews, which included a period of seriously contemplating conversion to Judaism, reflects his restless search for a voice and model.

One of Berryman's earliest successes was his short story "The Imaginary Jew" (1945), published in the *Kenyon Review* and winner of the magazine's story contest for that year. The story is a first-person narrative by a nameless character who has no preconceptions about Jews; he is from "a part of the South where no Jews had come, or none had stayed."[38] While at college he realizes that nearly everyone he spends time with turns out to be Jewish, and, as he gradually learns of the persecution of Jews in post-1933 Germany, he develops a "special sympathy and liking for Jews" (246). We learn this as background for a singular and uncanny event that befalls him on the streets of New York in the summer of 1941, an event that Berryman repeatedly assured interviewers actually happened to him. Having moved to New York City, the narrator finds himself listening in on a fierce street-corner debate

---

[38] John Berryman, "The Imaginary Jew," reprinted as appendix to *Recovery* (New York: Farrar, Straus & Giroux, 1973), 246.

on the question of American intervention in the war. When he breaks into the discussion to defend the idea of going to war against Hitler, the isolationist in the debate, a cruel man whom the text identifies as Irish, accuses the narrator of being a Jew: "You look like a Jew. You talk like a Jew. You *are* a Jew" (250). Though he protests that he is no Jew at all, the narrator soon discovers in himself an impulse to change his blood, if only to defy his accuser and to distance himself from what turns out to be their shared Irishness: "Shame, shame: shame for my ruthless people. I will not be his blood. I wish I were a Jew" (252). The story concludes with a postscript in which the narrator reflects that, for the sake of the exchange with the Irishman, he had in fact *become* a Jew, as much a Jew in the eyes of the antisemite as any real Jew.

"The Imaginary Jew" suggests that the Jew that is hated is always a figment in the mind of the hater, as we learn in the story's final declaration: "every murderer strikes the mirror, the lash of the torturer falls on the mirror and cuts the real image, and the real and the imaginary blood flow down together" (252). Thus the story discovers a particular logic – the logic of unconscious self-hatred – in acts of violence in general and in antisemitism in particular. Under these conditions, the Jew – even the falsely identified Jew – becomes a walking index for the pathologies of the gentile. "The Imaginary Jew" discovers the essence of Jewishness in the experience of being reviled by the non-Jew, which was also Jean Paul Sartre's point in *Anti-Semite and Jew*, originally published a year before Berryman's story.[39]

But Berryman invests palpable meaning within Jewishness as well, particularly in subsequent writings that call attention to the cultural strategies that have enabled Jews to survive their tribulations. An example is a work entitled "from *The Black Book*" (1958), a cycle of three poems depicting scenes of excruciating violence and torture during the Holocaust – a grandfather being stamped down in the mud, a girl being raped, a group of Jews in "long-lockt cattle-cars."[40] In their focus on physical violence and bodily disfigurement, these poems recall Plath's evocations of the Holocaust in the poems we have seen as well as other works about the Holocaust by non-Jewish poets of Berryman's generation, such as Randall Jarrell and Anne Sexton.[41] But Berryman is more interested than these other poets in exploring the inner lives of the Jews who are victimized by the Nazis. As a collective image for the Jews, Berryman evokes the image of the "luftmensch," a term of derision in much Zionist (and Nazi) discourse, but in the context of postwar America a badge of spiritual refinement. The second poem in

---

[39] Jean Paul Sartre, *Anti-Semite and Jew*, trans. George Becker (New York: Schocken Books, 1948).
[40] John Berryman, *Short Poems* (New York: Farrar, Straus & Giroux, 1967).
[41] See Randall Jarrell, "The Refugees," in *The Complete Poems* (New York: Farrar, Straus & Giroux, 1969), and Anne Sexton, "After Auschwitz," in *The Complete Poems* (Boston: Houghton Mifflin, 1981).

the cycle begins with these lines: "Luftmenshen dream, the men who live on air, / of other values, in the blackness watching / peaceful for gangs or a quick raid" (107). Even while the Jews here watch out for the violent hordes, they remain in an illuminated state, dreaming of "other values." If they "live on air" it is not because they have no productive form of labor (as the phrase was generally interpreted to mean), but rather because they see the "air" as imbued with meaning. Berryman's Holocaust poems confer a spiritual dignity to the suffering Jews.

Jewishness provides a model for Berryman himself at key moments in his most innovative and celebrated work, the "Dream Songs," which make up two separate books, *77 Dream Songs* (1964) and *His Toy, His Dream, His Rest* (1968). The central character is a witty, traumatized, sexually obsessed, and occasionally misanthropic poet named Henry, whose life experiences are identical to Berryman's though Berryman insists he be read as a "character." Among the numerous poems about fellow writers and literary critics, there are twelve powerfully felt elegies to Delmore Schwartz, who was a close friend of Berryman, as he had been of Lowell. In these elegies, Henry comes to the brink of despair, as if Schwartz's ignominious death, alone in the Chelsea Hotel (where his body lay a full day before being discovered), symbolized the death of part of Henry himself and a judgment on the fate of poets in postwar America. The elegies move from descriptions of Schwartz's death to recollections of their years of friendship, including one memory from the period when both were instructors at Harvard:

> unstained, I saw him thro' the mist of the actual
> blazing with insight, warm with gossip
> thro' all our Harvard years
> when both of us were becoming known
> I got him out of a police-station once, in Washington, the world is *tref*
> and grief too astray for tears.[42]

Schwartz is so close to the realm of the imagination that he is not really identified with his physical body at all. He is another version of the luftmentsch, a spiritual being whom Berryman glimpses "thro' the mist of the actual." The episode Berryman is recalling here involved a time Schwartz was held in jail for six hours after partly destroying a hotel room in Washington, D.C., in actuality more the result of mania than of drunkenness, which, however, was taken to be the cause. Like Lowell's "Memories of West Street and Lepke," here too the Jew is depicted as a figure moving against the grain of American society, so much so that he has been taken into police custody. As Berryman recalls Schwartz's legal and spiritual conflicts with this world, he names the world a *tref* (i.e., nonkosher) place, thus

---

[42] John Berryman, *His Toy, His Dream, His Rest: 308 Dream Songs* (New York: Farrar, Straus & Giroux, 1969).

incorporating Yiddish, ostensibly Schwartz's language, into his own poetic discourse. The effect of this unexpected Yiddish term is to wrench the poem momentarily out of its elevated "poetic" register and to lend it an air of the vernacular, the ethnic, and the urban. This movement downward in terms of diction is reversed once again in the final line of the stanza, which alludes to the concluding lines of William Wordsworth's "Intimations of Immortality" ode (compare Berryman's "grief too astray for tears" with Wordsworth's "Thoughts … too deep for tears"). The inclusion of Yiddish alongside this allusion to British romanticism enables Berryman to make his poem a play between registers, demonstrating his freedom from poetic discourse as traditionally construed. (Instructively, at other moments in the *Dream Songs*, Berryman also writes in a dialect marked as African American, which once again signifies a movement downward from the elevated diction that predominates elsewhere.)[43]

In a subsequent elegy to Schwartz, Berryman portrays his poet-protagonist Henry in the act of writing, trying to block out any distractions that would dilute the intensity of his meditations: "Let no activity / mar our hurrah of mourning." In order to capture the properly elegiac tone, he suggests that it may be necessary to become or at least impersonate a Jew himself, as if Jews were the quintessential mourners: "let's all be Jews bereft, for he was one." Here Berryman echoes and extends Schwartz's analogy linking poets and Jews we saw in Schwartz's 1951 essay "The Vocation of the Poet in the Modern World." If the perspective of the true poet is analogous to the perspective of "the Jew," becoming a true poet requires installing oneself in the position of the Jew.[44]

These various invocations of Jews, Judaism, and Jewishness in works by Lowell, Plath, and Berryman do not add up to the construction of a single, unchanging "Jewish type." What we find instead are multiple fantasies, with Jews standing, on the one hand, for the experience of abject suffering and, on the other, for a range of positive qualities, including verbal expressiveness, emotional sensitivity, moral courage, intellectual sophistication, and the ability to affirm value in an anxiety-ridden age. By identifying with Jews, these poets lay claim to a heightened kind of poetic authority, which supports their agenda of disclosing the horrific underside of midcentury American life. Thus, even as Jews were being welcomed into the expanding middle class as "white" Americans, the Jew also became a symbol in various kinds of literary texts for resistance to the status quo – in the argot of

---

[43] For a discussion of the language of minstrelsy in the *Dream Songs*, see Katherine Davis, "'Honey Dusk Do Sprawl': Does Black Minstrel Dialect Obscure *The Dream Songs?*" *Language and Style* 18, no. 1 (Winter 1985): 33–4.

[44] This fantasy of becoming Jewish resurfaces in Berryman's unfinished autobiographical novel, *Recovery*, published posthumously in 1972.

the time, they were seen as quintessentially "marginal," which in an age of conformity was seen as a badge of honor.

CONCLUSION

How does this pattern of references to Jews relate to other patterns of racial and ethnic reference in American literature? Many groups besides Jews have fascinated American writers – from African Americans to Native Americans to Spanish bullfighters to hoboes. What, then, distinguishes the fantasies woven around Jews from those woven around other groups? One helpful point of reference is offered here by the critic Michael North, who argues in *The Dialect of Modernism: Race, Language, and Twentieth-Century Literature* that high modernist writers engage in a practice he calls "rebellion through racial ventriloquism."[45] Surveying canonical figures such as Gertrude Stein, William Carlos Williams, Ezra Pound, and T. S. Eliot, North argues that these writers make use of an invented form of black speech, often mediated by the minstrel show, in order to free themselves from the straitjackets of standard language and white identity. At a moment in the 1920s when the movement for the standardization of English had emerged as a powerful political force, these writers discovered in black dialect a model for a more expressive, liberated form of discourse. In the case of Eliot, his personal correspondence is strewn with phrases in imitation black dialect, and he wrote satirical poems about an African character "King Bolo" as well as an unfinished play starring a black minister. North argues that black dialect presented itself as a "safety valve for [the young Eliot who was] sick of scholarly trivia and ... the cramped language of references and citations." It also offered a "prototype of the audacious poetry [he] was to write instead of academic philosophy."[46]

This analysis relates in a limited way to the patterns of Jewish reference in work of the confessional poets. Most generally, as in North's analysis of the role of African Americans for the modernist imagination, for Lowell, Plath, and Berryman the impulse to identify with Jews follows from an impulse to rebel against the conventions of the white Christian world. Moreover, these poets all link Jewishness with a distinctive kind of *voice*. Lowell reports to Elizabeth Bishop that the New York Jews speak an ecstatic and almost unrecognizable form of English and that beside them everyone else is speechless and dead; Plath recalls that she began to "talk like a Jew"; and Berryman has his hostile Irishman in "The Imaginary Jew" accuse the protagonist of speaking like a Jew. In Berryman's later poetry, he incorporates Yiddish as one of various

[45] Michael North, *The Dialect of Modernism: Race, Language, and Twentieth-Century Literature* (Oxford: Oxford University Press, 1994).
[46] Ibid., 10.

strategies for liberating his language from the controlled, academic verse of his early career.

Nevertheless, there are crucial differences between the turn toward black vernacular by modernist writers that North describes – their black-face performances – and the varieties of "Jewface" we have explored. Most notably, African Americans almost always stand for the primitive, a mode of existence that is prior to or wholly removed from the traditions and canons of Western civilization. (This applies equally to the work of the high modernist writers and to that of contemporaries of the confessional poets such as Jack Kerouac.) While Plath recalls this trope when she links the Jew to the Gypsy, a figure on the fringes of European society, Lowell and Berryman emphasize precisely the Jew's *insider* status when it comes to Western culture. The point about the Jews is their deep and authoritative grasp of European high culture. Still, theirs is a version of cultural sophistication liberated from the buttoned-down regime of the official institutions of culture; Jews' easy familiarity with high culture enables a spontaneous repossession of its ethos and authoritative texts. Thus Lowell yammers metaphysics with Abramowitz in the West Street Jail and discusses Freud and Joyce with Delmore Schwartz in his garret located at some remove from Harvard. Borrowing the terms of Philip Rahv's description of the two poles of American consciousness, we might say that in the figure of the Jew the "paleface" and the "redskin" overlap; the high cultural sophisticate and the untamed radical are one.[47]

A further point is that unlike the modernist figures North examines (and unlike their contemporaries, the Beat writers), Lowell, Plath, and Berryman did not eschew academic institutions and the road of professional normality they represented. Whereas the quintessential modernist was an expatriate, the typical confessional poet of the 1950s and 1960s was a college professor (Lowell and Berryman both taught at Harvard, among other places; Plath taught at Smith). But while Lowell, Plath, Berryman, and others became "respectable," it is evident that the concessions to decorum required by this transition did not always sit easily with them. One of the premises of their poetry, after all, was that the middle-class existence offered up as the good life during the postwar boom was in many ways a hollow promise. What they sought to articulate were the underground emotions, traumatic memories, and psychic pain that prosperity could hardly undo. This ambivalent relationship to mainstream American life (university life, the family, etc.) provides a context for understanding the unique appeal of Jews. By straddling the worlds of the paleface and redskin, of the sophisticated intellectual and the untrammeled savage, the Jew represented a mode of existence that was both inside and outside the

---

47 Philip Rahv, "Paleface and Redskin," in *Image and Idea: Fourteen Essays on Literary Themes* (Norfolk, CT: New Directions, 1949).

mainstream. Recall that Lowell meets Delmore Schwartz in his room in Cambridge, not in some far-flung café on the Left Bank. The Jew thus represents a realm of relative, not absolute, freedom. Jews are in this sense an ideal model for intellectual and literary engagement in an age of complexity, in which fantasies of escape into some fantasy of primitivistic freedom were losing traction. The insights the Jews were to offer – and that admiring American writers sought to make their own – illuminated the world *as it had become*, in all of its complexity and brutality. As this period of anxious introspection gave way to the radical impulses of the 1960s, the Jewish intellectual gradually ceased to embody an exemplary mode of engagement. New models, emphasizing ideological certainty and forthright action, came into vogue, dimming the luster of the image of the ambivalent, alienated Jew.

12

"It's All in the Bible"

Evangelical Christians, Biblical Literalism, and Philosemitism in Our Times

Yaakov Ariel

In 1982, Israel's prime minister, Menahem Begin, bestowed a medal on Jerry Falwell, one of the better-known American evangelists at the time.[1] To many, Begin's choice seemed weird, as did the friendship that had developed between Israelis and evangelical Christians in general. Surprisingly, mission-oriented conservative Christians have become friends and supporters of Jewish causes, mustering political and economic support for the state of Israel, as well as helping needy Jews in Israel and elsewhere. Messianically oriented evangelical Christians have become Israel's most dedicated friends, involving themselves with the well-being of the Jewish people and the Jewish state. While evangelical Christians have not fully abandoned well-rooted cultural stereotypes of Jews, they consider themselves to be ardent philosemites who care deeply about the Jews and their future.

The evangelical Christians' concern over the well-being of the Jews and their wish to see the Jews return to their ancestral homeland have a long history. From the perspective of conservative evangelical Christians, their philosemitic standing is an outcome of their biblical-pietist faith, their outlook on Jews meshing well with their larger worldview on the Bible and on the course of history. The pietist and evangelical advocacy of Jewish restoration to Zion affected the development of the Zionist ideal in the nineteenth and twentieth centuries and influenced the attitudes of governments, mostly in the English-speaking world, toward Zionism and the state of Israel. Support for Zionism, however, has been only one aspect of the manner in which philosemitic evangelicals have related to the Jews. Theirs has been a complicated relationship, which includes patronizing elements, as well as attempts to educate the Jews as to what evangelicals have considered to be the Jews' real purpose in history. At times those

---

[1] On Jerry Falwell and the Jews, see Merrill Simon, *Jerry Falwell and the Jews* (Middle Village, NY: Jonathan David, 1984).

philosemites have been disappointed at the Jews' unwillingness to play the part that the evangelicals had assigned them. This chapter aims at exploring the contemporary evangelical philosemitic attitude toward the Jews in all its variety and complexity. Among other things, it intends to explore the meaning of philosemitism in our time and to point to its vital role in the development of the Zionist movement and the state of Israel. In order to understand the rise and development of contemporary Christian philosemitism, one has to look at the roots of the movement, its theology, and its messianic vision.

EVANGELICAL CHRISTIAN MILLENNIAL FAITH AND THE JEWS

The messianic millennial hope, which has served as the source of evangelical interest in the Jews, draws on a long Christian messianic tradition.[2] In its early development, Christianity was a messianic faith, its followers expecting the imminent return of Jesus of Nazareth to establish the Kingdom of God on earth.[3] With the transformation of Christianity into the dominant religion in the Mediterranean world in the fourth and fifth centuries, the major Christian trends became amillennial, relegating the return of Jesus to the remote future. Christian thinkers began interpreting biblical passages with messianic overtones as symbolic or allegorical. According to this approach, during the present era the church has replaced Jesus; its mission is to instruct Christian believers and ensure their salvation. However, some millennial groups that expected the imminent return of Jesus to earth came about during the Middle Ages, drawing on messianic passages in Christian biblical tracts, such as Daniel and the Revelation of John, and predicting the end of the world as we know it.[4]

Apocalyptic speculation became widespread in the wake of the Protestant Reformation in the sixteenth century, especially among the more radical Protestant groups.[5] Reading the Old Testament in a new manner, a number of messianic thinkers expected the Jews to play an important role in the events of the end-times, which they believed were about to begin. Not only radical reformers, but at times other Protestants too looked upon the Jews as heirs and continuers of historical Israel. This view has been prevalent among leaders and thinkers of the Reform tradition (often known as Calvinist, after the most known member of that movement). The Reform

---

[2] Cf. Norman Cohn, *The Pursuit of the Millennium* (New York: Oxford University Press, 1970).

[3] Cf. Bart Ehrman, *Jesus: Apocalyptic Prophet of the New Millennium* (New York: Oxford University Press, 1999).

[4] Cohn, *Pursuit of the Millennium*.

[5] George Williams, *The Radical Reformation* (Philadelphia: Westminster, 1970).

tradition influenced French, Dutch, Swiss, and British Protestantism as well as Protestant colonies overseas. The English revolution in the mid-seventeenth century also stirred messianic hopes and gave rise to premillennialist groups in Britain. Some of them took a keen interest in the Jewish people and viewed their return to Palestine as an event to take place prior to the arrival of the Messiah. Messianic hopes played a part in the deliberations on the return of the Jews to England in the 1650s.[6] Likewise, premillennialist Christians in Britain and Holland closely followed the messianic movement stirred by Shabbatai Zvi in the 1660s, hoping it might hasten the return of the Jews to Palestine.[7]

The roots and early beginnings of Christian support for Zionism can be traced back to such seventeenth-century Protestant messianic yearnings. Even at this stage some of the characteristics of philosemitic interest in the Jewish people and their return to Palestine emerged. These Christians tended to read their sacred texts in a literal manner. In contrast to other branches of Christianity, they viewed the Jews as continuators of biblical Israel, heirs to the covenant between God and Abraham, and the object of biblical prophecies about a restored Davidic kingdom in the land of Israel. In their messianic scenarios, the return of the Jews to Palestine was the first step in the advancement of the messianic timetable. In many cases such Christians depicted the Jews and their role in history without ever encountering actual Jews, and with no knowledge of the realities of Jewish life and Jewish struggles and aspirations. Their image of the Jews was often mixed and ambivalent, based in part on the sacred scriptures and in part on popular stereotypes of the Jews in Western European culture. Such images can be noticed in English writings of the sixteenth and early seventeenth centuries, including those of William Shakespeare, during a period in which almost no Jews resided in Britain or in the Anglo-American colonies.

Christian Zionism resurfaced with a vengeance during the early decades of the nineteenth century, with the rise of the evangelical movement in Britain and a new wave of fascination with prophecy there and elsewhere.[8] Two brands of Christian messianic faith gained prominence in the nineteenth century, "historical" and "futurist," differing as to when the events of the end-times were to begin. For the most part, both messianic schools held common notions of the role of the Jews and the Holy Land in God's

---

[6] David Katz, *Philosemitism and the Return of the Jews to England* (Oxford: Clarendon Press, 1982); Douglas J. Culver, *Albion and Ariel: British Puritanism and the Birth of Political Zionism* (New York: Peter Lang, 1995).

[7] Cf. Gershom Sholem, *Shabbatai Zvi: The Mystical Messiah* (New York: Schocken Books, 1970).

[8] Cf. Yaakov Ariel, "The French Revolution and the Reawakening of Christian Messianism," in Richard Cohen, ed., *The French Revolution and Its Impact* (Jerusalem: Zalman Shazar, 1991), 319–38.

plans for humanity.[9] Similarly, adherents of both schools became supporters of initiatives to restore the Jews to Palestine, as well as of missionary
activity among the Jews.[10] But the differences were also significant. In
Europe, the predominant messianic school was historical, identifying current events with biblical passages, while in America the premillennialist
faith in its futurist, dispensationalist form became widely accepted during
the latter decades of the nineteenth century. This latter premillennialist
messianic faith has become part and parcel of a conservative evangelical
creed, functioning as a philosophy of history for conservative Christians
and meshing well with their outlook on contemporary culture. It has also
served to provide hope and reassurance in the face of uncertainty, including during the nuclear threat of the Cold War.[11]

In the predominant version of contemporary premillennialist understanding of the course of human history, God has distinct plans for the
Jews, the church, and the rest of humanity. Evangelical Christians define
the church as the body of the true believers, composed of those who have
undergone inner experiences of conversion and have accepted Jesus as
their personal savior. They alone will be saved and spared the turmoils
and destruction that will precede the arrival of the Messiah. According to
the messianic faith predominant among contemporary evangelicals, messianic times will begin with the Rapture of the church. The true Christian
believers will be snatched from earth and meet Jesus in the air. Those
Christians who die prior to the Rapture will rise from the dead and join
the living in heaven. These saintly persons will remain with Jesus in heaven
for seven years (according to some versions, for three and a half years) and
thus be spared the turmoils and miseries that will be inflicted on those
who remain on earth during that period. For the latter, this time will be
marked by natural disasters such as earthquakes, floods, and famines, as
well as wars and murderous dictatorial regimes. By the time Jesus returns
to earth, about two thirds of humanity will perish.[12]

According to this messianic evangelical faith, for the Jews the seven years
that stand between the current era and the messianic times will be known
as the "Time of Jacob's Trouble." The Jews will return to their ancient
homeland "in unbelief," without accepting Jesus as their Savior, and will
establish a political commonwealth in Palestine. This political entity will

[9] Ernest Sandeen, *The Roots of Fundamentalism: British and American Millenarianism, 1800–
    1930* (Grand Rapids, MI: Baker Book House, 1978).
[10] For example, Barbara Tuchman, *Bible and Sword: How the British Came to Palestine* (London:
    Macmillan, 1982).
[11] A. G. Mojtabai, *Blessed Assurance: At Home with the Bomb in Amarillo, Texas* (Boston: Houghton
    Mifflin, 1986).
[12] For details on this eschatological hope, see, for example, Hal Lindsey's best seller *The
    Late Great Planet Earth* (Grand Rapids, MI: Zondervan, 1971), or Tim LaHaye and Jerry B.
    Jenkins, *Left Behind: A Novel of the Earth's Last Days* (Wheaton, IL: Tyndale, 1995).

not yet be the millennial Davidic kingdom, but is nonetheless a necessary step in the advancement toward the messianic timetable. Antichrist, an impostor posing as the Messiah, will appear and seek to establish a universal dictatorial government. He will inflict a reign of terror, directed at, among others, Jews, who during this period will gradually accept the belief in Jesus. During the nineteenth and twentieth centuries, most premillennialist thinkers had assumed that Antichrist would be a Jew who would reign from Jerusalem and rebuild the Temple. At the turn of the twenty-first century, premillennialst writers decided to choose a new Antichrist. Responding to Jewish sensitivities, but not resorting to the Antichrist of the Protestant Reformation, the authors of the best-selling *Left Behind* series depicted Antichrist as a Romanian secretary of the United Nations, who rules from New York.

The arrival of Jesus at the end of the great tribulation will end Antichrist's rule. Jesus will crush this satanic ruler and his armies and will establish the millennial kingdom. The minority of Jews who survive the turmoil and terror of the great tribulation will accept Jesus as their Savior. There will follow a period of a thousand years marked by the righteous rule of Christ on earth. Jesus will establish a global government with Jerusalem serving as the world capital. The millennium will be an interim period in which humanity prepares itself for the eternal age of total peace and righteousness. At long last the Jews will be redeemed and live safely in their land, assisting in the reeducation and evangelization of humanity.

EVANGELICAL PHILOSEMITES AT WORK: CHRISTIAN ZIONISM

The special place Jews occupy in the evangelical messianic faith can well explain the interest those holding such beliefs have shown in the Jews and the prospect of their national restoration. In the nineteenth century, premillennialist evangelical Christians devised a series of initiatives intended to bring about the national restoration of the Jews in Palestine. Such persons were motivated by a biblical Christian faith that viewed the Jews as heirs and continuers of biblical Israel and by the belief that a Jewish commonwealth in the land of Israel was a necessary stage in the preparation of the way for the return of Jesus of Nazareth to earth. Evangelical Christians have, at times, been more enthusiastic over the prospect of a Jewish restoration to Palestine than Jews, who often were more interested in their coreligionists' well-being and survival than in heroic missions.

Evangelical political efforts to promote the building of a Jewish commonwealth in Palestine predated the rise of political Zionism. A number of evangelical Christians in Britain advocated initiatives to restore the Jews to Zion, trying to persuade the British government to intercede with the Ottoman Turks and propose the creation of a Jewish state in Palestine.

In 1840, the leader of the evangelical party in Britain, Lord Ashley Cooper, the seventh earl of Shaftesbury, petitioned the British foreign minister, requesting that Britain initiate the establishment of a Jewish state in Palestine.[13] A number of Protestant clergymen, writers, businessmen, and politicians supported, and at times labored actively, for the restoration of the Jews to Palestine and the establishment of a Jewish state and would be instrumented in persuading British statesmen to support the Zionist cause. At the least, they helped counterbalance negative sentiments and opposition to British sponsorship of a Jewish homeland in Palestine.[14] As a rule, Zionist narratives have overlooked the role of Christians in promoting Zionist ideas and causes.

American Christian Zionists have also formulated similar initiatives. Fifty years after Shaftsbury's attempts, an American evangelist, William Blackstone (1841–1935), organized a petition to the president of the United States, urging him to convene an international conference that would decide to grant Palestine to the Jews. A businessman from Oak Park, Illinois, Blackstone decided to dedicate his life to evangelism and the promotion of the dispensationalist messianic faith. He visited Palestine in 1889 and was impressed by the developments that the first wave of Zionist immigration had brought about in a country he had considered to be a desolated land. He viewed the agricultural settlements and the new neighborhoods in Jerusalem as "signs of the time," indications that an era was ending and the great events of the end-times were to occur very soon.[15] His remark about the Jews and Palestine, "A people without a land and a land without a people," was adopted by Zionist leaders and came to explain and justify in one sentence the Zionist endeavor.

Following his visit to Palestine, Blackstone decided to take an active line and help bring about Jewish national restoration to Palestine. In 1891 he organized a petition to the president of the United States requesting that the American government convene an international conference of the world powers that would give Palestine back to the Jews. More than four hundred prominent Americans signed the petition – congressmen, governors, mayors, publishers and editors of leading newspapers, notable clergymen, and leading businessmen. Although it failed to persuade the

---

[13] On Ashley Cooper, the seventh earl of Shaftesbury, and his proto-Zionist efforts, see Tuchman, *Bible and Sword*, 175–207.

[14] On the background to the issuing of the Balfour Declaration see Franz Kobler, *The Vision Was There: A History of the British Movement for the Restoration of the Jews to Palestine* (London: Lincolns-Praeger, 1956); Tuchman, *Bible and Sword*; Friedman, *The Question of Palestine*, 1914–1918 (New Brunswick, NJ: Transaction, 1992); Leonard Stein, *The Balfour Declaration* (Jerusalem: Magnes Press, 1983); Paul L. Merkley, *The Politics of Christian Zionism, 1891–1948* (London: Frank Cass, 1998), 37–53.

[15] See William Blackstone, *Jesus Is Coming*, 3rd ed. (Los Angeles: Bible House, 1908), 211–13, 236–41.

American government to take meaningful action regarding its request, the petition suggested the warm support that the idea of the Jewish restoration to Palestine might receive among American Protestants influenced by a biblical outlook on the Jewish people and Holy Land.[16]

Blackstone devised a theory that has become a cornerstone of American Christian supporters of Zionism and Israel ever since. The American evangelist asserted that the United States had a special role and mission in God's plans for humanity: that of a modern Cyrus, to help restore the Jews to Zion. God has chosen America for that mission on account of its moral superiority over other nations, and America is going to be judged according to the way it carries out its mission.[17] This theory amalgamates messianic beliefs and philosemitic and pro-Zionist agendas with a strong sense of American patriotism. Although conservative evangelicals have often criticized contemporary American culture, they have remained loyal citizens of the American commonwealth. British Christian Zionists have also tried to tie the promotion of the Zionist causes with British interests.

When Theodore Herzl, the father of political Zionism, began his efforts in the late 1890s to secure international recognition for the idea of a Jewish state, a number of messianically oriented Christians showed interest in the new movement and offered support. William Hechler, a German British clergyman who believed in the imminent Second Coming of Jesus, became an adviser to Herzl and his liaison to the Protestant Christian rulers of Europe.[18] Hechler introduced Herzl to the grand duke of Baden, who reacted sympathetically to Herzl and Hechler and promised to support the Zionist plans. The grand duke referred Herzl to the German emperor, whom Herzl tried to turn into a patron of the Zionist cause. When the first Zionist congress convened in Basel in 1897, a number of Christians attended as guests to show support and assess the new movement and its meaning for the advancement of history. One of them was Jean Henry Dunant, a Swiss banker and the founder of the International Red Cross, whose Calvinist Swiss upbringing lent itself to a literal reading of biblical

---

[16] See Yaakov Ariel, "An American Initiative for a Jewish State: William Blackstone and the Petition of 1891," *Studies in Zionism* 10 (1989): 125–37; on American Protestants, the Jews, and the Holy Land, see Robert T. Handy, ed., *the Holy Land in American Protestant Life, 1800–1948* (New York: Arno Press, 1981); Peter Grose, *Israel in the Mind of America* (New York: Alfred A. Knopf, 1983); Lester I. Vogel, *To See a Promised Land: Americans and the Holy Land in the Nineteenth Century* (University Park: Penn State University Press, 1993); John Davis, *The Landscape of Belief: Encountering the Holy Land in Nineteenth Century American Art and Culture* (Princeton, NJ: Princeton University Press, 1996).

[17] In a letter to Woodrow Wilson, November 4, 1914, and in a telegram to Warren G. Harding, December 10, 1920, Blackstone Personal Papers, Billy Graham Center, Wheaton, Illinois.

[18] On Hechler and his relationship with Herzl, see Claude Duvernoy, *Le Prince et le Prophète* (Jerusalem: Agence Juive, 1966); Amos Elon, *Herzl* (Tel Aviv: Am Oved, 1975), 212–19, 296, 321–3, 438; Merkley, *Politics of Christian Zionism*, 3–43.

prophecies.[19] Like Blackstone and Shaftesbury, Dunant too proposed initiatives to resettle the Jews in Palestine.

The peculiar relationship between the philosemitic supporters of Zionism and the Zionist leadership started at that time. Typical of this relationship, Theodor Herzl did not comprehend at first what motivated Christians to support the fledgling Zionist movement, but he became convinced that Hechler and Durand were genuine friends, interested in helping his cause, and that was all that mattered to him. More generally, Zionist leaders tended to turn a blind eye to the theological details of the Christian Zionist doctrines. When they did encounter the premillennialist Christian theology, they did not always take it seriously, viewing it as a somewhat eccentric belief system and focusing instead on the support that the Christians provided to their cause.[20] Christian Zionists, for their part, had mixed feelings about the Zionist movement. Their immediate reaction to the Zionist endeavor was supportive, and throughout the years their reports on the rise of the Zionist movement and the Jewish settlements in Palestine were reminiscent of those of Jewish supporters of the Zionist cause. They were, however, disappointed by the secular character of the movement and frustrated that the Zionists were unaware of what the Christian supporters considered to be the real significance of the Jewish return to Palestine, that is, the preparation of the ground for the Second Coming of Jesus to earth.

Christian Zionists were, at times, instrumental in promoting Zionist causes. For example, in 1916–17, Christian Zionists lobbied in the English-speaking countries in favor of a Jewish Commonwealth in Palestine. Historians have taken notice of the Christian Zionist efforts in Britain and their effect on the British government.[21] A number of historians have pointed out that the issuing of the Balfour Declaration in 1917, in which Britain expressed its support for the building of a Jewish national home in Palestine, resulted from a mixture of political calculations and Christian millenarian support in Britain for Jewish restoration in Palestine.[22] Few, however, have taken notice of the American Christian Zionist success in influencing the American government. In 1916–17, William Blackstone was again active in promoting the idea of a Jewish state in Palestine. In this instance, he coordinated his efforts with those of the American Zionist

[19] Cf. Martin Gumpert, *Dunant: The Story of the Red Cross* (Oxford: Oxford University Press, 1938); Michael J. Pragai, *Faith and Fulfillment: Christians and the Return to the Promised Land* (London: Valentine Mitchell, 1985).
[20] See Yaakov Ariel, "William Blackstone and the Petition of 1916: A Neglected Chapter in the History of Christian Zionism in America," *Studies in Contemporary Jewry* 7 (1991): 68–85; Merkley, *Politics of Christian Zionism*, 75–96.
[21] Franz Kobler, *Vision Was There*; Tuchman, *Bible and Sword*; Friedman, *Question of Palestine*; Stein, *Balfour Declaration*.
[22] Cf., for example, Tuchman, *Bible and Sword*.

leadership. In 1916 Blackstone organized a second petition calling upon the president of the United States to help restore Palestine to the Jews. Major Protestant churches endorsed his plan. Blackstone's efforts, coupled with petitions by Protestant churches, helped convince Woodrow Wilson to allow the British to issue the Balfour Declaration. Wilson himself did not want his negotiations with Zionist leaders and their Christian supporters to become public knowledge and preferred to make pro-Zionist moves behind closed doors.[23]

American Zionist leaders, such as Louis Brandeis, Steven Wise, Jacob de Haas, and Nathan Straus, saw the Christian efforts as beneficial to the Zionist cause and established a warm relationship with Blackstone. Blackstone did not keep his premillennialist motivations secret from his Jewish friends, but the Zionist leaders were not bothered by his prediction that years of turmoil were awaiting the Jews when the events of the end-times would begin to unfold. They did not expect the Rapture to take place and saw the help that Blackstone was providing them as the only concrete outcome of his messianic faith.

Evangelical and pietistic Christians continued to demonstrate a profound interest in the events that were taking place in the life of the Jewish people, and especially in the development of the Jewish community in Palestine. They welcomed the Balfour Declaration and the British takeover of Palestine at the end of World War I, interpreting these developments as further indications that the ground was being prepared for the arrival of the Messiah. They gave expression to their joy over the British takeover of Palestine in two "prophetic conferences" that took place in Philadelphia and New York in 1918.[24] In the years that followed, they saw the struggles and turmoil that befell the Jewish nation in the period between the two world wars in light of their eschatological beliefs. Evangelical and pietistic journals with pro-Zionist leanings, such as *Our Hope*, the *King's Business*, the *Moody Monthly*, and the Pentecostal *Evangel*, regularly published news on developments that took place in the life of the Jewish people, the Zionist movement, and especially the Jewish community in Palestine. Christian Zionists were encouraged by the new wave of Zionist immigration to Palestine in the years of the British administration of the country, and events, such as the opening of the Hebrew University in 1925 and the new seaport in Haifa in 1932, were publicized in their periodicals. They interpreted these developments as signs that the Jews were energetically

[23] Cf Ariel, "William Blackstone and the Petition of 1916."
[24] William L. Pettingill, J. R. Schafler, and J. D. Adams, eds., *Light on Prophecy: A Coordinated, Constructive Teaching, Being the Procedings and Addresses at the Philadelphia Prophetic Conference, May 28–30, 1918* (New York: Christian Herald Bible House, 1918); Arno C. Gaebelein, ed., *Christ and Glory: Addresses Delivered at the New York Prophetic Conference, Carnegie Hall, November 25–28, 1918* (New York: Publication Office "Our Hope," 1919).

building a commonwealth in their ancient homeland and that the great events of the end-times were to occur very soon.[25] Excited by the prospects of an imminent Second Coming of Jesus to earth, they expressed dismay at the restrictions on Jewish immigration and settlement that the British were imposing. They also criticized the Arabs for their hostility toward the Zionist endeavor and for their violence against the Jews. They saw attempts at blocking the building of a Jewish commonwealth in Palestine as equivalent to putting obstacles in the way of God's plans for the end-times. Such attempts, they asserted, were futile.[26] Premillennialists were not the only ones in Protestant circles voicing their opinions. In the 1930s, a pro–Palestinian Arab liberal Protestant lobby organized in the United States as well, although a number of liberals took a pro-Zionist attitude.

Christian Zionists in Britain continued in their efforts to shape British policy in Palestine, although the British government in London and the British administration in Palestine in the period 1918–48 had other considerations in governing Palestine besides philosemitic concerns.[27] However, Christian Zionists did succeed at times in modifying policies that they considered harmful to the Zionist cause. A philosemite British officer, Orde Wingate (1903–44), helped train independent units of Jewish fighters in Palestine.[28] Wingate grew up in a family of ardent premillennialists, associated with the Plymouth Brethren, one of the first dispensationalist groups in Britain. Daily readings of the Bible were part of his routine. An intelligence officer in the British administration in Palestine in 1936–9, Wingate was convinced that the Jews were heirs and continuers of the children of Israel, who were returning to their land in preparation for the events of the end-times. He established a special Jewish unit, the Night Squad, in which he trained young members of the Hagana, a paramilitary Jewish organization backed by the Zionist leadership in Palestine. Among his disciples were Yigal Alon and Moshe Dayan, who later became generals in the Israeli army and implemented some of his techniques.

Wingate's pro-Zionist stand was not the norm. During that period, the 1920s–40s, conservative evangelical and pietistic political power was on the decline, and Christian Zionist political influence, both in Britain and in America, weakened considerably. In Britain, the evangelical movement was just a shadow of what it had been a century earlier, and in America, after the Scopes trial of 1925, conservative evangelicals withdrew, to a large

---

[25] See, e.g., George T. B. Davis, *Fulfilled Prophecies That Prove the Bible* (Philadelphia: Million Testaments Campaign, 1931), and Keith L Brooks, *The Jews and the Passion for Palestine in Light of Prophecy* (Los Angeles: Brooks Publications, 1937).

[26] James Gray, Editorial, *Moody Bible Institute Monthly* 31 (1931): 346.

[27] Norman Rose, *The Gentile Zionists: A Study in Anglo-Zionist Diplomacy, 1920–1939* (London: Frank Cass, 1973).

[28] Cf. Jill Hamilton, *God, Guns and Israel: Britain, the First World War and the Jews in the Holy City* (Stroud, UK: Sutton, 2004), 223.

degree, from the political arena. Evangelical leaders did not see themselves as influential national figures whose voices would be heard by the policy-makers in Washington or as people who could advance a political agenda on the national or international level. On the European continent, the rise of the Nazis to power in 1933 subdued, if it did not completely crush, pro-Zionist pietistic activity. In a very crucial moment in the life of the Jewish people, its Christian supporters were weak.

During the 1930s–40s, it was often progressive Protestants who lent active support for the Zionist cause.[29] A number of America's leading Protestant clergymen and public figures joined the American Palestine Committee, a pro-Zionist organization, which Jews and Christians established in 1932 to promote Jewish and Zionist causes. However, it is questionable that such Christian supporters, in spite of their dedication to Jewish causes, could be described as philosemitic. The liberal Protestants who supported the Zionist cause did so on humanitarian and political bases. Few of them considered their support for a Jewish national home to be an outcome of their obedience to the word of God. Their support of Zionism was conditional on a particular humanitarian and political predicament. In latter years, especially after the Six-Day War of 1967, many of the progressives turned against Israel.[30]

While Christian sympathizers could not prevent the Holocaust and failed to persuade the British to open Palestine to unrestricted Jewish immigration, they resurfaced after World War II and the birth of the state of Israel and again played an important role in mustering political support, especially in America, for the Jewish state.

PHILOSEMITE CHRISTIANS AND A JEWISH STATE

Christian Zionists responded favorably to the establishment of the state of Israel in 1948. Pietist and evangelical journals published sympathetic articles and followed the progress of the fledgling state with great interest. While they were displeased by the secular character of Israeli government and society, some of the things they saw, such as the mass immigration of Jews to Israel, from Asian, African, and East European countries, intensified their messianic hopes.[31] In their eyes, this was a significant

---

[29] Cf. Merkley, *Politics of Christian Zionism*, 100–16.

[30] Garth Hewitt, *Pilgrims and Peacemakers* (Oxford: Bible Reading Fellowship, 1995); Michael Prior, ed., *They Came and They Saw* (London: Melisende, 2000); Donald E. Wagner, *Dying in the Land of Promise* (London: Melisende, 2003).

[31] Louis T. Talbot and William W. Orr, *The New Nation of Israel and the Word of God* (Los Angeles: Bible Institute of Los Angeles, 1948); M. R. DeHaan, *The Jew and Palestine in Prophecy* (Grand Rapids, MI: Zondervan, 1954); Arthur Kac, *The Rebirth of the State of Israel: Is It of God or Men?* (Chicago: Moody Press, 1958); George T. B. Davis, *God's Guiding Hand* (Philadelphia: Million Testaments Campaign, 1962).

development, one that had been prophesied in the Bible, and a clear indication that the present era was terminating and the events of the end-times were beginning.

Contrary to a common perception, Christian supporters of Zionists did take notice and showed concern over the fate of hundreds of thousands of Palestinian Arabs who lost their homes in 1948 and became refugees in Arab lands. Although they criticized the Arabs' hostility toward Israel and supported the Israeli state in its struggles with its Arab neighbors, they expressed a belief that the land of Israel could maintain an Arab population alongside its Jewish inhabitants and that Israel had an obligation to respect human rights and treat the Arabs with fairness.[32] A few conservative Protestant churches, such as the Southern Baptists, the Christian and Missionary Alliance, the Assemblies of God, and the Plymouth Brethren, have worked among Palestinians, offering relief and educational services. In striving to reconcile premillennialist teachings with the hopes and fears of Arab congregants and potential converts, philosemite supporters of Israel emphasized that the ingathering of the Jews in the land of Israel and the eventual reestablishment of the Davidic kingdom did not necessitate the banishment of Arabs from that land. In spite of such reassurances, only rarely did pietist or evangelical Arabs become Christian Zionists.[33]

The Six-Day War, in June 1967, had a dramatic effect on evangelical and pietist theologies. Since the French Revolution in the last years of the eighteenth century and the Napoleonic Wars at the beginning of the nineteenth, no political-military event has provided as much fuel to the engines of Christian prophetic belief as did the short war between Israel and its neighbors in 1967, which led to the takeover by Israel of the historical sites of Jerusalem. The dramatic Israeli victory and the accompanying territorial gains strengthened the premillennialists' conviction that the state of Israel had a mission in history and would play an important role in preparing for the arrival of the Messiah.[34]

During the 1970s–2000s, conservative evangelicals have been Israel's most ardent supporters in the American public arena.[35] Likewise, the growing evangelical population in Latin America has turned, at the turn of the twenty-first century, into a powerful philosemitic pro-Israeli constituency. In addition, evangelical and pietistic groups in countries such as the

---

[32] John Walvoord, *Israel in Prophecy* (Grand Rapids, MI: Zondervan, 1962), 19.

[33] An outstanding Palestinian Christian Zionist tract is that of Sahri Huri, *Udat al Masiah* (Jerusalem: El Mia el Hia, 1939).

[34] For example, L. Nelson Bell, "Unfolding Destiny," *Christianity Today* (1967): 1044–5.

[35] See, e.g., Peter L. Williams and Peter L. Benson, *Religion on Capitol Hill: Myth and Realities* (New York: Oxford University Press, 1986); Allen D. Hertzke, *Representing God in Washington* (Knoxville: University of Tennessee Press, 1988); Mark Silk, *Spiritual Politics* (New York: Touchstone, 1989); Michael Lienesch, *Redeeming America: Piety and Politics in the New Christian Right* (Chapel Hill: University of North Carolina Press, 1993).

Netherlands and Finland have served as pro-Zionist lobbies, counterbalancing anti-Israeli sentiments in their countries. The growth of the evangelical community in Korea has also turned that country into a Christian Zionist stronghold. Christian supporters of Israel all around the globe involved themselves, in the 1970s–80s, in such Jewish causes as the demand to facilitate Jewish immigration from the Soviet Union.

Especially in America, Christian Zionists have turned into a pro-Israel lobby that has used its political power to promote policies favorable to the interests of the Jewish state. The decades following the Six-Day War were marked by massive American support for Israel in terms of money, arms, and diplomatic backing. Many conservative Christians in America have viewed their pro-Israeli stand as in accord with America's historical role, as well as going hand in hand with what conservative Christians have conceived to be American political interests. During the 1960s–80s, many Americans, conservative evangelical or not, saw Israel as a valuable ally in the global struggle of the United States against the Soviet Union. The Israeli-American alliance began before the rise of evangelicals to power in America but was enhanced considerably with the growth in evangelical influence.

The years following the 1967 war saw a dramatic rise in evangelical influence in America. Growing in numbers and self-confidence, evangelicals have become more visible and aggressive. In 1976, when Jimmy Carter was elected president, many Americans who identified with liberal causes discovered in surprise that evangelicalism had grown considerably and was much more influential than they had assumed. The liberal Carter was, however, a disappointment to conservative evangelicals. Carter did take an interest in the Middle East and induced Egypt and Israel to negotiate a peace treaty, but the role he played was that of an enlightened American statesman rather than that of a Bible-believing evangelical Christian. The messianic agenda of paving the way for the Davidic kingdom was not his concern, and he did not give preference to Israeli interests over and against Egyptian ones.[36]

Ronald Reagan, who replaced Carter as president in 1981, was influenced in forming his Middle East policy by Christian Zionist pressure, if not by his own premillennialist understanding of the course of history.[37] During Reagan's presidency, America supplied Israel with generous military and financial aid as well as political backing. Reagan's policy toward Israel was adopted by his successor, George H. W. Bush, who was also close to Christian Zionist evangelicals and relied on their support. A friendly attitude toward Israel has been part and parcel of the conservative evangelical

---

[36] On Jimmy Carter's political views see Ron Richardson, ed., *Conversations with Carter* (Boulder, CO: Lynne Rienner, 1998).

[37] See Martin Gardner, "Giving God a Hand," *New York Review of Books*, August 13, 1987, 22.

vision for America's global policy. While other considerations, too, determined Reagan's and Bush's policy toward Israel, the favorable evangelical
attitude and the Christian Zionist insistence that America should assist the
Jewish state played a significant part.[38]

Bill Clinton's relationship with Israel, although not lacking in warmth
and goodwill, was different from that of Reagan or Bush. Although nomi-
nally an evangelical Christian himself, Clinton did not receive much support from conservative evangelicals, who have seen him as representing
the liberal values they oppose. While in Arkansas, Clinton had remained,
however, a member of a Southern Baptist church. Upon his election as
president, his pastor delivered a sermon that included the message that the
newly elected president should not neglect his obligation to protect Israel.
This tells us perhaps more about the effect of premillennialist thinking
on Baptists in Arkansas than it does about Clinton's personal faith. Yet it is
important to be aware of the fact that the roots and cultural background of
the American president, who opened his administration to Jews more than
any president before him and showed deep concern for Israel, were in the
American Bible Belt with its scriptural vision of Israel.

Even more than previous presidents, George W. Bush's administration
was strongly influenced by the conservative evangelical agenda including
its pro-Israeli sentiment. A committed conservative evangelical Christian
himself, Bush relied heavily on conservative evangelical support and was
reluctant to initiate diplomatic moves that might upset premillennialist
supporters of Israel.

The evangelical premillennialist understanding of Israel exerted an
impact, at times more openly, on the attitudes of other prominent American
public figures toward Israel. One noted example is that of Jesse Helms from
North Carolina, who served as a U.S. senator during the 1980s, 1990s, and
early 2000s. A convinced premillennialist, Helms, who, as the powerful
chair of the Senate's Foreign Affairs Committee, generally labored to limit
American financial support abroad, nevertheless approved the extensive
financial support that the United States offered Israel.

Helms's supportive attitude toward Israel was not unique. In the 1970s–
2000s, dozens of pro-Israeli Christian Zionist organizations emerged in
the United States as well as other countries with a sizable number of evangelical or pietist constituencies. Besides mustering political support for
Israel, leaders of pro-Israeli groups also have lectured in churches, distributed material on Israel, and organized tours to the Holy Land. A number
of such groups have also been engaged in evangelization efforts among the
Jews. For many premillennialist Christians these two programs, missions

[38] Cf. Silk, *Spiritual Politics;* Liensch, *Redeeming America;* Irvine H. Anderson, *Biblical
Interpretation and Middle East Policy: The Promised Land, America, and Israel, 1917–2002*
(Gainesville: University of Florida Press, 2005).

to the Jews and pro-Zionist activity, have been inseparable. They have seen both activities as means to express goodwill toward the Jews, become involved in the life of that people, and influence its fate.

The years following the Six-Day War also saw an increase in the actual presence and activity of philosemitic Christian in Israel. Tours of evangelical and pietistic groups to that country increased, as did the numbers of field-study seminars and of volunteers going to kibbutzim. Evangelical Christians even established institutions of higher education in Israel, one of these being the Holy-Land Institute, set up by Douglas Young, a philosemitic premillennialist.

The most visible and best known Christian Zionist organization in Israel is the International Christian Embassy in Jerusalem (ICEJ). Its story tells us a great deal about philosemitic Christian interest in the Jews and Israel, about Christian Zionist activity, and about the relationship that has developed between the Christian Zionist community and Israeli society and government. In the 1970s, Christian Zionist activists in Jerusalem, expatriates from Western countries, founded a local fellowship that saw its aim as galvanizing support for Israel. The participants met weekly, prayed, sang, and discussed means to promote support for Israel in order to counterbalance growing anti-Israel sentiments in the Christian world. One of the leaders of the group, the Dutch minister Jan Willem van der Hoeven, suggested organizing large annual gatherings of Christian supporters of Israel from all over the world during Sukkoth, the Jewish harvest festival commemorating the tent sanctuaries, or tabernacles, used during the Exodus. His theological rationale was that according to the Bible (Zechariah 14:15) gentiles were also commanded to gather in Jerusalem during the festival. In October 1979 the group launched its first yearly Tabernacles festival, a week-long assembly of Christian supporters of Israel, highlighted by a march through the streets of Jerusalem.

In 1980, these Christian Zionist activists in Jerusalem announced the creation of the International Christian Embassy, as an act of sympathy and support for Israel on the part of Christians.[39] The embassy chose as its logo two olive branches hovering over a globe with Jerusalem at its center. "This symbolizes the great day when Zechariah's prophecy will be fulfilled, and all nations will come up to Jerusalem to keep the Feast of Tabernacles during Messiah's reign on earth," the Embassy's leaders announced.[40] Israeli officials, including the Jerusalem mayor at the time, Teddy Kollek, noted the propaganda value of the embassy's creation and welcomed the new organization. It made the point, they believed, that even though many

---

[39] James McWhirter, *A World in a Country* (Jerusalem: B.S.B. International, 1983), 160–74; interviews with Marvin and Merla Watson, Jerusalem, October 16, 1992, and Menahem Ben Hayim, Jerusalem, October 14, 1992.

[40] Van der Hoeven, "If I Forget Thee O Jerusalem," Sukkoth brochure (Jerusalem: International Christian Embassy, 1984), 4.

countries had removed their embassies and consulates from Jerusalem because of Arab pressure, the Christian world backed Israel.[41]

The embassy's major work has been promoting support for Israel among pietistic and evangelical Christians worldwide as well as initiating various philanthropic programs in Israel. The embassy wishes to represent "true Christianity" and has made great efforts to open branches and gain supporters in as many countries as possible. In the United States, its activity meshes with that of other pro-Israel groups, but in European, Asian, African, and South American countries the ICEJ is often the largest and most vigorous pro-Israeli Christian group.[42]

The embassy's international work focuses on lecturing, mostly in churches, about Israel's role in history and the work of the embassy on behalf of Jewish immigration and settlement in that country. "Embassies" around the globe distribute ICEJ journals, brochures, leaflets, and audiocassettes of "Davidic music" and sermons. Embassy representatives also recruit pilgrims for the annual Tabernacles gatherings and collect money for the embassy's philanthropic enterprises in Israel. The day-to-day work of the embassy in Israel is devoted to this international mission. The Jerusalem headquarters supervises the work of the representatives in various countries, administers the finances, maintains public relations and publications departments, and oversees the production of DVDs and audiocassettes in a number of languages, including English, German, Dutch, Finnish, and Russian. A special department produces material for Latin American countries in Spanish and Portuguese. The radio department prepares a special program, *A Word from Jerusalem*, which is broadcast on evangelical radio stations.

The embassy also provides welfare services in Jerusalem, distributing money and goods to new immigrants as well as other needy Israelis. Aware that many Jews are suspicious of Christian charitable enterprises, ICEJ often distributes its parcels through Israeli public agencies.[43] This aspect of Christian Zionist support for Israel is relatively new. Christian missions to the Jews had historically offered material support to needy Jews. At the turn of the twenty-first century, Christian supporters of Zionism also began to provide such support, often in cooperation with Jewish philanthropic agencies. Along with the Holy Land Fellowship of Christians and Jews, the embassy was the first Christian institution to donate money systematically to Jewish and Israeli enterprises.

---

[41] Interview with Haim Schapiro, correspondent for religious affairs of the *Jerusalem Post*, Jerusalem, October 6, 1992.

[42] A typewritten list of ICEJ international representatives, February 1992, included representatives in Florida, Georgia, Mississippi, South Carolina, Texas, Maryland, California, and Wyoming.

[43] On the various activities of the embassy, see its brochure, "The Ministry of the International Christian Embassy Jerusalem" (Jerusalem: International Christian Embassy, 1992); Arlynn Nellhaus, "Go Tell It on the Mountain," *Jerusalem Post Magazine*, October 9, 1992, 6–7.

The Feast of Tabernacles serves as the focal point of the year for the International Christian Embassy. A major convocation of thousands of supporters from around the world, it provides an opportunity to present the embassy and its message to the Israeli public. Activities include tours of the country for the pilgrims, a march through Jerusalem's main streets, a "biblical meal" served and celebrated on the shore of the Dead Sea, and assemblies in Jerusalem. Some of the gatherings take place in Binyanei Ha'Uma, the largest convention hall in Jerusalem; booths exhibit publications and feature programs and enterprises promoted by the embassy.

During the 1980s–2000s, Jan Willem van der Hoeven, who was the embassy's leading ideologue, emerged as one of the better known spokesmen on Israel and its role within history in the Christian Zionist camp.[44] Van der Hoeven adhered to the premillennialist vision of Israel as a necessary development on the messianic road. Accordingly, the Jewish political entity will exist in rebellious unbelief until the arrival of Jesus. At the same time, its existence and security represent a positive, even reassuring, stage in the unfolding of history, and it is therefore essential that Israel be protected against forces seeking to undermine its existence. Philosemitic conservative Christians have seen Arab hostility toward the Zionist enterprise as an attempt to jeopardize the advancement of God's plan. In Van der Hoeven's view, Palestinian resistance organizations are instruments of Satan, and he has insisted that Arabs who are true Christian believers must support the Israeli cause.[45]

Like that of many Christian philosemites, van der Hoeven's attitude toward the Jews has been ambivalent. He has firmly believed that the Jews are the heirs of biblical Israel, God's chosen people, destined for a glorious future in the messianic age, but he also has displayed negative attitudes toward the Jews, including feelings of frustration, disappointment, and anger. He has expressed bitterness, for example, that so many Israelis have been unwilling to support a firmer, more right-wing political agenda. In order to be accepted by the liberal decadent West, he complained, they appear willing to compromise their national aspirations and, in so doing, betray their historical role.[46] In a speech delivered during the embassy's 1989 Tabernacles celebration, he attacked moderate and left-wing Israeli politicians, declaring that giving up the territories Israel had occupied since 1967 would mark the second time the Jews rejected God.[47] For him, "land

[44] On van der Hoeven's views on Israel, see his book, Jan van der Hoeven, *Babylon or Jerusalem* (Shippensburg, PA: Destiny Image, 1993).

[45] *Le Maan Tzion Lo Echeshe* [in Hebrew] (Jerusalem: International Christian Embassy, 1990), 13.

[46] Interview with Jan Willem van der Hoeven, Jerusalem, August 19, 1991.

[47] Interview with the Reverend Michael Krupp; see also Michael Krupp, "Falsche Propheten in Jerusalem," unpublished article from October 3, 1988, sent to the Protestant religious press in Germany.

for peace" has not been a pragmatic political decision aimed at enhancing the well-being of the region; on the contrary, such a decision could have disastrous cosmic consequences and would impede the divine plan for human redemption. The Jews are not just another people able to make its own choices according to perceived political needs: they bear a burden, a duty, and purpose in history. To refuse to play this role would constitute unforgivable treachery toward humankind. Van der Hoeven's words convey the bitterness felt by many Christian supporters of Israel regarding the Jewish refusal to accept Jesus as the savior. In their view, the Jews should have been the first to recognize him as Messiah. A second refusal to accept Jesus as Messiah, or to prepare the ground for his arrival, would be even worse than the first, for the Jews would miss their second opportunity for redemption.

Over the years the International Christian Embassy has become one of the more controversial of the Christian groups and agencies that work in the Middle East or take an interest in its fate. Middle Eastern churches, as a rule, are pro-Palestinian and reject the embassy's message. Middle Eastern Christianity generally holds to "replacement theology," the claim that the Christian Church is the heir of biblical historical Israel and that Judaism has no further purpose in God's plans for humanity. Most of these churches have Arab constituencies, are sympathetic to Arab national feelings, and have expressed support for the Palestinian cause. They see the Christian embassy as an institution offering one-sided support to Israel and, as members of the Middle East Council of Churches, have signed petitions condemning its activities.[48]

The International Christian Embassy has also aroused resentment among liberal Protestants, who have little patience for conservative Christianity and the premillennialist messianic conviction. Liberal Protestants have often developed a negative attitude toward the Israeli occupation of Arab territories and have taken exception to Israeli policies. Mainline Protestant churches are committed, in principle, to social and political justice, supporting movements of national liberation and expressing sympathy for the Palestinians' quest for independence from Israeli rule. Their declared opinion has been that the existence of Israel has nothing to do with biblical

---

[48] On Middle Eastern churches and their relation to Zionism and Israel, see Dafna Tsimhoni, "The Arab Christians and the Palestinian Arab National Movement," in Gavriel Ben Dor, ed., *The Palestinians and the Middle East Conflict* (Ramat Gan: Turtledove Publications, 1978); Paul Charles Merkley, *Christian Attitudes towards the State of Israel* (Montreal: McGill-Queens University Press, 2001), esp. 9–102, 161–94; Gabriel Zeldin, "Catholics and Protestants in Jerusalem and the Return of the Jews to Zion" (PhD diss., Hebrew University, 1992); "Signs of Hope," 1988 Annual Report of the Middle East Council of Churches, Cyprus, July 1989; *What Is Western Fundamentalist Christian Zionism?* (Limosol, Cyprus: Middle East Council of Churches, April 1988, rev. ed. August 1988). The second, revised edition is somewhat more moderate than the first.

prophecies and that Israel should be judged, like all other countries, on the basis of its policies.[49]

While Arabs and pro-Arab Christian churches often criticize Christian Zionist activity, the Israeli leadership has welcomed its unexpected allies with open arms.

ISRAELIS AND CHRISTIAN PHILOSEMITES

In general, the Israeli leadership has not fully comprehended the nature of the attitudes of Christian supporters toward the Jewish state and has therefore overlooked elements in the Christian Zionist theology and activity to which, in principle, it objects. Israeli officials could not always tell the difference between mainline Christian supporters, who showed sympathy for Israel on the basis of political or humanitarian considerations, and conservative evangelical or pietist philosemitic supporters, whose attitudes have been rooted in a biblical messianic faith.[50] They have certainly been unaware of the details of the Christian eschatological hopes and probably never heard of such theological terms as "the Great Tribulation" or the "Time of Jacob's Trouble." For the most part, they also have not wished to acquaint themselves with the details of Christian premillennialist supporters.

Israel's first prime minister, David Ben-Gurion, is a case in point. Ben-Gurion believed that Christian supporters viewed the establishment of the state of Israel as the ultimate fulfillment of biblical prophecies rather than as a step toward the realization of the millennial kingdom,and gave expression to such views in an address he wrote for the opening of an international Pentecostal conference that convened in 1961 in Israel. Israeli officials who sat at the opening session were puzzled by the coolness of the Pentecostal reaction to the prime minister's speech.[51] They certainly were not aware that messianic hopes encouraged not only support for Zionism and for Israel but also and primarily a belief that Israel was a means to an

[49] In some cases, such as in the Netherlands, mainline Protestant church members often have more positive attitudes toward Israel than their leadership; consequently the embassy, which is regarded as representing pro-Israel sentiments, enjoys support even when the church establishment is hostile to its activities: interview with the Reverend Simon Schoon and the Reverend Geert Cohen-Stuart of the Dutch Reformed Church, Southampton, July 14, 1991.

[50] A striking example of this failure to understand can be found in Michael Pragai's book *Faith and Fulfillment* (London: Valentine Mitchell, 1985). The author, who served as the head of the department for liaison with the Christian churches and organizations in the Israeli Ministry of Foreign Affairs for many years, demonstrated a complete lack of knowledge of the nature of the evangelical support of Zionism and of the differences between conservative and mainline/liberal churches.

[51] Yona Malacy, *American Fundamentalism and Israel* (Jerusalem: Institute of Contemporary Jewry, 1978), 106–11.

end, a necessary development on the messianic road. Likewise they have not always seen the connection between Christian support for Israel and aggressive missionary activity among the Jews.

A major feature of the Christian philosemite relation to the Jews has been the mission. Since the rise of the pietist movement in central Europe at the beginning of the eighteenth century and the evangelical movement in Britain at the beginning of the nineteenth century, missions to the Jews have occupied an important place on the Christian philosemitic agenda and have come to characterize the messianic-oriented Christian inter-action with the Jews even more than pro-Zionist activity.[52] The mission's meaning for evangelicals and pietists goes far beyond attempts to capture Jewish souls. These Christians see evangelism among the Jews as taking part in the divine drama of salvation. Propagating Christianity among the Jews means teaching the people of God about their role and purpose in history, as well as saving some of them from the suffering of the great tribulation.

Often, the same individuals have been active on both fronts, promoting support for Zionism and evangelism of Jews at the same time. Missions to the Jews have seen it as their goal to increase support in the Christian com-munity for the idea of the centrality of the Jews in God's plans for human-ity and the need to evangelize that nation. For institutions such as the American Messianic Fellowship or the Friends of Israel, the two aims are inseparable.[53] Their premillennialist convictions motivate both their pro-Israel stands and their zeal to evangelize God's chosen nation. An impor-tant part of their work is lecturing in churches and distributing written or recorded material in which they advocate their outlook on the Jewish people's historic role and the importance of supporting Israel and evan-gelizing the Jews. The best known of today's missions, Jews for Jesus, also works to promote pro-Israel sentiments, calling its official concert band the "Liberated Wailing Wall."[54] Support for Jews for Jesus is from conser-vative evangelical Christians who consider themselves to be philosemites, and their attempts to convert the Jews a demonstration of love and com-passion. Missions to the Jews have emphasized since the 1970s that becom-ing Christian does not work to eradicate Jewish identity. On the contrary, it produces "complete Jews," true to the intended purpose of the Jewish people. During the 1970s–2000s, a Christian-Zionist movement associated with the missionary movement came into being: Messianic Judaism. As

[52] A. E. Thompson, *A Century of Jewish Missions* (Chicago: Fleming H. Revell, 1905).

[53] Interview with the Reverend William Currie, former head of the American Messianic Fellowship, Jerusalem, September 16, 1991. Currie had little appreciation for the embassy.

[54] Cf. Yaakov Ariel, "Counterculture and Missions: Jews for Jesus and the Vietnam Era Missionary Campaigns," *Religion and American Culture* 9, no. 2 (Summer 1999): 233–57.

Jewish converts to evangelical Christianity, Messianic Jews see themselves as overcoming the historical differences between Judaism and Christianity and amalgamating the Christian faith with the Jewish tradition.

Secular Israeli leaders have not been particularly bothered by Christian missionary activities. Their view of such activities has often been cynical, convinced they are doomed to futility.[55] The Israeli government has tried to build good relations with Christian groups and considered it essential to assure them that the government will not interfere with their work.[56] Christian missionaries have continued their operations in Israel without interruption.[57] Orthodox Jewish activists have protested against the missionaries' work in Israel, and some Jews have occasionally attempted to harass missions, but the government has refused to change its policy, and the police have been given the task of protecting missionary centers.[58]

Since the late 1970s, as the evangelical pro-Zionist influence on American political life has become ever more apparent, the Israeli government has taken greater notice of this segment of Christianity and taken measures to establish contact with it.[59] Among other things, Prime Minister Menachem Begin (1977–83) appointed a special liaison for evangelical Christians. Israeli officials have spoken at evangelical conferences, and evangelists have met with Israeli leaders as part of their touring schedules in Israel. After the Israeli bombing of the Iraqi atomic plant in 1981, Begin called Jerry Falwell, leader of the conservative Christian group the Moral Majority, and asked him to back Israel. During the 1980s to 2000s, Israeli officials have relied on the International Christian Embassy as a vehicle to reach the Protestant Christian community, believing that it represents a large segment of Christianity.[60] Israeli leaders have met frequently with embassy leaders and granted the ICEJ permission to hold gatherings in the courtyard of the Israeli parliament, the Knesset, as part of its Tabernacles celebrations.[61] In April 1990, the speaker of the Knesset presented the embassy with the Quality of Life Award, in recognition of the positive role it has played in Israeli life.

[55] For example, David M. Eichorn, *Evangelizing the American Jew* (Middle Village, NY: Jonathan David, 1978).
[56] Cf. Uri Bialer, *Cross on the Star of David: Israeli Policy towards the Christian Churches, 1948–1967* (Bloomington: Indiana University Press, 2005).
[57] For example, Robert L. Lindsey, *Israel in Christendom* (Tel Aviv: Dugit, 1961).
[58] Per Osterlye, *The Church in Israel* (Lund: Gleerup, 1970).
[59] "Israel Looks on U.S. Evangelical Christians as Potent Allies," *Washington Post*, March 23, 1981, A11.
[60] "Israel's Leaders Greet the Embassy," in *Prepare Ye the Way of the Lord* (Jerusalem: International Christian Embassy, 1991).
[61] For a photograph of such a gathering, see Tzipora Luria, "Lelo Tasbichim: Notztim Mechuiavim LeYesha" [Without inhibitions: Christians committed to Judea and Samaria], *Nekuda*, 17 March 1989, 31.

Ironically, many of the more enthusiastic Jewish allies of the Christian Zionists are in the nationalist-religious wing of Israeli society. In 1988 the magazine *Nekuda* (Settlement), an organ of the Jewish settlements in Judea and Samaria, published a favorable article on the International Christian Embassy in Jerusalem entitled "Without Inhibitions: Christians Committed to Judea and Samaria." Emphasizing that the embassy had no missionary intentions, *Nekuda* described the embassy as a Christian pro-Israel group that, unlike many Jews, realized that the Bible authorized the Jews to settle their land.[62]

One example of the Israeli ignorance of the nature of philosemitic Christian Zionism took place in the late 1970s and involved one of the Begin government's earliest acts of legislation. Not realizing that mission-ary activity was carried out by the same elements in Christianity with whom it was trying to establish a friendly relationship, the government proposed a law in 1978 at the demand of Orthodox members, which forbade the offering of economic incentives in exchange for conversion. Little came of the legislation. Contrary to Jewish myths, missionaries were not "buying" converts, and, at any rate, the Israeli government was reluctant to enforce the law.[63]

In the 1990s, antimissionary sentiments were again running high, and a number of Orthodox and non-Orthodox members of the Knesset proposed initiatives to outlaw missionary activity.[64] In 1996, an initial, first-round, proposal to curtail missionary activity in Israel passed the Knesset vote. But then the complex nature of the relationship between the evangelical community and Israeli society became unprecedentedly clear. Missionaries operating in Israel called upon their supporters around the globe to raise their voices against the impending law. "We call upon the international Christian community to join us in our opposition to this law," read one of the appeals; "as Christian believers in the God of Israel and in Jesus the Messiah and Savior of the world, we have a special respect and apprecia-tion for the Jewish people and the nation of Israel. We seek and pray for the welfare of all of God's people in the land. We view with grave concern the erosion of Israel's democratic freedom by this proposed law."[65] Israeli embassies and consulates in countries with evangelical populations were virtually flooded with letters of protest against the law. Many wrote directly to the prime minister in Jerusalem. The standard letters emphasized that they were written by friends of Israel who wished the country well and were

[62] Luria, "Lelo Tasbichim,"30–4.
[63] Cf. Ariel, *Evangelizing the Chosen People*, 277–8.
[64] Daniel Ben Simon, "Doing Something for Judaism," *Haaretz*, December 18, 1997, English ed., 1–2.
[65] For example, a letter circulated through the Internet by Noam Hendren, Baruch Maoz, and Marvin Dramer, March 1997.

writing to warn the government that the passing of such a law would turn its current supporters against it. Prime Minister Benjamin Netanyahu, who at first offhandedly supported the bill, changed his mind and promised evangelical activists he would oppose it.[66] The aborted attempts at curtailing missionary activity in Israel highlighted the paradoxical nature of the relation of philosemitic Christians toward Jews: the evangelization of a people they see as chosen and whose country they strongly support. It also points to the nature of Israeli realpolitik: accepting help from Christians, some of whose values and agendas contradict their own.

CHRISTIAN SUPPORTERS OF JEWISH BUILDERS OF THE TEMPLE

One of the important outcomes of the Six-Day War for Christians expecting the Second Coming of Jesus has been the Israeli takeover of the territory on which the Temple could be rebuilt and the priestly sacrificial rituals reinstated. The Temple, or rather the prospect of its rebuilding, excited premillennialist Christians as the one event standing between this era and the next.[67]

A striking demonstration of the prominence of the Temple in Christian messianic thought can be found in Hal Lindsey's *The Late Great Planet Earth*, an evangelical Christian best seller of the 1970s. Lindsey, like other premillennialist Christians, was strongly impressed by the Six-Day War and its consequences and placed Israel at the center of the eschatological drama.[68] For him, the rebuilding of the Temple and the rise of Antichrist to power were major components of the great tribulation, without which the coming of the Messiah could not take place.

There remained, however, a number of obstacles to the advancement of this stage in the prophetic timetable, the most striking being a lack of interest among the Jews, including highly pious ones, in building the Temple. Many Israelis understood the outcome of the Six-Day War in messianic terms, but most of them did not wish to rebuild the Temple.[69] There was the unavoidable reality that the Temple Mount was a Muslim site, with magnificent mosques and administered by the Muslims. The Israeli minister of defense at the time, Moshe Dayan, designed a policy of maintaining the status quo on the Temple Mount as well as in other Muslim and Christian sites. In addition, a number of rabbis declared that Jews were forbidden

---

[66] Ibid.

[67] Raymond L. Cox, "Time for the Temple?" *Eternity* 19 (January 1968): 17–18; Malcolm Couch, "When Will the Jews Rebuild the Temple?" *Moody Monthly* 74 (December 1973): 34–5, 86.

[68] Lindsey, *Late Great Planet Earth*, 32–47.

[69] Cf. Alan Mairson, interview with Rabbi Getz, "The Three Faces of Jerusalem," *National Geographic* 189, no. 4 (April 1996): 30.

to enter the Temple Mount. Most rabbinical authorities have viewed the
Temple Mount as being as sacred as it was when the Temple was standing. The Mishnah, the postbiblical compilation of law, outlined the various
degrees of sanctity of areas on the Temple Mount and the rituals of puri-
fication people needed to perform in order to enter these areas.[70] All Jews
are required to purify themselves with the ashes of the Red Heifer before
entering the mount, and there are currently no Red Heifers to be found.[71]
Rabbis also feared that Jews might step on restricted sacred ground, such
as the Holy of Holies, which ordinary Jews, and even ordinary priests, were
not allowed to enter. Most observant Jews at the time accepted the rabbinical ban and saw entrance to the Temple Mount as taboo.[72]

An Australian premillennialist Christian, Dennis Michael Rohan,
decided to change the existing reality. After spending some time as a vol-
unteer in an Israeli kibbutz, where he fell in love with his Hebrew teacher,
Rohan visited Jerusalem in July 1969 and there, convinced that God had
designated him for that task, planned and executed the burning of the
El-Aqsa Mosque on the Temple Mount in an attempt to secure the necessary ground for the building of the Temple.[73] The mosque was damaged
and Arabs in Jerusalem rioted. Rohan was arrested, put on trial, found
insane, and sent to Australia to spend the rest of his life in an asylum.[74]

Most premillennialist Christians have not taken the law into their own
hands but instead have sought legal and peaceful means to advance their
agenda. A number of Christian premillennialist groups and individuals
in the 1970s–2000s have promoted the building of the holy Jewish shrine
through a variety of activities, most of them centered on encouraging Jews
to prepare for the building of the Temple. During the 1970s and 1980s,
premillennialist Christians discovered groups of Orthodox Jews interested in the building of the Temple. Some of these groups promoted their
agenda publicly, while others prepared more quietly for the reinstatement
of the sacrificial system in a rebuilt Temple.[75] Such Jews, who were studying
the Temple rituals, manufacturing utensils to be used for sacrificial purposes according to biblical or Talmudic measures, or trying to breed a new
variety of heifers, served to sustain the Christian messianic imagination.
Premillennialist Christians marveled at these groups and their activities,

[70] Mishna, *Seder Taharot*, Masehet Kelim (Jerusalem: Mosad Biakik, 1958), 1, 8–9; cf. "Har Ha
Bayit," in *Ha-Encyclopedia Ha-Talmudit*, vol. 10 (Jerusalem, 1966), 575–92.
[71] Cf. Numbers 19.
[72] Cf. Ehud Sprinzak, *The Ascendance of Israel's Radical Right* (New York: Oxford University
Press, 1991), 279–88.
[73] I am indebted to Avinoam Brog for sharing with me information and impressions on
Rohan's stay in the kibbutz and his motive for burning the mosque.
[74] See Jerusalem District Court Archive, Criminal File 69/173.
[75] On the Jewish groups aiming at building the Temple, see Sprinzak, *Ascendance of Israel's
Radical Right*, 264–9, 279–88.

viewing them as "signs of the time," indications that the current era was ending and the apocalyptic events of the end-times were near.[76] One of the evangelical philosemites who took interest in the rebuilding of the Temple is Chuck Smith, a noted minister and evangelist whose Calvary Chapel in Costa Mesa, California, has, since the 1970s, been one of the largest and most dynamic charismatic churches in America. Smith supported Jewish efforts of rebuilding the Temple and invited Stanley Goldfoot, leader of the Temple Mount Foundation, to California to lecture in his church. Smith also secured financial support for exploration of the exact site of the Temple.[77] An associate of Smith, Lambert Dolphin, a California physicist and archaeologist and leader of the "Science and Archeology Team," took it upon himself to explore the Temple Mount.[78] Dolphin used sophisticated technological devices and methods, such as wall-penetrating radar and seismic sounding, in his search for the ruins of the previous Temples. In both taking his sophisticated instruments into Israel and preparing to explore the Temple Mount, Dolphin worked in cooperation with and received help from Goldfoot. His attempts to research the Temple Mount to find conclusive evidence regarding the Temple's exact location were frustrated by the Israeli police, who, confronted by Muslim protests, refused to allow the use of such devices on or under the Mount.[79] Yet a number of premillennialist Christians refused to wait for conclusive findings by Dolphin and embraced the theory that the Temple was originally located between the two major mosques, El-Aksa and the Dome of the Rock. The Temple, they concluded, could therefore be rebuilt without destroying the existing mosques, thus providing a "peaceful solution" to the dilemma of how to build the Temple at a site that is holy to Muslims.[80]

Christian proponents of building the Temple have not limited their efforts to discovering the exact site of the Temple. Some have searched for the lost ark, a quest that inspired a number of novels and a movie based in part on a real-life figure.[81] Some premillennialists have also

---

[76] Cf. Grant R. Jeffrey, *Armageddon: Appointment with Destiny* (New York: Bantam, 1990), esp. 108–50. For example, see Don Stewart and Chuck Missler, *The Coming Temple: Center Stage for the Final Countdown* (Orange, CA: Dart Press, 1991), 157–70.

[77] On Chuck Smith, see Donald E. Miller, *Reinventing American Protestantism* (Berkeley: University of California Press, 1998).

[78] On Dolphin and his premillennialist thinking and connections, see Dolphin's extensive Web site, www.Ldolphin.org; see also a series of tracts the Californian physicist has published, copies in Yaakov Ariel's collection.

[79] Stewart and Missler, *Coming Temple*, 157–70.

[80] See Yisrayl Hawkins, *A Peaceful Solution to Building the Next Temple in Yerusalem* (Abilene, TX: House of Yahweh, 1989).

[81] On the premillennialist fascination with the lost ark, see Doug Wead, David Lewis, and Hal Donaldson, *Where Is the Lost Ark?* (Minneapolis: Bethany House, n.d.); Don Stewart and Chuck Missler, *In Search of the Lost Ark* (Orange, CA: Dart Press, 1991).

searched for the ashes of the Red Heifer, necessary in order to allow Jews to enter the Temple Mount, while others have supported attempts at breeding red heifers.[82] A new interest has arisen in Christian conservative circles in the Temple building, its interior plan, and its sacrificial works, as well as in the priestly garments and utensils.[83] The rebuilt Temple has also played an important role in the literature, including the novels, published by the movement. The most popular of them has been the *Left Behind* series, which was published in the late 1990s and early 2000s and has sold millions of copies. The series takes place in the aftermath of the Rapture. It describes the struggles of those left behind, not least of which is the rise to power of the Antichrist, one of whose "achievements" is orchestrating the removal of the mosques to New Babylon.[84]

One of the Israeli groups that have established a working relationship with premillennialist Christians is the Temple Mount Faithful. Since its inception in the 1970s, the Temple Mount Faithful has become the best known of all the Jewish groups aiming at rebuilding the Temple. Its periodic attempts to organize prayers on the Temple Mount, not to mention its plans to install a cornerstone for the rebuilt Temple, have enjoyed considerable media coverage.[85] Pat Robertson, the founder of the Christian Coalition and longtime host of the *700 Club* and a one-time presidential hopeful, offered his support and hospitality to Gershon Solomon, the leader of the Temple Mount Foundation. In August 1991, the *700 Club* aired an interview with Solomon. Robertson described Solomon's group as struggling to gain the rightful Jewish place on the Temple Mount. "We will never have peace," Robertson declared, "until the Mount of the House of the Lord is restored."[86] Solomon, for his part, described his mission as embodying the promise for a universal redemption of humanity. "It's not just a struggle for the Temple Mount, it's a struggle for the ... redemption of the world," he declared.[87]

[82] Lawrence Wright, "Forcing the End," *New Yorker*, July 20, 1998, 42–53; Jewish Telegraph Agency, September 2, 1999, posted at http://www.jta.org/sep99/02-cows.htm.

[83] See, for example, C. W. Sleming, *These Are the Garments* (Fort Washington, PA: Christian Literature Crusade, n.d.); Wead, Lewis, and Donaldson, *Where Is the Lost Ark?*; Stewart and Missler, *In Search of the Lost Ark*; Thomas Ice and Randall Price, *Ready to Rebuild* (Eugene, Or: Harvest House, 1992).

[84] LaHaye and Jenkins, *Left Behind*. The series has sold more than 20 million copies. On the Temple, see, for example, *Left Behind*, 415; *Nicolae: The Rise of Antichrist* (1998), 369; *Tribulation Force* (1996), 208, 277.

[85] On the different Jewish groups that advocate the building of the Temple, see Matti Inbari, *Jewish Fundamentalists and the Temple Mount: Who Will Build the Third Temple?* (Albany, NY: SUNY Press, 2009).

[86] Quoted in Robert I. Friedman, *Zealots for Zion* (New York: Random House, 1992), 144.

[87] Ibid., 144–5.

Peace negotiations between the Israelis and the Palestinians, including the Oslo peace agreement, and the Israeli promise to evacuate settlements have not always pleased Christian Zionists,[88] but the hopes of most Christians for the Second Coming of Jesus and the rebuilding of the Temple have remained strong.[89] One cannot tell what would happen if Israel were to give up its official control of the Temple Mount. Would Christian philosemites be disappointed with Israel and the Jews and their attitude dramatically change?

CONCLUSION

Evangelical Christian philosemitism has been an unusual phenomenon in the history of the relationships between religious communities. In no other case have members of one religious community considered members of another religious tradition to be God's first nation and to hold a special role in the drama of human redemption. The unique nature of Christian philosemitism is especially remarkable when one bears in mind the bitter history of the relationship between Judaism and Christianity. For most of its history, the major trends in Christianity have seen Judaism as replaced by the church. However, the centrality of the Hebrew Bible for pietists and evangelicals and the more literal manner in which they have read the Old Testament can explain, at least in part, their infatuation with the Jewish people.

The almost incredible relationship that has developed between Christian philosemites and Jews can be compared to a marriage of convenience. Christian philosemites have perceived the rebuilding of the Jewish state and the Temple by the Jews as necessary stages toward the realization of the messianic age but have not always been admirers of the Jews. Similarly, Jewish statesmen have not cared for the Christian messianic faith more than Christian premillennialist groups have appreciated the Jewish faith, but they have seen such details as being beside the point. In recent years, however, one can detect some warming of heart as evangelical Christians and Jews have come to interact with each other more often than before. Among other things, premillennialist Christian writers are more careful when they write about Jews. The phenomenon of Christians supporting Jewish and Zionist causes is full of paradoxes. Being committed, indeed fervent, evangelicals or pietists, Christian supporters of Israel insist on the exclusivity of their faith as the only true fulfillment of God's commands and as the only means to assure people's salvation. The Christian philosemite relations to the Jews have therefore been characterized by two conflicting

---

[88] Cf. articles in the *Middle East Intelligence Digest*, a publication of the International Christian Embassy in Jerusalem, in the 1990s.

[89] Cf., for example, the series *Left Behind*.

sentiments, one supportive and appreciative, and the other critical and patronizing.

While evangelical and pietist Christians have enthusiastically supported Zionist initiatives, they have viewed the Jews as a people who failed to recognize and accept the true Messiah, thus depriving themselves of both eternal life and sound moral guidelines. Christian philosemites have maintained, therefore, many of the stereotypes held of Jews in Western Christian culture while expecting Jews to regain their ancient position as the leading nation in the millennial kingdom. Mixed, dual opinions have characterized the attitudes of pro-Zionist Christian activists, who, while supporting Jewish causes politically and genuinely showing love and kindness toward the Jews, also express unfavorable opinions of them.[90] Viewing the Jews as a people in need of improvement, pietist and evangelical philosemites have been active in the building of missions to the Jews, busily spreading the Gospel among the children of Israel. Missions to the Jews have become the twin sister of Christian Zionism, deriving from the same theological roots. The missions themselves have become Christian Zionist agencies par excellence, promoting support for the Zionist cause or for Israel.

In no other realm has the paradoxical nature of the relationship of contemporary philosemitic Christians to Jews demonstrated itself as much as in the Christian attempts to help traditionalist Jews rebuild the Temple. Christians expecting the Second Coming of Jesus have formed historically unprecedented friendships and alliances with Jewish groups that would have been difficult to imagine at other times and places. There is, therefore, something surreal about Christian support of Jewish religious causes in the sense that such actions transcend the historical dynamics of Jewish-Christian interaction. The unique relationship that has developed between Jews and Christians over the building of a Jewish state in Palestine, and the hopes that such Christians have placed on Jews' preparing the ground for the arrival of the Messiah, have brought about scenes that border on the fantastical, including Christians marveling at and receiving reassurance for their messianic faith from Orthodox Jews taking steps toward the building of the Temple. Although the groups have had different visions for the messianic times, for the near future they all share the same agenda.

One has to conclude that the Christian interest in the Jewish resettlement of Palestine in the nineteenth and twentieth centuries and Christian support of the Jewish Zionist cause have derived first and foremost from

---

[90] Charles Y. Glock and Rodney Stark, *Christian Beliefs and Antisemitism* (New York: Harper Torchbooks, 1966); cf. also L. Ianniello, press release by the Anti-Defamation League, New York, January 8, 1986, which announced remarkable improvement in evangelical attitudes toward Jews.

Christian messianic hope, and a specific mode of interpretation of biblical passages. Pro-Israel sentiments and concern for the physical well-being of Jews derive from the function of the Jews in the advancement of history toward the arrival of the Lord. While such Christians have often shown dedication and warmth toward Jews and Israel, they see themselves as supporting and working toward a great cause, in fact the greatest of all, the unfolding of the messianic age and the establishment of the kingdom of God on earth.

PART V

PHILOSEMITISM IN POST-HOLOCAUST EUROPE

13

What Is the Opposite of Genocide?

Philosemitic Television in Germany, 1963–1995

Wulf Kansteiner

Philosemites had a tough time after 1945. Their professions of love for Jewish culture and the Jewish people met with considerable skepticism in the aftermath of the Nazi genocide. Where had all these philosemites been when Hitler and his followers perpetrated the "Final Solution?" The lack of credibility was particularly pronounced in West Germany, where political leaders eagerly embraced philosemitic stereotypes without being able to dispel serious doubts about the sincerity of their pro-Jewish sentiments. To contemporary intellectual observers, the philosemitism that blossomed in West Germany's public sphere appeared to be a particularly egregious example of political opportunism. By embracing philosemitic values West German elites appeared to be currying favor with their Allied overlords, who worried about the denazification of Germany. Moreover and more disturbingly, the belated enthusiasm for everything Jewish seemed to be intrinsically linked to antisemitic dispositions of previous decades and centuries.[1]

The field of Jewish studies has generally confirmed this negative judgment. Most experts argue that the public display of pro-Jewish attitudes represented a convenient way for Germans to distance themselves from the Nazi past, identify with the new political status quo, and resume their lives and careers without significant self-reflection.[2] In their scholarly opinion, there is no need to study philosemitism as a phenomenon sui generis, least of all as a model of dealing with ethnic and social diversity

---

[1] Ernst Bloch, "Die sogenannte Judenfrage," in *Literarische Aufsätze* (Frankfurt: Suhrkamp, 1965), 549–54, 552.

[2] Frank Stern, *The Whitewashing of the Yellow Badge: Antisemitism and Philosemitism in Postwar Germany* (Oxford: Pergamon, 1992); see also Lars Rensmann, *Demokratie und Judenbild: Antisemitismus in der politischen Kultur der Bundesrepublik* (Wiesbaden: VS, 2004); Michal Bodemann, *Gedächtnistheater: Die jüdische Gemeinschaft und ihre deutsche Erfindung* (Berlin: Rotbuch, 1996).

that is worth emulating. I am offering the following case study on West German philosemitic television as a corrective to these dominant trends in Jewish studies. The study of contemporary philosemitism provides important research opportunities for historians, sociologists, and media studies experts. Postwar philosemitism shaped gentile-Jewish relations, especially in Germany. It has played an important role in the construction of the memory of the Holocaust and represents an integral part of the success story of the Federal Republic, which, if we believe the dominant emplotment of that story, turned a collective of Nazis and antisemites into a nation of Holocaust-conscious democrats. I will probe the West German success story later in this essay but would first like to point out that there is more at stake than the German case, however important it may be. Scholars in the humanities and the social sciences have only recently begun to unravel the complicated processes of collective identity and memory formation in media societies. We have known for some time that the social and political effects of mass media products rarely directly reflect the qualities of and intentions behind these products. But we are only now trying to reconstruct and understand the multiple ways in which media representations and communication about media coverage shape our understanding of society and our roles within society.[3]

West German philosemitism was developed in the 1950s and introduced into public TV in the 1960s. Philosemitic television consisted of nonfiction programs, especially features and documentaries, that address three different, more or less closely related topics. In the 1960s, the programs summarized centuries of German Jewish history and (re)introduced viewers to Jewish life in contemporary Germany. In the 1970s, philosemitic TV shifted focus and dealt primarily with the history and legacy of German Jewish immigration to Israel. The engagement with Israeli society and German Jewish history continued in the 1980s and 1990s but occurred now against the background of a rising interest in the Holocaust. As a result, philosemitic television lost its status as a marginal yet independent type of nonfiction programming.

Philosemitic television follows a simple, yet highly contradictory set of discursive rules. First, the narrative world of philosemitism only permits positive statements about Jews, who appear primarily in the roles of devout worshippers, scholarly geniuses, financial wizards, energetic settlers, and innocent victims. But since the programs strive for reconciliation, non-Jews – variously identified as Germans or Christians or German Christians – cannot be presented in an unequivocally negative light. Therefore, philosemitic

[3] See, for instance, the volumes compiled by Melvyn Stokes and Richard Maltby, eds., *Going to the Movies: Hollywood and the Social Experience of Cinema* (Exeter: University of Exeter Press, 2007), and *Identifying Hollywood's Audiences: Cultural Identity and the Movies* (London: BFI, 1999).

programs acknowledge antisemitic crimes but never focus on the Holocaust. Second, while philosemitic TV emphasizes the accomplishments and specificity of Jewish culture and religion, its inquiries into Jewishness tirelessly preach the utopia of peaceful Jewish-gentile coexistence. As a result, in the philosemitic universe of West German TV, Jews come in two attractive, nonthreatening flavors. For the most part, "the Jew" is simply depicted as a better, more innocent version of its other; the majority of TV Jews are well educated, culturally and linguistically German individuals who fit perfectly into postwar European society. Starting in the 1970s, these symbolic Jews pick up another intriguing quality. As West German TV reaches out to Israel and tracks down German-speaking Jews in Mediterranean settings, TV Jews also become suitable objects for the West German touristic gaze and its sense of exotic alterity. All of these characteristics turn philosemitic TV into a highly unstable discourse that constantly vacillates between identity and difference, symbiosis and antibiosis.

Philosemitic programs do not make for great television: they lack drama, visual focus, and entertainment potential. Obviously, these shortcomings apply to the whole genre of philosemitic media coverage, although the TV stories differ in one important respect from many other routine philosemitic products. What appears as an abstract anonymous entity in the public speeches of politicians could not remain so ephemeral in the work of TV executives. The latter had to deal with concrete people – concrete Jews – and that fact sometimes made producers and audiences quite nervous. This nervousness and the inherent instability of the discourse caused a number of strange faux pas, Freudian slips, and contradictions during the production and reception of philosemitic TV that are often more interesting and entertaining than the programs themselves. We will follow these communication mishaps over three decades by analyzing the communication processes surrounding the production and reception of 18 philosemitic programs that the powerful German public TV network Zweites Deutsches Fernsehen (ZDF) broadcast between 1963 and 1995.[4] The analysis reveals particularly vivid examples of philosemitic stereotypes as well as their semantic discontents.

SELF-PITY AND CULTURAL APPROPRIATION

The second weekend in November 1963 marked the fortieth anniversary of Hitler's amateurish power grab in Munich, which catapulted him onto the national political stage, and the 25th anniversary of Kristallnacht. ZDF marked the occasion by broadcasting a critical inquiry into lingering

---

[4] ZDF was the latecomer of West Germany's two public television networks. It was founded in 1961 and commenced broadcasting in March 1963; see Hans Bausch, *Rundfunkpolitik nach 1945* (Munich: dtv, 1980).

right-wing political proclivities in Bavaria's capital and a pessimistic report
on the lives of Jews in contemporary Germany entitled *Jews in Germany
Today: Taking Stock of a Loss.*[5]

No copy of the *Jews in Germany Today* has survived in the archives, but the
communication about the program elicited a number of typical philosemitic
phrases and attitudes. First, there is the broadcast's title, which exudes self-
pity. After all, the loss that is being acknowledged refers to the loss of lives
but also the "loss of intellectual and human substance" for the German
nation, as the reviewer for the *Abendzeitung* put it rather bluntly.[6] Moreover,
drawing up the balance sheet of genocide was accompanied by an eager
appropriation of the few remaining "assets" through study and catalogu-
ing. The program announcement for *Jews in Germany Today* clearly reflects
this objective by emphasizing that the TV feature provides answers to a
wide range of essential questions, including "How many Jews are still living
among us? How do they live? How many Jewish communities will still exist
in the Federal Republic in 10 to 20 years? Will the German-Jewish partner-
ship to which we owe so much come to an end in the near future?"[7] This list
of questions nicely illustrates the disturbing continuities between Nazi and
postwar culture. The text only reaches safe philosemitic ground with the
fourth question; questions one through three could function in all kinds
of ideological contexts that pay specific attention to Jews, including the
pseudoscientific efforts of Eichmann and Co. The reviewer for the *Kölner
Stadtanzeiger* encouraged such possessive inclinations, albeit in a rather
contradictory fashion. He pointed out that "contemporary philosemitism
makes the Jews uncomfortable" but nevertheless wholeheartedly endorsed
the ZDF's call to its viewers "to come to know the purpose of life for the
Jews, study their religion, and visit their synagogues and religious services
in order to not completely lose contact with them" – apparently without
noticing the obvious tension in his two-hundred-word review.[8]

Self-pity and appropriation of Jewish culture went hand in hand
with awkward silences and the essentializing of Jewishness as the
other of Germanness. The critic of the *Stuttgarter Zeitung* nicely captured these central characteristics of public communication in postwar
Germany: "Whenever the conversation turns to the fate of the Jews in
Germany a certain uptightness appears unavoidable – despite the best

[5] ... *und ihr habt nicht gesiegt: 9. November 1923–9. November 1963,* ZDF, November 9, 1963;
   Juden in Deutschland – heute: Bilanz eines Verlustes, ZDF, November 8, 1963.
[6] "Am Wochenende," *Abendzeitung,* November 11, 1963; on philosemitic self-pity in postwar
   Germany see also Erica Burgauer, *Zwischen Erinnerung und Verdrängung: Juden in Deutschland
   nach 1945* (Reinbek: Rowohlt, 1993).
[7] *ZDF-Programm* for November 8, 1963; on the eager attention that philosemites pay to
   Jews see also Wolfgang Benz, *Zwischen Antisemitismus und Philosemitismus: Juden in der
   Bundesrepublik* (Berlin: Metropol, 1991).
[8] "Mahnende Spuren," November 11, 1963.

intentions on both sides."⁹ The review from Stuttgart also reflected the best of intentions. By acknowledging the existence of "two sides," the critic insisted on the distinction between victims and perpetrators, a distinction that was often systematically obfuscated in Germany's historical culture, including on television. In the first decades after World War II Germans paid more attention to fallen Wehrmacht soldiers and victims of Allied bombing and expulsion than to the millions of innocent people who had been killed all over Europe as a result of the Nazi campaign of terror and genocide.¹⁰ In this cultural context philosemitism represented an important, albeit indirect and timid attempt to set the record straight and remember the Nazi crimes and some of its victims. At the same time, by gently insisting on the difference between victims and perpetrators philosemitism kept dividing the world into us and them and thus inadvertently reproduced the ideological vectors of Nazi antisemitism.

Finally – and this is the most frequently overlooked and puzzling component of postwar German philosemitism – many philosemites strove for and occasionally achieved a laudable degree of self-reflexivity. Philosemites recognized the problematic nature of their cultural profiling as they struggled to get a handle on "the Jews" in the new political climate. But they stuck to their stereotypes and sought engagement with Jews on the basis of these constructed images. In the end, the persistence paid off, although not necessarily in the way it was intended. The philosemitism that developed in this fashion marked an important departure from earlier decades because it was hardly the ideological, let alone the political equivalent of antisemitism. Philosemitism was so fraught with internal contradictions, so overburdened with helpless and hopeless self-reflexivity, and at the same time structurally so closely related to antisemitism that it helped render postwar antisemitism politically dysfunctional – at least when compared to Nazi antisemitism, which had played such a frightfully effective role in mobilizing the citizens of the Third Reich.

It is easy to highlight the complexities of postwar philosemitism and speculate about possible positive effects of philosemitic TV. It is much more difficult to document such effects conclusively because the available sources tell us frustratingly little about the reception of programs like Jews in Germany Today. We do know, however, that any learning process could not have occurred on a large scale. The late broadcast and the unpopular topic of the program explain why only 6 percent of television households tuned in to watch Jews in Germany Today.¹¹ We also know

⁹ Bilanz eines Verlustes, November 12, 1963.
¹⁰ William Niven, ed., Germans as Victims: Remembering the Past in Contemporary Germany (Basingstoke, UK: Palgrave Macmillan, 2006).
¹¹ The political magazine Weltspiegel, which was broadcast on the ARD channel in the same time slot as Juden in Deutschland – heute, attained ratings of 43 percent of TV households; see Infratest report for August 11, 1963.

that many of the viewers who stayed up late to watch *Jews in Germany Today* had already absorbed key lessons of philosemitism and knew how to keep their mouths shut. Researchers at Infratest who conducted qualitative interviews with viewers after the broadcast reported that many audience members who actually watched *Jews in Germany Today* were in principle opposed to all programs related to the Nazi past because they "do not want to hear or see anything about it anymore."[12] Somewhat surprisingly, the very same audience members also rated the program satisfactory but declined to go into any specifics. The experts at Infratest, who apparently could not imagine or did not want to admit that anybody would lie to them, drew the optimistic conclusion that viewers refrained from expressing a negative opinion because they found *Jews in Germany Today* so compelling that they were willing to set aside their negative prejudices.[13]

FLIGHT INTO HISTORY AND FOLKLORE

Until the mid-1980s, when the first commercial TV stations went on the air in West Germany, ZDF and ARD (Arbeitsgemeinschaft der öffentlich-rechtlichen Rundfunkanstalten der Bundesrepublik Deutschland) were the only games in town. The TV executives and staff members in both public networks proudly accepted their paternalistic responsibilities and, among other objectives, tried to instill in their viewers a properly Western democratic worldview.[14] The majority of the audience responded to these pedagogical efforts by focusing on entertaining TV fiction and avoiding didactic nonfiction as much as possible.[15] The evening of October 11, 1968, offers a good example of the audience's slalom run through the obstacle course of patriarchal television. At the beginning of the evening, ARD and ZDF were running neck and neck in the ratings, but the picture changed drastically at 9 P.M., when ARD broadcast the popular British crime series featuring the character Simon Templar (*The Saint*) and ZDF screened *The Jews of Prague.*[16] While more than thirty million people followed the adventures of Simon Templar, an intimate group of about one million viewers (70 percent vs. 3 percent of TV households) gathered in front of the ZDF

[12] See the detailed Infratest report for *Juden in Deutschland – heute* published in *Infratest-Index Abendprogramm* for August 11, 1963, 56–7.
[13] Ibid.
[14] Knut Hickethier, *Geschichte des deutschen Fernsehens* (Stuttgart: Metzler, 1998).
[15] Knut Hickethier, "Zwischen Einschalten und Ausschalten: Fernsehgeschichte als Geschichte des Zuschauens," in Werner Faulstich, ed., *Vom Autor zum Nutzer: Handlungsrollen im Fernsehen, Geschichte des Fernsehens in der Bundesrepublik Deutschland*, vol. 5 (Munich: Fink, 1994), 237–306, 274.
[16] *Die Juden von Prag*, ZDF, October 11, 1968; *Simon Templar und der Senkrechtstarter*, ARD, November 10, 1968.

screen to be enlightened about the long history of the Jewish community in Prague.[17]

The Jews of Prague contains a few explicit philosemitic statements, praising for instance the "penetrating intelligence" of the Jewish people (32:40 minutes into the program). In addition, the script of the documentary assumes a general philosemitic orientation in the way it positions its audience vis-à-vis the history of antisemitism. Kurt Kofron, the author of *The Jews of Prague*, identifies only two ardent antisemites, Hitler and Maria Theresa, in the long history of the Jewish community of Prague. Kofron stresses the parallels in the anti-Jewish legislation of both leaders and links them in a more ominous and somewhat disingenuous way by relating the name of Theresienstadt to the crimes committed there by the Nazis. Yet with the exceptions of the empress and the führer, Jews seemed to have experienced no animosity from their gentile neighbors during the 1,000 years that they lived in Prague.[18]

But the images of the documentary tell a very different story. The visual aesthetics of the documentary undermine the comfortable tourist perspective and render the Jewish community of Prague strange and even threatening. First, the film features unusually long segments from an Orthodox Jewish service without translation or commentary (41:15–43:40 minutes into the program).[19] The Hebrew liturgy and the concurrent German silences, lasting as long as two and a half minutes, must have been an alienating experience for the prime time audience. Another disconcerting passage depicts a chorus of male singers (again no translations or comments offered) from a top-down, askew camera angle and shot through the strings of a harp, which the viewer only recognizes as the image slowly comes into focus (25:30–26:45). Finally, the director uses hand-held cameras and unusual cuts that provide little information but are emotionally very evocative. At one point, for instance, the camera follows a member of the Jewish community through the narrow streets of the old town focusing on his feet and never revealing who this person is and where he is going. The walk ends, in fact, in front of a distorting mirror and the camera delivers a close-up of the warped reflection of the Jew's face before cutting to excerpts of Paul Wegener's expressionistic film about the famous Prague rabbi, Judah Loew, and his legendary Golem (17:00–18:00). On the visual level, *The Jews of Prague* thus presents a small, mysterious, anachronistic, and ethnically and culturally foreign

[17] Infratest report for Friday, October 11, 1968, 18–19.

[18] Kofron's positive assessment of Czech-Jewish relations did not please the reviewer of the *Allgemeine Jüdische Wochenzeitung*; see "Die Juden von Prag," 25 October 1968.

[19] The reviewer of *Die Welt* admonished this religious excess that "transposed historical facts into the realm of the irrational" ("Mehr Requiem als Report," 14 October 1968); compare to the favorable reviews "Prag und die Juden," *Aachener Volkszeitung*, 14 October 1968, and Günther Grack, "40 Generationen," *Tagesspiegel*, October 14, 1968.

community, which ekes out a precarious existence in the margins of modern-day Prague. The images belie Kofron's optimism about the future of the Czech Jewish congregation and undermine his philosemitic agenda. The expressionistic excess might explain why the reviewer in the TV guide *Gong*, straining to provide flattering comments, fell straight into stereotyped clichés about Jews that hover somewhere between philo- and antisemitism: "One always has to admire the achievements, the intelligence, and the tough, unerring persistence with which the Jews pursue their goals." Feeling apparently threatened by this persistence, the reviewer then applauds the ZDF film for "casting a wide and controlling gaze over the great history" of the Jewish community of Prague.[20]

The next folkloristic excursion into Jewish culture, which ZDF offered its viewers at 10 P.M. on October 26 1969, caused another ratings debacle, and understandably so. Only 4 percent of TV households suffered through *Yiddish: The German Language of the Jews*, and the critics had a field day.[21] The producer, Gottfried Edel, had called his feature an "entertaining report."[22] But the eclectic, superficial selection of a few Yiddish language cabaret performances, opera tunes, and pieces of medieval music, combined with long-winded, stilted comments, was neither entertaining nor particularly informative.[23] Eckhart Kroneberg of *epd/Kirche und Fernsehen* blasted the producers for presenting Judaism and Yiddish in ways that are normally reserved for topics like the world of the Incas: "far from us, exotic, and, with the exception of a few isolated relics, no longer part of contemporary history." Kroneberg also objected to what he perceived as the producers' "timid, apologetic efforts to prove the 'Germanness' of Jewish culture."[24]

The German Language of the Jews did not cause any extraordinary linguistic malapropisms with the possible exception of the words chosen by the

[20] "Die Juden von Prag," *Gong*, November 1968.
[21] *Jiddisch: Die deutsche Sprache der Juden*, ZDF, October 26, 1969; for ratings see Infratest Tagesanalyse, November 26, 1969.
[22] *ZDF Programm* for November 26, 1969.
[23] *Jiddisch: Die deutsche Sprache der Juden* does contain a few inadvertently funny scenes. At one point, for instance, a master of ceremonies announces an "ecstatic performance" of an Eastern European medieval song that, he intimates, requires the musicians to use their whole body. Then a somber-looking singer appears on stage whose ecstatic physical performance involves his standing around stiff as a poker and slowly lifting his arms a couple of times (21:30–23:00).
[24] Eckhart Kroneberg, "Nebbich: 'Jiddisch' – ein unterhaltender Bericht von Edel," *epd/Kirche und Rundfunk*, 1 November 1969. The reviewer of the *Süddeutsche Zeitung* called *Jiddisch* a "one-man stuttering with archival footage": "Jiddisch," *Süddeutsche Zeitung*, 28 October 1969; compare to Wilhelm Eisenbarth, "Vergessenes," *Die Rheinpfalz*, 28 October 1969.

reviewer of the *Lübecker Nachrichten*. This journalist, with the byline "jh," welcomed the younger generation's interest in Yiddish as an act of symbolic retribution performed on behalf of their fathers but then went on to describe Yiddish as a "peculiar, colorful, and also grotesque mixture of Hebrew and Middle High German."[25]

EXPORTING PHILOSEMITISM TO ISRAEL

Philosemitism in West Germany took a new, very productive turn after the Six-Day and Yom Kippur Wars. The mournful contemplation of past Jewish glory and German-Jewish symbiosis gave way to a celebration of Israel as an invincible melting pot. On a symbolic level, Zionism and philosemitism complemented each other beautifully, and the new ideological union provided German journalists with fabulous travel opportunities to the Middle East. ZDF producers and directors flew to Israel; returned with footage of palm trees, desert landscapes, ancient architecture, modern Israeli institutions, and scenes of Hebrew everyday life; and subsequently crafted these images into picture-perfect illustrations of Judaic exoticism. At the same time, the Zionist society of the 1970s still offered many opportunities to depict Israel as a success story made in Germany. Most "Jeckes" (as East European Jews referred to their German coreligionists) might not have left their homeland on their own account, but their Germanic industriousness and reliability could now be presented as invaluable assets during the colonization of the tough and allegedly unpopulated desert landscape of Palestine. Philosemitic Zionism was a great mixture of *Heimat* and orientalism.[26]

The feature *Nahariya: A German City in Israel* from 1972 approaches the topic of German immigration in a lighthearted, pre-Holocaust frame of mind.[27] The Israelis Gerhard Herm and Freddy Duna begin their report from Nahariya with a nice anecdote that gives them a chance to toy with German nationalistic and Nazi lingo (and inadvertently reveal the lack of Holocaust consciousness among Israel's settlers of German extraction). According to the story they tell, when the British contemplated dividing Palestine into a Jewish and a Palestinian sector in 1945 and making Nahariya part of the Palestinian sector, the inhabitants of the city sent an

---

[25] "Jiddisch," *Lübecker Nachrichten*, 28 October 1969.
[26] On a few occasions, ZDF journalists tracked down Jewish exoticism in locales other than Israel. In 1976 ZDF broadcast, for instance, a feature designed to familiarize viewers with the "involuntary, sometimes grotesque, but always tragic adventures" of German Jews who found refuge from Nazism in Santo Domingo: *Die Juden von Santo Domingo*, ZDF, May 16, 1976, quote from *ZDF Programm* for May 16, 1976.
[27] *Nahariya: Eine deutsche Stadt in Israel*, ZDF, May 28, 1972.

adamant letter of protest to the British governor insisting that "Nahariya remain German!"[28] The same playful, seemingly naive, and provocative approach to questions of German identity informs the very next scene. The off-screen commentator sets the tone with the words "under euca-lyptus trees people at ease with their past" as the camera pans over the said eucalyptus trees and settles on a large group of "Jeckes" engaged in animated conversation with a reporter and clearly excited about being filmed by German TV.[29] Talking about "people at ease with the past" cre-ates a sharp contrast to Germans who are often told that they yet have to come to terms with their past. But before the German viewer might be offended, the reporter and MC quickly asks all those present about their cities of origin in Germany and produces a truly heart-stopping hom-onym in an exchange with one of the "Jeckes" – heart-stopping at least for Germans steeped in politically correct, constitutional patriotism of the postnational, antinationalistic type epitomized by the philosopher Jurgen Habermas.

"So where are we from?"

"From Karlsruhe."

"From Karlsruhe – also born in Karlsruhe?"

"Yes, also born in Karlsruhe."

"And the parents?"

"The parents from Markt close to Karlsruhe."

"That means purely German?"

"Yes, purely German."

"Purely German – and the husband?" (4:09–4:20)

But I am mistranslating here. The woman and the reporter do not really say "purely German," that is, "rein deutsch." They are not speaking about racial or other types of imagined, untainted identities. Instead, they use the phrase "Rheindeutsch," meaning Rheinland-German. But the two expres-sions sound identical and the exchange thus creates a pointed climax to the tongue-in-cheek, Israeli-administered lesson in German nationalism for the benefit of nationally handicapped viewers sitting in front of the ZDF screen. In *Nahariya*, the German side of the philosemitic coin is subjected to a benevolent, ironic treatment that affirms German national identity

---

[28] "Nahariya bleibt deutsch" invokes nationalistic slogans circulating in the German media after World War I and World War II and insisting on the allegedly irrevocably German character of places like Memel, Saar, Danzig, or Königsberg: *Nahariya*, 2:53–3:13.

[29] The words "unter Eukalyptusbäumen bewältigte Schicksale" correspond and stand in contrast to the phrase "unbewältigte Vergangenheit," which became an important con-cern for German elites in the 1960s, *Nahariya*, 3:25–3:29; see also Grete Klingenstein, "Über Herkunft und Verwendung des Wortes 'Vergangenheitsbewältigung,'" *Geschichte und Gegenwart* 4 (1988): 301–12.

while offering the TV audience temporary relief from the task of coming to terms with Nazism.[30] Watching "Jeckes" proudly claim their German heritage without regret and recrimination might have helped their peers in Germany make peace with their own past and the troublesome legacy of their fatherland.

The next ZDF feature about German Jewish migration, entitled *Jews along the Rhine* and broadcast on the afternoon of Good Friday 1973, presents Jewish history from a thoroughly Zionist perspective.[31] The scriptwriter Anton Keim and the director Claus Hermans corroborate Leo Baeck's famous postwar assertion that "the epoch of Jews in Germany has come to an end" and are similarly outspoken in their support for Israel.[32] Throughout the program, they intercut segments about Jewish suffering in Central Europe since the Middle Ages with scenes of bustling everyday life in Israeli cities (5:00–7:20; 14:00–15:20). The footage from Europe focuses on dilapidated Jewish cemeteries and deserted architectural marvels like the reconstructed Romanesque synagogue of Worms. The images from Israel feature relaxed, self-confident Sabras and trace the history of immigration from Germany in the 1930s and 1940s. Keim and Hermans show that German Jewish immigrants played an important role in establishing cities like Naharya but that their German traditions have not been communicated to subsequent generations. Israel thrives, but the epoch of German Jews in Israel is also coming to an end.[33]

Jews along the Rhine had an unusual production history, which includes a major communication mishap. The idea for the program was first pitched to the director general of ZDF, Karl Holzamer, by none other than the director general of Israeli Television, Shmuel Almog, in May

---

[30] Judging by their lighthearted approach to the topic of German identity the Israeli filmmakers probably believed that the process of coming to terms with the Nazi past had been more or less successfully brought to a close. They were not alone in that assessment. Even many self-critical members of the German elite felt in the early 1970s that the postwar years were over and all accounts had been settled; see Wulf Kansteiner, "Losing the War, Winning the Memory Battle: The Legacy of Nazism, World War II, and the Holocaust in the Federal Republic of Germany," in Ned Lebow, Wulf Kansteiner, and Claudio Fogu, eds., *The Politics of Memory in Postwar Europe* (Durham, NC: Duke University Press, 2006), 102–48, 120–4.

[31] *Juden am Rhein*, ZDF, April 20, 1973. The documentary received a decent rating of 16 percent; see Infratest report for April 20, 1973.

[32] Baeck's statement is invoked three times, twice verbatim, in *Jews along the Rhine*, 14:38–14:45; 36:40–38:08; 45:04–45:13.

[33] The program *Pioniere nach Mass: Bericht über die jüdische Jugend-Aliyah* broadcast by ZDF on the afternoon of March 25, 1973, contains a very similar message. The producers Helmut Greulich and Hermann Engel describe how the Youth Aliyah managed to save 15,000 Jewish children and adolescents from Nazi Germany and Nazi-occupied Europe and turn them into productive Israeli citizens unencumbered by Old World cultural baggage.

1972.[34] Almog also proposed that ZDF and Israeli Television should collaborate in the production of *Jews along the Rhine*. Both suggestions met with Holzamer's enthusiastic approval, and he passed the idea along to the head of the ZDF main division, "Culture," one day after the meeting with Almog.[35] One of the key documents of the production file, the application for permission to develop new program content, explicitly mentions the director general's wish to develop the program as a coproduction with Israeli television.[36] However, while the production moved forward without a hitch, the cooperation with Israeli Television never occurred. One wonders whether the ZDF staff members in charge of the project decided that a coproduction would be simply too cumbersome or else did not feel comfortable shaping their philosemitic visions in close cooperation with representatives of Israeli TV.[37]

The miscommunications about *Jews along the Rhine* did not cause a major setback in relations between ZDF and Israeli television. A few years later, in 1978, Israeli TV officials warmly welcomed the opportunity to broadcast another ZDF program, which cast a woeful, nostalgic glance over centuries of German Jewish traditions and their relatively abrupt end in Israel.[38] The documentary, with the appropriate title *The Jeckes*, was produced by the Israeli filmmaker Nathaniel Gutman and aired by ZDF in May 1979.[39] Gutman, himself the son of Jewish immigrants from Berlin, captured on film conversations with and among the remaining elderly Jeckes who had lived for decades in the margins of Israeli society. As he visited them in their homes, clubs, and restaurants he documented their lifelong appreciation of German culture and European bourgeois etiquette, which always seemed out of place in Israel. Gutman's cultural archaeology of his childhood pays tribute to Jeckes as a special breed of Jews, "who live in a past that never had a future."[40]

---

[34] Internal memo from Hans Ölschläger, head of the ZDF Culture and Society division, addressed to a certain Kimmel in the ZDF International Affairs division and dated December 1, 1972. This document, as well as others cited later, are part of the editorial file of *Juden am Rhein*, which is archived at the ZDF under the production number 6354/0455.

[35] Internal memo from the office of the director general addressed to the head of the main Culture division, Brobeil, dated May 17, 1972.

[36] "Vorlage zur Stoffzulassung," dated June 27, 1972.

[37] When Ölschläger was later forced to apologize for the unusual occurrence that explicit wishes of the director general had been ignored, he offered no explanation other than his absence from the office due to illness for an extended period in 1972; see memo Ölschläger to Kimmel and the letter from Ölschläger to Amos Goren, the representative of Israeli Television in Bonn, dated November 29, 1972.

[38] In a handwritten letter addressed to his contact at ZDF, "Christoph," the director of *Die Jeckes*, Nathaniel Gutman, reports that "our film was very, very well received by Israeli TV." The letter is included in the editorial file of *Die Jeckes* (production number 6336/1062).

[39] *Die Jeckes*, ZDF, May 24, 1979.

[40] This bon mot was featured prominently in *Die Jeckes* and cited in many reviews of the program; see, for example, Heinrich von Nussbaum, "Tagträume über Utopia," *Frankfurter Allgemeine Zeitung*, 26 May 1979.

At first glance, there is nothing unusual about *The Jeckes*. The documentary represents just another late-night, low-budget, routine exercise in philosemitic broadcasting on a Christian holiday.[41] As often before, reviewers wholeheartedly supported the effort while viewers paid little attention to the program.[42] Yet the impression of philosemitic business as usual is somewhat misleading. *The Jeckes* was broadcast in a post-*Holocaust* environment (ARD had aired this American miniseries in January 1979), at a time when many West Germans were enthusiastically joining in efforts to come to terms with the past. As a result, Gutman and some of his interview partners "received an awful lot of letters and phone calls (!) from Germany."[43] The emotional flashpoint of the program seems to have been a certain Professor Markus who lived all by himself in a big villa in Ramat Gan, surrounded by his dogs and his books but otherwise completely isolated and tottering on the brink of senility.[44] In his helplessness and harmlessness Markus stirred the post-Holocaust philosemitic sensibilities of West German *Bildungsbürger* of Jewish and non-Jewish background, who sent him books, sought his didactic advice, told him their family histories, and even inquired in not so subtle terms whether he was interested in a long-distance romantic relationship.[45]

One of Gutman's correspondents also clearly identified the main ideological benefit of German spiritual tourism to Israel. The philosemitic ambassadors from Germany, who traveled to the Middle East courtesy of their ZDF expense accounts or who passed through vicariously via ZDF television, were welcomed in Israel with open arms because their seemingly naïve, uncritical appreciation of everything Jewish offered a nice break from the determined anti-Jewish attitudes of many other foreign observers of Israeli politics. But when the virtual travelers disembarked again in Germany they appear to have acquired, through the detour of "Jecke-culture," an equally uncritical appreciation of everything German that had otherwise largely been excised from the West German cultural-political scene. In the following remarks,

---

[41] *Die Jeckes* was screened at 9:55 P.M. and produced on a budget of 80,000 marks; see "Application for Production Authorization" dated November 13, 1978; May 24, 1979, was Ascension Day. For a similar program broadcast in the 1980s see *Denk ich an Deutschland in der Nacht ... Jüdische Emigranten erinnern sich*, ZDF, October 10, 1988.

[42] See, for example, "Neugier geweckt," *Frankfurter Rundschau*, 26 May 1979, and Andreas Wild, "Die Jeckes," *Die Welt*, 26 May 1979. Only 7 percent of TV households tuned in, and only four viewers called the station with routine questions or comments; see *Telejour* (Allensbach & Infas) for May 24, 1979, and "Protokoll des Telefondienstes," May 24, 1979.

[43] Letter of Gutman to Christoph.

[44] In his letter to Christoph, Gutman reports that Markus cannot answer his fan mail: "He is extremely excited but at the same time too old and senile! The interview on film was a miracle!"

[45] ZDF had released Gutman's address to viewers upon request, and Gutman sent copies of a few of the letters back to Mainz; that is how they found their way into the editorial file.

Ilse F. from Hannover beautifully captures this aspect of the German Jewish heritage exchange (and demonstrates in the process that she does not understand how marginal German traditions in Israel really are):

Your documentary shows that over all these years you have carefully and lovingly maintained the common cultural heritage. Here [in Germany (WK)] many things have been subjected to overcritical scrutiny with notorious thoroughness: the pathos of Schiller, the cruelty of the fairy tales of the brothers Grimm ... not to mention such things as spiked helmets. Therefore, the heritage has not been transmitted on a large scale. I take it from your account that in Israel, which did not have to deal with similar taboos, many things have stayed alive with which whole generations are no longer familiar here.[46]

TESTING THE LIMITS OF PHILOSEMITISM

On a few occasions, ZDF journalists dared to test the limits of philosemitism by criticizing the Jewish community in West Germany or by calling into question the soundness of Israeli policies. ZDF staff members were less aggressive in this regard than their colleagues at some of the ARD stations, especially at the Left-leaning WDR in Cologne or NDR in Hamburg.[47] Only two programs in the ZDF sample either straddle the border or clearly violate the rules of philosemitic programming. One of them is a two-part documentary entitled *A Fight about Palestine: The Path to the Jewish State*, which ZDF broadcast in February 1977.[48] In many respects Lothar Ruehl, the political journalist who produced *A Fight about Palestine*, very effectively toed the line; the documentary is hardly a radical piece of programming. But at the beginning of the second part Ruehl also documents in impressive detail the terror tactics that the Jewish secret service employed in the years before the founding of the state of Israel.[49] These segments can be interpreted as a thinly veiled critique of Jewish aggression; for several minutes Ruehl tells stories about Jews that would have been inadmissible or unimaginable in a thoroughly philosemitic narrative universe. *A Fight about Palestine* thus illustrates that, starting in the 1970s, TV officials faced an interesting choice in their representation of Israel. They could produce programs that offered a comprehensive engagement with the history of Israel and retained credibility with large segments of German TV audiences – but only at the price of

[46] Letter of Ilse F. addressed to Nathaniel Gutman and dated May 26, 1979.

[47] That applies, for instance, to some political magazines broadcast by ARD; see Gerhard Lampe, *Panorama, Report und Monitor: Geschichte der politischen Fernsehmagazine 1957–1990* (Konstanz: UVK Medien, 2000).

[48] *Ein Kampf um Palestina oder Der Weg zum Judenstaat*, two parts, ZDF, February 6 and February 10, 1977.

[49] Hans Joachim Fischer, "Ein Kampf um Palestina," *Frankfurter Allgemeine Zeitung*, 12 February 1977, and "Viele Legenden," *Frankfurter Rundschau*, 12 February 1977.

violating the rules of philosemitic discourse. Or, they could stay within the philosemitic paradigm and choose to focus on small segments of Israeli history, for instance, the record of immigration from Germany. At ZDF most staff members clearly chose the second option.

The second deviation from philosemitic standards occurred in 1971 when ZDF broadcast the feature *Young Jews in the Federal Republic*.[50] Screened at 10 P.M. on a Sunday night, the program was another off–prime time affair, which began with another exercise in ethnic accounting.[51] A few minutes into the program the audience learns that 26,354 Jews are registered in West Germany and that 6,412 of them are less than thirty years of age.[52] But the program is more remarkable for reminding us why philosemitic rules of media conduct were so important in the first place. The feature presents its viewers with an intriguing generational matrix that circumvents the philosemitic rule to "tell no evil about Jews" by inviting young Jews to testify against their parents.

The audience is first introduced to the older non-Jewish German generation, that is, the Nazis, who quickly reveal their true colors in a conversation about Jews in Germany. A well-fed, smirking fifty-five-year-old man with a military haircut tells the invisible interviewer: "If there are still some left alive? Yes, I assume so, don't you? Eh?" (00:34–00:41). Having met the ugly German, the audience can now mingle with the good Germans. The producers have lined up a fair number of relaxed, well-spoken young adults who profess to know little about Jews, stress that they harbor no ill feelings toward them, and approach the topic with attitudes ranging from benign indifference to mild curiosity. The Jewish peers of the good Germans largely share their upbeat assessment of the state of religious and ethnic tolerance among postwar generations. Nevertheless, the extensive interviews with young Jews in Germany quickly reveal a serious problem. The young Jews are not integrated into West German society, and many are already planning their emigration to Israel. An expert who is occasionally brought in (without being properly identified) introduces in this context the term "psychological ghetto" (17:50–18:02).

The producers quickly present a culprit for this unfortunate development by very effectively cutting together a string of statements by their young interviewees that all point in the same direction: the young Jews have become the victims of their irrational parents. The disturbing image that is artfully

---

[50] *Junge Juden in der Bundesrepublik*, ZDF, March 7, 1971.

[51] *Junge Juden in der Bundesrepublik* received perfectly acceptable ratings of 15 percent of television households, thus narrowly defeating *Zu Protokoll*, an ARD interview program; see Infratest report for March 7, 1971.

[52] The producers apparently attributed a lot of importance to the numbers game. The figures are not just mentioned in the off-screen commentary but also appear twice in print on the full screen, *Junge Juden*, 06:03 and 49:15. In addition, the figures are cited in the first line of the official program announcement; see *ZDF-Programm* for March 7, 1971.

assembled here tells of survivors who have decided to settle in Germany because they are not cut out for the tough life in Israel and also "for monetary reasons" (28:49–28:52). However, despite having chosen Germany as their better option, the parents remain deeply suspicious of German society and aggressively prevent their children from making Germany their homeland. They keep their children in separate Jewish educational and cultural institutions, compel them to attend synagogue, and discourage them from dating and marrying non-Jews.[53] One of the young Jews, who has apparently escaped the psychological ghetto and is dating a gentile, calls the parents' behavior irrational, "reverse antisemitism" (26:18–26:45).

With its emphasis on non-German guilt *Junge Juden* made things easy for reviewers. Only one critic doubted that all of the interview subjects had spoken their true mind in front of the camera and suggested that ethnic relations in Germany might be less relaxed than the film implied.[54] Everybody else jumped on the "it's-not-us-it's-them" bandwagon, celebrating the lack of prejudice among German youths and regretting the self-imposed isolation of their Jewish peers – often by embracing the term "psychological ghetto."[55] Yet despite this near consensus and the film's clear message, a veteran reviewer lost his way in the semantic jungle of philosemitism and Nazi memory. Eike Wolf from the *Stuttgarter Zeitung* tried to pay the producers a compliment, but the result registers somewhere between impenetrable and ambivalent: "Through compelling and painstaking analytical work the sad complex of 'the German guilty conscience,' personified in Judaism, was liberated from the poisonous fog of irrationalism and revealed in all its constitutive components."[56] In contrast, five of the actual viewers of *Junge Juden* proved anything but ambivalent when they called ZDF during the broadcast. Having emphasized that they were members of the young generation who share no responsibility for Nazi crimes, the callers demanded that the media stop depicting all Germans as anti-Jewish criminals and encouraged "the young Israelis" to grow up in their own state."[57] Apparently, these viewers had not paid much attention to the program. Moreover and more important, they clearly demonstrated that not all German youths were models of tolerance and that Jews were well advised to keep their distance from at least some of them.

---

[53] In this context, the film contains an almost perfidious aside. The off-screen commentary points out that two-thirds of recent weddings involving Jews in Germany have not been conducted in a synagogue because one of the wedding partners was not Jewish. The commentator then adds that the registry office option does not exist for weddings in Israel: *Junge Juden*, 24:28–24:47.
[54] "Kommentar fehlte," *Süddeutsche Zeitung*, 9 March 1971.
[55] See, for example, "An den Jungen liegt es nicht," *Frankfurter Rundschau*, 9 March 1971; "Einfach natürlich sein," *Rheinische Post*, 9 March 1971.
[56] "Junge Juden in der Bundesrepublik," 9 March1971.
[57] "Protokoll des Telefondienstes" for March 7, 1971.

Junge Juden in der Bundesrepublik paints a completely unfair picture of the survivors, who are never invited themselves to present their point of view. The program's remarkable lack of empathy makes one wish that its producers had exercised a little more philosemitic tact. Moreover, the 1971 program illustrates that the subsequent rise of Holocaust consciousness in Germany, despite its serious limitations, would mark a decisive change in the history of German collective memory. By the 1980s, the type of passive-aggressive criticism of survivors found in *Junge Juden*, exceptional even in the early 1970s, had been excluded from mainstream media. Such images were deemed incompatible with philosemitic Holocaust memory and the importance it attributes to the survivors of the "Final Solution." A careful, critical look at the vicissitudes of Holocaust culture also reveals, however, that attributing central importance to the survivors does not necessarily mean paying them respect and that the rise of Holocaust consciousness is not always a sign of ethical maturity and political progress.

PHILOSEMITIC HOLOCAUST MEMORY

Philosemitic television changed subtly yet persistently in the late 1970s and 1980s. And since the shift predates the invention of the Holocaust paradigm proper, the transformation of philosemitic discourse in the late 1970s probably helped pave the way for the surprising curiosity with which audiences, critics, and TV personnel approached the history and legacy of the "Final Solution" in the 1980s. The first wave of ZDF philosemitic programming in the 1960s had presented Jews as representatives of certain groups and types. Even in interview settings, TV directors hoped to elicit information on "the young generation," "the Israeli," or "the German-Jewish immigrant." The specific autobiographical experience of the interview partners (as well as their names) did not count and rarely made it into the final product. In the mid-1970s, the focus shifted toward the individuals in front of the camera, whose past suffering was now interpreted as the central experience of their lives.[58]

Starting in 1978, before the screening of *Holocaust* in Germany, ZDF began to broadcast a number of nonfiction programs that focused specifically on the survivors of the "Final Solution."[59] With the stunning success of *Holocaust* in January 1979, that trickle turned into a flood of dozens of fiction and nonfiction programs per year. ARD and ZDF now produced and

---

[58] For a program on the threshold between the two paradigms see *Herbst der Welt: Samuel Bak – ein Maler aus Israel*, ZDF, February 8, 1976; the feature pays close attention to the survivor Bak but primarily to tell a story of German-Jewish reconciliation, not a story about the Holocaust. See also *Juden in Deutschland 1 and 2*, ZDF, March 26 and 27, 1978.

[59] See, for example, *Beschrieben und vergessen: Simon Wiesenthal oder ich jagte Eichmann*, ZDF, March 6, 1978; *Es verfolgt mich bis auf den heutigen Tag: Ein deutsch-jüdisches Schicksal*, ZDF, March 6, 1978; *Wenn ich wieder ins Leben zurückkehre: Fania Fenelon und die Jahre nach*

purchased a large number of programs dealing with the history and memory of the "Final Solution."[60] Consequently, all of this philosemitic programming was produced and perceived against the background of a sustained and successful wave of Holocaust stories and images. Before 1980, philosemitic TV shows played only a marginal role in the context of German national television broadcasting, although these shows represented a considerable percentage of television communication about Jews. After 1980, German viewers saw Jews primarily in their roles as victims of Nazi anti-Jewish policies and, even more frequently, as survivors of the Holocaust who were most likely to appear on TV if they had made their peace with Germany.[61]

Philosemitic television in the era of Holocaust consciousness resulted in fewer gaffes and contradictions. Reviewers now had the Holocaust to contend with and therefore paid less attention to philosemitic programming. Moreover, since the Holocaust paradigm offered new, more stable, and less contradictory rules of discursive conduct, communication about Jews was less likely to end up in uncharted linguistic territory. Media professionals quickly acquired a set of routine phrases and images for the representation of Nazi genocide. They eloquently attested to the uniqueness of the Holocaust, crafted moving stories about Holocaust survivors, and effectively garnished their reports with photos of watchtowers, barbed wire, mountains of shoes, and other Holocaust icons.[62] But the belated recognition of the enormity and irreversible consequences of Nazi genocide temporarily extinguished any remaining hope for a return to the cultural status quo ante. As a result, philosemitic discourse assumed a new sense of finality and hopelessness.

In *Once upon a Time: A Trip to Old Jewish Centers* the director Robert Hartmann takes the viewers on a whirlwind tour of European Jewish neighborhoods where Yiddish culture thrived in the 1920s and 1930s.[63] The trip takes 135 TV minutes; covers Paris, Vienna, Amsterdam, Antwerp, Prague, Warsaw, Moscow, and East Berlin; and was presented to ZDF viewers on three nights in June and July 1985. Hartmann finds death and decline everywhere. In one cemetery after another, the camera lingers over graves of famous and not so famous Jewish artists and intellectuals.

Auschwitz, ZDF, March 9, 1981; and ... *damit es nie wieder geschieht: Die Ueberlebenden des Holocaust in Israel*, July 21, 1981.

[60] Wulf Kansteiner, *In Pursuit of German Memory: History, Television, and Politics after Auschwitz* (Athens: Ohio University Press, 2006), 109–30.

[61] For an excellent example of a Holocaust reconciliation story see *"Hier sind meine Wurzeln, hier bin ich zuhaus ... ": Das Leben der Gerti Meyer-Jorgensen, geb. Salomon*, ZDF, March 3, 1991; compare to *Deutsch ist meine Muttersprache: Deutsche Juden in Israel erinnern sich*, ZDF, April 18, 1990.

[62] On the development of visual and discursive strategies for Holocaust representation in West Germany in the 1980s see, for example, Kansteiner, *In Pursuit of German Memory*, 41–5, 115–18, 256–7.

[63] *Wus Gewejn ... es war einmal: Eine Reise durch alte jüdische Zentren*, ZDF, June 17, June 19, and July 1, 1985.

In each neighborhood, Hartmann tracks down the last Yiddish speakers, who woefully recall the homogeneous culture of their childhoods and view their current surroundings with considerable suspicion. It is not surprising then that Hartmann also feels compelled to break the philosemitic mold and instead emphasize death camp iconography in his report. Having traced the path of the deported Berlin Jews to the Grunewald train station, Hartmann abruptly shifts gears and briefly flashes photographs of corpses and emaciated inmates. Afterward, without explanation or comment, the film reassumes its elegiac pace and almost apologetically explores the snow-covered, picturesque ruin of the largest Berlin synagogue, which provides Hartmann with a particularly suitable metaphor of doom (39:00–41:00). Since Hartmann shuns complexity and contradiction in his thematically and aesthetically consistent lament, he misses a number of interesting opportunities. In Paris, for instance, he spends no time and expends not an inch of film on any exploration of the thriving Sephardic Jewish community. In Berlin, he reports from the diamond wedding anniversary celebrations of a blind and deaf couple in the East Berlin synagogue but does not even mention the lively Jewish congregation of West Berlin.

Once upon a Time was hardly an audience success; it triggered a handful of antisemitic phone calls and reached only 7 percent of TV households.[64] But critics paid considerable attention to Hartmann's ambitious documentary. Most reviewers stayed with the philosemitic message; they criticized the program's alleged superficiality or praised the sensitive camerawork in measured, appropriately solemn words.[65] Yet a minority of critics reacted very differently to Hartmann's unusually uninhibited reflections on Jewish death and Yiddish decline. Hartmann's modest effort to shatter taboos inspired them to follow suit and explore the topic in similarly blunt although considerably more haphazard ways. It seems as if the rise of the Holocaust paradigm had loosened some critics' pens, and they now started to chat about death and destruction in a process of free association.

Gudrun Ziegler of *Funk-Korrespondenz*, for instance, spent the first paragraph of her one-page review on a discussion of Harry Kemelman's murder mysteries featuring detective Rabbi Small.[66] That approach did not offer any insights into Hartmann's film, but Ziegler must have felt that her excursion fit the overarching theme of Jews and death. Elisabeth Bauschmidt, writing in the *Süddeutsche Zeitung*, first warned her readers not to react to the destruction of Yiddish culture with self-pity "like a child who murdered mother and father and is now crying because he is an orphan." Then she incongruously compared Hartmann's endeavor to the task of "following a

[64] The content of the phone calls is recorded in the "Protokoll des Telefondienstes" for June 17, June 19, and July 1, 1985. For the ratings see GFK-Fernsehforschung for the same dates.
[65] See, for example, "Dürftig," *Frankfurter Rundschau*, 24 June 1985, and compare to Horst Jansen, "Auf den Spuren einer verlorenen Welt," *Westdeutsche Allgemeine Zeitung*, 3 July 1985.
[66] Gudrun Ziegler, "Sightseeing der Zufälligkeiten," *Funk-Korrespondenz*, 5 July 1985.

trail of blood that is still wet." Finally, Bauschmidt took inspiration from the title of the program and started playing with fairy tale language: "Once upon a time. The old fairy tale phrase does not apply. They do not live; they are dead. And if they have not died yet, they will die soon."[67]

The combination of Holocaust curiosity, philosemitic values, and the overcoming of important representational taboos and inhibitions caused yet another interesting twist in the German media's infatuation with Jews and inadvertently revealed the drawbacks of Holocaust culture. Since a considerable share of Germany's elite had been engaged in memory work for a number of years now, television could report on particularly laudable exemplars of the new species of self-reflexive Germans and their philosemitic deeds.[68] A particularly revealing program about good Germans entitled *Temporary Grandchildren: German Conscientious Objectors in Prague* was broadcast in 1995 and illustrates that the best intended memory work may yet have unwelcome consequences.[69]

For ten days a ZDF camera team observed three German conscientious objectors who provided essential social services to Holocaust survivors in Prague. But six minutes into the program the producers felt the need to share with their viewers a harmless slip of the tongue that they had caught on tape. The conscientious objector Fabian and the survivor Ms. Ernstowa appear side by side on an outdoor bench while the interviewer asks the young man whether he finds any important differences between knowing abstractly about the Holocaust and sitting next to a survivor who has lived through the actual events. Fabian dutifully confirms the difference and adds that in fact he finds it impossible to relate the two:

Fabian:	It is something different and somehow I cannot integrate these two images. Ms. Ernstowa as a living women [she is laughing, he is blushing] as, I mean, lively in terms of her personality ...
Ms. Ernstowa (interrupting quietly):	Yes, I know, yes.
Fabian:	and the reports that have so much hopelessness about them and that are just on paper.

---

[67] Elisabeth Bauschmidt, "Das Bilderverbot der Grossväter missachten," *Süddeutsche Zeitung*, 3 July 1985; Bauschmidt had used similar language in a previous, very short review of the program lamenting that "the dead are dead and the murderers multiply": "Kein Trost," *Süddeutsche Zeitung*, 19 June 1985.

[68] In this vein, in 1988, ZDF highlighted the path-breaking memory efforts of twenty-five German adolescents who had helped build a synagogue in Lyon in the 1960s; see *Kontext: Reise in die Vergangenheit: 1963 – Junge Deutsche bauen eine Synagoge in Lyon*, ZDF, September 28, 1988.

[69] *Enkel auf Zeit: Deutsche Zivis in Prag*, ZDF, December 10, 1995. The feature by Michael Koechlin was originally scheduled for 9:15 P.M. on July 21, 1995, but postponed on short notice; see *ZDF-Programm* for July 21, 1995, and December 10, 1995. It was watched by 1.4 million viewers, representing 3 percent of TV households in unified Germany.

While Fabian's lapse appears not to have damaged his good relationship with Ms. Ernstowa, one cannot help but wonder about the psychological fallout from another scene included in *Temporary Grandchildren*.

The interviewer has already asked the Auschwitz survivor how important Fabian's daily visits are for her. He has already encouraged her to comment about the fact that she was tortured by young Germans and now has a young German in her apartment. As a result of these not-so-subtle inquiries, the interviewer has already elicited from her explicit statements affirming Fabian's innocence and his superior work ethic. But the interviewer has a very specific plan in mind – in fact, it seems that he has already decided on the title of his film – and therefore digs deeper. The camera first offers a close-up of an old red and black photograph depicting three Soviet soldiers and two women in camp uniform. The camera then slowly moves up the arm of the person holding the photograph before coming to rest on the tattoo on the women's left forearm. After a cut the camera provides a top-down close-up of the face of Ms. Pechanova, an old, small woman who sways awkwardly back and forth (the viewers already know that she walks with the help of a cane). The scene is accompanied by voice-over comments before we hear Ms. Pechanova herself. For the duration of the scene the camera remains closely trained on her face:

Comment:	A Russian soldier took this photo. The bowed down Hedwiga Pechanowa during the liberation of Auschwitz on her 30th birthday. The concentration camp number 74901 is the external sign for that which has changed her life forever.
Ms. Pechanova:	There is, there is in me … I had during the Heydrich years here, I had tragically lost both parents, both parents and 52 relatives. Now I am all alone in the world.
Interviewer:	Is it under these circumstances particularly important that Fabian comes by every day?
Ms. Pechanova:	Yes, it is very important.
Interviewer:	What kind of relationship do you have to him? How would you describe it?
Ms. Pechanova	(swaying more intensely and briefly leaving the field of vision of the camera, then laughing a little): Very friendly …
Interviewer:	If the war, the persecution, and the Nazi period had not occurred, a grandchild, perhaps one's own grandchild would come to you. Is Fabian …
Ms. Pechanova	(swaying, interrupting the interviewer quickly, speaking fast then remaining silent): Yes, yes, yes, no. It is like you say it.
Interviewer:	What kind of, what kind of grandchild is he? Is he a good grandchild?
Ms. Pechanova	(nodding and laughing a little, then remaining silent): Good, good, good, good, good. (21:53–23:43)

A camera, a good conscience, and steadfast dedication to the cause of coming to terms with the past can create a sanctimonious or even violent mix. The scriptwriter and interviewer of *Temporary Grandchildren* seem strangely reticent when they refer to Nazi crimes in general terms (e.g., "that which has changed her life") but pull no punches when engaged in the face-to-face questioning of survivors. The interviewer cannot quite make himself say "your grandchild," but he otherwise forces Ms. Pechanova to walk the line established by his script and his underlying assumptions. Watching *Temporary Grandchildren* one has to wonder whether the history of German memory politics is really one of unequivocal progress. Are the self-righteous memory professionals of the 1990s with their allegedly postallosemitic disposition (that is, neither philo- nor antisemitic) really more open and self-aware than the inhibited, hypocritical philosemites of the 1960s? Both groups are apparently masters of flowery, circumspect communication about German crimes and German guilt, but at least the philosemites of the earlier period did not seize the opportunity to verbally abuse survivors on national television.

A MEDIA MICROHISTORY OF PHILOSEMITISM

The lapses and contradictions analyzed in this essay transgress and on occasion even call into question the philosemitic discourse from which they originate, especially when they occur with such surprising frequency, surprising, at least, in the context of the highly regulated discursive environment of German public television. Obviously, some of the lapses and plays on words in the eclectic mix only become noticeable from a Holocaust point of view. Did viewers hear "rein deutsch" or "Rheindeutsch," did they draw a connection between the two terms, and if so what kind of connection was it? But I assume that other mistakes were already obvious in their contemporary settings. One probably could have convinced the respective authors that "grotesque" is an inappropriate characterization of the Yiddish language, that praising Jews for "their unerring persistence" might not be a good idea, that failing to follow through on a decided German-Israeli collaboration taints the ZDF's philosemitic track record, and that presenting a close-up of a hideously distorted face of a Prague Jew may be great aesthetic fun but is not necessarily good educational television. We do not know how many viewers noticed the linguistic and visual slip-ups and drew conclusions from them. Most communication from viewers displays a disconcerting lack of self-reflexivity about these matters. But I am counting on the many professionals inside and outside the TV stations who were involved in the production and reception of philosemitic discourse and certainly paid close attention to the programs. They might have thought, "Oops, that's an embarrassing mistake. Let's try to avoid it." On the basis of that speculation, I would like to offer a microhistorical addendum to the history of West German philosemitism.

The field of German memory studies offers two vantage points from which to conceptualize communication processes about Nazism, the Holocaust, and philosemitism. Some historians contend that West Germans acquired philosemitic attitudes from positive role models. They point to individuals like Theodor Heuss, the first president of the Federal Republic, who often displayed favorable opinions about Jews in the postwar media and might have convinced his fellow citizens to imitate his public persona.[70] Other scholars argue that West Germans mended their antisemitic ways because they learned from negative examples. According to this explanation, West German media consumers have been regularly confronted with scandalized news stories about the antisemitic activities of prominent politicians and regular citizens. Germans quickly understood that they better keep their antisemitic opinions to themselves, and, in the course of several decades and generations, these acts of self-censorship undercut the reproduction of the antisemitic attitudes and behavior.[71] Without dismissing the insights provided by either model, I would like to add a more complex, microhistorical explanation that focuses specifically on the ways that members of the elite dealt with their own ideological pasts but probably also applies to other settings. Instead of envisioning the relative decline of antisemitism as a top-down process, involving enlightened elites that taught Germans to abandon the values of National Socialism, I am interested in showing how journalists taught themselves philosemitic virtues while they imagined themselves in the roles of national moral trailblazers.

For media professionals and a fairly small segment of the general TV audience, philosemitic media output offered a well-circumscribed, unobtrusive arena for modest memory work. The excursions into the history and rituals of Judaism, which were distributed through television and other media outlets, provided Germans with a counterfactual narrative universe in which they could try out new ideas, often in the privacy of their living rooms, that differed substantially from the Nazi values that many of them had held just a few years before. The mediated encounters with Jews did not directly confront the disturbing legacies of the Third Reich. The programs refrained from visualizing the Holocaust, carefully avoiding images of the "Final Solution" and the Nazi camps that had been widely circulated in the immediate postwar years.[72]

[70] Ulrich Baumgärtner, *Reden nach Hitler: Theodor Heuss – Die Auseinandersetzung mit dem Nationalsozialismus* (Stuttgart: Deutsche Verlags-Anstalt, 2001).

[71] Werner Bergmann, *Antisemitismus in öffentlichen Konflikten: Kollektives Lernen in der politischen Kultur der Bundesrepublik 1949–1989* (Frankfurt: Campus, 1997).

[72] Habbo Knoch, *Die Tat als Bild: Fotografien des Holocaust in der deutschen Erinnerungskultur* (Hamburg: Hamburger Edition, 2001).

But somewhere in the mix of desire and denial, the new vision of a Jewish-German symbiosis intersected with half-buried memories of deportations, "aryanization," and racial warfare, and, for people willing or required to deal with these programs, the clash between the two cultures could cause a profound sense of unease. Feelings of helplessness and displacement are particularly noticeable in the writings and reactions of TV producers, journalists, reviewers, and viewers who for professional, political, or ethical reasons chose to be involved in the construction of the new philosemitism. Thus, the communication processes surrounding West Germany's philosemitic media coverage offer a rare glimpse into the trials and tribulations of the postfascist mind-set. They render explicit the awkward encounters between past and present that might have taken place in many German minds and illustrate how the unlearning of Nazism took place on the level of everyday life.

Philosemitism worked as a tool for reeducation because it helped some Germans rearrange their minds and memories. Most Germans had no interest in learning philosemitic formulas with which they could garnish their language. But they certainly needed help in managing the radical reversal of values after 1945, and philosemitic media production furthered that process in indirect and sometimes rather peculiar ways. Philosemitic stories constituted homeopathic stumbling blocks; they offered an opportunity to watch others struggle with the new system of values, and that struggle had particular educational value because many former citizens of the Third Reich did not manage to adopt a democratic Western frame of mind, and the corresponding rules of social and discursive conduct, in a smooth, graceful, and compelling fashion. Maybe the situation is best expressed in a metaphor: For the average producer, reviewer, and consumer, abstract presidential speeches and the big antisemitic scandals of the postwar years functioned as large traffic signs pointing toward the West and announcing a destination that most Germans already identified with but did not quite know how to reach. In that situation the experience of watching their fellow travelers losing their way westward, sometimes sliding into antisemitic terrain, provided useful and entertaining guidance; these communication mishaps represented the little, unspectacular signposts that line our highways and that, especially under conditions of poor visibility (as in the aftermath of a national catastrophe), help us stay on the road even if we cannot see the big signs, even if we are unable to steer in a straight line and are not sure where the trip will ultimately end.

In other words, some Germans learned by watching others mess up in unspectacular ways; they profited from the awkward silences, little contradictions, slips into Nazi lingo, and accompanying moments of self-consciousness that have occurred and still occur in conversations about the Nazi past in German society. In this sense, Germans really learned by example, but not only from the Sunday speeches of West German politicians or the indictments handed down by hypocritical judges against incorrigible Nazis. They profited from the experience of fellow Germans who, often media savvy and with the best intentions, failed to master the slippery terrain between anti- and philosemitism. These experiences taught the contemporaries of the Third Reich how to weather the transition to democracy. Studying their struggles with the benefit of hindsight helps us gauge the social effects of philosemitism. Moreover and more important, we understand in concrete terms how Germans managed to engage with the past in a selective and dishonest fashion while laying the foundation for a surprisingly self-critical historical culture. This complex process becomes even a little messier and more interesting in hindsight, if we remind ourselves that a significant number of the creators of philosemitic media texts were themselves Jews and, philosemitic utopias notwithstanding, neither immune to collective self-praise or self-loathing nor to other types of ethnic stereotyping.

14

"Non-Jewish, Non Kosher, Yet Also Recommended"

Beyond "Virtually Jewish" in Postmillennium Central Europe

Ruth Ellen Gruber

Froehlich's pastry shop is in the heart of Budapest's former main Jewish quarter, a few steps away from the city's central Orthodox synagogue. A sign in Hebrew at its door declares its wares to be kosher, and the shop is the haunt of Budapest Jews sipping tea and nibbling on sweets, as well as visiting tourists seeking to sample local Jewish specialties.[1] Here, amid the cherry strudel and cabbage pasties, you can often find other items for sale: miniature Jews made out of marzipan. The tiny figures, just three inches high, sport the black suits, black hats, earlocks, and dangling ritual fringes worn by Hasidic or other ultra-orthodox Jews of East European origin. Beardless, they apparently represent boys, *Yeshiva bochers*; as far as I can tell, they are sold as Bar Mitzvah cake decorations or party favors. Each is in a clear plastic container. Produced by Jews and directed at a Jewish market, they are a humorous, even self-ironic take on a Jewish reality: kitschy, to be sure, but by no means malevolent. At the same time, however, these Jewish self-representations clearly embody the same stereotypical markers so often used to depict Jews in far less flattering contexts. I bought a couple to place beside a hook-nosed Jewish puppet I had bought in Prague and bearded figurines of Jewish peddlers I got in Poland. In 2006 I added a new figure to the collection – a miniature Jew molded out of some sort of plastic, little more than an inch in height, smiling behind his red beard and clutching a real Polish coin in his hands. I got him at Anatewka, a popular "Jewish" (or "Jewish-style") restaurant in Łódź, Poland, where he – and dozens of other figurines like him – were placed on tables and given out to patrons as souvenirs.

---

[1] The title phrase comes from the menu of the restaurant U Fryzjera, Kazimierz Dolny, Poland. Much this chapter is drawn from my essay "Kitsch-Juden," in Hanno Loewy, ed., *Gerüchte über die Juden: Antisemitismus, Philosemitismus und aktuelle Verschwörungstheorien* (Essen: Klartext Verlag, 2005), 287–99.

314

The miniature Jews I found at Froehlich's and Anatewka illustrate the ambiguities inherent in the popular representation of Jews in a world that straddles the Jewish and non-Jewish community and where stereotypes and shorthand often take the place of nuanced definitions. Boundaries between insider and outsider, believer and nonbeliever, devotee and ironic observer can sharply delineate the differences between kitsch and caricature, art and artifice, stereotype and homage. But perspectives shift, and the boundaries often blur. The images and their meaning are often decidedly in the eyes of the beholder. And they are frequently dictated by changing religious realities, an often engineered nostalgia, and the powerful exigencies of the marketplace.

Much has been written about the marketing or, as some put it, the "commodification" of Jewish culture and, particularly in places where few Jews live today, the transformation since the fall of communism of prewar Jewish neighborhoods into tourist attractions.[2] These transformations, with their Jewish-style cafés, Jewish souvenirs, klezmer music concerts, and Jewish-themed galleries and cultural attractions, have, through the years, caused uneasiness among many Jews, who have decried what was sometimes termed the creation of "Jewish Disneylands."[3] Even today, Jewish visitors to some of these places may see little behind the commercial infrastructure and kitsch and express outrage at what they regard as a sellout of Jewish culture and Jewish tragedy by entrepreneurs whose only aim is to make a buck.

In a review of Jan T. Gross's 2006 book *Fear: Anti-Semitism in Poland after Auschwitz*, for example, Ruth Franklin, a senior editor at the *New Republic*, wrote about Kazimierz, the former Jewish quarter of Krakow, which since the early 1990s has developed as one of the major centers of Jewish-themed tourism in East Central Europe. Franklin slammed what she termed the "much ballyhooed renaissance of Jewish culture in Poland, complete with sold-out klezmer festivals and a popular brand of spirits called 'Kosher Vodka.' Half a dozen Jewish-themed hotels welcome visitors to Kazimierz, with names like 'Alef' and 'Ester' and 'Klezmer Hois'; the 'Eden' sports mezuzahs on every door and advertises 'the only *mikveh* bath in Poland,' as if it were a Jacuzzi." She goes on, "This grim carnival of Holocaust tourism and Western capital is neither a sign nor a symptom of a greater change in Polish society. It is evidence only of the Polish national schizophrenia on the subject of Jews. It is lovely to restore old buildings and to cherish a culture that has perished. But the celebration of the Jews of Poland cannot

---

[2] See, for example, Monika A. Murzyn, *Kazimierz: The Central European Experience of Urban Regeneration* (Krakow: International Culture Center, 2006).

[3] See, for example, Iris Weiss, "Jewish Disneyland: Die Vermarktung des Jüdischen," in haGalil, April 2001, posted at www.hagalil.com/archiv/2001/01/jewish-disney.htm (in English, as "Jewish Disneyland – the Appropriation and Dispossession of 'Jewishness,'" posted at http://www.hagalil.com/golem/diaspora/disneyland-e.htm).

substitute for a genuine confrontation with the manner of their disappearance: when, where and by whom. There is no indication that the consumers of 'Kosher Vodka' are interested in engaging in such a reckoning any
time soon."[4]

Franklin's indignation echoes that expressed by other writers and visitors to Krakow – and elsewhere. To me, though, the unmitigated finality
of these expressions seems blinkered, even dated. These critiques tend to
zoom in on a set of specificities, confounding several overlapping but quite
different trends or manifestations within a broad phenomenon that continues to grow and change as Jewish-themed tourism becomes (for better or
worse) a recognized niche and open Jewish or "Jewish-style" expression –
religious, cultural, or otherwise – becomes part of the mainstream. To be
sure, some people just want to drink vodka, dance to klezmer music, and
have a good time. But others want to understand, to learn, to appreciate.
There is a blurry line here between what I have begun to think of as the
realms of "semites" and "semitism": that of "semites" implying those manifestations that deal with Jews and Jewish culture as living entities; that of
"semitism" implying those that treat, and sometimes separate, them as an
isolated, exotic, or even codified category: "Jewish" as a brand. There are
"positive" and "negative" expressions within each broad category, and both
categories may include organic development as well as artificial models
and stereotypes. There may be an echo of "us" versus "them" – but the idea
of who is "we" and who is "they" is often quite blurred, with Jews and non-
Jews playing roles in each sphere. The Eden Hotel, whose advertisement
for its mikveh so disturbed Franklin, is in fact run by a Jew and caters to
observant Jews; the mikveh has been used for local conversions to Judaism,
and Orthodox Jews on group tours to Poland sometimes line up to use it
by the dozen.

In this essay I will discuss some of the trends along these lines that
have emerged in the more than two decades since the fall of communism.
Parts of the background discussion are drawn from my book *Virtually
Jewish: Reinventing Jewish Culture in Europe* (2002), which deals with non-Jewish interest in Jews and Jewish culture, primarily in post-Holocaust countries like Poland, where few Jews live today.[5] In particular, however, I want
here to look at phenomena that I may call "Beyond Virtually Jewish," that
is, some of the ways the trends I described in that book have evolved in the
past four or five years. These include, in some areas, a "mainstreaming" of
Things Jewish, as well as a continuing interest in and even enthusiasm for

---

[4] Ruth Franklin, "The Epilogue," *New Republic*, October 2, 2006, posted at http://www.tnr.
   com/article/the-epilogue.
[5] Ruth Ellen Gruber, *Virtually Jewish: Reinventing Jewish Culture in Europe* (Berkeley: University
   of California Press, 2002). Some of the material here is also drawn from my essay "Kitsch-
   Juden."

Jewish culture and markers among sectors of non-Jewish society, characterized by efforts that both exalt and cut through preconceptions.

MODELS

As the miniature Jews in Budapest and even tinier Jews in Łódź illustrated, many of the markers identified with Jewishness have religious overtones that have long laid the basis for both antisemitic stereotypes and nostalgic yearning for the "authentic" Jewish experience of the East European shtetl. Signs and symbols of Jewish holidays and domestic observance, and the beards, side curls, black hats, yarmulkes, fringes, and other outward trappings of the traditional Orthodox or Hasidic Jew spell "Jewish" – even to Jews – in a way that, for example, the physical attributes of Jews such as the actress Natalie Portman or the actor Kirk Douglas do not. A case in point is a T-shirt sold online at the www.judaicaheaven.com Web site. It features the slogan "Don't Worry, Be Jewish" under a big yellow "smiley face" that is topped by a kippah and long, dangling earlocks. The image, the Web site states, "shows off Jewish pride." Likewise, the banner for the Habad Lubavitch Hasidic movement's "Ask the Rabbi" stand at Budapest's huge annual "Sziget" music festival shows a grinning Hasid, wearing sunglasses and a sunhat and with a beard down his knees: the image is not dissimilar to the tiny bearded, coin-clutching "Jew" I got at Anatewka.

The equation of traditional Orthodox shtetl imagery with authenticity is by no means new. In the nostalgic recollection of urbanized (or urbanizing) Jews in central and other parts of Europe in the nineteenth century, the twin image of the shtetl and traditional Jewish ways of life had already achieved mythic status. Jewish artists, as well as some non-Jews, embraced the romance and portrayed traditional Jews in a positive or sentimental way in literature and painting. "The vanishing past was to be recalled and recorded by collecting Judaica, visualizing Jewish religious life, describing its family setting and emotions and even imagining a return to Jerusalem," wrote Richard I. Cohen in his book *Jewish Icons: Art and Society in Modern Europe*.[6]

The same sorts of stereotypical, religion-based markers, of course, can spell "different," "exotic," and "weird," as well as romantic, and as such they have long become the stock in trade of antisemites, who twist them, exaggerate them, and combine them with somatic and behavioral characteristics that are also used to define "the Jew" in negative terms – everything from big noses and sad eyes to a special relationship with money. Above my desk, hanging side by side, are several souvenir postcards of nineteenth-century Hasidic rebbes from northeastern Hungary. All wear head covering and all

---

[6] Richard I. Cohen, *Jewish Icons: Art and Society in Modern Europe* (Berkeley: University of California Press, 1998), 185.

have long noses, long beards, and long hair that dangles in front of their ears. Just beside these devout images, I have tacked a postcard I bought in Germany in 1997. It shows an elderly man with the same "typically Jewish" facial characteristics as the rebbes, but the artist has dressed him as Santa Claus, twisted his features into a lascivious grin, and portrayed him rubbing his hands in a greedy gesture – a modern take (deliberate or not) on a traditional antisemitic image.

As early as 1887, the London *Jewish Chronicle* noted that one of the aims of the Anglo-Jewish Historical Exhibition, a huge Jewish-organized exhibition of Jewish art, ritual objects, memorabilia, documents, portraits, and other material that was one of the first of its kind, was to combat such stereotypes by clearing the air and removing "something of the mystery which somehow seems in the mind of the outside world to environ all that is Jewish."[7] Richard I. Cohen notes that there was even some "antisemitica" among the exhibits, arguing that the exhibition "confronted Jews with questions about their self-image and their image in the eyes of English society."[8] These questions persist, and not just in England. Today, Judaica stores, Web sites, galleries, souvenir shops, and even street kiosks in many parts of the world feature a wide variety of items that bear or embody the physical image of the Jew. They range from dolls to T-shirts, from puppets to postcards, from portraits and gadgetry even to ritual objects such as Hanukkah menorahs. No matter where these outlets are located, and no matter whom the market comprises, the image tends to be some variation on the traditional Orthodox figure. The logo of a Web site called www.yidworld.com, for example, is a cartoon of a Hasidic man with a big beard, black hat, and dangling fringes, standing tall on top of the world and making a "typical" Jewish shruglike gesture, his hands and arms splayed open, as if to say: "Nu?" The insider-outsider equation means that an item, a caricature – or even a joke – that is seen as irreverent, self-ironic, totally kitsch, or just plain fun when produced by Jews for a primarily Jewish audience can embody an ambiguous and sometimes overtly antisemitic expression when produced and/or directed "outside the family."[9]

These issues have particular implications in places where there is no substantial internal Jewish market, or even much of a visible Jewish population. In Venice, for example, where the historic Jewish ghetto is one of the most important complexes of Jewish physical and spiritual heritage in Europe, Jewish tourists are by far the largest living Jewish presence in the

---

[7] Ibid., 195.
[8] Ibid.
[9] The Jewish Museum in Hohenems, Austria, explored Jewish kitsch and antisemitic kitsch in exhibitions in 2005–6. The volume Loewy, *Gerüchte über die Juden*, which includes my essay "Kitsch-Juden," from which parts of this chapter are drawn, was published to accompany one of these exhibitions.

city. Their numbers, estimated in the tens or even hundreds of thousands annually, dwarf the four hundred–odd Jews who make up the local Jewish community. Jewish tourists, by and large, are physically indistinguishable from other tourists, and local Venetian Jews are, by and large, physically indistinguishable from any other Italians. The most prominent, public Jewish face in Venice, however, is that of Habad Lubavitch, the American-based Hasidic movement, whose adherents, with their beards, black hats, and ritual fringes, conform to the stereotypical image of "the Jew." A big portrait of the late Lubavitcher Rebbe looms from the picture window of a Habad House and outreach center on the Gheto Novo, the main piazza of the Ghetto.[10] A few steps away is a Habad Yeshiva and synagogue, whose dozen students, mainly from Israel and the United States, stroll around the district in the traditional Hasidic attire. "People say it is a breath of fresh air to see a Jewish *bocher* walking around," Rabbi Ramy Banin, the Habad emissary in Venice, told me in 2005. (Some years ago, however, complaints by non-Jewish neighbors about the yeshiva's noisy singing made newspaper headlines.)

The Ghetto has a kosher pizzeria and a kosher bakery selling local pastries, and around the corner, overlooking one of the Venice canals, there is a Habad-run kosher restaurant, Gam-Gam, that offers free Shabbat meals for anyone who wants to partake – in the high tourist season, several hundred tourists may attend, eating in shifts; Habad in Venice says that the Habad House there draws bigger crowds than anywhere else in the world. At Sukkoth, Habad erects a public sukkah outside the restaurant and also on the Gheto Novo square. In addition, it builds a sukkah on a boat and cruises the Venice canals, stopping at intervals to offer free glasses of kosher wine to passersby. For Hanukah it erects a twenty-five-foot public menorah and also places a menorah on a gondola and sails it through the city.[11]

Souvenir shops respond to these realities, to expectations of Jewish imagery, and to the market. Venice is famous for its hand-blown Murano glass, and Judaica shops in the Ghetto sell everything from glass kiddush cups and Hanukah menorahs to refrigerator magnets and mezuzahs. Among them are handmade glass figurines of Jews. Almost all are humorous caricatures of Hasidic-looking rabbis gesticulating as they carry out various activities, from religious rituals to a game of golf. The figures do not look much like local Venetian Jews: they wear knee-length black garments, a

---

[10] In 2006, the Habad House was one of the few places in the area with free Wifi Internet access; the Wifi field stretched into the ghetto square, and it was not unusual to see the benches in the square populated by individuals piggybacking onto the service and pecking out e-mails on their laptop computers.

[11] See my articles "Chabad Now the Jewish Face of Venice," *Jewish Telegraphic Agency – JTA*, April 26, 2005, and "In Venice, a Jewish Disconnect between Locals and Visitors," *JTA*, June 16, 2010. Habad now (2010) also runs a kosher pizzeria and bake shop, called Gam-Gam Goodies.

rippling tallis, and a black hat of some sort. They wear long beards and dangling side curls and have exaggerated noses.[12]

These are quirky curios, sold in Jewish-run shops and primarily designed for the Jewish tourist market (a chess set, for example, pits Ashkenazi against Sephardic Jews). But some evidently were also specifically aimed at crossover trade. One figurine I saw several years ago showed a rabbi figure/Santa Claus, carrying a Hanukah menorah, above a sign reading, "Merry Hanukah, Happy Christmas." Another showed two figures, physically indistinguishable from each other except for their costume and the color of their beards. One was Santa Claus, in his red suit and white beard. The other was a rabbi, in his black beard, black garb, and tallis. The rabbi wore a red Santa Claus hat and carried Santa's sack of toys. Santa Claus, in turn, carried a Hanukah menorah. Again, a sign read, "Merry Hanukah, Happy Christmas."[13] In some cases, however, these trinkets were also promoted as a way to connect not just with the tourist market, but with Judaism itself (or at least with one form of Judaism). In November 2006 I found a display of four typical glass Jewish figures, grouped around a Sabbath table, in the window of the Gam-Gam restaurant. A small sign taped to the window described the figures as the work of the "master in glass" Gianni Toso, who, it said, was from a long line of Venetian glassblowers but now had a studio in Baltimore. "Join Gianni Toso in supporting the revival of Jewish Life in Venice," the sign said. "When you purchase a unique piece of Gianni's art, proceeds will go toward our many programs." "Our" in this case meant Habad, the proponent of a form of Orthodoxy whose physical appearance was reflected by the figures. The sign noted that today's Habad House on the Ghetto square had once been Toso's studio in Venice, which he had sold to Rabbi Banin "through a divinely inspired chain of events."

MARKETPLACE

The issue of the representation and self-representation of Jews took a new turn when the fall of communism enabled efforts to revive Jewish communal life in countries devastated by the Holocaust and at the same time opened up historic East Central European Jewish homelands to mass tourism.[14] Thousands of Jews – including people who suddenly claimed long-dormant or previously unknown Jewish roots – stepped forward to grapple with, and eventually, in some cases, to form, new models of Jewish self-image and Jewish identity, from the spiritual to the physical. Most of those

---

[12] They can also be viewed and purchased online. See the Web site for David's Shop, located on the Ghetto Novo, posted at www.davidshop.com/c/49/Murano_glass_figurine.html.

[13] In April 2010 these no longer appeared in David's Shop's online catalog.

[14] I discuss this at length in *Virtually Jewish*, from which some of the following material is drawn. In particular see chap. 7, "The Tourist Track."

who became religiously observant or otherwise affiliated with the emerging Jewish communities remained acculturated in their dress and habits. But some, too, adopted the garb and religious lifestyle of the traditional Orthodox Jew or Hasid, giving a recognized "Jewish" look to newly recognized "Jewish spaces." (A religiously observant Jew in Warsaw told me in 2005 that he made it a point to wear a sweater or a sports jacket to services in the city's Nozyk synagogue, in order to make a visual statement countering the strict black garb affected by a core group of newly Orthodox congregants.)

Meanwhile millions of tourists, Jewish and non-Jewish alike, eagerly rushed to visit places that the Iron Curtain had made either off-limits or off the beaten track for many decades. Among castles, cathedrals, and old town squares, Jewish heritage sites, and also sites of Holocaust memory, quickly became tourist attractions in places where few, if any, Jews now lived and where those who did live generally did not conform to the stereotypical image.

The display, representation, and exploitation of Jewish heritage and heritage sites, as well as the creation of infrastructure and services by tourism providers and facilitators, had to fulfill the needs and expectations of very diverse markets, ranging from people with a casual, primarily abstract or literary interest in Things Jewish; to those who knew nothing whatsoever about the Jewish experience; to those for whom every town, building, and square inch of earth had a hallowed place in personal or collective memory; to those newly seeking to contact or discover such tradition, style, and memory.

Souvenirs, knickknacks, keepsakes, and mementos quickly became part of the equation – an integral part of the touristic experience that meant different things to different purchasers and partakers. In Prague in particular, the tourist influx engendered a fierce and sudden market competition that produced an unprecedented market for Jewish-themed souvenirs, postcards, books, T-shirts, and other tourist mementos aimed at both Jewish and non-Jewish purchasers. Already in the early 1990s such diverse items as fold-out paper greeting cards of the Old Jewish Cemetery, good luck "pet rocks" painted with stars of David, candles in the shape of Franz Kafka's head, Jewish puppets, and figurines representing the Golem crammed shops and streetside kiosks. And living Jews – particularly when they conformed to stereotype – sometimes became "objects" for the touristic gaze. "[Prague's] Jewish Quarter has become a veritable Jurassic Park of Judaism, a Williamsburg for the conscience of Europe," the American Eli Valley wrote in the *Forward* newspaper in 1995, foreshadowing Ruth Franklin's critique of Poland's Kazimierz more than a decade later. "On the street you can purchase a Jewish doll, complete with black robe and jumbo nose, for $50. In the eyes of the tourists, Jewish Prague is a circus of the dead. On the infrequent occasions that a Chasidic family visits the area,

visitors abandon the dead religious objects and take out their cameras....
And when I stand outside the Old-New Synagogue, wearing my yarmulke,
I too am gawked at by the bemused mobs."[15]

But the intense exploitation was not confined to *Jewish* Prague. Virtually
all of historic Prague attracted swarms of tourists and generated similar
kitsch. For most visitors, Jewish and non-Jewish, Prague's Jewish sites and
tacky take-aways simply became parts of a kaleidoscopic whole. Not only
that, the 1,500-member Prague Jewish community drew rent from some of
the souvenir stands and other commercial space, and local Jews (and some
Israelis) were among the entrepreneurs cashing in on the crowds. The
insider-outsider boundary among purchasers, producers, and partakers
became quite blurred. Over the years the market – and its offerings – have
mutated and evolved, both to meet the demands of more discriminating
visitors and to reflect a growing maturity among local producers, promoters, and advocates of Jewish culture. The Prague Jewish Museum, which has
emerged as one of Central Europe's leading Jewish cultural institutions, has
played a key role in this process, and the development of at least five active
Jewish congregations, ranging from Reform through modern Orthodox to
Habad, has also influenced the scene. The museum's 100th anniversary, in
2006, was marked by an extraordinary "Year of Jewish Culture," which saw
scores of exhibitions, lectures, concerts, and other Jewish cultural events
programmed in numerous locations around the country throughout the
year. In Prague, vendors now offer good-quality Judaica and tasteful souvenirs alongside the junk. And exhibition spaces, including, in particular, the Prague Jewish Museum's new Robert Guttmann Gallery, spotlight
contemporary Jewish art, music, and cultural production, creating new
Jewish paradigms alongside the historical exhibitions, evocations of the
Kafkaesque, and legends of the Golem. "In contrast to the museum's traditional visitors, who are in the large part foreign, the [Robert Guttmann]
gallery draws a hip Czech crowd with an interest in Jewish themes, modern
art or both," the Prague-based American journalist Dinah Spritzer wrote
in 2006.[16] Michaela Hajkova, who in 2002 founded the Jewish Museum's
"Jewish Presence in Contemporary Art" series, told Spritzer that she wanted
to "wake people up, wake them from the illusion that Jewish means past
tense. ... People were used to something different from the museum, something traditional. But why shouldn't we also let the Jewish present and all

[15] Eli Valley, "Letter from Prague," *Forward*, 17 March 1995. See also the chapter "The Jurassic
Park of Judaism" in Eli Valley's book, *The Great Jewish Cities of Central and Eastern Europe*
(Northdale, NJ: Jason Aronson, 1999), 53ff. Ironically, while in Prague, Valley worked for
a while as a tour guide. Also see the chapter on Prague in my book *Upon the Doorposts of Thy
House: Jewish Life in East-Central Europe, Yesterday and Today* (New York: John Wiley & Sons,
1994), for a detailed description of the tourist scene in Prague in the early 1990s.
[16] Dinah Spritzer, "Czech Curator Bucks Traditional Art," *Jewish Telegraphic Agency – JTA*,
22 October 2006.

the questioning that goes with it have a voice in Prague?"[17] This emphasis on the contemporary extends to the café-restaurant located in the Jewish Museum building complex that also houses the Guttmann gallery. With jazzy music playing low in the background, the sleek, rather stark design of the establishment (which is not run by the Jewish Museum) tips no hat to the nostalgic or archaic; nor does the menu hark to any Jewish tradition other than, say, that of trendy downtown New York.

In Poland, the country that once had Europe's largest Jewish population, the evolution of Jewish and Jewish-themed tourism was closely linked to the unique place held both by Poland in Jewish history and memory, and by Jews in Polish history and memory. Some 3.5 million Jews lived in Poland before World War II, and most Jews in North America trace their ancestry to Polish lands. More than three million Polish Jews were murdered in the Holocaust. Even after the fall of communism, Jewish travelers went to Poland for highly specific reasons, and with concrete expectations, that – unlike in Prague – had nothing whatsoever to do with conventional tourism. Few Jews visited Poland simply to sightsee – and even fewer to have a good time. Jews went to Poland to mourn and remember – and they remembered Polish antisemitism as well as the Nazi annihilation. Many were emotionally prepared to expect nothing but negative experiences and mentally armed to view every contemporary Pole as an antisemite. Mainstream Poland, in effect, was, to the general Jewish view, not just a world of "outsiders" but a world of hostile outsiders.[18]

Many Jews, thus, looked extremely askance at the Jewish-themed tourism that began to develop in Poland, and particularly in Kazimierz, the old Jewish quarter of Krakow, in the early 1990s. Many, like Ruth Franklin, were repulsed, rather than enchanted, by the new Jewish-style cafés, restaurants, and galleries that wrote their names in Yiddish-style letters and appealed to nostalgia for a past that had been destroyed. Until relatively recently, few foreign Jews attended the popular summer Festival of Jewish Culture, which was founded in 1988 by non-Jews for an overwhelmingly non-Jewish audience.[19]

Many of the Jews who visited Poland after 1990 were particularly disturbed by the plethora of Jewish souvenirs that went on sale – and especially by the carved wooden figures of Jews, sold by the thousands at sidewalk kiosks, craft stalls, and souvenir shops. These figurines are in all sizes, from

[17] Ibid.
[18] See Jack Kugelmass, "The Rites of the Tribe," in Jack Kugelmass, ed., *Going Home: YIVO Annual 21* (New York: YIVO Intitute for Jewish Research, and Evanston, IL: Northwestern University Press, 1993), 395–453.
[19] See my article "The Krakow Jewish Culture Festival," in Michael C. Steinlauf and Antony Polonsky, eds., *Polin: Studies in Polish Jewry*, vol. 16, *Jewish Popular Culture and Its Afterlife* (Oxford: Littman Library of Jewish Civilization, 2003), 357–67.

a few centimeters tall to nearly life-sized. Almost all are representations of
Jewish men, in the iconic, stereotypical form of the Hasid. They are generally portrayed wearing long black garb, black beards, side curls, and either
black hats or the fur streimel worn by some Hasidic sects. Some have exaggerated "melancholy" eyes; most have oversized noses. Some hold musical
instruments – and some even scraps of parchment from desecrated Torahs.
The figures, their meaning, and their history within both Polish popular
tradition and contemporary tourist commercialization move uneasily back
and forth between the realms and realities of antisemitism, nostalgia, souvenir sentiment, and, by now, also insider irony. As Erica Lehrer pointed
out in her essay "Repopulating Jewish Poland – in Wood," carved figures
of Jews have been a part of Polish folk culture since the nineteenth century and have long coexisted with folk carvings of other iconic religious
and secular figures – Jesus, Mary, the devil, nativity figures, and the like.[20]
Prewar representations of Jews were based on actual living models, though
they also reflected the superstitious role assigned to Jews by Polish peasants
and the grassroots Catholic antisemitism that permeated society. Lehrer
notes that even as late as the early 1990s the carved figures of Jews were
"meaner caricatures ... echoing Nazi wartime propaganda: sneering lips
framing a single tooth, money-clutching fists, a nose threatening to topple
the piece forward." Yet the postwar carvings also represented figures from
a destroyed world and thus were also steeped in nostalgia; they were figures based on literature, imagination, superstition, and memory, rather
than current physical realities: English non-Jewish friends of mine who
purchased several wooden Jewish dolls in Krakow and displayed them in
their home along with other Polish folk carvings had no inkling of the baggage attached to the figures. They saw them simply as examples of folk art
that were conduits to past history.

In the early 1990s, the figurines were still, in large part, individually
crafted pieces of peasant artisanship, produced by non-Jews for a non-
Jewish market. Today, with a greatly expanded – and expanding – tourist
market that increasingly includes many Jews, most of the figures appear to
be more standardized, and many are clearly mass produced. Nonetheless,
a Polish Jewish friend reminded me recently that among non-Jewish Poles,
the figures are still often referred to as "Zydki" – a pejorative term for Jews.
A new and apparently popular line of Jewish figures clutching real coins,
such as the miniature figurine I got at the Anatewka restaurant, channel
the antisemitic stereotype that Jews are greedy money-grubbers, but they
also have other, more ambiguous, meanings.[21]

[20] Erica Lehrer, "Repopulating Jewish Poland – in Wood," in *Polin: Studies in Polish Jewry*, vol.
     16 (Oxford: Littman Library of Jewish Civilization, 2003), 335–54.
[21] I find the number of such "money-clutching" figures, particularly in certain shops, now
     striking. In addition to the tiny standing figures, there is a line of coin-clutching, dancing

In May 2006, the American artist Jack Sal, who was then in Kielce, north of Krakow, at work on the city's first public sculptural memorial to the 1946 pogrom there that left forty-two Jews dead, e-mailed me a photograph of a painting he had seen at a local art exhibition. It was the portrait of a "Jew" – a man with a dark beard, long nose, and a skullcap, peering closely at a thick coin he held between thumb and forefinger. Sal told me he had come across the painting when he attended the opening of an exhibition of flower paintings and abstractions at the Kielce Society of Artists' gallery. He had been invited by the vice president of the society, who was also the director of the Art Academy of Kielce and who had overseen the project of the pogrom monument as well as an earlier exhibit Sal had had in Kielce.

"While standing outside to 'get some air' I saw in the window of the gallery a painting of a bearded middle aged man wearing a skull cap!" Sal wrote me in the e-mail:

When I re-entered the gallery I saw displayed, in a prominent place, the painting photographed. [That is, the portrait of the Jew peering at the coin.] There were 2 other paintings all by the same artist including another one of a Jew with a coin in his hand. I approached the professor & the president of the Society & asked how such paintings could be allowed to be shown in the gallery. I was told that the artist was a member in good standing of the Society and had other works on display (indeed, his landscapes were also exhibited) and that the paintings were part of a "long" tradition of Polish people placing pictures of Jews with money in their hands near the entrance doors of their homes as a good luck omen. I pointed out that it was still a stereotype-antisemitic image & should be viewed as such, in Kielce of all places. I brought up the example of Black Jockey American lawn ornaments & their disappearance as an example. But I was told I was taking it the "wrong way" & that no harm was meant.

Some ten minutes later I was approached by the 2 again & they agreed that I might have a point; the president thought that perhaps Poles could be offended by a painting of Polish men around a table strewn with empty Vodka bottles, [implying] all Poles were drunks.[22]

Still, for Jewish tourists seeking a souvenir, the carved figures can play to their own ingrained images of Jewish authenticity and the nostalgic *Fiddler on the Roof* world of the shtetl. Many of the exaggerations, too, can be seen as comical, rather than sinister, reflecting the same humorous take on the same sorts of stereotypes so often found in Jewish insider contexts, as I

Jews as refrigerator magnets. Also, in 2010 I saw rows of small portraits of rabbis, with coins glued to the frame.

[22] Personal e-mail from Jack Sal, May 8, 2006. In a similar, more recent development, a Chicago-based Jewish lawyer, who also maintains an office in Poland, told me that when a town councillor of a Polish city came to visit him in Chicago, he brought, as a present, a portrait of a rabbi counting money, with a dollar bill stuck in its back. This also was meant to be a token of good feeling and of best wishes for good luck; the councillor appeared to be totally unaware of any negative connotations with the imagery.

noted earlier. Perhaps if a Jew buys a Polish Jewish carving and displays it in a Jewish home or other Jewish setting, the mere fact of purchaser and final display place – that is, the fact that a Jew now "controls" the object, its meaning, and its setting – can somehow transform the ambiguous into the (typically Jewish) self-ironic.[23] "I have to go to the market and get myself a 'Jew!'" a performer taking part in his first Krakow Jewish Culture Festival exclaimed to me in 2007. (Not long ago I myself succumbed and bought a money-clutching dancing Jew refrigerator magnet.) Moreover, as Lehrer writes, given the fact that the figures are on sale in Poland, the site of so much Jewish tragedy, some Jewish purchasers also apparently view the figurines almost as talismans, minimemorials to the Holocaust: "Most now are deemed by Jewish tourists as 'melancholy': with 'sad eyes,' 'drooping,' 'gaunt,' 'haunted' faces – 'prayerful' or 'resigned' – even as some play tiny violins or accordions. Through the lens of the Holocaust, these Jews seem to know their fates."[24]

The physical development of Kazimierz as a site of Jewish-themed tourism began in the early 1990s, after the fall of communism and on the heels of an interest in Jewish culture that had already been manifested in Poland for a decade or more. The Festival of Jewish Culture began formally in 1988, two years after a Jewish film festival had been staged in the town. The vast array of Jewish-themed offerings in Kazimierz we find today, thus, did not by any means appear overnight. And much of it did originate in an attempt by local Poles to come to terms with the annihilation of Polish Jewry. In a sense, the blasé attitude of locals to the Jewish-themed tourist industry noted by Ruth Franklin in 2006 is at least partly the fruit of what is by now familiarity with a phenomenon that has been in the making for years: the kosher vodka craze peaked in the mid- to late 1990s, when "kosher" was seen as "pure" and set such vodkas aside from ordinary brands; vodka connoisseurs today have a variety of new luxury labels to choose from. And the student-aged young Poles who dance to klezmer music at the Festival of Jewish Culture have few if any direct memories of Kazimierz before the festival existed or when no Jewish (or Jewish-style) cafés plied their trade.

Developed over the course of two decades, the efforts to reconnect to a lost or destroyed Jewish world by now form what I would call a "new authenticity" that creates rather than recreates. As part of this process,

---

[23] It is clearly this sense of irony that impelled me to purchase, in Texas, a thirteen-inch "talking action figure" doll representing the satiric Jewish writer and singer Kinky Friedman, who in 2006 staged an unsuccessful campaign for the state governorship. The doll portrays Friedman – once frontman for a band called the Texas Jewboys – in a black hat and vest not unlike those worn by Polish Jewish figurines. And he sports long sideburns, not unlike side curls. If you push a button on the doll, it spouts Kinky's one-liners, including mocking takes on Jewish stereotypes, such as, "As the first Jewish governor of Texas, I'll reduce the speed limit to $54.95."

[24] Lehrer, "Repopulating," 336.

it has created its own models and shorthand stereotypes. And the ersatz can be compellingly, even devastatingly, blatant. On a visit to Kazimierz in 2006, I saw a newly renovated building that included, on its brand new doorpost, a newly made groove reproducing a scar like those not long ago found on many derelict buildings in Kazimierz showing where a mezuzah had been affixed before World War II: gentrification has by now done away with many, if not most, of the "real" such scars.[25]

MENUS

In much of East Central Europe, "Jewish" in terms of café and restaurant décor draws on a literary image of a lost Jewish past. Dining rooms are furnished with antiques, or quasi-antiques, and walls are covered with paintings, many of them showing Jewish themes. Lights are low and klezmer music plays in the background. These conventions – and by now they are conventions – play on nostalgia but, in the best cases, are achieved with sensitivity and good taste. Jews sometimes use them, too. The café Tuwim in Łódź, a kosher restaurant located in the city's Jewish communal complex, opened in April 2005. The dim light, antiques, and old photos form an ambience resembling that of the Krakow cafés, and the Tuwim hosts Jewish cabaret programs and concerts of klezmer music. The proprietor, Malgosia Keller, admits the influence but stresses that there is a difference. "Many of the people who have cafés in Krakow's Kazimierz are our friends," she told me a year after the café opened. But, she added, "Our style I think is from [actual] remembrance; the photos and furnishings come from our parents, our grandparents." Her own great-great-grandfather, she told me, had run a hotel in Lublin. "It's good that the tradition has moved on to me."[26]

The Jewish, or what I would call "Jewish-style," café conventions extend beyond Poland. In Kiev, the Tsimmes restaurant, which opened in 2003, looks "Jewish in the nostalgic, Old World way of many Jewish restaurants in the former Eastern Bloc," the (non-Jewish) Ukrainian journalist Yulianna Vilkos wrote in an American Jewish publication. "The décor draws heavily

---

[25] In recent writing and presentations, I have elaborated this concept into that of "new authenticities" and "real imaginary spaces," comparing – and contrasting – the "virtually Jewish" with another phenomenon I have been exploring, the multifaceted "imaginary Wild West in Europe." Both phenomena feed on myth and stereotype but also create their own tropes and traditions. See in particular my essays "Beyond Virtually Jewish: New Authenticities and Real Imaginary Spaces in Europe," *Jewish Quarterly Review* 99, no. 4 (Fall 2009): 487–504, and "Beyond Virtually Jewish … Balancing the Real, the Surreal and Real Imaginary Places," in Monika Murzyn-Kupisz and Jacek Puchla, eds., *Reclaiming Memory: Urban Regeneration in the Historic Jewish Quarters of Central European Cities* (Krakow: International Cultural Center, 2009), both of which include some of the discussion presented here.

[26] On Jewish and Jewish-style cafés, see my essay "Juedische und 'juedische' Cafés," in Michal Friedlander and Cilly Kugelmann, eds., *Koscher & Co. Ueber Essen und Religion* (Berlin: Nicolai, 2009).

on Marc Chagall, there's live Jewish music on weekends and the menu is
sprinkled with Yiddish humor that is impossible to translate."[27] Founded
by Lena Stolyarova, who Vilkos said "grew up in a secular Jewish family,"
Tsimmes, located in a city that is home to as many as seventy thousand
Jews, swerves wildly across the line of insider-outsider ambiguity; on a visit
in 2006, I found it a far cry from the city's two kosher restaurants, the
upscale King David and the Makkabi snack bar, neither of which affected
nostalgic tropes. The restaurant's logo, deliberately or not, reproduces the
picture from the label of Cymes (pronounced "Tsimmes") brand Polish
vodka – a brand that, in the 1990s, did not declare itself to be kosher but
used Jewish imagery to cash in on the then-popularity of kosher vodka.
The picture is a caricature portrait of a Jew, with beard, hat, and side locks,
winking and making a "that's good" gesture with his thumb and forefinger.
The waitresses wear old-fashioned long dresses, and the restaurant is deco-
rated with Chagall-style stained glass, Hebrew writing, Israeli flags, and
dozens of wooden carvings of Jews, some of them caricaturish and many of
them Jews carrying or counting money – an almost life-sized such figure of
a seated, red-bearded Jew counting coins stands outside on the sidewalk.
The overtness of it all made me somewhat uneasy, but the friend who took
me there, a prominent Kiev Jew, did not seem troubled by the imagery.
Indeed, about half of the patrons are believed to have some sort of Jewish
connection. Local Jews are said to "celebrate engagements, weddings and
other family occasions" there, and in 2005 the Kiev branch of Hillel, the
Jewish students' organization, held its Passover seder at the restaurant. "I
go to different restaurants, but Tsimmes is special. I feel at home here,"
the twenty-four-year-old president of the Hillel business club told Vilkos.
Stolyarova said she had been inspired to open Tsimmes by the Jewish restaurant culture in Krakow. At that time, Kiev had just one Jewish (or Jewish-
style) restaurant. Even though Krakow's Jewish population – at only two
hundred souls – was far smaller than that in Kiev, there were more Jewish
restaurants there, she said. "Why, she asked herself, shouldn't Kiev's much
larger Jewish community support at least a second Jewish restaurant?"[28]

Wojtek Ornat and his wife, Malgosia, have been leading figures in the
revival (or indeed creation) of new Jewish and Jewish-style authenticities
in Krakow's Kazimierz for nearly twenty years, and their take on what is
"Jewish" has been one of the most important in helping shape contemporary conventions and expectations of local Jews and non-Jews as well
as tourists.[29] Today they are the proprietors of the popular Klezmer Hois

---

[27] Yulianna Vilkos, "Eating Jewish in Kiev," *Jewish Telegraphic Agency – JTA*, December 26,
   2005. Vilkos made a point in the article of noting that she is not Jewish.
[28] Ibid.
[29] "So much of the tiny amount of Jewish culture that exists in Poland does so under the direct
   or indirect influence of the Jewish heritage industry." Lehrer, "Repopulating," 340.

café/restaurant/hotel. They also run Austeria, a publishing house that specializes in Jewish-themed books, and a well-stocked Jewish bookstore, also called Austeria, that offers Jewish-themed publications in several languages.[30] In April 2006 Wojtek Ornat reflected on the impact of his ideas. "People from villages now turn to me for advice on how to make a Jewish restaurant," he told me. "There are two questions – business and emotions. These are two different things. In the beginning, these places had another face; the situation was different," he said. "Now, this is life, it is not a presentation, but life – this is the future, too. I think that this represents a big success. It's life, living; not just for foreigners, but for young people, young Jews."

I first discussed the possibilities for the development of Kazimierz in 1993, with a variety of interested people, including Jewish representatives, city officials, and some of the first private entrepreneurs, Ornat among them.[31] At the time, the district was a rundown slum that attracted few visitors. Among the few foreigners who visited were Orthodox Jews visiting the tombs of sages in the Old Jewish Cemetery and other religious sites. The issue of "what to do with Kazimierz" was a hot topic, and everyone I talked to had his or her idea of how the district should be developed. At that time, the only Jewish-themed café was the Ariel, located at one end of Szeroka Street, the main Jewish square, near the Gothic Old Synagogue, which already was a Jewish museum. The Ariel formed a thriving oasis amid the derelict buildings. Originally founded as a gallery specializing in Judaica, it was transformed into a coffeehouse in 1992. Back then, Ornat was the Ariel's manager. "Some people think it's sick to have a café here, but I disagree," he told me. "Forty years have passed now," he said. "Until recently, you couldn't think of doing something like this. Kazimierz spatially is identical to how it was before the war. Now Jews are coming back to visit here; they recognize places where they were as children. Now I can open a café." So isolated a venture was the café that Jewish visitors, he said, occasionally mistook it – with its Hebrew-style signage – for a synagogue or other religious facility. He made a telling prediction: "Eventually," he said, "this will become a very snobby, elegant neighborhood, with very expensive property prices.... It will be gentrified." Likewise Krakow-born Stanislaw Zohar, the then-director in Krakow of the American Jewish Joint Distribution Committee, made remarks that, in retrospect, seem prescient.

[30] Both Ornats have Jewish roots but were not raised as Jews. Austeria published a book of mine, *Letters from Europe (and Elsewhere)*, in February 2008.

[31] The following is drawn from the chapter on Krakow in my book *Upon the Doorposts of Thy House*, chiefly 206–29. For a very rich and detailed discussion of the urban regeneration of Kazimierz over the past twenty years – in all its facets – see Monika A. Murzyn, *Kazimierz*; also see Jack Kugelmass and Annamaria Orla-Bukowska, "If You Build It They Will Come: Recreating an Historic Jewish District in Post-Communist Krakow," *City and Society Annual Review* (1998): 315–53.

"I've drunk gallons of coffee with people who have ideas about what to do with Kazimierz," he told me. "There's room on Szeroka Street for a good Jewish bookstore, and there's a need for a good book on Kazimierz, on Krakow Jewry, in English, Polish, and Hebrew. There needs to be a good kosher restaurant, too ... and a hotel catering to Jews.... I'd like to see a Jewish hotel with a kosher kitchen – a forty room hotel would have seventy to eighty percent occupancy all year round. That's the way you can make Kazimierz alive."

Such a hotel today is the Eden, with its mezuzahs on every door and its mikveh. Kazimierz has come alive in other ways, too, that have built on but also transcended the "Jewish" attraction. Jewish visitors still make up a small minority of people who attend the nine-day annual Festival of Jewish Culture, which by 2009 had grown to encompass more than two hundred events, including concerts, lectures, workshops, and guided tours. Still, participants and performers each year include some of the top international names in Jewish art, music, and scholarship. And in recent years, organizations such as the American Jewish Committee and the Taube Foundation, which funds Jewish cultural development in Poland, have used the festival as an opportunity to take over delegations to experience a positive embrace by enthusiastic Poles. In July 2006, Michael Steinlauf, an American academic expert on Yiddish culture and Polish-Jewish relations and the author of the book *Bondage to the Dead: Poland and the Memory of the Holocaust* (1997), commented that during the festival, Szeroka Street formed a symbolic "headquarters of the Diaspora" thanks to the numerous cultural events and the many international Jewish artists, performers, and fans who attended. I spoke to him after he had enjoyed Friday night dinner with friends and family at one of the Szeroka Street restaurants – a newly opened "normal" restaurant, not one of the Jewish-style cafés. "We had a table for 11 and lit the candles," he told me. "The couple from the next table came over saying 'Shalom Aleichem.' I've never done this anywhere else. It's never been as easy to be a Jew than on Szeroka street the night before [the festival's outdoor final concert there]." Meanwhile, the latest wave of development in Kazimierz has seen the area, and in particular the old Jewish marketplace, Plac Nowy, become the hub of trendy local youth culture, lined with late-night clubs and music bars that have nothing to do with "semitism" or "semites" – and irritate local residents with the noise and partying that spill out into streets and squares. Some of the new clubs feature sleek, contemporary decor. In fact, Jewish-style locales today make up only a minority of the venues in the district. Szeroka Street itself now features an Indian and an Italian restaurant as well as other, non-Jewish establishments.[32]

[32] See Murzyn, *Kazimierz*, for a detailed analysis of this development.

LITTLE MEN

Even more than Tsimmes in Kiev, Anatewka in Łódź embodies, as far as I am concerned, the "Platonic ideal" of "Virtual Jewishness," the zenith of the realm of "Semitism." Though clearly modeled on the Jewish-themed restaurants in Krakow, Anatewka seems more about marketing and branding than about sensitivity – or about Jews in any sense of the real world. It offers "Jewish" as a brand – but also "nostalgia" as a brand. Its décor consists of an almost standardized set of items that spell out "Jewish" as a commercial category.[33]

I first visited Anatewka in March 2005 during a book tour to promote the Polish edition of *Virtually Jewish*. My presentation took the form of a public conversation in a little theater with a (non-Jewish) journalist who has studied local Jewish history and written extensively about it, including a walking tour guidebook to the wartime Łódź ghetto. After the event, she and I and the organizers went out to dinner. I chose the restaurant after hearing a description of it from my companions. Anatewka, of course, is the name of the fictional shtetl that was home to Sholom Aleichem's Tevye the Milkman – and a Fiddler on the Roof. On that first visit, a giant carved wooden Jew greeted us at the door. The waiter was dressed up in Hasidic costume, including a black hat and ritual fringes dangling from under his white shirt and black vest. He sat us at a round table and brought something to munch on – matzo, accompanied by flute glasses of sparkling wine. Paintings of bearded sages and saintly rabbis looked down from the walls – they were "old style" but looked so freshly finished I could almost smell the paint. There were candles, old furniture, a piano, old books, an old sewing machine: all off-the-shelf markers signifying the "Jewish" brand. In the main room, a sort of thatched roof affair stretched across

[33] The Ariel café/restaurant in Krakow's Kazimierz also represents an increasingly crass example. Its walls bear the same sort of new-looking, old-style, off-the-shelf paintings as found at Anatewka – including dozens and dozens of portraits (or imaginary portraits) of rabbis. Long shunned by many in the "Jewish revival" scene for its commodification and commerciality (see Kugelmass and Orla-Bukowska, "If You Build It," and their discussion of the "good" Ariel and the "bad" Ariel), it caters to tour groups and sells souvenir wares that, to my eye, cross the line well into the antisemitic. In addition to the debatable Jews clutching money, these include refrigerator magnets in the form of the heads of Jews – one of which, in profile, appears identical to the type of caricature printed in Nazi era publications such as *Der Sturmer* – each bearing the legend "Kazimierz Krakow." When I once asked a (surly) waiter why these were sold, his response was that it was "a Jew." He and the man at the counter selling the items refused to discuss them with me beyond that. I also found these magnets sold at stands on the street, outside the Remuh synagogue, in 2009. An even more extreme example, in some senses, was found at the "At the Golden Rose" café in L'viv, Ukraine, which I visited in November 2008. Here, no prices were listed – patrons were supposed to haggle (i.e., like Jews) over what to pay. And the hat rack included black hats with long, dangling sidelocks that patrons were encouraged to try on.

one wall. Beside it, on a platform attached to the wall, a young woman sat – playing Yiddish tunes on a fiddle. Aha! I opened my notebook to record the "Jewish style" names of dishes on the menu, but the proprietor stopped me – "You don't have to write anything down," he told me; "everything is on our web site." True virtuality![34]

It was Friday night – Shabbes – and the place was hopping with prosperous looking patrons enjoying a pseudoexotic dining experience in an ambience whose characteristics they recognized as "Jewish" in the same way that patrons of the Polish chain of American Wild West restaurants called "Sioux" recognize boots, spurs, swinging doors, and Stetsons as trappings of the American frontier. Sioux, which has several branches around the country, sells T-shirts with a head-dressed Native American face on them, and its waitresses wear fringed, miniskirted uniforms. As the Web site for the chain's Krakow restaurant puts it, "All of it is happening in Wild West where Indians, handsome cowboys, and beautiful squaws walk around all the time!!!"[35]

Everything, I remember thinking, could have come off the shelf, filed under "J" for "Jewish." A write-up in a local travel guide emphasized this: "Celebrate Łódź's rich Jewish heritage in this superb effort found tucked just off Piotrkowska. Mannequins complete with prayer shawls and Hassidic locks, a couple of menorahs and general bric-a-brac lie scattered around, while Klezmer tunes play in the background. Delicious dishes like the duck served in cherry sauce. A must visit."[36] It was so standardized that I wondered whether – and when – Anatewka might become a chain or franchise like Sioux. In fact, Anatewka did indeed open a second branch at a huge new shopping mall, Manufaktura, which opened in May 2006 in the transformed former textile factory of nineteenth-century Łódź's wealthiest Jewish industrialist, I. K. Poznanski. Describing it as the "sister restaurant" of the original Anatewka, the same guide advised, "you can expect a clone of the original; from the same top-mark food, to a Jewish-themed interior that comes with menorahs, stirring Klezmer anthems and lacy frills. An absolute hit."[37]

---

[34] www.anatewka.pl.

[35] See http://www.sioux.krakow.pl/index_eng.php. See also my *Jewish Quarterly Review* article, "Beyond Virtually Jewish."

[36] Posted at www.inyourpocket.com/instant/lodz-instant-guide.pdf. Now changed to http://www.inyourpocket.com/poland/lodz/restaurants/jewish/Anatewka_20722v. The blurb has also been changed: "Celebrate Łódź's Jewish heritage inside an atmospheric venue scattered with prayer shawls, menorahs and general bric-a-brac, and don't forego a visit in the evening, when the live music recitals involve violinists sitting on a chair suspended half way up a wall. A team of flighty waitresses take the orders, and the chef does the rest coming up trumps with a range of traditional Jewish dishes, including rather good goose."

[37] Posted at http://www.inyourpocket.com/poland/lodz/manufaktura/category/60491-wheretoeat.html. The link is now http://www.inyourpocket.com/poland/lodz/manufaktura/wheretoeat/Anatewka_21079v and the blurb now reads: "Sister restaurant of the highly recommend Anatewka found on Łódź's ul. Sierpnia, and though this place isn't nearly as good it's still a decent stop when you're Manufaktura bound."

I obtained my miniature Jew at the original Anatewka, a year after I had first been there. This time, I found the waiters no longer dressed in explicit Hasidic costume, but the tiny figurines were placed on each crowded table like souvenir party favors. One table was full of Japanese guests – experiencing "Jewish," perhaps, as Westerners experience "Japanese" at a sushi bar.

As I write this, I am looking at the miniature Jew I was given that night; it is perched on a speaker next to my computer. He is a cute little fellow with a big smile on his face behind a rust-red beard that covers his little chest. He is bald but has red side locks that match his beard, and on his head is balanced a tiny, wide-brimmed hat. He wears a baggy black suit with a high collar, brown shoes, and a white shirt. The coin in his hands, a brass one-grosz piece, comes up above his trouser top, like an apron. He looks like a cartoon character, not even really human. There is nothing specifically malevolent about him, except the context of his production and proliferation. The somatic stereotypes are not all that dissimilar to those of the little Yeshiva bocher from the kosher pastry shop in Budapest, which I have also placed on the speaker. If anything, the Budapest figure looks more sinister – he is rather bulky and awkward, like a Golem, with a strange stovepipe hat and staring eyes.

POSTSCRIPT

There are no "typical" Krakow-style Jewish trappings at Budapest's best-known "Jewish" café, Siraly, which opened in October 2006 at the edge of the city's historic old downtown Jewish quarter, the Seventh District. Hungary has the highest number of Jews in any postcommunist state outside the former Soviet Union, with as many as ninety thousand Jews in the capital. There is a very small, traditional Orthodox community, but the dominant religious stream is Neolog, a type of conservative-reform. The vast majority, however, are secular or totally assimilated; Budapest Jews prided themselves on their Magyar identity already in the nineteenth century. In Budapest, definitions of what is "Jewish" are often linked not with shtetl nostalgia but with liberalism and cultural values – even, as a Jewish artist friend once told me, to what books one had on one's bookshelves. And he did not mean prayer books or sacred texts.

Siraly's design and that of several other new cafés in the neighborhood that are run by young Jews and attract a young Jewish clientele reflect these markers and these conventions. On my first visit to the café, just two months after it opened, Siraly (its name means "Seagull" but also, in local slang, "fantastic") looked as if it had been there for years. Its main area, on the ground floor, was a spacious room with a high, barrel vaulted ceiling and walls painted a dirty, cream-colored tan, except for the wall behind the wooden bar, which was painted a distressed rusty red. The lighting was low and diffused by cigarette smoke; patrons – including shaggy-looking men with beards and ponytails, sat at small, round-topped wooden tables. The furnishings exuded the look of scarred experience, a lifetime of tobacco, coffee, and conversation. A few framed blow-ups of old photographs of Budapest hung on one wall; another bore a brownish tapestry. Black chalkboards listed drink offerings and events, and bulletin boards fluttered with notices. Low background music was playing – Latin sounds, and then a compilation of African pop: in the several times I dropped in over the course of a week, I heard no klezmer music whatsoever.

A big mezuzah was – and still is – positioned prominently on the front doorpost, however. Upstairs, in another room equipped with WiFi Internet, wooden shelves proffer an array of Jewish books and magazines. Tucked away there, too, is the office of Marom, a Jewish youth group that co-runs the place. Walls are usually hung with Jewish-themed exhibitions, and each year the café hosts a week-long series of concerts, parties, and other events to mark Hanukkah: every night the candles are lit on a menorah set up on the bar. The aim, Adam Schoenberger, the rabbi's son, then twenty-six, who heads Marom and is Siraly's program director, told me at our first meeting, is to integrate Jewish cultural content into a general-style café. "Everyone comes here, lots of young Jews and non-Jews, a certain type of Hungarian intellectual," he said. "In Budapest, Jewish people don't go into a 'just Jewish' place. In a mixed place like this, everyone can come. This is Siraly's identity."

Schoenberger's insistence on lively Jewish integration and the prevalence of nonreligious (or at least nontraditional) markers indicating what is Jewish – like the hip new ambience of Prague's Robert Guttmann Gallery in Prague – reflect the confidence of younger generations looking for new models and new ways of both displaying Jewish identity and attracting interest in Things Jewish. These efforts eschew nostalgia; Jews and Jewish culture, they declare, are living entities at home – in Europe – in the twenty-first century, not sentimental relics of the past, or entities that only live on elsewhere, in places like North America and Israel. Indeed, Schoenberger himself is part of a band with a Jewish name, HaGesher – whose music is a sort of hip-hop/rap/klezmer/funk fusion.

That is not to say that nostalgia will not retain an appeal, nor that the old imagery will not continue to exert a potent pull, among Jews and non-Jews alike – as the success of Jewish-style cafés in various places demonstrates. Still, I found it significant, and telling, that when Wojtek Ornat, the pioneering entrepreneur of Jewish style in Krakow, decided to set up a branch of his business in the former Jewish quarter of Budapest, he opened, in August 2007, not a nostalgia-driven café but a well-stocked, multilingual Jewish bookstore.[38]

[38] Alas, though the bookstore was located a couple of blocks from the Siraly café and across the street from a kosher restaurant, it failed to draw business, and Ornat closed it at the end of 2009.

In Krakow itself there are also signs of continuing change. The open-ing of a modern, state-of-the-art Jewish Community Center (JCC) in 2008 was an institutional milestone.[39] "Our primary goal is to serve, strengthen and build the Jewish community here, as well as to educate non-Jews about Judaism," the New York–born JCC director, Jonathan Ornstein, told me. I found it indicative that he preferred to meet for cappuccino at a café on Plac Nowy, with its youthful counterculture vibe, rather than at one of the "Jewish-style" cafés on Szeroka. "People talk about Kazimierz as being the 'former' Jewish quarter of Krakow," he said. "But I say, why former? I think that it is the present Jewish quarter of Krakow. You can't measure it in num-bers, but in feeling. Here, we have an intact Jewish quarter. Jews live freely; people know things about Judaism and Jewish traditions; there's a Jewish studies program at the university; there's the Festival. And now the JCC is a magnet. People are finding their way back." He continued, "Nobody alive today has a good memory of Kazimierz when it was better than it is now. There was the war, and then after the war it was derelict for decades. Now, it's the hippest place in the city. The whole 'former' thing is based on history, not living memory."[40]

[39] Financed mainly by the JDC and World Jewish Relief, the JCC was inspired by Britain's Prince Charles, who visited Krakow in 2002 and wanted to help the elderly, poor Jewish community. Charles attended the inauguration and helped affix a mezuzah to the door.

[40] See my article "Scenes from a Krakow Café," *Moment*, January–February 2010.

Index